THE COMPLETE JOHNNY CASH

THE COMPLETE JOHNNY CASH

LYRICS FROM A LIFETIME OF SONGWRITING

LYRICS BY JOHNNY CASH
ESSAYS BY MARK STIELPER
FOREWORD BY JOHN CARTER CASH
CURATED BY SANDRA STILLWAGON AND MARK STIELPER

VORACIOUS
Little, Brown and Company
New York Boston London

Voracious / Little, Brown and Company
Hachette Book Group
1290 Avenue of the Americas, New York, NY 10104
voraciousbooks.com

First North American Edition: October 2025
Published simultaneously in the UK by Orion Books

Voracious is an imprint of Little, Brown and Company, a division of Hachette Book Group, Inc. The Voracious name and logo are trademarks of Hachette Book Group, Inc.

All images are courtesy of the John R. Cash Revocable Trust, except the following: p. ii courtesy of Sony Music Entertainment, Al Clayton, photographer; p. 56 by Don Hunstein © Sony Music Entertainment; p. 686 by Marty Stuart; pp. 101, 105, 194, 197, 245–46, 249–50, 252, 256, 259, 265, 269, 272, 275, 293, 297, 304, 307, 309, 371, 389, 455–56, 489, 493, 499–500, 504, 509, 511, 515, 517, 525, 529, 534, 541, 545, 549, 555, 563, 578, 595, 609, 620, 631, 635, 637, 641, 645, 660 (top), 669, 690, 693 courtesy of Julien's Auctions.

Print book interior design by Bart Dawson
Project management by Sandbox Succession

ISBN 9780316503549
LCCN 2025937830

Printing 1, 2025

LSC-C

Printed in the United States of America

CONTENTS

INTRODUCTION

John Carter Cash

WHO WAS MY father?

My father was the writer. This distinction set him apart from so many of his peers. Surrounded as he was by some of the greatest talent in music history, in those early days at Sun Records, Dad nevertheless stood out. How? What made him different and memorable? It was that voice, of course. But more, it was what that voice *said*. He wrote his own music and lyrics, and they were like no one else's. He captured the essence of the human condition and touched head, heart, and soul. His words put him on the path to Forever.

Dad read the Bible as a boy, sang Southern gospel songs, and began writing as early as twelve years old. He would go on to write his whole life through. One defining element of his works from the very beginning was humor, from his youth until his final recording, "Like the 309," which all in all laughs in the dreadful and enormous face of death. Another is hope, and perhaps the most significant is love.

Poetry and song were my father's lifeblood, their gravitas conducting his soul. His creativity was his vital and essential companion from his childhood onward, through it all, even past my mother's death.

It is not well known, but my father was functionally blind the last few months of his life. Even when he could no longer read the books from his treasured library, poetry and words were still there for him. His last recording session was ten days before his passing.

From the very first thoughts of creating a book to contain my father's writings, I felt the immense need for it not to be abbreviated but for it to be complete and reside in a solid and purposeful tome. With this edition, he may be that much more nobly and soundly known.

Who was my father? By reading his words you will experience the very essence of his soul. This book is far more than a companion piece for his music. It is his whole story.

A NOTE ON METHODOLOGY

THIS BOOK CATALOGS over a half century of Johnny Cash's songs, poetry, prose, and musings, from his childhood in rural Arkansas, across the highways and high points (and low ones, too) of his public career and personal life, through to his last days. It encompasses more than 500 compositions, from the 1940s to 2003.

Cash was a prodigious writer and thinker, and the quest to capture "it all" involved casting a wide net. He claimed, like many artistic types, that he discarded as many of his creations as he retained. Based on the trove that posterity now possesses, it is a wonder he had the time or strength to live the storied life he did.

As masters do, Cash used the world as his palette. The search for the "complete" Johnny Cash entailed examining ragged old scraps from notepads as well as leather-bound diaries, elegant pronouncements, and his most private pages. Those words are presented here, many in his own handwriting, just as he set them down. He wrote masterpieces on postcards, scribbled eternal phrases on the corners of airplane sickness bags, and scratched profundities in the margins of greeting cards and on scores of pages of hotel stationery. He even carved a couplet into the bark of a tree trunk. As the reader will see, what he wrote and what he sang often evolved, sometimes almost immediately. Part of the adventure is taking that journey with him and marveling at where it took him — and us. For those who like their Cash set in stone, we remind them of the man's own declaration on that topic: "Don't tell anybody how I feel about anything unless I told you in the last few days." Here are fifty-five years' worth of "the last few days" as they happened.

Documenting these treasures required stepped-up detecting and deducing, akin to an archaeological dig. Cash's artifacts were found in every one of his several homes, in file cabinets and closets, inside books and journals, in dusty trunks and coat pockets. Some lyrics were placed (hidden?) in a pair of his tall black boots. We are fortunate for the times when a shelf was closer than a trash can. Few pieces have dates on them, which invited questions: How do you date an *idea*? Is a piece considered "written" when it is started, or completed? Do we say the ceiling of the Sistine Chapel was painted in 1508, when Michelangelo began, or 1512, when he was able to come down from the scaffolding for good? Cash would start works and then set them aside, forgetting about them for years, before returning to them. Many in this collection have their genesis long before they were published, performed, or simply put away. We have chosen to start at the beginning when assigning years (or, when they could not be determined, decades) to Cash's grand tour.

The sticklers out there might quibble at whether a particular work should be classified as a "song" or "poem" or merely a meander. Rather than visit that mire, the entirety of the Cash canon is on display without arbitrary labels. It all came from the same mind and the same pen, myriad threads weaving a whole cloth. Everyone is invited to sing — or talk — along as new insights into Johnny Cash are discovered. Let's hope he left even more.

THE COMPLETE JOHNNY CASH

ONE

✵ DAWN ✵

1940s–1957

THE GREAT DEPRESSION gutted the lives and souls of generations of American families. The people of the tiny hamlet of Kingsland, in Cleveland County, deep in south-central Arkansas, scarcely noticed. Such had already been their lot for decades. The forest was impenetrable; the land, unforgiving; the heat, snakes, and rampant disease, ruinous.

The outmatched settlers who ventured into this no-man's-land in the latter nineteenth century were not people of letters. An ability to read and write was not a prerequisite, which was fortunate, since few could do so. Many of the earliest land grants contain nothing more than stray markings, passing for signatures, of weary old soldiers, hopeful, but often failed, farmers, or simply run-of-the-mill, out-of-their-depth adventurers pursuing what could never be gotten. By the 1920s in Kingsland, with its total area of one square mile and population only in the hundreds, residents could not remember when prosperity had ever shown its face.

Ray Cash, the youngest child (of twelve) in a once semi-successful family of growers, and his wife, Carrie Rivers, a solemn woman of the soil who had seen three younger siblings die on the frontier before she turned eight years old, felt the wrath of economic and natural calamities. By 1932, a dozen years and three children into a marriage as hard and unforgiving as the ground that mocked their existence every day, the Cashes were typical of the time and place. They were dependent on others for their sustenance and had little agency of their own.

Like millions of others, they were reduced to tenant farming — obliged to endure the scourge of sharecropping on someone else's land, living in a clapboard shack, barely eking out a minimal existence in a system that guaranteed poverty and hopelessness. Resolute that her fourth child would not be born on such cursed soil, even if it meant delivering in an unheated shed room with a dirt floor behind her father's isolated house outside town in the middle of winter, Carrie did just that. These are the improbable — almost unfathomable — circumstances that form the foundation of the life of Carrie Cash's third son, born on February 26, 1932. She named him John R. Cash.

The Cashes moved from Kingsland when J.R. was only three years old — probably a little young to have formed permanent memories — but the short time spent in his birthplace had a profound impact on Johnny Cash's worldview and songwriting. The wail of a locomotive's whistle, harkening a welcome arrival or a heartbreaking goodbye; a hardscrabble existence that demanded awe for nature, which took away more easily than it gave; unshakable faith in the promise of an uncloudy day (generations of Cash forebears were ordained fundamentalist ministers) — he would return to these themes time and time again. They were his foundation.

In 1935, the Cash family was accepted into a federal government "agricultural relief and resettlement program," whose mission was to give indigent farmers a way out of their plight via a quasi-socialistic (but genuinely quixotic) scheme to take these poverty-stricken, largely uneducated, rural Americans and turn them into self-sufficient entrepreneurs.

Built out of a snake- and mosquito-infested swamp in the sunken Delta lands of northeast Arkansas, the Dyess Colony was an audacious experiment in social engineering that ultimately failed. Homesickness, lack of knowledge in proper planting techniques, droughts, fires and floods, World War II, and endless, backbreaking work all contributed to its demise. The promise of stability gave way to the reality of debt and impermanence. Until 1947, not a single boy finished the Dyess school. Little wonder, then, that the tally of people giving up on the dream quickly exceeded the dreamers. Dyess was no place for dreamers.

Ray and Carrie Cash had nowhere and nothing to go back to, so they stayed — for fifteen years, until their third son did, in fact, graduate from high school (he was the senior class vice president). The paradox is that, against every odd imaginable, the Colony was the incubator of Johnny Cash's intelligence, sensitivity, honesty, and even uproarious humor. He grew up in an environment where choices, and life itself, were stark and limited. His earliest poetry and musings were plainspoken and direct, just as they would ever be, their subjects taken from everyday life. But they also exhibited an imagination and whimsy that belie later caricatures of an unrelentingly dark soul. It was the embodiment of the human condition.

In middle age, he looked back on those formative years:

> I didn't play basketball or football on the Dyess team. There was always work to do in the fields after school. In the spring it was plowing and hoeing. In the fall and winter it was picking. I never saw a mechanical cotton picker when I lived on the farm. It was all done by hand.
>
> In school I spent a lot of time daydreaming, then began putting my daydreams on paper. I wrote short stories, poems, drew pictures of tall buildings in cities I'd never seen.

I sang at school assembly. They asked me to sing things like "Trees" [by Joyce Kilmer] and "Whiffenpoof Song"... which I did, though it wasn't what I wanted to sing. I wanted to sing a country, or hillbilly, song, as our music was called then. Or, let me do a gospel song... How about a poem? One I wrote.

When I consider
Why that I
Was made to live
And made to die
And know no more
Than what I'm told
And what the Book says
Centuries old
My mind goes flying
Far away
To those six great
Creation days
When light first shone
And trees first grew
When waters ran
And eagles flew
Then He saw fit
To make me last
To live a life
And then it's passed
There must have been a reason

Staying in Dyess after high school "was not an option," so Cash spent the next four years in the United States Air Force, assigned to its security service as a radio intercept operator. The military venture — conducted primarily in Europe — blew the farm boy's world wide open, exposing him to sounds, cultures, and experiences he could scarcely have imagined at his school desk or in the cotton field. Much of his early songwriting would call on these essential, pivotal years for themes and inspiration.

Although Johnny Cash became one of the most renowned singers and musical stylists in history, many of his early peers, and indeed he himself, characterized him as a songwriter first and foremost. "I started singing as a way to get what was in my head out," Cash later said. "It was how I could communicate."

Memphis's Sun Records was the vehicle and outlet for all that communicating. A phenom from his initial release in 1955, Cash immediately stood out from his labelmates in his composing virtuosity. His first single included "Hey, Porter!," an exuberant account of a Southern boy's anxious train ride back home after an absence, echoing his own return from the service less than a year before. That was followed by "Folsom Prison Blues," inspired (at least partially) by a movie he had viewed in Germany two years prior, a dark piece that placed the "lonesome whistle" of a train flat up against a prisoner's guilty conscience. Then it was "I Walk the Line," an ode to fidelity for his young wife, and next, another locomotive coming down the line with "Train of Love." By 1957 and the classic "Big River," centered on the mighty waterway that dominated so much in its namesake Mississippi County, home to the Dyess Colony, Cash had already established a written canon that rivaled his recorded hits, and nearly all were based on his own personal résumé.

While Sun released only eight singles during Cash's tenure with the label (every one of which featured at least one Cash composition), his pen was even more prolific. He would publish over a dozen other songs from 1955 to 1958, ranging from silly ditties about his own band ("Luther Played the Boogie") and a ferocious feline ("Mean-Eyed Cat") to a lament about a dying prisoner lying beside a railroad track ("Give My Love to Rose," a song with so much pathos and power that it would earn Cash a Grammy forty-five years after it was first recorded) and even a few (semi-successful) attempts at rock and roll.

Taken together, this was sunrise, Genesis, the rise of the curtain. Long before the advent of the singer-songwriter era, Johnny Cash started out in a high school in the middle of a swamp and in less than a decade had not only set the stage but also defined it.

THE FAMILY TREE

1940s

There's a wonderful family
On our family tree
I've been forever wondering
What they'll make of me

Ma's enlisted in the "WACs"
Daddy carries mail
Sister's married, got nine kids
Brother, he's in jail!

The family Tree

There's a wonderful family
On our family tree
I've been forever wondering
what they'll make of me
Ma's enlisted in the "WACS"
Daddy carries mail
Sisters married, got nine kids
Brother, he's in jail!

J R Cash

THE FLIGHT BEFORE CHRISTMAS

1940s

'Twas the flight before Christmas and all
down below
Not a thing was I seeing, not even the snow
Visibility was zero, no stars were in sight
It was promising to be a heck of a night

The copilot was sleeping, but not in his bed
While visions of Broadway danced in his head
The rest of the crew was just sitting around
Thinking of life in the old hometown

And I, in my cockpit, had set the controls
Hoping the fuel was going to hold
When on engine "4" there arose such a clatter
I started checking the dials to see what's the
matter

And doing so, this instantly came to my mind:
The RPM was only half-time!
With the old intercom I yelled, "Pilot to crew!
Number 4 is kapoot [kaput]. You know what
to do."

I opened the throttle on old number 4
But only three engines were making her roar
So I set up the crate so she'd run on the three
And told the radio operator to get on the key
I knew that our field must be pretty near
If it wasn't, then we'd never see the New Year

After minutes of sweating they finally came
through
And said their visibility was zero, too!

So they picked us up with their radar eyes
And started giving us instro to fly

"Two degrees to the left and keep on the line.
You don't see us, but you're coming in fine.
Drop her a little now, and drop her slow.
There's just about four more minutes to go.

"Altitude 300, you're coming in, roger!
The strip's just ahead so, buddy, don't dodge her."
Visibility zero, I still couldn't see
But thank God the GCA man saw me

Then the final command:
"Gear down and roll."
I rubbed Mother Earth
And we'd reached our goal

When we came to a stop
And finally unpacked
I felt like Santa Claus
Opening his sack

And when I crawled in my sack
At the end of day
And I was thanking my God for GCA

And I heard the boys say
When they turned off the light,
"Merry Christmas to all
And, brother, what a night."

(GCA: Ground-Controlled Approach)

The Flight Before Christmas.

'Twas the flight before Christmas and all down below,
Not a thing was I seeing, not even the snow.
Visibility was zero, no stars were in sight.
It was promising to be a heck of a night.
The Co-Pilot was sleeping, but not in his bed
While visions of Broadway danced in his head.
The rest of the crew was just sitting around.
Thinking of life in the old home town.
And I, in my cockpit had set the controls
Hoping the fuel was going to hold.
When on engine "4" there arose such a clatter
I started checking the dials to see what's the matter.
And doing so, this instantly came to my mind;
The R.P.M. was only half time!
With the old inter-com I yelled "Pilot to crew!
Number 4 is kapoot! You know what to do."
I opened the throttle on old number 4
But only three engines were making her roar.
So I set up the crate so she'd run on the three.
And told the Radio Operator to get on the key.
I knew that our field must be pretty near,
If it wasn't, then we'd never see the new year.
After minutes of sweating they finally came through
And said thier visibility was zero, too!
So they picked us up with thier radar eyes,
And started giving us instrs. to fly.
"Two degrees to the left, and keep on the line.
You don't see us, but you're coming in fine."
Drop her a little now, and drop her slow.
There's just about 4 more minutes to go."
Altitude, 300, you're coming in Roger!
The strip's just ahead, so buddy don't dodge her.
Visibility Zero! I still couldn't see.
But thank God the G.C.A. man saw me.
Then the final command, "Gear down and roll!"
I rubbed mother earth, and we'd reached our goal

When we came to a stop, and finally unpacked
I felt like Santa Clause opening his sack.
And when I crawled in my sack the end of the day,
I was thanking my God for G.C.A.
And I heard the boys say, when they turned off the light
"Merry Christmas to all, and brother what a night!"

GCA. Ground Controlled Approach

THE SCHOOL BUS

1940s

The great big bus that always stops
And picks up brother Les
Comes clean across from the other side
Of Emmerville, I guess

I like to hear it squeak and stop
It makes the funniest sounds
It sounds like all of Emmerville
Was tumblin' to the ground

Some day, Ma says, I'll go to school
And learn to read and write
I'll probably be the president
Now, won't I be a sight!

My brother, Les, is really smart
He's went to school ten years
So now he's in the seventh grade
And learnin' fast, I hears

I sure wish I could go to school
And ride that bus around
That big old yellow squeaky bus
That makes the funny sounds

Guess I'm too young to go to school
'Cause I'm only four
But Uncle Bill don't go to school
I'll bet he's forty, or more

But I'll just wait and then someday
I'll ride that yellow thing
Clean t'other side of Emmerville
Where you hear the school bell ring!

THE SCHOOL BUS

J. R. Cash

The great big bus that always stops
And picks up brother, Les,
Comes clean across from the other side
Of Emmerville, I guess
I like to hear it squeek and stop
It makes the funniest sounds
It sounds like all of Emmerville
Was tumblin' to the ground
Some day, ma says I'll go to school
And learn to read and write
I'll probably be the president
Now wont I be a sight!
My brother, Les is really smart
He's went to school ten years
So now hes in the <u>seventh</u> grade
And learnin fast, I hears
I sure wish I could go to school
And ride that bus around
That big old yellow squeeky bus
That makes the funny sounds. (contd)

Guess I'm to young to go to school
Cause I'm only four
But uncle Bill don't go to school
I'll bet he's forty, or more
But I'll just wait and then someday
I'll ride that yellow thing
Clean t'other side of Emmerville
Where you hear the school bell ring!

by
J R Cash

I dont want to be a gun totin' Texan
Rather see 'em in the moving picture show
And I dont want to be a singin' cowboy
Rather hear the popular songs on the radio
Want a soft, fluffy place to lay my head
Don't want any snakes nor cactus beds
Rather ride my girl in my Caddilac
Than to ride a smelly horse's back
Hope I wont get tanned from riding a mule
I'll get my tan in a swimming pool.
I'm a tenderfoot from the city
But I'm livin' just the same

I'm a tenderfoot from the city
and I live a life of ease.
I wear my silk and satin
and go just where I please

TENDERFOOT FROM THE CITY

1940s

I don't want to be a gun-totin' Texan
Rather see 'em in the moving picture show
And I don't want to be a singin' cowboy
Rather hear the popular songs on the radio

Want a soft, fluffy place to lay my head
Don't want any snakes or cactus beds
Rather ride my girl in my Cadillac
Than to ride a smelly horse's back

No, I won't get tanned from riding a mule
I'll get my tan in a swimming pool
I'm a tenderfoot from the city
But I'm livin' just the same

I'm a tenderfoot from the city
And I live a life of ease
I wear my silk and satin
And go just where I please

THE THINGS WE'RE FRIGHTENED AT

1940s

When I was just a little kid
And played a lot at night
Back in our country village
Where we didn't pay for light

Then I could see behind each tree
An Indian standing there
And, say, how I'd shake and holler!
It would fairly raise my hair

And when I grew to be a man
I knew it more and more
That half the fun was knowing not
What I was running for

And I used to go to town
Every night for Paw
I'd go down the road just lickety split!
Until my feet were raw

I had a little cousin
(He was scary, too)
He's worse than I am
He's scared of ghosts. Are you?

Once I heard my cousin
Just outside a-yellin'
He wouldn't tell me what it was
I said there ain't no telling

THE THINGS WERE FRIGHTENED AT

WHEN I WAS JUST A LITTLE KID
AND PLAYED ALOT AT NIGHT
BACK IN OUR COUNTRY VILLAGE
WHERE WE DIDNT PAY FOR LIGHT
THEN I COULD SEE BEHIND EACH TREE,
AN INDIAN STANDING THERE
AND SAY, HOW I'D SHAKE AND HOLLER!
IT WOULD FAIRLY RAISE MY HAIR
AND WHEN I GREW TO BE A MAN
I KNEW IT MORE AND MORE
THAT HALF THE FUN WAS KNOWING NOT
WHAT I WAS RUNNING FOR
AND I USED TO GO TO TOWN
EVERY NIGHT FOR PAW
I'D GO DOWN THE ROAD JUST, LICKEDY SPLIT!
UNTIL MY FEET WERE RAW
I HAD A LITTLE COUSIN
(HE WAS SCARY, TOO)
HE'S WORSE THAN I AM
HE'S SCARED OF GHOSTS ARE YOU
ONCE I HEARD MY COUSIN JUST OUTSIDE
A YELLIN'
HE WOULDN'T TELL ME WHAT IT WAS
I SAID THERE AINT NO TELLING

But when I awoke the morrow morn
I found this beggar gone.
And he left a piece of paper
With these words so true and plain
"You have carried someone's burdens
You have not lived life in vain."
And if it was before me,
I would do it o'er again
Just to help some weary pilgrim
And not live life in vain.

by

J R Cash
1948

NOT LIVE LIFE IN VAIN

1948

But when I woke the morrow morn
I found this beggar gone
And he left a piece of paper
With these words so true and plain

"You have carried someone's burdens
You have not lived life in vain."
And if it was before me
I would do it o'er again

Just to help some weary pilgrim
And not live life in vain

LITTLE JOEY

1949

I've got a little brother
Almost as big as me
Ma says he'll soon be five
But what a boy is he!

Joey, that's my brother's name
He's tough as our old horse
Why, he could eat a hive of bees
And never feel the worse

He cut his toe just yesterday
The big one, on the right
Ma, she put on liniment
And wrapped the bandage tight

In just about an hour then
The bandage, it was gone
And he was wading in the ditch
His toe cut to the bone

And eat! Lordy, how he eats!
There's nothing that will fill him
I guess that boy won't ever die
I don't know what could kill 'im!

3-31-49

Little Joey

by J R Cash

Nita Faye Hambull

I've got a little brother
 Almost big as me
Ma, she says he'll soon be five
 But what a boy is he!
Joey, thats my brothers' name
 He's tough as our old horse
Why, he could eat a hive of bees
 And never feel the worse
He cut his toe just yesterday
 The big one on the right
Ma, she put on liniment
 And wrapped the bandage tight
In just about an hour then
 The bandage, it was gone
And he was wading in the ditch
 His toe cut to the bone
And eat! oh Lordy, how he eats!
 Theres nothing that will kill 'im
I guess that boy wont ever die
 I dont know what could kill 'im!

BELSHAZZAR

1954

Well, the Bible tells us about a man
Who ruled Babylon and all its land
Around the city he built a wall
And declared that Babylon would never fall

He had concubines and wives
He called his Babylon "Paradise"
On his throne he drank and ate
But for Belshazzar, it was gettin' late

For he was weighed in the balance and found wanting
His kingdom was divided, couldn't stand
He was weighed in the balance and found wanting
His houses were built upon the sand

Well, the people feasted and drank their wine
And praised the false gods of his time
All holy things, they scorned and mocked
But suddenly all their mocking stopped

For on the wall there appeared a hand
Nothing else, there was no man
In blood the hand began to write
And Belshazzar couldn't hide his fright

For he was weighed in the balance and found wanting
His kingdom was divided, couldn't stand
He was weighed in the balance and found wanting
His houses were built upon the sand

Well, no one around could understand
What was written by the mystic hand
Belshazzar tried but couldn't find
A man who could give him peace of mind

But Daniel the prophet, a man of God
He saw the writing on the wall in blood
Belshazzar asked him what it said
And Daniel turned to the wall and read:

"My friend, you're weighed in the balance and found wanting.
Your kingdom is divided, it can't stand.
You're weighed in the balance and found wanting.
Your houses are built upon the sand."

MY TREASURE

1954

I saved a lot of money
My fortune was untold
And like a fool I idolized
My silver and my gold

My earthly treasures mounted
But when I counted through
I realized the treasure
I had overlooked was you

My treasure, unmeasured
But forsaken of the treasures
That come from above
My treasure, unmeasured
But it don't hold a heart
Of the one that I love

TWO TIMIN' WOMAN

1954

I woke up this morning
In a terrible mood
Now, you talk about a woman
Treating a good man rude

She had me talking to myself
Gazing at that mean ol' wall
She had another daddy waiting down
At the end of the hall

She changes with the weather
Like the leaves, I recall
She blossoms in the spring
But then she's gone in the fall

A two timin' woman
With a heart of solid stone
She tells me that she loves me
But her heart's a little undergrown

She drifts around the country like
A steamboat on a foam
She said she'd never leave me
But she'd got the urge to roam

She never changes course
She just goes along that same old way
Well, I hope she keeps a-drifting
Rolls along back home someday

Because if I ever find her
Going to chain her to the floor
And tell her, "Now sit there, woman,
You ain't leaving no more.

"I'm going to tame you, mama,
Until you're eating from my hand.
It's not that I don't love you, honey,
It's just to make you understand."

YOU'RE MY BABY (LITTLE WOOLY BOOGER)

1954

Hey, I love that hair, long and black
Hanging down in the middle of your back
Don't you cut it off, whatever you do
'Cause I need it to run my fingers through

'Cause you're my baby
You're my sugar
Don't mean maybe
Little wooly booger

I got a guitar, got six strings
And a guitar pick that a-make 'em ring
Every string got a note or two
That I'm gonna use to serenade you

'Cause you're my baby
You're my sugar
You drive me crazy
Little wooly booger

Well, I got a dollar that I saved
Saved it up for a rainy day
Everybody's calling for bills that's due
But if they don't catch me, I'll spend it on you

'Cause you're my baby
You're my sugar
Don't mean maybe
Little wooly booger

Well, I had me a gal, she said she's mine
But she run around on me all the time
Now she's gone I'm glad we're through
'Cause I'm plumb goggle-eyed over you

'Cause you're my baby
You're my sugar
You drive me crazy
I don't mean maybe
Little wooly booger

FOLSOM PRISON BLUES

1955

I hear the train a-comin'
It's rollin' 'round the bend
And I ain't seen the sunshine
Since I don't know when

I'm stuck in Folsom Prison,
And time keeps draggin' on
But that train keeps a-rollin'
On down to San Antone

When I was just a baby
My mama told me, "Son,
Always be a good boy.
Don't ever play with guns."
But I shot a man in Reno
Just to watch him die
When I hear that whistle blowin'
I hang my head and cry

I bet there's rich folks eatin'
In a fancy dining car
They're probably drinkin' coffee
And smokin' big cigars
Well, I know I had it comin'
I know I can't be free
But those people keep a-movin'
And that's what tortures me

Well, if they freed me from this prison
If that railroad train was mine
I bet I'd move it on a little
Farther down the line
Far from Folsom Prison
That's where I'd want to stay
And I'd let that lonesome whistle
Blow my blues away

Folsom Prison Blues

I hear the train a comin'
It's rollin' round the bend
And I aint seen the sunshine
Since I dont know when
I'm stuck in Folsom Prison and time keeps draggin' on
But that train keeps a rollin' on down to San Antone

When I was just a baby
My mama told me, son
Always be a good boy
Dont ever play with guns
But I shot a man in Reno just to watch him die
When I hear that whistle blowing I hang my head an cry

I bet there's rich folks eatin
In a fancy dinin' car
They're probably drinkin' coffee
And smokin' big cigars
I know I had it comin' I know I cant be free
But those people keep amoving and thats what tortures me

If they freed me from this prison
If that railroad train was mine
I bet I'd move it on
A little farther down the line
Far from Folsom prison, thats where I want to stay
And I'd let that lonesome whistle blow my blues away

Johnny Cash
1955

CRY, CRY, CRY

1955

Everybody knows where you go when the sun goes down
I think you only live to see the lights uptown
I wasted my time when I would try, try, try
'Cause when the lights have lost their glow you're gonna cry, cry, cry

Soon your sugar daddies will all be gone
You'll wake up some cold day and find you're alone
You'll call for me but I'm gonna tell you bye, bye, bye
When I turn around and walk away you'll cry, cry, cry

You're gonna cry, cry, cry and you'll cry alone
When everyone's forgotten and you're left on your own
You're gonna cry, cry, cry

I lie awake at night to wait 'til you come in
You stay a little while and then you're gone again
Every question that I ask I get a lie, lie, lie
For every lie you tell you're gonna cry, cry, cry

When your fickle love gets old, no one will care for you
Then you'll come back to me for a little love, that's true
I'll tell you no and you'll ask me why, why, why
When I remind you of all of this, you'll cry, cry, cry

You're gonna cry, cry, cry and you'll want me then
It'll hurt when you think of all the fool you've been
You're gonna cry, cry, cry

HEY, PORTER!

1955

Hey, Porter! Hey, Porter!
Would you tell me the time?
How much longer will it be 'til we
cross
That Mason-Dixon line?

At daylight, would you tell that
engineer
To slow it down?
Or better still, just stop the train
'Cause I want to look around

Hey, Porter! Hey, Porter!
What time did you say?
How much longer will it be
'Til I can see the light of day?

When we hit Dixie, will you tell that
engineer
To ring his bell?
And ask everybody that ain't asleep
To stand right up and yell

Hey, Porter! Hey, Porter!
It's getting light outside
This old train is puffing smoke
And I have to strain my eyes

But ask that engineer
If he will blow his whistle, please
'Cause I smell frost on cotton leaves
And I feel that Southern breeze

Hey, Porter! Hey, Porter!
Please get my bags for me
I need nobody to tell me now
That we're in Tennessee

Go tell that engineer to make
That lonesome whistle scream
We're not so far from home
So take it easy on the steam

Hey, Porter! Hey, Porter!
Please open up the door
When they stop the train
I'm gonna get off first
'Cause I can't wait no more

Tell that engineer I said thanks a lot
And I didn't mind the fare
I'm gonna set my feet on Southern soil
And breathe that Southern air

I JUST DON'T CARE ENOUGH (TO CARRY ON)

1955

I had a dozen others before I ever met you
And there'll be that many more when you're gone
You're just one out of many, it's easy to forget you
'Cause I just don't care enough to carry on

I haven't broken every heart that chanced to come my way
I haven't cherished any love or begged one girl to stay
So don't think that you only stay away, don't phone me
'Cause I just don't have the time to fool with you

Of all the dozen others I knew before I met you
I only said, "Well, maybe she's the one."
But true love wouldn't cheat me, but you did and I let you
You proved untrue so now leave me alone

I thought you surely were the one I wanted for my wife
But I can't stand a cheating heart to live with all my life
I've only been your pastime, so darling, for the last time
I just don't have the time to fool with you

I'LL CRY FOR YOU

1955

Take me in your arms and hold me
Give me just a minute more
To help me over all the days
That I'll be blue

Take my lips and kiss me gently
'Cause I know that like before
When you leave me all alone
I'll cry for you

I haven't got the right to ask for love or sympathy
After I did all the things I shouldn't do
But all I'm asking for is just a little memory
'Cause I know that when you go I'll cry for you

I'll sit and watch the window and I'll pray that you will come
But at the end of every day I'll still be blue
I'll think of all the chances that I had to keep you mine
And like I've done a million times I'll cry for you

Memories that come and linger make me wish we'd never met
Because it seems they're gonna break my heart in two
Either give me love forevermore or help me to forget
'Cause when you're gone far away I'll cry for you

I'll sit and watch the window and I'll pray that you will come
But at the end of every day I'll still be blue
I'll think of all the chances that I had to keep you mine
And like I've done a million times I'll cry for you

LUTHER PLAYED THE BOOGIE

1955

We were just a plain ol' hillbilly band with a plain ol' country style
We never played the kind of songs that'd drive anybody wild
Played a railroad song with a stomping beat
We played a blues song, kinda slow and sweet
But the thing that knocked them off of their feet was, ooh-wee

When Luther played the boogie-woogie
Luther played the boogie-woogie
Luther played the boogie-woogie
Luther played the boogie-woogie
Luther played the boogie-woogie
Luther played the boogie-woogie
Luther played the boogie-woogie
Luther played the boogie in the strangest kind of way

Well, we did our best to entertain everywhere we'd go
We'd nearly wear our fingers off to give the folks a show
Played jumping jive to make 'em get in the groove
We played sad songs, real slow and smooth
But the only thing that'd make 'em move was, ooh-wee

When Luther played the boogie-woogie
Luther played the boogie-woogie
Luther played the boogie-woogie
Luther played the boogie-woogie
Luther played the boogie-woogie
Luther played the boogie-woogie
Luther played the boogie-woogie
Luther played the boogie in the strangest kind of way
Now didn't Luther play the boogie strange

MEAN-EYED CAT

1955

I gave my woman half my money at the general store
I said, "Now buy a little groceries, and don't spend no more."
Then she paid ten dollars for a ten-cent hat
And got some store-bought cat food for her mean-eyed cat

When I give her ten more dollars for a one-way ticket
She was mad as could be
Then I bet ten more that if she ever left
She'd come a-crawling back to me

When I woke up this morning and I turned my head
There wasn't a cotton-picking thing on her side of the bed
I found a little note where her head belonged
It said, "Dear John, honey, baby, I'm long gone."

When I heard a whistle blowing, and the big wheels a-turning
I was scared as I could be
I put on my overalls and I headed for town
Gonna bring her back with me

I asked the man down at the station if he'd seen her there
I told him all about her pretty eyes and long, blond hair
He spit his tobacco, said, "I'll be dad-blamed.
I believe I did see her leaving on the eastbound train."

I bought a round-trip ticket on the eastbound train
I was broke as I could be
But when I come back, I gotta buy another ticket
Gonna bring her back with me

Well, I got off the train somewhere in Arkansas
And I worked up the guts to call my mother-in-law
She said, "I'll tell you where she is if you act right.
She's working four to twelve at Trucker's World tonight."

Well, when I walked in, she saw me and she took off her apron
And she grabbed her going-home hat
She bought a ticket with her tips, now we're curled up on the sofa
Me and her and that mean-eyed cat

PORT OF LONELY HEARTS

1954

A ship came in, but it was empty
And then it sailed back out to sea again
Now there's a sail on the horizon
And now I wait until your ship comes in

And I'll be waiting in the port of lonely hearts
Watching for your topsail on the sea
Praying that my ship of love will come
To the port of lonely hearts where I will be

I'll brave the storm until you're with me
'Cause wind and rain can't change a love that's true
I'll be alone until you anchor
And then I'll leave this lonely port with you

'Til then I'm waiting in the port of lonely hearts
Watching for your topsail on the sea
Praying that my ship of love will come
To the port of lonely hearts where I will be

ROCK 'N' ROLL RUBY

1955

Well, I took my Ruby jukin' on the outskirts of town
She took her high heels off and rolled her stockings down
She put a quarter in the jukebox, to get a little beat
Everybody started watching all the rhythm in her feet

She's my rock and roll Ruby, rock and roll
Rock and roll Ruby, rock and roll
When Ruby starts a-rockin'
It satisfies my soul

Well, Ruby started rockin' 'bout one o'clock
And when she started rockin', she just couldn't stop
She rocked on the tables and she rocked on the floor
And everybody yelled, "Ruby, rock some more."

She's my rock and roll Ruby, rock and roll
Rock and roll Ruby, rock and roll
When Ruby starts a-rockin'
It satisfies my soul

It was 'round about four and I thought she would stop
She looked at me and then she looked at the clock
She said, "Wait a minute, Daddy, now don't get sore.
All I want to do is rock a little bit more."

She's my rock and roll Ruby, rock and roll
Rock and roll Ruby, rock and roll
When Ruby starts a-rockin'
It satisfies my soul

One night, my Ruby left me all alone
I tried to contact her on the telephone
I finally found her about twelve o'clock
She said, "Leave me alone, Daddy,
'Cause your Ruby wants to rock."

She's my rock and roll Ruby, rock and roll
Rock and roll Ruby, rock and roll
When Ruby starts a-rockin'
And it satisfies my soul

SO DOGGONE LONESOME

1955

I do my best to hide this low-down feeling
I try to make believe there's nothing wrong
But they're always asking me about you, darling
And it hurts me so to tell them that you're gone

If they ask me, I guess I'd be denying
That I've been unhappy, all alone
But if they heard my heart, they'd hear it cryin'
Where's my darling, when's she coming home?

I ask myself a million times what's right for me to do
To try to lose my blues alone or hang around for you
Well, I make it pretty good until that moon comes shining through
And then I get so doggone lonesome

Time stands still when you're a-waiting
Sometimes I think my heart is stopping, too
One lonely hour seems forever
Sixty minutes more to wait for you

But I guess I'll keep waiting 'til you're with me
'Cause I believe that loving you is right
But I don't care if the sun don't rise tomorrow
If I can't have you with me tonight

Well, I know I'll keep on loving you
'Cause true love can't be killed
I ought to get you off of my mind
But I guess I never will

I could have a dozen others
But I know I'd love you still
'Cause I get so doggone lonesome

WIDE OPEN ROAD

1954

Well, you said you had enough
You said that you were leaving
I said, "Shove off, honey, baby, I ain't grieving.
Pack your bags and pull out this evening.
There's a wide open road."

Early this morning, you were nowhere about it
And so I searched the town but you had done pulled out
I looked north, east, and west and then a-leading south
I saw a wide open road

There's a wide open road
It's leading south from my abode
If you stick around and turn your damper down
There's a wide open road

Well, the reason I was looking for you all over town
Was to tell you that your kitty cat is still around
And you left your wedding ring when you went down
That wide open road

If you gonna stay away then, honey, let me know
How to cook hot biscuits, how to roll a dough
Everything's gone crazy since I told you to go
Down that wide open road

There's a wide open road
And, honey, I want you to know
You can look down south or you can turn back home
And there's a wide open road

ALL MAMA'S CHILDREN

with Carl Lee Perkins

1956

There was an old woman that lived in a shoe
Had so many children, she didn't know what to do
They were doin' all right, 'til she took 'em to town
The kids started pickin' 'em up and puttin' 'em down

Now all your children wanna rock, mama
All your children want to roll
They wanna roll, wanna rock, wanna bop 'til they pop
All your children want to rock

Well, we're not tryin' to live too fast
But we might as well try to live in class
We better move out before the rent comes due
'Cause we wanna live in a blue suede shoe

All your children wanna rock, mama
All your children want to roll
Wanna roll, wanna rock, wanna bop 'til they pop
All your children want to rock

Well, every night when it's quiet and still
You can hear it echoing through the hill
To a blue suede shoe on a mountaintop
All of mama's young'uns are doin' the bop

All them children wanna rock, mama
All your children wanna roll
They wanna roll, wanna rock, wanna bop 'til they pop
All your children wanna rock

GET RHYTHM

1956

Hey, get rhythm
When you get the blues
Come on, get rhythm
When you get the blues

Get a rock and roll feeling in your bones
Put taps on your toes, and get goin'
Get rhythm
When you get the blues

A little shoeshine boy, he never gets low-down
But he's got the dirtiest job in town
Bending low at the people's feet
On a windy corner of a dirty street

Well, I asked him while he shined my shoes
How'd he keep from getting the blues
He grinned as he raised his little head
He popped his shoeshine rag, and then he
said

"Get rhythm
When you get the blues.
Come on, get rhythm
When you get the blues.

"A jumpy rhythm makes you feel so fine.
It'll take all your trouble from your worried
mind.
Get rhythm
When you get the blues.

"Get rhythm
When you get the blues.
Come on, get rhythm
When you get the blues.

"Get a rock and roll feeling in your bones.
Put taps on your toes, and get goin'.
Get rhythm
When you get the blues."

Well, I sat and I listened to the shoeshine boy
And I thought I was gonna jump for joy
Slapped on the shoe polish left and right
He took his shoeshine rag and he held it tight

He stopped once to wipe the sweat away
I said, "You're a mighty little boy to be
a-workin' that way."
He said, "I like it," with a big wide grin
Kept on a-poppin' and he said again:

"Get rhythm
When you get the blues.
Come on, get rhythm
When you get the blues.

"It only costs a dime, just a nickel a shoe.
It does a million dollars' worth of good for
you.
Get rhythm
When you get the blues."

I WALK THE LINE

1956

I keep a close watch on this heart of mine
I keep my eyes wide open all the time
I keep the ends out for the tie that binds
Because you're mine, I walk the line

I find it very, very easy to be true
I find myself alone when each day is through
Yes, I'll admit that I'm a fool for you
Because you're mine, I walk the line

As sure as night is dark and day is light
I keep you on my mind both day and night
And happiness I've known proves that it's right
Because you're mine, I walk the line

You've got a way to keep me on your side
You give me cause for love that I can't hide
For you I know I'd even try to turn the tide
Because you're mine, I walk the line

I keep a close watch on this heart of mine
I keep my eyes wide open all the time
I keep the ends out for the tie that binds
Because you're mine, I walk the line

I Walk the Line

by Johnny Cash

E B7
I keep a close watch on this heart

E E B7
of mine — I keep my eyes wide

E
open all the time — I keep the

A E
ends out for the tie that binds —

B7 E
Because you're mine, I walk the line.

A E A
I find it very very easy to be true

A E A
I find myself alone when each day's thru

D A
Yes I'll admit that I'm a fool for you

E A
Because you're mine, I walk the line

Because you're mine I walk the line

Johnny Cash © 1956

STRAIGHT A'S IN LOVE

1956

Well, a-reading and a-writing and arithmetic
Never did get through to me
It ain't because I'm square or thick
'Cause I learned my ABC's

But when I graduated from the grammar
school
And I moved one grade above
I began to be a snook at books
But I made straight A's in love

Now, the teacher would say to learn your
algebra
But I'd bring home C's and D's
How could I make an A when there's a
swinging maid
On the left and on the right and in the back
and the front of me

Oh, my grades are low on my card, I know
But they oughta give me one above
If they'd give me a mark for learning in the
dark
I'd have straight A's in love

Now, in my senior year with graduation near
I did my homework every night
And when my mama said I oughta go to bed
I'd turn out all the lights

But my sweetie pie was waiting right outside
She'd be a-cooing like a dove
Though I did my best, I failed semester test
But I made straight A's in love

Now, the teacher would say to learn your
algebra
But I'd bring home C's and D's
How could I make an A when there's a
swinging maid
On the left and on the right and in the back
and the front of me

Oh, my grades are low on my card, I know
But they oughta give me one above
If they'd give me a mark for learning in the
dark
I'd have straight A's in love

THERE YOU GO

1956

Well, here I am and there you go, you're gone again
I know you're gonna be the way you've always been
Breakin' hearts and telling lies is all you know
Another guy gives you the eye and there you go

There you go, you're gone again
I should have known, I couldn't win
There you go, you're by his side
You're gonna break another heart
You're gonna tell another lie

Because I love you so, I take much more than I should take
I want you, even though I know my heart is gonna break
You build me up and for a while I'm all a-glow
Then your fickle heart sees someone else and there you go

There you go, you're gone again
I should have known, I couldn't win
There you go, you're by his side
You're gonna break another heart
You're gonna tell another lie

TRAIN OF LOVE

1956

Train of love's a-coming, big black wheels a-humming
People waiting at the station, happy hearts are drumming
Trainman, tell me maybe, ain't you got my baby?
Every so often, everybody's baby gets the urge to roam
But everybody's baby but mine's coming home

Now, stop your whistle blowing, 'cause I got ways of knowing
You're bringing other people's lovers, but my own keeps going
Train of love's deceiving, when she's not gone she's leaving
Every so often, everybody's baby gets the urge to roam
But everybody's baby but mine's coming home

Train of love's now hasting, sweethearts standing waiting
Here and there and everywhere, they're gonna be embracing
Trainman, tell me maybe, ain't you got my baby?
Every so often, everybody's baby gets the urge to roam
But everybody's baby but mine's coming home

Train of love's a-leaving, leaving my heart grieving
But early or late, I sit and wait, because I'm still believing
We'll walk away together, though I may wait forever
Every so often, everybody's baby gets the urge to roam
But everybody's baby but mine's coming home

BIG RIVER

1957

Now, I taught the weeping willow how to cry
And I showed the clouds how to cover up a clear blue sky
And the tears that I cried for that woman are gonna flood you, Big River
And I'm gonna sit right here until I die

I met her accidentally in St. Paul, Minnesota
And it tore me up every time I heard her drawl, Southern drawl
Then I heard my dream went back downstream, cavortin' in Davenport
And I followed you, Big River, when you called

Then you took me to St. Louis later on, down the river
A freighter said she's been here but she's gone, boy, she's gone
I found her trail in Memphis, but she just walked up the bluff
She raised a few eyebrows and then she went on down alone

Well now, I pulled into Natchez the next day, down the river
And there wasn't much there to make a rounder stay very long
And when I left it was raining, so nobody saw me cry
Big River, why is she doing me that way?

Now, won't you bat it down by Baton Rouge, River Queen, roll it on
Take that woman on down to New Orleans, New Orleans
Go on, I've had enough, dump my blues down in the Gulf
She loves you, Big River, more than me

Now, I taught the weeping willow how to cry, cry, cry
And I showed the clouds how to cover up a clear blue sky
And the tears that I cried for that woman are gonna flood you, Big River
And I'm gonna sit right here until I die

COUNTRY BOY

1957

Country boy, ain't got no shoes
Country boy, ain't got no blues
Well, you work all day while you're wantin' to play
In the sun and the sand, with the faces tanned
But at the end of the day, when your work is done
You ain't got nothing but fun

Country boy, ain't got no ills
Country boy, don't owe no bills
You get a wiggly worm and then you watch him squirm
While you put him on a hook and you drop him in a brook
And if everything's gonna turn out right, you're gonna fry fish tonight

Country boy, you're lucky, free
Country boy, I wish I was you, and you was me

Country boy, got work to do
Country boy, in the mornin' dew
You gotta cut the weeds, you gotta plant the seeds
There's many a row you know you gotta hoe
But when it's quittin' time, and your work is through
There's a lot of life in you

Country boy, got a shaggy dog
Country boy, up a hollow log
Well, he comes in a run, when you pick up your gun
And with a shell or two, and your dog and you
When you get your rabbit, you'll skin his hide
He's gonna be good fried

Country boy, you got a lot to lose
Country boy, how I wish I was in your shoes

Management
ROLAND M. HOWELL
JERRY L. JOHNSON

312 S. E. SECOND AVENUE
MIAMI, FLORIDA

Country Boy, aint got no shoes
Country Boy, aint got no blues
Well you work all day
While you're wantin to play
In the sun and the sand
With a face that's tanned
But at the end of the day
When your work is done
You aint got nothin but fun

Country boy aint got no ills
Country boy dont owe no bills
You get a wiggle worm
And you watch him squirm
While you put him on a hook
And then you drop him in the brook
And if everythings gonna turn out right
You're gonna fry fish tonight
Country boy you're lucky free
Country boy I wish I was you
And you was me

Country Boy got a shaggy dog
Country Boy up a holler log
Well he comes in a run
When you pick up your gun
You get a shell or two
And with your dog and you
When you get your rabbit
You'll skin his hide
He's sure gonna be good fried.

Country Boy, you got work to do
Country Boy, in the early dew
You gotta cut all the weeds
You gotta plant the seed
There's many a row
That you know you gotta hoe
But when it's quittin time
And your work is through
There's sure lot of life in you
Country Boy you've got a lot to lose
Country Boy I wish that I was
in your shoes

1

COME IN, STRANGER

1957

She said, "Come in, stranger,
It's good to have you home.
I hurried through 'cause I knew it was you
When I saw your dog wagging his tail.
Honey, why didn't you let me know by mail?
You've been gone so long."

She said, "Come in, stranger,
I know you're weary from all the miles.
Just sit right there in your easy chair
And tell me all about the places you've been
And how long it'll be before you leave again.
I hope it's a long, long while."

She said, "Come in, stranger,
Everything around home is fine.
I've watched and I've waited for you to get back
And I missed you all the time."

She said, "Come in, stranger,
Oh, how I miss you when you're gone.
I walk the floor and I watch the door
And when I lie awake and wonder where you can be
I'd give anything to have you here with me.
I get so lonesome all alone."

She said, "Come in, stranger,
And won't you listen to my plea?
Stay long enough, so that the one I love
Is not a stranger to me."

DON'T MAKE ME GO

1957

You take my hand and smile at me
But I can tell you'd rather be
Alone or with somebody else you know
And when your eyes look into mine
That old-time love light doesn't shine
But let me try again, don't make me go

I want you, don't make me go
My heart would break, I'd miss you so
Trading love for sympathy is old to me
What's this lovesick heart to do when it cries for only you?
Hold me close, I love you so, don't make me go

I'm sorry that I never knew the way to show my love for you
I took too much for granted all the time
Two hearts in love must give and take
When one heart fails, the other breaks
Don't make me go, I wanna show this love of mine

I want you, don't make me go
My heart would break, I'd miss you so
Trading love for sympathy is old to me
What's this lovesick heart to do when it cries for only you?
Hold me close, I love you so, don't make me go

GIVE MY LOVE TO ROSE

1957

I found him by the railroad track this morning
I could see that he was nearly dead
I knelt down beside him and I listened
Just to hear the words the dying fellow said

He said, "They let me out of prison out in Frisco.
For ten long years, I've paid for what I'd done.
I was trying to get back to Louisiana
To see my Rose and get to know my son.

"Give my love to Rose, please, won't you, mister?
Take her all my money, tell her, buy some pretty clothes.
Tell my boy that Daddy's so proud of him
And don't forget to give my love to Rose.

"Won't you tell them I said thanks for waiting for me?
Tell my boy to help his mom at home.
Tell my Rose to try to find another
'Cause it ain't right that she should live alone.

"Mister, here's a bag with all my money.
It won't last them long the way it goes.
God bless you for finding me this morning
Now, don't forget to give my love to Rose.

"Give my love to Rose, please, won't you, mister?
Take her all my money, tell her, buy some pretty clothes.
Tell my boy that Daddy's so proud of him
And don't forget to give my love to Rose."

HOME OF THE BLUES

with Douglas Glenn Tubb and Lily McAlpin

1957

Just around the corner, there's heartache
Down the street that losers use
If you can wade in through the teardrops
You'll find me at the home of the blues

I walk and cry while my heartbeat
Keeps time with the drag of my shoes
The sun never shines through this window of mine
It's dark at the home of the blues

Oh, but the place is filled with the sweetest memories
Memories so sweet that I cry
Dreams that I've had left me feeling so bad
I just want to give up and lay down and die

So if you've just lost your sweetheart
And it seems there's no good way to choose
Come along with me, misery loves company
You're welcome at the home of the blues

Just around the corner, there's heartache
Down the street that losers use
If you can wade in through the teardrops
You'll find me at the home of the blues

I STILL MISS SOMEONE

with Roy Cash Jr.

1957

At my door the leaves are falling
A cold wild wind will come
Sweethearts walk by together
And I still miss someone

I go out on a party
And look for a little fun
But I find a darkened corner
'Cause I still miss someone

No, I never got over those blue eyes
I see them everywhere
I miss those arms that held me
When all the love was there

I wonder if she's sorry
For leaving what we'd begun
There's someone for me somewhere
And I still miss someone

LEAVE THAT JUNK ALONE

1957

Well, you come home feeling
For the knob on the door
You better pick up your feet
You're gonna fall on the floor
I keep on telling you
I'll tell you some more

You better leave that junk alone
And drink water
Lord, that liquor is hot
Drink water
You don't wanna be a sot
You better lay down the bottle
And put on the top
And drink cool H_2O

Well, your eyes are baggy
And a bloodshot red
It's been a week or two
Since you've been in bed
You better pay attention now
To what I said

You better leave that junk alone
And drink water
Lord, that liquor is hot
Drink water
You don't wanna be a sot
You better lay down the bottle
And put on the top
And drink cool H_2O

Well, now I'll forgive you
For your running around
If you just promise
That you come unwound
I'll buy you anything
You want in town

If you'll leave that junk alone
And drink water
Lord, that liquor is hot
Drink water
You don't wanna be a sot
You better lay down the bottle
And put on the top
And drink cool H_2O

NEXT IN LINE

1957

The next in line will be someone who loves you
The next in line is me, 'cause it's my time
Now, how long will it be, 'til you end my misery?
You better be prepared to linger, when you get to me

The time has come for you to love me, if you ever are
Come to me now, so I can make you mine
I watched them rush to you so fast
I waited so I'd be the last
It's my time, 'cause I'm the next in line

The next in line will want your love forever
The next in line is me and here I am
Give me a day or two and I'll get through to you
You'd been my baby long ago, if you'd turned down a few

This old heart can't take much more waiting for your love
I'm tired and we're running short of time
I'll make you love me more than everyone before
It's my time to try, 'cause I'm the next in line

I stood and watched you take their hearts and break 'em one by one
My time was coming, so I waited while you had your fun
Now I'm through a-waiting way behind
It's my time, 'cause I'm the next in line

THAT'S RIGHT

with Carl Lee Perkins

1957

I get off on 4 o'clock, just a little 'fore it's dark
Standing on my steps at 4:05 sharp
Lucy gal, you better get that dog
You better tell old lover boy to get checked
out

'Cause that's right
Well, that's right

I got a funny feeling, I wanna go home
When I get there, I found you on Mister Bell's
telephone
A lot of people been telling me what to do
But when it comes to loving, gal, that's me
and you

Ain't that right
That's right
Well, that's right
That's right

In my vocabulary you've been reading fine
But it seems to me I've been walking the line
When it comes to loving, I'm dumb in spots
But when I get mad, gal, I sure get hot

Ain't that right
That's right

If what they say is true and there is another
joker
Well, you's a number five in this game of
poker
When I find that cat who's getting my sugar
It's gonna be rough when I catch that bugger

That's right
That's right
Well, that's right
That's right

Do you ever stop to think about
When something's right
It's just flat right, honey
That's right
That's right
That's right
That's right

Johnny Cash

TWO

✷ MOVEMENT ✷

1958–1963

CASH'S TENURE AT Sun Records ended fairly quickly, a casualty of a collision between the artist's burgeoning aspirations and the small label's limited abilities to help further them. Columbia Records, the biggest record company in the world, offered Cash an opportunity to expand past the singles and jingles of the pop-oriented Sun, where he was often awkward and uncomfortable and felt constrained. At the new label, Cash found himself among an international roster of renowned artists, which gave him cachet of his own. He used the freedom that provided in unexpected ways.

Cash's outlook — and output — seemed to transform almost overnight. This is where the iconic, haunting "I Still Miss Someone," a song that endures more than sixty years and hundreds of interpretations later, went from paper to posterity. Listeners could scarcely believe this was the same would-be teenybopper who gave the world that "Little Wooly Booger" just an eyeblink ago. Even "I Walk the Line" — widely regarded as one of the greatest country songs ever written — almost sounded like merely a prelude. Then, in "Don't Take Your Guns to Town," Cash presented a morality tale that serves as a template for the discourses on responsibility and consequences that distinguish his career. Record buyers pushed the saga of a reckless, naive young cowboy who ends up bleeding out on a dusty barroom floor to number one on the charts for over a month. There is a through line to Johnny Cash's march into virtually every Hall of Fame that exists, and it begins here.

Even as Cash pushed the envelope on his artistry, he called again on his bedrock for foundation, to enormously great and lasting effect. Dyess was firmly in the rearview, but it would never be far away. First-person accounts of his childhood on the farm — "Five Feet High and Rising," "Pickin' Time," and "The Man on the Hill" — were all composed during this pivotal era, taking permanent places in the great American songbook. He relied less on the train allusions but did continue to return to nostalgic themes, even as his ambitions led him toward more contemporary pursuits, such as movies and television. These paradoxes made it difficult for others to assign him a specific, if confining, musical identity, leaving Cash without a default home base. Still, he was content to straddle these various worlds on his own terms — come what may.

No world was more incongruous for a rising teen idol than gospel music, and Sun strove mightily to keep the young Cash pining for lost loves and not searching for a home far beyond the skies. Once he was at Columbia, however, this grandson and great-grandson of Missionary Baptist preachers threw off the shackles, recording a hymn — "It Was Jesus," which he wrote himself — at his first recording session with the new label and releasing an entire album of gospel songs soon after. Even as the new guy, Cash was confident enough in his own skin (and evidently his convictions) that he penned four original hymns for that album and boldly placed them alongside traditional classics like "Swing Low, Sweet Chariot." *Hymns by Johnny Cash* was an unexpected commercial success that reinforced the appeal of his highly personal, unconventional approach to his craft. He would eventually record nine gospel and religious albums.

Among the fortuitous, if unheralded, circumstances that made all this exploration possible was Johnny Cash's immediate embrace of the long-play album format as a forum for his music. Columbia had already become the preeminent proponent (and seller) of the big vinyl records, and was known to encourage its artists to extend past perceived limitations in commercial viability in the quest for quality or perhaps cultural significance. Such vision was not part of Sun Records' DNA, where music was made in a hurry and patience was a vice, not a virtue. It is inconceivable that Cash's *Hymns,* or dozens of his other artistic triumphs and breakthroughs, could have been made at Sun.

Leaving the label that birthed his career could have resulted in him burying his originality and uniqueness, especially since moving on also entailed moving out, with Memphis being replaced by the machines of Los Angeles and Nashville. This was not a bad thing to someone whose eyes were on a much bigger prize, so Cash went all in, simultaneously changing recording studios and residences. Home became a series of ever-changing addresses in California (at least partially the result of a family that would grow to include four daughters and a weary, worried wife). He lost focus. He almost lost it all.

The story of one-time wonder boy Johnny Cash and the klieg lights of the City of (often fallen) Angels is not a particularly happy one. Too fast, too far, too much. His writing became much more introspective as he retreated deep within himself. Sad, lonely, homesick, guilty. What happened to the buoyant young man on the train who couldn't wait to "breathe that Southern air"?

Although storm clouds had gathered, waiting to let loose a torrent that would nearly drown him, Cash's troubled times were, in many ways, his most creative. The despair he felt as the California dream crumbled led him to seek stability with new friends, different traditions, and fresh inspirations, which brought changed perspectives and some of his best work. The California folk music community, with its respect for rural values and honoring of uncomplicated ways and days, guided Cash's return to his roots.

In *Songs of Our Soil,* an especially "realistic" (to others, that read: dark) collection of "earth songs," he wrote no fewer than seven of the tracks. A reprise of the railroad theme was used to great effect in his masterful travelogue *Ride This Train,* for which he wrote another half dozen. *Ride This Train* is regarded as Cash's first concept album (and his professed favorite of all his works) and *Blood, Sweat and Tears* among the best—more products of his attachment to the long-play record, which allowed him immense space to devote entire volumes to his histories, narratives, lessons, and epics. Although Cash was not the progenitor of the concept album, he raised it to an art form. And, as in the past, he surely would not have had that opportunity if not for Columbia, and the world would not have felt their impact without California, warts and all.

ALL OVER AGAIN

1958

Every time I look at you, I fall in love
All over again
Every time I think of you, it all begins
All over again

One little dream at night and I can dream all day
It only takes a memory to thrill me
One little kiss from you and I just fly away
Pour me out your love until you fill me

I wanna fall in love, beginning from the start
All over again
Show me how you stole away my heart
All over again

One little dream at night and I can dream all day
It only takes a memory to thrill me
One little kiss from you and I just fly away
Pour me out your love until you fill me

I wanna fall in love, beginning from the start
All over again
Show me how you stole away my heart
All over again

DON'T TAKE YOUR GUNS TO TOWN

1958

A young cowboy named Billy Joe grew
restless on the farm
A boy filled with wanderlust who really meant
no harm
He changed his clothes and shined his boots
And combed his dark hair down
And his mother cried as he walked out,
"Don't take your guns to town, son.
Leave your guns at home, Bill,
Don't take your guns to town."

He laughed and kissed his mom and said,
"Your Billy Joe's a man.
I can shoot as quick and straight as anybody
can.
But I wouldn't shoot without a cause.
I'd gun nobody down."
But she cried again as he rode away,
"Don't take your guns to town, son.
Leave your guns at home, Bill,
Don't take your guns to town."

He sang a song as on he rode, his guns hung
at his hips
He rode into a cattle town, a smile upon his
lips
He stopped and walked into a bar
And laid his money down
But his mother's words echoed again:
"Don't take your guns to town, son.
Leave your guns at home, Bill,
Don't take your guns to town."

He drank his first strong liquor then to calm
his shaking hand
And tried to tell himself at last he had become
a man
A dusty cowpoke at his side
Began to laugh him down
And he heard again his mother's words:
"Don't take your guns to town, son.
Leave your guns at home, Bill,
Don't take your guns to town."

Filled with rage, then Billy Joe reached for his
gun to draw
But the stranger drew his gun and fired before
he even saw
As Billy Joe fell to the floor
The crowd all gathered 'round
And wondered at his final words:
"Don't take your guns to town, son.
Leave your guns at home, Bill,
Don't take your guns to town."

DON'T TAKE YOUR GUNS TO TOWN

(alternate version)

1980s

A young man of propriety
Found life to be a bore
He had studied politics and law
Psychology and more

He felt cold and jaded
Overall, and all around
On impulse, he picked up a gun
In the sleazy part of town

But a lady who understood him said,
"Don't let the hammer down, Joe.
Leave the thing at home, no,
Don't take the gun to town."

They fussed and he said,
"Please, don't underestimate your man.
I can do and be and dare
As anybody can.

"Sweetheart, there are people
Who need silencing, and so
I shall avenge society.
Definitely I'll go
And take my gun to town."

He named a politician
Who had long been on his list
And a singer and an actor
And others I won't miss

"The preachers with their promises
Are plastic, bogus clowns."

But a kind, sweet voice kept haunting him:
"Joe, don't take your gun to town.

"Do not draw the gun.
Let God's peace rule the day.
Throw the gun away, Joe,
Let this obsession go."

The happy, cheering crowd, unaware
Watched the motorcade move on
With a change of heart, Joe
Stood with his sweetheart, alone

Then they walked to the river bridge
Where, midway, he sat down
He dropped the gun
And the water made a laughing sound

The cold steel blue for killing
Settled in the mud, deep down
And never will be found

Thank God for the woman
Who went out into the night
And quietly corrected
This great wrong and made it right

The intent of the gun
And Joe, with love, she turned around
A tragedy, unsound
And heaven answered down,
"Don't take your guns to town."

Dont Take Your Gun to Town

A young man of propriety
found life to be a bore
He had studied politics and law
Psychology and more
He felt cold and jaded
Over all, and all around
On impulse he picked up a gun
In the sleazy part of town
But a lady who understood him said
Dont let the hammer down Joe
Leave the thing at home, no –
Dont take the gun to town.

They kissed and he said please
Dont underestimate your man
I can do and be and dare
As anybody can
Sweetheart there are people
Who need silencing and so
I shall avenge society of hypocrites, so,
Definitely I'll go, and
Take my gun to town –

He named a politician
Who had long been on his list
A singer and an actor
And the preachers with their promises
Are plastic bogus clowns
But a kind sweet voice kept haunting
Joe dont take your gun to town

Stay here with me dont go no
Dont take the gun to town –
In suit of double knit and tie
He drove down to the square
The famous man would soon arrive
And Joe'd be waiting there
He felt the cold steel in his coat
Full loaded cocked and primed
The motorcade appeared
But he heard her voice one more time
Dont take your gun to town Joe
Let your heart beat with mine please
Dont take your gun to town

The limousine approached
And he could glimpse the man inside
Waving smiling bowing to the
Tributes on each side –
Remorse and fear came over Joe
But he would not be bound
He muffled out the inner voice
Dont take your gun to town
Throw the thing away, I pray
Dont take your gun to town

The time was suddenly right
For him to slay the V.I.P.
Trembling he said
All these admirers wont change me
His hand went for the weapon
Then he felt a tender touch
She firmly held his hand and said
True love can change so much Joe
Let this notion go, hon,

Do not draw the gun
Let Gods peace rule the day, Then
Throw the gun away Joe
Let this obsession go

The happy cheering crowd
Watched the motorcade move on
With a change of heart, Joe
Stood with his sweetheart alone
Then they walked to the river bridge
Where midway he sat down
He dropped the gun and the water
Made a laughing sound
The cold blue steel for killing
Settled in the mud deep down
And never will be found –
mod –
Thank God for the woman
Who went out into the night
And quickly corrected
This great wrong and made it right
The intent of the gun
With love she turned around
A tragedy unfound
And heaven answered down
Dont take your guns to town

DRINK TO ME

1958

Drink to me, drink to me
Drink to me, drink to me
Drink to me
A rose, a carnation, the lily, and an orchid
Make such a pretty bouquet

But only the orchid was worthy of you
So I threw all the others away

Then you took the orchid
And you breathed on its petals
And after a day or two
The flower still blooms
But the scent's not the orchid's
It carries the savor of you

So if you're gonna drink to me
Drink with your eyes
And I'll never cry for wine
Or leave a kiss in an empty coffee cup
Then pass it from your lips to mine

'Cause I've got a thirst burning
Way down in my soul
And honey from a sugar tree
Is not half as sweet
As the air that you breathe
Honey, come here and drink to me

FRANKIE'S MAN, JOHNNY

1958

Well now, Frankie and Johnny were
sweethearts
They were true as a blue, blue sky
He was a long-legged guitar picker
With a wicked, wanderin' eye
But he was her man nearly all of the time

Well, Johnny, he packed up to leave her
But he promised he'd be back
He said he had a little pickin' to do
A little farther down the track
He said, "I'm your man, I wouldn't do
you wrong."

Well, Frankie curled up on the sofa
Thinkin' about her man
Far away the couples were dancing
To the music of his band
He was Frankie's man, he wasn't doin'
her wrong

Then in the front door walked a redhead
Johnny saw her right away
She came down by the bandstand
To watch him while he played
He was Frankie's man, but she was far
away

He sang every song to the redhead
She smiled back at him
Then he came and sat at her table
Where the lights were low and dim
What Frankie didn't know
Wouldn't hurt her none

Then the redhead jumped up and
slapped him
She slapped him a time or two
She said, "I'm Frankie's sister
And I was checking up on you.
If you're her man, you better treat her
right."

Well, the moral of this story is be good
But carry a stick
Sometimes it looks like a guitar picker
Just can't tell what to pick
He was Frankie's man
And he still ain't done her wrong

I'LL REMEMBER YOU

1958

Come to me, sweetheart
And let me hold you
One minute more will help me through
The loneliness that's due

Give me another kiss
That I can dream on
Then you'll know that where I go
I'll remember you

Hold my hand
And tell me that you love me
Look at me the same old way
As only you can do

And when you're out of reach
My heart will know what to turn to
When you remember me
Remember, I'll remember you

I'll remember you
I'll remember you
Honey, how could I forget, when I love you
I'll remember you

You don't have to worry, I'll remember you
I'll remember you
Honey, how could I forget, when I love you
I'll remember you

IT WAS JESUS

1958

Well, a man walked down by Galilee
So the holy book does say
And a great multitude was gathered there
Without a thing to eat for days

Up stepped a little boy with a basket
"Please take this, Lord," he said
And with just five loaves and two little fishes
Five thousand had fish and bread

Who was it everybody? It was Jesus
Who was it everybody? It was Jesus
Who was it everybody? It was Jesus
It was Jesus Christ, our Lord

Now pay close attention, little children
It's somebody you ought to know
It's all about a man that walked on earth
Nearly two thousand years ago

Well, He healed the sick and afflicted
And He raised them from the dead
Then they nailed Him on an old rugged cross
And put thorns on His head

Who was it everybody? It was Jesus
Who was it everybody? It was Jesus
Who was it everybody? It was Jesus
It was Jesus Christ, our Lord

Well, they took Him down and they buried Him
And after the third day
When they came to His tomb, well, they knew He was gone
'Cause the stone was rolled away

"He's not here, for He is risen,"
The angel of the Lord then said
And when they saw Him walking with His nail-scarred hands
They knew He came back from the dead

Who was it everybody? It was Jesus
Who was it everybody? It was Jesus
Who was it everybody? It was Jesus
It was Jesus Christ, our Lord

KATY TOO

with Jack Clement

1958

I'm not the going steady kind
I miss 'em all, all the time
I told Annie I'd be true
But I still think about Katy too
Katy too, Katy too
I still think about Katy too

If you should see Miss Mary Ann
Just tell her I'm her loving man
Give my love to Jane and Sue
But don't forget ol' Katy too
Katy too, Katy too
I still think about Katy too

I like Sadie's chicken stew
And Suzie's good at stitching
wool
I like Mary's barbecue
But I still like ol' Katy too
Katy too, Katy too
I still think about Katy too

Now, girls, I'm not the flirty kind
But I just can't make up my mind
I'd like to marry all of you
But I still miss ol' Katy too
Katy too, Katy too
I still think about Katy too

To all the girls I make this toast
I love you, everyone the most
But don't ask me to say "I do"
'Cause I still miss ol' Katy too
Katy too, Katy too
I still think about Katy too

Cupid, you been good to me
I got more girls than I can see
But if you give me all but two
Then let's squeeze in ol' Katy too
Katy too, Katy too
Let's squeeze in ol' Katy too

LEAD ME, FATHER

1958

When my hands are tired
And my step is slow
Walk beside me and give me
The strength to go

Fill my face with Your courage
So defeat won't show
Pick me up when I stumble
So the world won't know

Lead me, Father, with the staff of life
Give me the strength for a song
That the words I sing
Might more strength bring
To help some poor, troubled
Weary worker along

When my way is light
But I still can't see
With a strong hand
Strike out the blindness in me

Show me work that I should
Carry on for Thee
Make my way straight and narrow
Like You want it to be

Lead me, Father, with the staff of life
Give me the strength for a song
That the words I sing
Might more strength bring
To help some poor, troubled
Weary worker along

LIFE GOES ON

with Jack Clement

1958

My baby left me just the other day
I guess that things will never be the same
But I must forget that she is gone
Because time goes by and life goes on

Making plans, shaking hands
Try to prove that I'm a man
It's hard to do, but I must try
Because life goes on and so will I

It's been kind of tough these last few days
Trying to act normal and be gay
It's not easy to be all alone
But time goes by and life goes on

If I see her anywhere
I hope she thinks that I don't care
For after night there comes the dawn
Yes, time goes by and life goes on

MAMA'S BABY

1958

I met a girl out in a town that tore all my resistance down
I thought, What a dream this oughta be
I went with her a month or two and like any boy in love will do
Asked her if she would marry me

But she was a mama's baby, mama's baby
Though she loved me like she never loved another
She was a mama's baby, mama's baby
And she said that she just couldn't leave her mother

Then I said, "Well then, probably the only thing that's left for me
Is to go and come back in a year or so."
A year passed away and then I tried to win her hand again
She even packed her clothes, but she wouldn't go

'Cause she was a mama's baby, mama's baby
Though she loved me like she never loved another
She was a mama's baby, mama's baby
And she said that she just couldn't leave her mother

Well, I hung around 'til finally I persuaded her to marry me
Her mother said that it would be all right
We bought ourselves a little home and I finally got her off alone
But she stays with her mother every night

'Cause she's a mama's baby, mama's baby
Though she loved me like she never loved another
She's a mama's baby, mama's baby
And she said that she just couldn't leave her mother
Well, she said that she just couldn't leave her mother

OH, WHAT A DREAM

1958

I dreamed I walked in a field of flowers
Oh, what a dream
The houses all were silver towers
Oh, what a dream

Beside the road an angel sat
I said hello and I tipped my hat
And stopped when I saw her smile
And set me down a while
I set me down a while

I tried the angel for a kiss
But she turned away and my lips missed
She said, "Sir, I'll have you know
I met you just a while ago.
You're welcome for to sit
But calm yourself a bit, sir,
Calm yourself a bit."

I fell in love like one, two, three
I asked the angel to marry me
She said, "Sir, I can't marry you
But I'm a dream that can come true.
There are dreams of much my worth
That live upon the earth, sir,
Live upon the earth."

Then I awoke and found my love
As heavenly as the one above
We'll marry in a sea of flowers
Home will be a silver tower
There'll be heaven in my life
With an angel for a wife
With an angel for a wife

PICKIN' TIME

1958

I got cotton in the bottom land
It's up and growin' and I got a good stand
My good wife and them kids of mine
Gonna get new shoes, come pickin' time
Get new shoes, come pickin' time

Every night when I go to bed
I thank the Lord that my kids are fed
They live on beans eight days and nine
But I get 'em fat, come pickin' time
Get 'em fat, come pickin' time

The corn is yellow and the beans are high
The sun is hot in the summer sky
The work is hard 'til layin' by
Layin' by, 'til pickin' time
Layin' by, 'til pickin' time

It's hard to see by the coal-oil light
And I turn it off pretty early at night
'Cause a jug of coal oil costs a dime
But I'll stay up late, come pickin' time
Stay up late, come pickin' time

My old wagon barely gets me to town
I patched the wheels and I watered 'em down
Keep her in shape so she'll be fine
To haul my cotton, come pickin' time
Haul my cotton, come pickin' time

Last Sunday mornin', when they passed the hat
It was still nearly empty back where I sat
But the preacher smiled and said, "That's fine.
The Lord'll wait 'til pickin' time.
The Lord'll wait 'til pickin' time."

RUN SOFTLY, BLUE RIVER

1958

Run softly, Blue River, my darling's asleep
Run softly, Blue River, run cool and deep
Oh, I thrill to her kisses and she thrills to mine
Run softly while she sleeps and dreams for a time

'Cause she dreams of tomorrow, when she'll be my wife
And I pray that as peaceful as you is our life
And if your murmuring soothes me 'til I'm sleeping, too
Run softly, Blue River, we'll both dream with you

Oh, I thrill to her kisses and she thrills to mine
Run softly while she sleeps and dreams for a time
'Cause she dreams of tomorrow, when she'll be my wife
And I pray that as peaceful as you is our life
And if your murmuring soothes me 'til I'm sleeping, too
Run softly, Blue River, we'll both dream with you

WALKIN' THE BLUES

with Robert Lunn

1958

Well, I went down to the store
I got some brand-new shoes
I told them make the leather tough
I gotta walk the blues

Walkin' the blues
I'm walkin' the blues all day, all day
I'm wearin' out my shoes
But I'm walkin' the blues away

Well, my baby's got a heart
Like the cold north wind
I'll walk until I find her
Bring her back again

I'm walkin' the blues
Walkin' the blues all day, all day long
I'm wearin' out my shoes
But I'm walkin' the blues away

Well, now the man down at the station
He won't even talk
He said, "If you ain't got no money, boy,
Then you gotta walk."

That's why I'm walkin' the blues
Walkin' the blues all day
I'm wearin' out my shoes
But I'm walkin' the blues away

WHAT DO I CARE

1958

When I'm all through, if I haven't been what they think I should be
If the total isn't high enough when they figure me
When I grow old, if there's no gray from worry in my hair
What do I care? What do I care?

What do I care, just as long as you were mine a little while?
When the road was long and weary, you gave me a few good miles
What do I care if I miss a goal because I make a slip?
I'll still be satisfied because I tasted your sweet lips

What do I care, if I never have much money?
And sometimes, my table looks a little bare
Anything that I may miss is made up for each time we kiss
You love me and I love you, so what do I care?

What do I care, just as long as you were mine a little while?
When the road was long and weary, you gave me a few good miles
What do I care if I miss a goal because I make a slip?
I'll still be satisfied because I tasted your sweet lips

What do I care, if I never have much money?
And sometimes, my table looks a little bare
Anything that I may miss is made up for each time we kiss
You love me and I love you, so what do I care?

YOU'RE THE NEAREST THING TO HEAVEN

with Jim Atkins and Hoyt Johnson

1958

I have sailed the peaceful waters of the ocean deep and blue
I held my breath and watched the western sunset's golden hue
I've flown above the mountain peaks and valleys wide and green
But you're the nearest thing to heaven that I've seen

You're the nearest thing to heaven, yes, you are
I have searched for happiness so long and far
But my search for love was through, the day that I found you
'Cause you're the nearest thing to heaven, yes, you are

I confess that I've been tempted by alluring, magic charms
When a smile was flashed my way, and stood before two open arms
But I turned and walked away because I love you like I do
You're the nearest thing to heaven, darling you

You're the nearest thing to heaven, yes, you are
I have searched for happiness so long and far
But my search for love was through, the day that I found you
'Cause you're the nearest thing to heaven, yes, you are

I have watched the silver raindrops fall to earth, to cool the day
Watched the rainbow at twilight, when the clouds had blown away
I love the pretty flowers, but they cannot buy their worth
'Cause you're the nearest thing to heaven on this earth

You're the nearest thing to heaven, yes, you are
I have searched for happiness so long and far
But my search for love was through, the day that I found you
'Cause you're the nearest thing to heaven, yes, you are

THE CARETAKER

1959

I live in the cemetery
Ol' caretaker, they call me
In the wintertime I rake the leaves
And in the summer I cut the weeds

When a funeral comes the people cry and
pray
They bury their dead, then they all go away
But through their grief I can still see
Their hate and greed and jealousy

And here I work and I somehow hide
From a world that rushes by outside
And each night when I rest my head
I'm contented as the peaceful dead

But who's gonna cry when old John dies?
Who's gonna cry when old John dies?

Once I was a young man
Dashing with the girls
Now no one wants an old man
I lost my handsome curls

But I wanna say when my time comes
Lay me facing the rising sun
Put me in the corner where I buried my pup
Tell the preacher to pray, then cover me up

Don't lay flowers where my head should be
Maybe God will let some grow for me
And all the little children that I love like my
own
Will they be sorry that old John's gone?

Who's gonna cry when old John dies?
Who's gonna cry when old John dies?

DON'T STEP ON MOTHER'S ROSES

1959

We all were called to come back
To the old home on the farm
Mother's passed away
What a mournful day
And as my daddy watched
His eyes were filled with pain and hurt
When someone stepped upon a rose
And crushed it in the dirt

"Don't step on Mother's roses,"
Daddy cried
"She planted them
The day she was my bride.
And every time I see a rose
I see her smiling face.
She made my darkest days look bright
Around the old home place.

"Don't step on Mother's roses.
Let them grow
The way they did
Since many years ago.
They will bloom for me each year
And I will have Mother near.
Don't step on Mother's roses.
Let them grow."

Years have passed away
And how the old home place has changed
Daddy had to go
We all miss him so
Children pick the roses
As they go along the way
But when their petals are abused
I hear my daddy say

"Don't step on Mother's roses,"
Daddy cried
"She planted them
The day she was my bride.
And every time I see a rose
I see her smiling face.
She made my darkest days look bright
Around the old home place.

"Don't step on Mother's roses.
Let them grow
The way they did
Since many years ago.
They will bloom for me each year
And I will have Mother near.
Don't step on Mother's roses.
Let them grow."

FIVE FEET HIGH AND RISING

1959

How high's the water, Mama?
Two feet high and rising
How high's the water, Papa?
She said it's two feet high and rising

We can make it to the road in a homemade boat
'Cause that's the only thing we got left that'll float
It's already over all the wheat and the oats
Two feet high and rising

How high's the water, Mama?
Three feet high and rising
How high's the water, Papa?
She said it's three feet high and rising

Well, the hives are gone
I've lost my bees
The chickens are sleeping
In the willow trees
Cow's in water up past her knees
Three feet high and rising

How high's the water, Mama?
Four feet high and rising
How high's the water, Papa?
She said it's four feet high and rising

Hey, come look through the windowpane
The bus is coming, gonna take us to the train
Looks like we'll be blessed with a little more rain
Four feet high and rising

How high's the water, Mama?
Five feet high and rising
How high's the water, Papa?
She said it's five feet high and rising

Well, the rails are washed out north of town
We gotta head for higher ground
We can't come back 'til the water goes down
Five feet high and rising
Well, it's five feet high and rising

GOING TO MEMPHIS

traditional, collected by Alan Lomax and Hollie Dew

adapted in 1959

Bring a drink of water, Leroy
Bring a drink of water
If I could get to the mercy man
He'd give me some, I know

I got a gal in Vicksburg
Bertha is her name
Wish I was tied to Bertha
Instead of this ball and chain
I'm going to Memphis

A dude took all my money
Wouldn't let me see the cards
I owe the boss about a hundred years
For sleeping in his backyard
I'm going to Memphis

Like a bitter weed
I'm a bad seed
But when that levee's through and I am, too
Let the honky tonk roll on
Come morning, I'll be gone
I'm going to Memphis

I never been to Chicago
But it must be a mighty fine place
I couldn't get past Tennessee
With Mississippi all over my face
I'm going to Memphis

A freezing ground at night
Is my own folding bed
Polk salad is my bread and meat
And will be until I'm dead

I brought me a little water
In a Mr. Prince Albert can
But the boss man caught me drinking it
And I believe he broke my hand

They all call me crazy
For sassing Mr. Scott
My brother was killed for a deed I did
But I didn't remember what

Well, another boy is down
The shovel burned him out
Let me stand on his body
To see what the shouting's about
I'm going to Memphis

Like a bitter weed
I'm a bad seed
But when that levee's through and I am, too
Let the honky tonk roll on
Come morning, I'll be gone
I'm going to Memphis

HANK AND JOE AND ME

1959

In the desert where we searched for gold
The days are hot, the nights are cold
Hank and Joe and me walked on
So bold and brave and free

For days and days we fought the heat
I got so thirsty and I got so weak
And when I fell 'cause I couldn't go
I heard Hank say to Joe

"He's dying
For water.
Hear him crying
For water.

"Well, lay him down in the dust and sand."
He said, "Joe, you know, he's a dying man.
Leave him there and let him die.
I can't stand to hear him cry for water."

I don't remember how long I lay
But when I awoke it was the break of day
Buzzards circled miles ahead
I knew Hank and Joe were dead

My eyes were dimmed, but I could see
A bed of gold nuggets under me
Now, I know that it won't be long
'Til they decorate my bones

'Cause I'm dying
For water
Can't help crying
For water

Well, they laid me down in the dust and sand
He said, "Joe, you know, he's a dying man.
Leave him there and let him die.
I can't stand to hear him cry for water."
He couldn't stand to hear me cry for water

HE'LL BE A FRIEND

1959

Well, God told Noah to build an ark
He said, "It's gonna rain, gonna be dark.
Call in the animals, two by two,
And don't let a sinful man go through."

So the flood came just like He said
And every evil thing on earth was dead
But Noah's faith was like a rock
God laid his ark on a mountaintop

He'll be a friend and guide you
He'll walk along with you
He'll feel it there inside you
He'll help you make it through

When things look dark, Noah saw the light
'Cause faith had told him right was might
If you need a friend, He'll guide you
He'll be a friend to you

Well, you've heard of Samson, the strong man
The mightiest man in all the land
There was one purpose for his might
He had to deliver the Israelites

By the Philistines he was overcome
They tied him up to carry him home
But Samson prayed and his bounds were gone
He killed a thousand with an old jawbone

He'll be a friend and guide you
He'll walk along with you
He'll feel it there inside you
He'll help you make it through

God showed Samson what to do
And it's the same God that stands by you
If you need a friend, He'll guide you
He'll be a friend to you

I CALL HIM

with Roy Cash Jr.

1959

Well, the blue's still in the water
And the blue's still in the sky
And way beyond the blue
There's someone watching from on high

My clothes may be ragged
And my shoes may be worn
But I've been a wealthy boy
Since I've been born

'Cause I call Him when I'm troubled
And I call Him when I'm weak
And He always pulls me through my troubles
Some way and I believe
He'll be there, He'll be there
Like He always is to answer when I call Him

My mother used to tell me
I should take it slow
The pace is not what matters
It's the direction that you go

Keep your feet upon the path
And your eyes upon the goal
You'll have all the joy
A heart could ever hold

And I call Him when I'm troubled
And I call Him when I'm weak
And He always pulls me through my troubles
Some way and I believe
He'll be there, He'll be there
Like He always is to answer when I call Him
Like He always is to answer when I call Him

I GOT STRIPES

originally by Huddie Ledbetter

adapted in 1959 with Charles Williams

On a Monday, I was arrested
On a Tuesday, they locked me in the jail
On a Wednesday, my trial was attested
On a Thursday, they said guilty and the judge's gavel fell

I got stripes, stripes around my shoulders
I got chains, chains around my feet
I got stripes, stripes around my shoulders
And them chains, them chains
They're about to drag me down

On a Monday, got my striped britches
On a Tuesday, got my ball and chain
On a Wednesday, I'm working, digging ditches
On a Thursday, I begged them not to knock me down again

I got stripes, stripes around my shoulders
I got chains, chains around my feet
I got stripes, stripes around my shoulders
And them chains, them chains
They're about to drag me down

On a Monday, my mama come to see me
On a Tuesday, they caught me with a file
On a Wednesday, I'm down in solitary
On a Thursday, I start on bread and water for a while

I got stripes, stripes around my shoulders
I got chains, chains around my feet
I got stripes, stripes around my shoulders
And them chains, them chains
They're about to drag me down

THE MAN ON THE HILL

1959

Will we get cold and hungry?
Will times be very bad?
When we're needing bread and meat
Where we gonna get it, Dad?

We'll get it from the man
In the house on the hill
Yes, we will
From the man on the hill

Plowin' time is over
Still the fields are bare
How we gonna make a living
With twenty acres to share?

I'll beg for more land
From the man on the hill
Yes, I will
I'll ask the man on the hill

I ain't got no Sunday shoes
That I can wear to town
Papa, reckon the boss
Has got a pair of hand-me-downs?

I'll go and ask the man
In the house on the hill
Yes, I will
I'll ask the man on the hill

Maybe he will help us
Maybe we'll get by
But who's gonna pay the dying bills
If we all should die?

We'll leave it to the man
In the sky, when we die
Yes, we'll leave it
To the man in the sky

OLD APACHE SQUAW

1959

Old Apache Squaw
How many long lean years you saw
How many bitter winter nights
Shivering in a cold teepee
Shivering in a cold teepee

Old Apache Squaw
How many hungry kids you saw
How many bloody warriors
Running to the sea
Fleeing to the sea

Well now, they tell me that you saw Cochise
When he made his last stand
He said, "The next white man that sees my face
Is going to be a dead white man."

Old Apache Squaw
How many broken hearts you saw
Have you had misty eyes for years
Could that mist be tears
Could that mist be tears

RESTLESS KID

1959

I came in like a restless wind
On a wagon train
But I'm gonna go like a July snow
Back to where I came from
Gonna leave this humdrum
It's too slow and tame

None of your business where I've been
Don't ask me what I've done
Run your ranch and punch your cows
And stay behind my gun, man
Colorado's right hand
Will put you on the run

I've got a gal in Denver town
That's crying over me
But I said goodbye and I let her cry
I miss her company, but
I'll get out of this rut
Rio Bravo's killing me

They got a man locked in a cell
That's a freer man than I
He's gonna laugh right in their face
When they lead him out to die, and
He's gonna leave these badlands
And ride off in the sky

You're gonna see old Colorado
Heading for the door
You better believe I'm gonna leave
Like the 904 train
Gonna breathe some air again
That ain't been breathed before

END

1960s

I have scars upon my arms
That show how I have lived
To tell you I once fell
I've forgiveness in my heart
Both given and received
I've a promise in my heart
That I won't go to hell

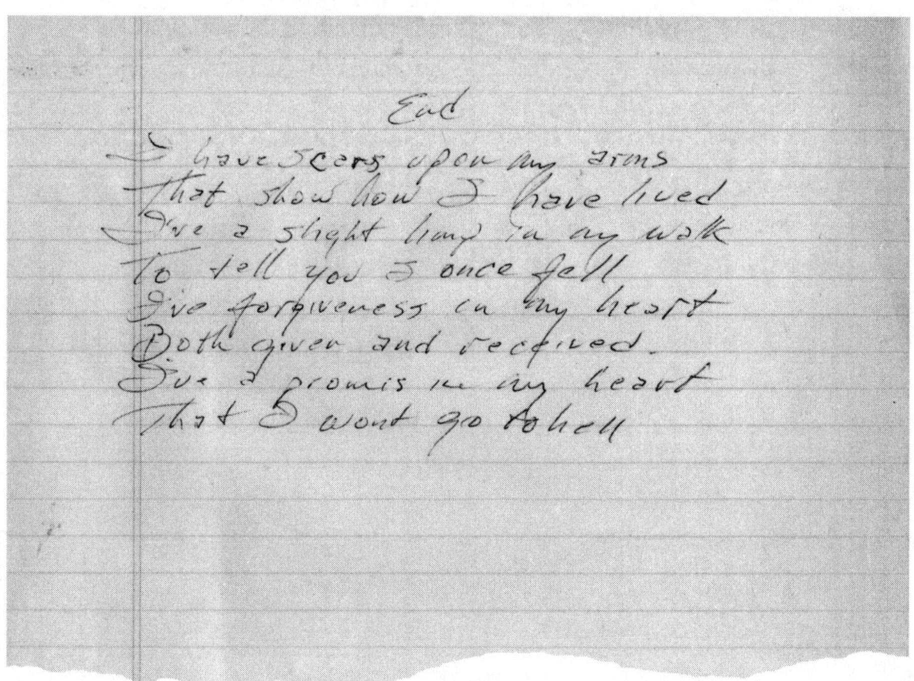

End

I have scars upon my arms
That show how I have lived
I've a slight limp in my walk
To tell you I once fell
I've forgiveness in my heart
Both given and recieved.
I've a promis in my heart
That I wont go to hell

DARK AND BLOODY GROUND

with Ruston Kelly

1960s

I been going like a chorus late at night
All busted down and burning for my bed
I've been thinking about a woman in a wild
Kentucky town
Where the mountains are high near Harlan

And the whirlpools twirl on down
There my secret can be found
In the dark and bloody ground
In the dark and bloody ground

Oh, how I've missed you
Oh, how I've cried
I'd like to lay you down by my side
Love you just once before I die

And I'd be gentle
And I'd never hurt you
And God might send a moonbeam
Lay us down, pleasant dreams

Whatsoever things are lovely
Whatsoever things are true
Whatsoever things are kind and pure
Thank you, these things
And I will send out a moonbeam
And lay us down to pleasant dreams

Dewey was my best friend and he was tall
Stood six foot nine against the wall
We both loved the same girl, but Dewey, he
went bad
And I guess you could say he made one mad

He didn't have to do
All those awful things to you
Yeah, Dewey made me sick
But I guess it takes two heels to click

I took my nine-pound hammer
Swung it hard and spun him 'round
I kicked him in the temple
Watched him fall to the ground

Oh, my blade found its mark
In the dark
And that blood flowed on the sand
From the tall Kentucky man

Oh, hell hath no fury like the blues
When a man's got on his killing shoes
In the dark and bloody ground

Dark and Bloody Ground

I've been going like a quarry slave at night
All busted down and burning to my bed
I've been thing 'bout a woman
In a wild Kentucky town
Where the mountains are high near Harlan
And the whirlpools twirl on down
There my secret can be found
~~[illegible]~~ in the dark and bloody ground

Chr Oh how I miss you, Oh how I've cried
I'd like to lay you down by my side
And love you just once before I die
Repeat And I would be gentle and I would never hurt you
And God might send a moonbeam
And lay us down to pleasant dreams
Whatsoever things are lovely whatsoever things are true
Whatsoever things are kind and pure, think upon these things
And God might send a moonbeam and lay us down to pleasant dreams

Dewey was my best friend he was tall — He stood six foot against the wall
We both loved the same girl but Dewey he went bad
And I guess you could say he made me mad
He didn't have to do all those awful things to you
Aw Dewey made me sick / and I guess it takes two heels to click
I took my nine pound hammer swung it hard and spun him round
Kicked him in the temple watched him falling to the ground
There my blade found its mark in the dark
And the blood flowed in the sand from that tall Kentucky man

Hell hath no fury like the Blues
When a man's got on his killing shoes

Repeat

GO WITH WHAT YOU'VE GOT

1960s

My friends called me the Southpaw
'Cause I pitched with my left
I was only twelve years old
And unsure of myself

We led the score, three to two
And I was on the mound
And I heard my daddy shout at me
I turned to look around

The bases were all loaded
But one strike and we'd win
I listened to my daddy's voice
And he said to me then

"Go with what you've got
And do the best that you can do.
Be the best that you can be
'Cause there ain't anyone like you.

Always be just what you are
If it's popular or not.
Throw the ball the way you know
You're sure to strike him out."
I threw the ball, it was strike three
Daddy's voice was like a shout

"Go with what you've got
And be the best that you can be.
You're the only you
That this old world will ever see.

"Do the best that you can do
And you may win or you may not.
You'll be proud of yourself
If you go with what you've got."

Go With What You've Got

My friends called me the Southpaw
Cause I pitched with my left
I was only 12 years old and unsure of myself.
We led the score three to two
And I was on the mound
I heard my daddy shout at me
And I turned to look around
The bases were all loaded,
But one strike and we'd win
I listened to my daddy's voice
And he said to me then

cho

Go with what you've got
And do the best that you can do
Be the best that you can be
Cause there aint anyone like you
Always be just what you are Throw the ball
If it's popular or not the way you know you're sure to strike him out
~~If you go with what you've got~~
I threw the ball, it was strike three
Daddy's voice was like a shout

2nd cho

Go with what you've got and be the best that you can be
You're the only you that this old world will ever see
Do the best that you can do and you may win or you may not
You'll be proud of yourself if you will go with what you've got.

Honeydew

Silver bark of birch
And green and yellow twig of willow
~~The~~ Emeralds were the lily pads
Upon the stream nearby
And purple was the (

I kissed you
And at once I know
That life was good
And you were true
~~But~~ And you were sweeter than the honeydew

HONEYDEW

1960s

Silver bark of birch
And green and yellow twig of willow
Gold was in your hair
And you were mine
And I was there

And sweeter than the honeydew
Were you, sweeter than the honeydew
Were you, sweeter than the honeydew
Were you, sweeter than the honeydew

With fingers intertwined
We laughed our way
Across the meadow
When we kissed I knew
You put to shame the honeydew

Just a kiss
And then I knew
Our love was right
And good and true

Your sweetness
Put to shame the honeydew
Quickly went the day
But those were minutes
Not for timing
In the honeydew
The only fragrance there
Was you

I REALLY HAD A BALL LAST NIGHT

1960s

Well, I really had a ball last night
I held all the pretty girls tight
I was feeling single, seeing double
Wound up in a world of trouble
But today I'll face the really big fight
But I really had a ball last night

Well, I came home from work this morning
My baby was feeling low
And she told me what was on her mind
And she told me where I could go

I didn't go where she told me to
'Cause the water was cold in the lake
Now, there's something fishy about this deal
I don't see where I made my mistake

Well, I really had a ball last night
I held all the pretty girls tight
I was feeling single, seeing double
Wound up in a world of trouble
But today I'll face the really big fight
But I really had a ball last night

When I woke up this morning
I could feel the summer sun
Well, I started walking the long way home
Just to think of an alibi

Well, I couldn't think of a doggone thing
That hasn't already been said
So I guess I better play it by ear
For I'm already dead
But I really had a ball last night

I'LL STILL LOVE YOU

with Elvis Costello

1960s

One of these mornings
I'm gonna rise up flying
One of these mornings
I'll sail away beyond the blue
I gotta promise there's a better world ahead
I want you to know that when I go
I'll still love you, I'll still love you

I won't be a stranger when I get to heaven
'Cause you gave me heaven
Right here on earth
If I get through heartache
With the edge of heart of gold
It's true, for what it's worth I still love you

One of these mornings, when my trouble's over
One of these mornings, when all my suffering is through
I'll go out singing, it'll be a day to sing about
And I'll guarantee for eternity
I'll still love you, I'll still love you
I'll still love you, I'll still love you

I'll Still Love You

One of these mornings
I'm gonna rise up flying.
One of these mornings
I'll sail away beyond the blue
I've got a promise
That there's a better world ahead
I want you to know that when I go
I'll still love you

One of these mornings
When my troubles over
One of these mornings
When all my suffering is through
I'll go out singing
It'll be a day to sing about
And I guarantee for eternity
I'll still love you

I wont be a stranger
When I get to heaven
Cause you gave me heaven
Right here on earth
If I get rewarded
With a mansion on a golden street
I want you to know
For what its worth
I'll still love you

I'VE GOT LOVE

1960s

I got arms to hold you tight
I got lips to kiss goodnight
I got a heart set to beat strong and true
I got love, love, love to give you

Get on your feet
And come a-runnin' here to me
And it's gonna be sweet, sweet, sweet
Oh, you don't know how sweet
The love I got for you can be

I got time, and I'll give you
All the time you need
I'm all yours
And satisfaction's guaranteed

I belong to you
And I'll do what you want me to
I got love, love, love to give you

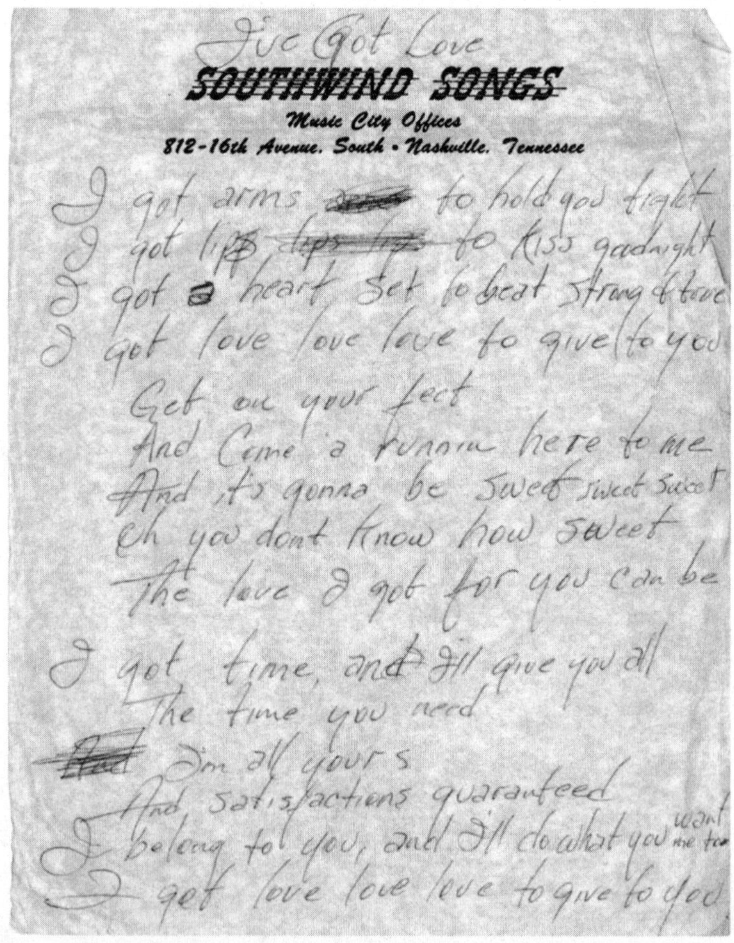

I've Got Love

~~SOUTHWIND SONGS~~

Music City Offices
812-16th Avenue, South • Nashville, Tennessee

I got arms to hold you tight
I got lips to kiss goodnight
I got a heart set to beat strong & true
I got love love love to give to you
Get on your feet
And Come a runnin here to me
And it's gonna be sweet sweet sweet
Oh you dont know how sweet
The love I got for you can be

I got time, and I'll give you all
the time you need
I'm all yours
And satisfactions guaranteed
I belong to you, and I'll do what you want me to
I got love love love to give to you

JUNE WAS GOIN' FOR A POET

1960s

June was goin' for a poet
A poet she would be
Four-line rhymes and sonnets
Quick as one-two-three

You never saw nothing like it
She sits there all day long
And I'm here, waitin' at the door
'Til she's through with her song

"June! Hey, honey, hey, baby!"
She never heard a word I said
She don't know I'm livin'
With rhymes goin' through her head

Then she says, "Honey, this poem's for you."
And I say, "I don't mind waiting
'Til you're through."

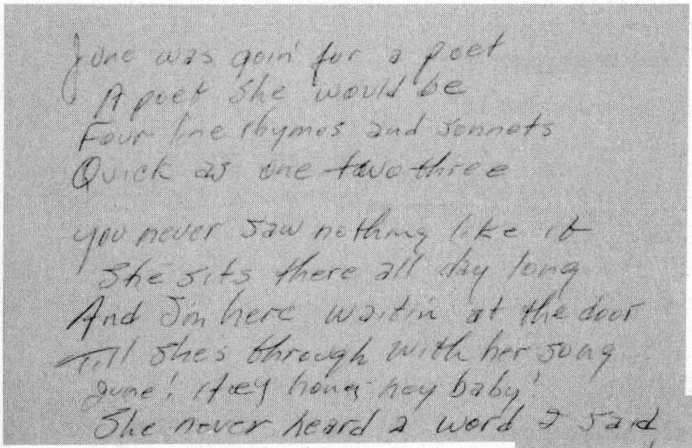

June was goin for a poet
A poet she would be
Four line rhymes and sonnets
Quick as one two three

you never saw nothing like it
She sits there all day long
And Im here waitin at the door
Till shes through with her song
June! Hey honey hey baby!
She never heard a word I said

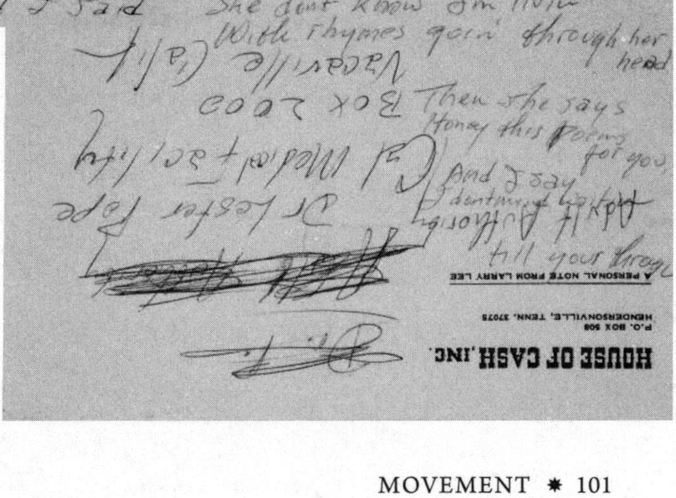

She dont know Im livin
With rhymes goin through her head
Then she says
Honey this poems for you
And I say
I dont mind waiting
till your through

HOUSE OF CASH, INC.
P.O. BOX 508
HENDERSONVILLE, TENN. 37075
A PERSONAL NOTE FROM LARRY LEE

JUNE'S SUNDOWN

with Carlene Carter

1960s

Another day is dropping westward, slipping away
Sounds of machines, motors, and men quieter now, less the din
Sundown, tally the pay
The laboring man welcomes the gray
Many a wife with a kiss at the door
New lipstick, not worn before

Sundown, a turn of your wheel
A plowboy whistling, back from the field
Many a mother counts one day less
'Til "someone" returns
May mothers be blessed

A voice to repeat, with a silent heart said
I prayed for them, receive daily bread
Millions of hearts beat as one sound
In love's perfection, together at sundown

Mothers, shepherds, count the table around
Thankful the lambs are all in at sundown
Sundown, desert, sand
Beginning to cool the hot face it tanned
He gave me this day, allowed me to live
At every sundown, thanks I give

So listen, and you will feel love universal
Personal reel
Just drift with the tide
Released and unwound
Love at sundown

June's Sundown

Sundown, another day
Is dropping westward, slipping away
Sounds of machines—motors—men
Quieter now, ... less the din

Sundown—Tally the day
The laboring man welcomes the gray
Many a wife with a kiss at the door
—A new lipstick not worn before

Sundown, a turn of your wheel
A plowboy whistling back from the field
Many a mother counts one day less
till "Someone" returns.
May mothers be blest.

Sundown....
The desert,
The sand
Beginning to cool,
The hot face it tanned
He gave me this day,
[illegible] Allowed me to live
At every sundown
Thanks I give

Millions of hearts
Beat as one sound
In love, in perfection
Together at Sundown

[illegible]

A voice to repeat
What the silent heart said,
I prayed for, and received!
"Our daily bread."

Mothers sweet sheppards
Count the table around
Thankful the lambs are all in,
At Sundown

Sundown,.....listen!
You also will [illegible] feel
Love universal,
Personal—real

Sundown.....open
your heart to the beat
The feeling will take you
Off of your feet

Drift with the tide
Released and enjoyed
At peace with yourself
Love
At Sundown

LAS VEGAS

1960s

Oh, oh, Las Vegas ain't a place for a poor boy like me
Oh, oh, Las Vegas ain't a place for a poor boy like me

Queen of spades is a friend of mine
The queen of hearts is a bitch
Someday I'll clean up my mind
And find out which is which

Spend all night with the dealer
Just trying to get ahead
Spend all day at the Holiday Inn
Trying to get out of bed

LET'S PUT IT TO MUSIC

1960s

How do you feel about me
Now that you've learned to know me
Why don't we both admit
That something is happening

And we would feel better
If we'd just tell each other
No need to keep it to ourselves
Let's put it to music

Let's put it to music
Let's sing about it
Laugh about it
Clap our hands
And shout about it

Let the whole world hear it
In a sweet, sweet melody
Let's put it to music
You and me

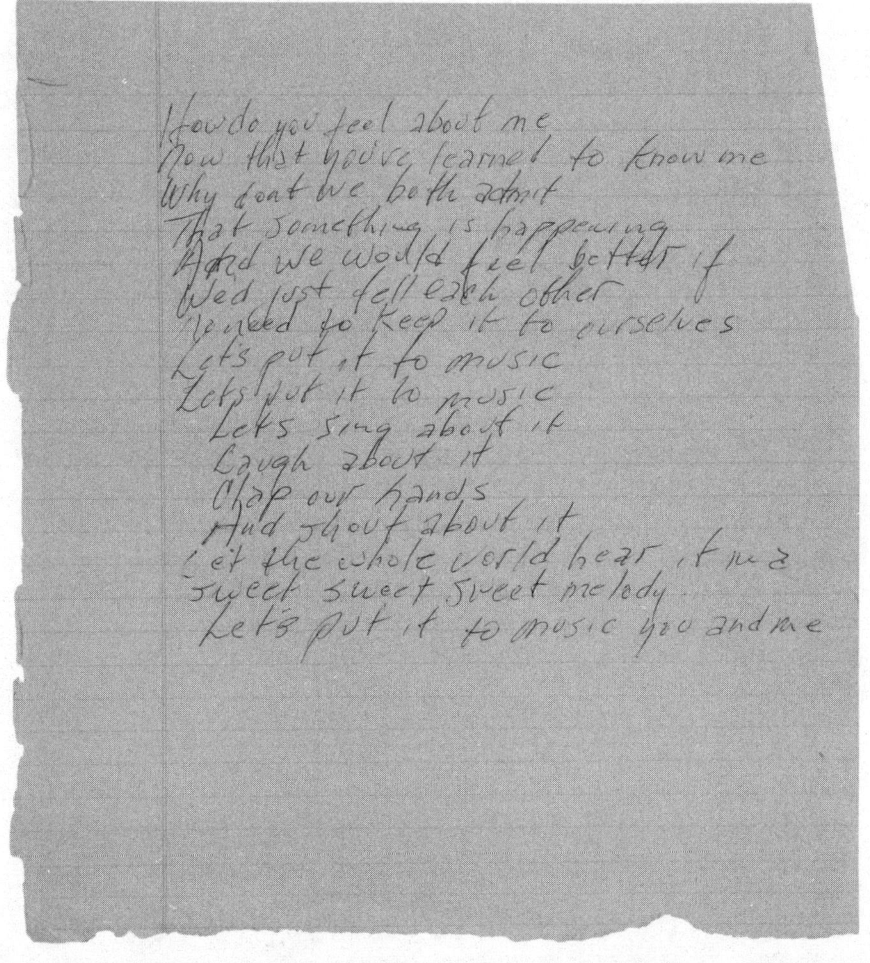

How do you feel about me
Now that you've learned to know me
Why dont we both admit
That something is happening
And we would feel better if
Wed just tell each other
No need to keep it to ourselves
Let's put it to music
Lets put it to music
Lets sing about it
Laugh about it
Clap our hands
And shout about it
Let the whole world hear it in a
sweet sweet sweet melody
Let's put it to music you and me

In the hotel room alone I was lying
In the night a man was softly crying

He grabbed his phone
And then he started screaming
I covered up my head and said,
I'm dreaming
The man said send someone
I know I'm dying
Come to 1702 the man was crying

In the darkness I reached for the light
But my hand couldn't penetrate the night
I left my bed, but didn't feel the floor
Then someone was knocking at my door
Thru the bolted door I slipped right thru
And we walked out of 1702

ROOM 1702

1960s

In the hotel room alone
I was lying
In the night
A man was softly crying

He grabbed his phone
And then he started screaming
I covered up my head
And said, "I'm dreaming."

The man said, "Send someone.
I know I'm dying.
Come to 1702."
The man was crying

In the darkness
I reached for the light
But my hand
Couldn't penetrate the night

I left my bed
But didn't feel the floor
Then someone was knocking
At my door

Through the bolted door
I stepped right through
And we walked out
Of 1702

"The Southwind"

She left me in Nashville today
The town is talkin' bout us
But I dont care
What they have to say
Off to Jacksonville again
~~And~~ heartache settled in
I caught a plane
To beat the train
I hear it comin' in
But We'll leave out again
On the high flyin'
Streamlined
Southwind

The big express
Took her south
But ~~[illegible]~~ I'll meet her at the gate
~~And~~ I can hardly wait
To ~~[illegible]~~ ask her back again
And ~~[illegible]~~ buy two one-way tickets
Back on the Southwind.

ON THE SOUTHWIND

1960s

She left me in Nashville today
The town is talkin' 'bout us
But I don't care
What they have to say
Off to Jacksonville again
And heartache settled in

I caught a plane
To beat the train
I hear it comin' in
But we'll leave out again
On the high flyin', streamlined Southwind

The big express
Took her south
But I'll meet her at the gate
And I can hardly wait
To ask her back again
And buy two one-way tickets back
On the Southwind

DORRAINE OF PONCHARTRAIN

1960

As I walked by the lake one day
By chance, my Dorraine passed my way
Then she and I walked hand in hand
On the banks of Ponchartrain

I pinned a flower on her heart
I swore we'd never be apart
She vowed her love forever
And, as I kissed her, did the same

Dorraine, my Dorraine
My dark-haired little angel
My belle of Ponchartrain

We sat down on the dock
And with our hearts and fingers locked
We laughed and talked and joked about
When our names are the same

And joking I said, "Honey,
Are you marrying me for money?"
And it took just one quick look
To tell it hurt my dear Dorraine

She jumped and stood above me
And she cried, "Why you don't love
me?
I'm rowing home across the lake.
You won't see me again."

I called and called some more
But she rowed fast from the shore
And the clouds brought by a wind
Began to rain on Ponchartrain

"Dorraine," I called. "Dorraine,
Come back my little angel,
My belle of Ponchartrain."

The storm should make her learn
That she should make a swift return
But as the rain fell harder
I lost sight of my Dorraine

As panic gripped my heart
I drew the oars and made my start
To look for her on raging waters
And the rain on Ponchartrain

At darkness I still called
But no one heard my cries at all
And when the daybreak came
Then others helped me look for my
Dorraine

But there was not a thing afloat
Except the oars from her rowboat
For all was lost upon the choppy waves
And rain on Ponchartrain

Now I come day after day
To where my sweetheart rowed away
And I gaze across the water
Of the rainy Ponchartrain

Just one thing and nothing more
Ever floated back to shore
Was this flower I hold
It is the one I pinned on my Dorraine

Dorraine, my Dorraine
My dark-haired little angel
My belle of Ponchartrain

THE FABLE OF WILLIE BROWN

1960

Well, I knew a boy named Willie Brown
He was a lover of our town
Wherever he went, the girls fell down
And cried for Willie Brown
Crazy 'bout Willie Brown

Tall and dark and lean and long
Big as a bull and twice as strong
He loved the girls and turned 'em down
A sheik was Willie Brown
Dashin' Willie Brown

Well, a new girl moved in on our street
We knew that she and Will would meet
But then when we inquired around
She'd not met Willie Brown
She said, "Who's Willie Brown?"

The prettiest girl you ever saw
Head to toe without a flaw
When they met one night in town
She fell for Willie Brown
In love with Willie Brown

But the trouble was that we all knew
Willie Brown was fallin', too
Then he announced when June comes 'round
She'll marry Willie Brown
She's in love with Willie Brown

But then the girl denied it all
She said, "It's true that I did fall
But he took my love for granted.
Now to heck with Willie Brown,
Conceited Willie Brown."

Willie Brown was shocked to learn
That his love had at last been spurned
So on a hill outside of town
We buried Willie Brown
We buried Willie Brown

FIVE MINUTES TO LIVE

1960

What all can you give
With five minutes to live?
Hear the tock tick tock
Of the laughing clock

What can you do or say?
Maybe you oughta pray
But you better think positive
You got five minutes to live

Time is flying by
Now, don't you sit there and let it fly
You better come on strong
You can't stay here long

That bell is gonna ring
This is a final fling
Ain't no alternative
You got five minutes to live

What all can you give
With five minutes to live?
Get dressed for your date
Or you're gonna be late

Live a little while you can
Don't you sit there and wring your hands
Here comes a great big sedative
You got five minutes to live

FORTY SHADES OF GREEN

1960

I close my eyes and picture
The emerald of the sea
From the fishing boats at Dingle
To the shores of Donaghadee

I miss the River Shannon
And the folks at Skibbereen
The moorlands and the meadows
With their forty shades of green

But most of all I miss a girl
In Tipperary town
And most of all I miss her lips
As soft as eiderdown

Again I want to see and do
The things we've done and seen
Where the breeze is sweet as shalimar
And there's forty shades of green

I wish that I could spend an hour
At Dublin's churning surf
I'd love to watch the farmers
Drain the bogs and spade the turf

To see again the thatching
Of the straw the women glean
I'd walk from Cork to Larne to see
The forty shades of green

But most of all I miss a girl
In Tipperary town
And most of all I miss her lips
As soft as eiderdown

Again I want to see and do
The things we've done and seen
Where the breeze is sweet as shalimar
And there's forty shades of green

GIRL IN SASKATOON

with Johnny Horton

1960

I left a little town
A little south of Hudson Bay
I couldn't find a thing
To make a rounder want to stay

I fought the wind
Across the barren waste
In the crystal doom
Going for to marry the girl in Saskatoon

I'm glad I realized that
No one could take her place
My heart was beating for her
Like the winter beat my face

But knowing that I'd see her
Made my spirit bright as June
I'm freezing but I'm burning
For the girl in Saskatoon

South and west and following
The cold December sun
I bedded down in the Carragana
When my daily trek was done

Then up and pressing onward
By the light of the morning moon
A prodigal returning
To the girl in Saskatoon

Then I found the trail
That had packed beneath the snow
I made the final miles
Where the prairie lilies grow

The steeple on a church
Glistened by the prairie moon
I'm freezing but I'm burning
For the girl in Saskatoon

My journey was forgotten
When I held her in my arms
My wanderlust was stifled
By possession of her charms

And even beneath the steeple
Where we couldn't wait 'til June
I found eternal spring
With the girl in Saskatoon

LOCOMOTIVE MAN

1960

I got a gal in Dallas
I wave at when I go through
I got a gal in Tulsa
That I toot my whistle to
Say, "How do?"

I got 'em all over the land
I'm a locomotive man

Left my heart in Omaha, Omaha
And I never did quite get it back
I got a Sue in Sioux City
Waiting by the railroad track
Keeps her money in a tater sack

I got 'em all over the land
I'm a locomotive man

Well, I left a little switch engine
'Bout forty miles south of Bangor, Maine
Couldn't keep the wheels a-turning
Shouldn't try to pull my train

I got 'em all over the land
I'm a locomotive man

Well, I had a gal in Jackson
And it sure broke my heart to turn her loose
When I checked my time and moved on
She's hooked on my caboose

I got 'em all over the land
I'm a locomotive man

THE LOSING KIND

1960

Lost my job and I lost my money
I turn my back and I lost my honey
Lord, I guess I'm just the losing kind

Lost my license, 'cause I drove too fast
Got in a game and I lost my cash
Lord, I guess I'm just the losing kind

Someday the cops are gonna come around
And turn me over to the lost and found
I was sitting on the porch the other day
And watched the finance man drive my car away

I'm too proud to crawl and too weak to run
I'd shoot myself, but I lost my gun
Lord, I guess I'm just the losing kind

Well, if it was raining dollar bills
And I was up on the highest hill
Clouds would break
And I know the sun would shine

The only way that I can win
Is pick a fight and bet on him
Lord, I guess I'm just the losing kind

Someday the cops are gonna come around
And turn me in to the lost and found
I just got a letter from a baby of mine
She's in Las Vegas and she likes it fine

I'm too proud to crawl and too weak to run
I'd shoot myself, but I lost my gun
Lord, I guess I'm just the losing kind

SLOW RIDER

1960

I ride an old Paint, he's on the weary side
And I am a saddle tramp about to cross the Great Divide
Where there's grass in the coulees and water in the draw
And the forty-pound saddle won't make us both raw

Slow rider, slow rider, move on a little more
The sky boss is waiting at the big ranch house door

I can't help but missing the daughters that I had
One went to Denver, the other went bad
My young wife died in a poolroom fight
But I try to keep singing from morning 'til night

Slow rider, slow rider, move on a little more
The sky boss is waiting at the big ranch house door

Whenever I die, take my saddle from the wall
Strap it on Snuffy, lead him out of the stall
Throw me on his back and turn him toward the West
He knows how to take me to the spot I love best

Slow rider, slow rider, move on a little more
The sky boss is waiting at the big ranch house door

SMILING BILL McCALL

1960

Well, the whole town listened to the radio
For the Smiling Bill McCall Show
Everyone in Nashville
Was listening to Bill

"I don't want to be laying in bed
When they pronounce me dead."
He'd stand and breathe in the microphone
With his guitar hanging to his knee bone

All the girls just sat and dreamed
When Bill began to sing
"I don't want my hat to be hung
When my last song is sung."

But he never let fame go to his head
"This is Smiling Bill McCall," he said
"Gonna pick and sing a song or two.
You all listen 'til I'm through.

"And if you're at the house or in your car
Tune in this time tomorrow."
To all the boys, he was a big hero
They'd glue their ears to the radio

Then talking a most unusual drawl
Imitating Bill McCall
"Daddy, can I get me a guitar?
'Cause I want to be a star."

The girls would say, of Bill McCall
"Why, I bet he's over six feet tall.
Handsomest man in Nashville."
They said, of Smiling Bill

"He won't be planting potato slips
When he cashes in his chips."
Then one day Bill didn't make the show
Didn't even show up for a week or so

The station's boss said to city hall,
"Find Smiling Bill McCall.
It won't be hard to track him down.
He's got the biggest feet in town."

Well, there's a creek that runs through Nashville
And on the bank, they found Smiling Bill
He's committing suicide
But they grabbed him before he tried

"Turn me loose, I want to jump," he screamed
"'Cause I can't stand that theme.
Let this be my final breath
'Cause I'm scared half to death."

The big brave Smiling Bill McCall
Is only four feet tall
"I'd rather be in the river, dead,
Than to hear them laughing at my bald head."

WHEN PAPA PLAYED THE DOBRO

1960

My Papa was a hobo, when they delivered me
We didn't have a doctor, 'cause he couldn't pay the fee
But when the going got too bad, to ease his misery
Papa played the dobro thisaway, and he'd go...

When company would come around, he kept the dobro hid
He knew he couldn't play the way the other players did
Why, the guitar's resonator was a gallon-bucket lid
But Papa played the dobro thisaway, and he'd go...

Well, now that Papa's gone away, it's hanging by the flue
The top of it is rusted and the strings are rusty, too
It won't ever sound the way that it did when it was new
When Papa played the dobro thisaway, and he'd go...

THE BIG BATTLE

1961

I think, sir, the battle is over
And the young soldier lay down his gun
I'm tired of running for cover
I'm certain the battle is done

For, see over there where we fought them
It's quiet for they've all gone away
All left is the dead and the dying
The blue lying alongside of the gray

So you think the battle is over
And you even lay down your gun
You carelessly rise from your cover
For you think the battle is done

Now, boy, hit the dirt, listen to me
For I'm still the one in command
Get flat on the ground here beside me
And lay your ear hard to the sand

Can you hear the deafening rumble?
Can you feel the trembling ground?
It's not just the horses and wagons
That make such a deafening sound

For every shot fired had an echo
And every man killed wanted life
There lies your friend, Jim McKinney
Can you take the news to his wife?

No, son, the battle's not over
The battle has only begun
The rest of the battle will cover
The part that has blackened the sun

The fight yet to come's not with cannon
Nor will the fight be hand-to-hand
No one will regroup the forces
No charge will a general command

The battle will rage in the bosom
Of mother and sweetheart and wife
Brother and sister and daughter
Will grieve for the rest of their lives

Now go ahead, rise from your cover
Be thankful that God let you live
Go fight the rest of the battle
For those who gave all they could give

I see, sir, the battle's not over
The battle has only begun
The rest of this battle will cover
The part that has blackened the sun

For though there's no sound of the cannon
And though there's no smoke in the sky
I'm dropping the gun and the saber
And ready for battle am I

SING IT PRETTY, SUE

1961

So you gave up all between us for a glamorous career
And with all your talent, you should be the big star of the year
Then you'll be public property, so I release my claim to you
Go on and give them all you've got, sing it pretty, Sue

I can't take just part of you and give the world a half
So smile for all the papers and give them autographs
Go on to all the cities, so your public can see you
But I'll watch on television, so sing it pretty, Sue

I hope you'll soon be on the top of every hit parade
I'll try to be excited 'bout the progress that you've made
I'll collect your pictures, like any fan would do
And I'll buy all your records, so sing it pretty, Sue

But I won't ever tell a soul that we have ever met
I'll just be one of millions who'll give the praise you get
And maybe every year or so, I'll drop a card to you
To tell you I'm still listening, so sing it pretty, Sue

TENNESSEE FLAT-TOP BOX

1961

In a little cabaret in a South Texas border town
Sat a boy and his guitar, and the people came from all around
And all the girls from there to Austin were slipping away from home
And putting jewelry in hock to take the trip to go and listen
To the little dark-haired boy that played the Tennessee flat-top box
And he would play…

Well, he couldn't ride or wrangle and he never cared to make a dime
But give him his guitar and he'd be happy all the time
And all the girls, from nine to ninety
Were snapping fingers, tapping toes, and begging him, "Don't stop."
And hypnotized and fascinated
By the little dark-haired boy that played the Tennessee flat-top box
And he would play…

Then one day he was gone, and no one ever saw him 'round
He vanished like the breeze, and they forgot him in the little town
But all the girls still dreamed about him
And hung around the cabaret until the doors were locked
And then one day, on the hit parade
Was the little dark-haired boy that played the Tennessee flat-top box
And he would play…

THE CHRISTMAS SPIRIT

1962

On Christmas Eve, I dreamed I traveled all around the earth
And in my dream, I saw and heard the ways the different people
Hail the king whose star shone in the east, and what a dream it was

In London Town, I walked around Piccadilly Circus
A mass of people moving here and there, I wondered where?
On every face at every place was, "Hurry up, I'm late."
But a kind old man at a chestnut stand said, "Merry Christmas, mate."
And I felt the Christmas spirit

In a little town nestled down in Bavaria, Germany,
I walked along to see what the feeling there would be
And here again was the busy din, the rushing, the yelling
But some kind boy said, "Fröhliche Weihnachten."
Not understanding the words, but getting the buying and selling,
I felt the Christmas spirit

In Bethlehem, I heard a hymn some distant choir sing
And with other tourists, I walked along to a church as its bells rang
Then I heard someone tell someone, "There's where Christ was born."
I wonder if He looked like our baby looked on that first morn
And then I really felt the Christmas spirit

From a businessman in the Holy Land at a sidewalk souvenir shop
I bought a little Bible since I'd already stopped
And it was in Paris, France, somehow by chance that I took the Bible out
And as I flipped the pages, I saw these words
And I knew what it was all about

For I read, "Fear not, for behold I bring you good tidings of great joy
Which shall be to all people.
For unto you, He was born this day in the City of David, a Savior
Which is Christ the Lord."

Then I took the little holy book, held it close and tight
I closed my eyes and visualized the glory of that night

So suddenly, it came to me for when I awoke on Christmas Day
I felt the Christmas spirit down deep inside to stay

FOURTEEN CARAT NOTHING

1962

I wore your ring around my finger
And your gold around my heart
For your sweet talk made me tremble
Like you planned it from the start

But your sweet talk turned sour
And your gold burned down and died
Had your golden ring refinished
While you memorized your line

Keep your fourteen carat nothing
I can see through everything
My heart cannot be molded
Nor adjusted by your ring

Keep your fourteen carat nothing
I won't miss it when it's gone
Save your sweet talk and your money
For a heart that's made of stone

Like a happy Cinderella
Trying on a wedding gown
You took my heart and dropped it
But you can't keep it down

For your dirty gold is worthless
Don't bother now at all
Your best attention-getter
Is the mirror on your wall

Keep your fourteen carat nothing
I won't miss it when it's gone
Save your sweet talk and your money
For a heart that's made of stone

HARDIN WOULDN'T RUN

1962

I know a man whose plow handle hand
Is quicker than a light
Wes Hardin is his name, they say
He travels in the night, for
He might have to kill, or
Walk around a fight

And if you ever saw Wes Hardin draw
You know he can skin his gun
He won't say how many tried and died
Up against the top hand
Up against the wrong man
'Cause Hardin wouldn't run

He rode in like a Texas wind
Took the eastbound train
Going, going, with Jane Bowen
'Til the lawmen caught up
"So long, Janie, chin up.
I'll be back again."

Off he went to Huntsville Prison
"So long, Janie," he cried
Fifteen years she waited
'Til her heart broke and she died, and
She left that bad land
To wait up in the sky

Free at last, the paying past
For all the wrong he did
First free air they let him breathe
Since he was a kid, so
Let him come and let him go
And let him deal and bid

Near the border in El Paso
Lawyer reads the sign
You won't find him there for business
Every day at nine
For business is real bad
One client's all he's had
In quite a long, long time

Then Sheriff Selman's boy broke in
To Wes's woman's place
Up she jumped and pistol-whipped him
Kicked him in the face
And John Selman demands
Revenge for this disgrace

You could see her every night by
candlelight
In Hardin's favorite bar
She'd be hanging on his arm
And very late they'd leave there
Headed for the Goose Hair
Glad it wasn't far

Right through the swinging doors
John Selman came with a blazing gun
Wes Hardin chug-a-luggin' red-eye
Got him in the back of the head
John Wesley Hardin fell dead
Hardin wouldn't run

A LITTLE AT A TIME

with Gordon Terry

1962

Stop loving me a little at a time
Let me lose you a little at a time
Walk away slow, like you don't want to go
Leave me a little at a time

For my benefit
Try to cry a little bit
For old times' sake
Give me a slow heartbreak
I put up a fight, but I'll be all right
If you stop loving me a little at a time

Hurt me a little at a time
Turn me away a little at a time
Walk away slow, like you don't wanna go
Leave me a little at a time

For my benefit
Try to cry a little bit
For old times' sake
Give me a slow heartbreak
I put up a fight, but I'll be all right
If you stop loving me a little at a time

A little at a time
A little at a time
A little at a time

SEND A PICTURE OF MOTHER

1962

After seven years behind these bars together
I'll miss you more than a brother when you go
If only I had not tried to escape
They'd pardon me with you I know, yes, I know

Won't you tell the folks back home I'll soon be coming
And don't let them know I never will be free
Sometimes write and tell me how they're doing
And send a picture of Mother back to me

Say hello to Dad and shake his poor hardworking hand
And send a picture of Mother, if you can

I am happy for you that you got your freedom
But stay with me just another minute or so
After all this sweating blood together
Who'll be my fighting partner when you go?

The hardest time will be on Sunday morning
Church bells will ring on Heaven Hill
Please, ask Reverend Garrett to pray for me
And send a picture of Mother, if you will

Say hello to Dad and shake his poor hardworking hand
And send a picture of Mother, if you can

SHAMROCK DOESN'T GROW IN CALIFORNIA

1962

Shamrock doesn't grow in California
And your shillelagh is a forty-five
It's the leaf of all the chiefs
But I can't keep it alive
'Cause shamrock doesn't grow in California

A letter came from my sweetheart in Ireland
The envelope was brimming full of tiny shamrock seeds
She said, "I'm sure you know, you can't make the shamrock grow.
Don't plant it over there beside the sage and jimson weed."

'Cause you know shamrock doesn't grow in California
And your shillelagh is a forty-five
It's the leaf of all the chiefs
But I can't keep it alive
'Cause shamrock doesn't grow in California

Well, I planted the shamrock seeds my sweetheart sent me
"My thumb is Irish green," I said. "For me, they are sure to grow."
My good friend Mike O'Shea came every day, for thirty days
When cactus grew instead, Mike said, "Why, I could've told you so."

Don't you know that shamrock doesn't grow in California?
And your shillelagh is a forty-five
It's the leaf of all the chiefs
But I can't keep it alive
'Cause shamrock doesn't grow in California

YOU REMEMBERED ME

1962

You were young and needed love
And I was wild and free
But every time you said a prayer
You said a prayer for me

Why, the ring upon your hand
We vowed fidelity
There were times when I forgot
But you remembered me

You remembered only
That wedding bells would ring
You remembered only
To count the days 'til spring

You knew only love and honor
But I couldn't see
I regret that I forgot
'Cause you remembered me

I believed that promises
Were made to break apart
But every time I broke a vow
I always broke your heart

So here's to you, God bless you now
Wherever you may be
There were times that I forgot
But you remembered me

You remembered only
That wedding bells would ring
You remembered only
To count the days 'til spring

You knew only love and honor
But I couldn't see
I regret that I forgot
'Cause you remembered me

THE GIFTS THEY GAVE

1963

Jesus our King, kind and good
Was humbly born in a stable of wood
And the lowly beasts around Him stood
Jesus our King, kind and good

"I," said the donkey, shaggy and brown
"I carried His mother up and down.
I carried His mother to Bethlehem town.
I," said the donkey, shaggy and brown

"I," said the ox, "this was my hay.
I gave Him my manger, 'twas here that He lay.
I gave Him my manger, 'twas here that He lay.
I," said the ox, "this was my hay."

"I," said the sheep with pearly horn
"I gave Him my wool for a blanket warm.
He wore my coat on Christmas morn.
I," said the sheep with pearly horn

"I," said the dove, from the rafters high
"I sang Him to sleep that He would not cry.
We sang Him to sleep, my love and I.
I," said the dove, from the rafters high

And so every heart, by some good spell
In the stable dark, was glad to tell
Of the gift that he gave to Emmanuel
Of the gift that he gave to Emmanuel

I'D STILL BE THERE

with Johnny Horton

1963

I overlooked a lot of things
I knew I should have done
I did things that I'm sorry for
I lived to have my fun

But now the world that once was bright
Is empty and bare
And if you wouldn't be ashamed of me
I'd still be there

I'd be with you
Where I belong
And nothing they could do or say
Could make me think it's wrong

If all the love that made you mine
Could make you still care
I'd be by your side
I'd still be there

I'd give the world if I could only
Have you close to me
I'd pray the Lord to keep you safe
Wherever you may be

Don't let anybody share
The things we used to share
If I only knew you loved me, too
I'd still be there

I'd be with you
Where I belong
And nothing they could do or say
Could make me think it's wrong

If all the love that made you mine
Could make you still care
I'd be by your side
I'd still be there

I'd be by your side
I'd still be there

THE MATADOR

with June Carter

1963

The crowd is waiting for the bullfight, Matador
My final fight, the place is packed once more
Anita won't throw me a rose this fight
The one she wears is not for me tonight

She's watching now with her new love, I know
Walk proud and slow
Be strong and sure and give the crowd their show
They want blood, you know

You're still their idol
As you were before
Kill just one more
Remind Anita you're the greatest Matador

Walk on out, forget Anita in the stand
Be a tall and brave and noble man
Be better than you've ever been before
Make this your greatest moment, Matador

She's watching now with her new love, I know
Walk proud and slow
Be strong and sure and give the crowd their show
They want blood, you know

You're still their idol
As you were before
Kill just one more
Remind Anita you're the greatest Matador

UNDERSTAND YOUR MAN

1963

Well, don't call my name out your window, I'm leaving
I won't even turn my head
Don't send your kinfolks to give me no talking
I'll be gone, like I said

You'd say the same old things that you've been saying all along
Lay there in your bed and keep your mouth shut 'til I'm gone
Don't give me that old familiar crying, cussing moan
Understand your man
Tired of your bad-mouthing
Understand your man

You can give my other suits to the Salvation Army
And everything else I leave behind
I ain't taking nothing that'll slow down my traveling
While I'm untangling my mind

I ain't gonna repeat what I've said anymore
While I'm breathing air that ain't been breathed before
I'll be as gone as a wild goose in winter
Then you'll understand your man
You hear me talking, honey
Understand your man

WE ARE THE SHEPHERDS

1963

So here is the stable and there is the manger
The new Savior sleeps on His first earthly night
The wise men brought riches, but we brought a candle
It's all that we have, but it gives a good light

We are the shepherds, we walked 'cross the mountains
We left our flocks when the new star appeared
Oh, the beautiful singing of heavenly choir
We had to come see Him, we had to come here

We beg You, forgive us for such a small offering
But our sheep are out there with wolves in the night
We bring You this candle, it's all we have with us
But with it, the new Savior has His first light

We are the shepherds, we walked 'cross the mountains
We left our flocks when the new star appeared
Oh, the beautiful singing of heavenly choir
We had to come see Him, we had to come here

We thank thee, kind Joseph, for bidding us enter
Please take our gift for the new babe to thine
'Tis only one candle, but it is our symbol
Of how we believe that His great life will shine

WHO KEPT THE SHEEP

with Ezra J. Carter

1963

The shepherds afar left their flocks by night
Followed the new star by its heavenly light
Did the lambs fear the wolves?
Did they lay down and sleep?
Who kept the sheep?
Who kept the sheep?

Did robbers not steal, or did they fear the light
That the shepherds had followed, night after night?
Did they not stray?
Did little lambs weep?
Who kept the sheep?
Who kept the sheep?

Under the new star, the new Savior lay
In His dim manger, He lay on the hay
The shepherds that came had a vigil to keep
But who kept the sheep?
Who kept the sheep?
Who kept the sheep?

THREE

* DISTRACTION *

1964–1968

BY AGE THIRTY, Cash had already passed through more phases than most artists could hope to realize, with each iteration the seeming culmination — or conclusion — of a pretty amazing run that surely had a shelf life. After all, not many putative teen princes last very long in the royal court of pop fame. It was just a matter of time before Cash would age out.

Except he did not. He abdicated his position on the dance floor, only to emerge during the folk music boom of the late 1950s, embodied by glee clubs, barbershop quartets, and varsity jackets, as a genuine son of the soil, who had both lived the source material and written penetrating sagas about it. Where his peers, many actually older than he, were leading sing-alongs to old murder ballads in college gyms, for example, Cash walked the dusty streets of yore, his interpretations often presenting as firsthand accounts of long-ago events. It was not a "reinvention" as much as a reincarnation of these historical figures. In his epic tales, like "Hardin Wouldn't Run," about the notorious outlaw John Wesley Hardin, or in his adaptations, such as "Mister Garfield" or "Hiawatha's Vision," Cash offered distant moments as relevant, current events. "On the Line" and "We All Miss You, Joe" spoke to a loneliness and unease that had begun to pervade the land as the conflict in Vietnam steadily escalated and losses mounted. Luther strangely playing the boogie-woogie, this was not.

Cash's writings took on a darker tone. His assumption of these characters, many of whom lived existences of alienation and outsider-ness, into his own persona can be seen as attempts to escape the personal trials that threatened to consume his career and his very being. His mental health devolved, treated by "professionals" using nearly lethal combinations of stimulants and depressants that not only failed to stabilize him but also left him addicted and physically wrecked. "Time" and "commitment" became irrelevant concepts. His marriage floundered, then collapsed.

Everything he did was frantic. For his 1965 album *Johnny Cash Sings the Ballads of the True West,* he described spending weeks "in the desert" — his own version of being tested in the wilderness:

> I followed trails in my Jeep and on foot, and I slept under mesquite bushes and in gullies. I heard the timber wolves, looked for golden nuggets in old creek beds, sat for hours beneath a manzanita bush in an ancient Indian burial ground,

> breathed the west wind and heard the tales it tells only to those who listen. I replaced a wooden grave marker of some man in the Arizona who "never made it." I walked across alkali flats where others had walked before me, but hadn't made it. I ate mesquite beans and squeezed the water from a barrel cactus. I was saved once by a forest ranger, lying flat on my face, starving. I learned to throw a bowie knife and kill a jackrabbit at forty yards, not for the sport but because I was hungry.

Little wonder he would write but four of the album's twenty tracks. He could not focus on composing, just as he could not focus on much of anything else. Was this the man who had the teenagers dancing to "It Was Jesus" on *Town Hall Party*?

Columbia released *Johnny Cash's Greatest Hits, Volume 1* in 1967. Only one Cash-written song dating from this period was included (although it was a big one: "Understand Your Man," a deranged, one-way rant that depicted the demise of his marriage), but it was a testament to the scope of his achievements over the prior decade, and it kept the fascination with this enigma going strong.

Greatest Hits — there was no consensus as to whether there would ever be a *Volume 2* (there was) — stormed onto the charts, racing to number one and spending three months in the Top 10. The album was still up there in January 1968 when Cash went to Folsom State Prison, in California, and recorded a live album in front of the inmates. The result was historic and life altering. Accompanying him at the show was June Carter, heir to the legacy of country music's most famous family, whom he would marry shortly after. The new couple traveled to Israel for their honeymoon, where they taped themselves at sacred sites, forming the foundation for Cash's gospel music triumph, an album titled *The Holy Land,* which included five self-penned tracks.

The confluence of these events — which all occurred within a matter of mere months — awakened a sleeping titan. Within this period, Cash wrote the classics "He Turned the Water into Wine" and "God Is Not Dead," as well as the essential love songs "'Cause I Love You" and "I Promise You." The pessimism of autobiographical works such as "California Poem" ("There's trouble on the mountain...") and the regret over lost chances in "Twelve Feet Tall, Again" gave way to a rebirth of Cash's vision, accomplishments, and — missing for some time — humor.

He was just beginning. Again.

AIN'T YOU ASHAMED

with June Carter

1964

Oh, you sit there and smile and you hold him by the hand
You'll make him a failure and break him as a man
You know, he was mine, yes, you took the things I claimed
Look into the mirror, woman, ain't you ashamed

Ain't you ashamed that you took all I owned
You lured him away from me with your sweet lies and song
Your kind's a dime a dozen, and you think that love's a game
Look into the mirror, woman, ain't you ashamed

These gray hairs I wear are not put there by age
In my book of life, your name's on many a page
Our fire of love was burning but you lured him from the flame
Look into the mirror, woman, ain't you ashamed

Ain't you ashamed that you took all I owned
You lured him away from me with your sweet lies and song
Your kind's a dime a dozen, and you think that love's a game
Look into the mirror, woman, ain't you ashamed

ALL GOD'S CHILDREN AIN'T FREE

1964

I'd sing more about more of this land
But all God's children ain't free
I'd open up every door I can
'Cause all God's children ain't free

I met a beaten, broken man
He shovels dirt but got no land
And he held out his hand to me
All God's children ain't free

I'd sing along to a silly song
But all God's children ain't free
I'm gonna sing the blues for the men they
  done wrong
'Cause all God's children ain't free

Mister, how 'bout the man you condemn
  to die
By taking everything that he's livin' by
And reject him from society
All God's children ain't free
No, reject him from society
All God's children ain't free

I'd be happy walking any street
But all God's children ain't free
I'd have a smile for all I meet
But all God's children ain't free

I'd whistle down the road, but I wouldn't
  feel right
I'd hear somebody cryin' out at night
From a sharecropper shack or penitentiary
All God's children ain't free
From a sharecropper shack or penitentiary
All God's children ain't free

APACHE TEARS

1964

Hoofprints and footprints
Deep ruts the wagons made
The victor and the loser came by here
No headstones but these bones bring Mescalero death moans
See the smooth black nuggets by the thousands lying here
Petrified but justified, are these Apache tears

Dead grass, dry roots, hunger crying in the night
Ghosts of broken hearts and laws are here
And who saw the young squaw
They judged by their whiskey law
Tortured 'til she died of pain and fear?
Where the soldiers lay her back are the black Apache tears

The young men, the old men, the guilty and the innocent
Bled red blood and chilled alike with fears
The red men, the white men
No fight ever took this land
So don't raise the dust when you pass here
They're sleeping, and in my keeping, are these Apache tears

THE BABY IS MINE

1964

Now, don't laugh at the condition the lady's in
She soon could wear a cocktail dress again
But we get along without cocktails mighty fine
This will be our first and I'm proud the baby is mine

Yes, I married her although I knew the kind of life she used to live
And 'cause I knew she loved me, too, it was easy to forgive
And if you just mind your own business, we'd be fine
Don't ever doubt I'm proud the baby is mine

She's awkward, yeah, but have you seen her face?
Where there once was shame, there's a sparkle in its place
And her conscience is clear, that's why her eyes shine
Mister, don't ever doubt I'm proud the baby is mine

I married her although I knew the kind of life she used to live
And 'cause I knew she loved me, too, it was easy to forgive
If you'd mind your own business, we'd make it fine
Tell all her old friends I'm proud the baby is mine

HOW DID YOU GET AWAY FROM ME

with June Carter and Anita Carter

1964

Oh, I hate it, but you made it
You're running, jumping, laughing, filled with glee
Oh, I told you that I'd hold you
Just how did you get away from me?

I had bars on the windows, had you chained to the floor
And a moss-covered monster at the door
Had a bottomless moat with a hole in the boat
And a big rattlesnake, if you tried to make the break
Had a swarm of bees, a gorilla in the trees
Just how did you get away from me?

Where did you get the sense
To get through the electric fence?
Your handcuffs are gone, you're running free
What happened to my sniper
With his high-powered rifle?
Just how did you get away from me?

Is it true that you really did make it through?
How 'bout the tiger in the car?
Did you go like a mole through a hole
Or did you sail like a quail on the pole?
Give it to the news on TV?
Oh, how did you get away from me?

I WANT YOU AGAIN

with Sheb Wooley

1964

'Cause I was too blind to see
You got away from me
You slipped through my hands like sand
Though I was too proud to cry
It wouldn't die
And I want you again

Oh, lonesome feeling
My head is reeling
From the heaven I was in
But I just can't go on
Can't take it alone
And I want you again

Now that I've been through the storm
My heart is tattered and torn
I know what a fool I've been
I just can't get by
Without a second try
And I want you again

Oh, what a feeling
My head is reeling
From the heaven I was in
But I just can't go on
Can't take it alone
And I want you again

A LONG WAY FROM THE COTTON FIELDS

1964

You're looking like a million
You always dress in style
You always go first class
Even if it's half a mile
I'm glad to see you made it
You really are a wheel
You're a long way from the cotton field

But I still wear the cotton dress
You gave me, way back when
Back when we missed every other meal
I will always be the way I was
When you loved me
But you're a long way from the cotton field

I hope you'll both be happy
Because I want the best for you
And I will never interfere
No matter what you do
I'll go back home and, maybe
In time, my heart will heal
'Cause you're a long way from the cotton field

But I still wear the cotton dress
You gave me, way back when
Back when we missed every other meal
I will always be the way I was
When you loved me
But you're a long way from the cotton field

SING, SING, SING

1964

I'm gonna sing
I'm gonna sing
Get the band upon the stand
And let the music ring

I'm gonna sing
I'm gonna sing
I'm gonna sing
I'm gonna sing, sing, sing, sing, sing

Farmer Brown has been down
For a month or two with the flu
The doctor's pills won't cure his ills
So he needs a song or two

I'm gonna sing
I'm gonna sing
I'm gonna sing
I'm gonna sing, sing, sing, sing, sing

We prayed for rain but it never came
And the fields are bare and hot
The sun is high and the creek is dry
And music's all we got

I'm gonna sing
I'm gonna sing
I'm gonna sing
I'm gonna sing, sing, sing, sing, sing

We can't go to the picture show
'Cause the money ain't comin' in
Sing it high up to the sky
And the rain will fall again

I'm gonna sing
I'm gonna sing
I'm gonna sing
I'm gonna sing, sing, sing, sing, sing

The fields will be green, the birds will sing
We'll make it, by and by
But until then, sing out again
Lift your voices high

2nd Verse (Tenor)
WE DONT GO TO THE PICTURE SHOW
CAUSE THE MONEY AINT COMIN IN
SING IT HIGH UP TO THE SKY
AND THE RAIN WILL FALL AGAIN
(BASS)
THE FIELDS WILL GREEN
THE BIRDS WILL SING
WE'LL MAKE IT BY AND BY
BUT UNTIL THEN, SING OUT AGAIN
AND LIFT YOUR VOICES HIGH

REPEAT CHO - TWICE

I'm gonna sing — I'm gonna sing
Get the band up on the stand
And let the music ring
I'm gonna sing — I'm gonna sing
" " " ", sing sing sing etc

BASS
1. Farmer Brown has been down
for a month or two with the flu
The Dr's pills wont cure his ills
So he needs a song or two

We prayed for rain, but it hasn't came
And the fields are bare and hot
The sun is high and the creek is dry
And music's all we've got
Cho

2. We can't go to the picture show
Cause the money ain't comin' in
Sing it high up to the sky
And the rain will fall again
Well ~~[illegible]~~
The fields will green, the birds will sing
We'll make it by & by. But until then
Sing out again. Lift your voices high

MY OLD FADED ROSE

with June Carter

1964

You have got them all hanging around
Like the fringes that's on your gown
You're picking them up
And laying them low
My old faded rose

Was it me that said you're getting old
And losing your appeal?
Was it me that said you're growing cold
And I wanted another deal?

Well, I see that you're not wilted
But you never did let it show
Why didn't I know about the fiery glow
In my old faded rose?

My old faded rose
With your petals hanging down
I didn't know I'd miss you so
My old faded rose

Look at them hanging around
Like the fringes that's on your gown
You're picking them up
And laying them low
My old faded rose

I didn't mean that the grass was green
While your leaves was turning brown
Don't take me so seriously
When I tell you don't hang around

But now I see that you don't need pruning
And who do you suppose
Is back in line for one more time
After his old faded rose?

My old faded rose
With your petals hanging down
I didn't mean I'd miss you so
My old faded rose

THE TALKING LEAVES

1964

Sequoia's winters were sixteen
Silent tongue, spirit clean
He walked at his father's side
Across the smoking battleground
Where red and white men lay all around
So many here had died

The wind had scattered around
Snow-white leaves upon the ground
Not leaves, like leaves from trees
Sequoia said, "What can this be?
What's the strange thing here I see?
From where come leaves like these?"

Sequoia turned to his father's eyes
And he said, "Father, you are wise.
From where come such snow-white leaves
With such strange marks upon these squares?
Not even the wise owl could put them there,
So strange these snow-white leaves."

His father, shielding his concern
Resenting the knowledge Sequoia yearned
Crumbled the snow-white leaves
He said, "When I explain, then it's done.
These are talking leaves, my son,
The white men's talking leaves.

"The white man takes a berry of black and red
And an eagle's feather from the eaglet's bed
And he makes bird track marks.
And the marks on the leaves, they say,
Carry messages to his brother far away
And his brother knows what's in his heart.

"They see these marks and they understand
The truth in the heart of the far-off man.
The enemies can't hear them."
Said Sequoia's father, "Son,
They weave bad medicine on these talking leaves.
Leave such things to them."

Then Sequoia, walking lightly
Followed his father quietly
But so amazed was he
If the white man talks on leaves
Why not the Cherokee

Vanished from his father's face
Sequoia went from place to place
But he could not forget
Year after year, he worked on and on
'Til finally he cut into stone
The Cherokee alphabet

Sequoia's hair by now was white
His eyes began to lose their light
But he taught all who would believe
That the Indians' thoughts could be written down
Just as the white men's, there on the ground
And he left us these talking leaves

TIME AND TIME AGAIN

with June Carter

1964

I wish my heart was stone
Because you're hard on flesh and bone
But even if my heart was stone
I couldn't stand it long

Because time and time again
You're gone with the wind
And even when you're here
I know you're making plans to go

You come back and I take you back
But you're like the shifting sand
And, like the sand, you shift
Right through my hands
Time and time again
I got you time and time again

You come back and I take you back
But you're like the shifting sand
And, like the sand, you shift
Right through my hands
Time and time again
I lose you time and time again

I want to be your man
So I give in all I can
And when I give in all I can
I give up time and time again

You take hold of my hand
And I look at where I stand
Then I say this is my last stand
Time and time again

You come back and I take you back
But you're like the shifting sand
And, like the sand, you shift
Right through my hands
Time and time again
I got you time and time again

Time and time again
I lose you time and time again
Time and time again
I got you time and time again

YOU WILD COLORADO

1964

Oh, you wild raging river
Like my woman's lips, you lure me
Pied piper of the desert
Roll on to the sea

You're the same, at noon or midnight
And I follow where you go
But you're planning no returning
You wild Colorado

If I had no love of life
I'd become part of your flow
But I fear the place you'd take me
You wild Colorado

Oh, you wild raging river
From the fountains of the mountains
You ripple down the valleys
Growing wide and swift and deep

With what power you cut your canyons
How long ago
You're as wayward as my woman
You wild Colorado

A CERTAIN KINDA HURTIN'

1965

I've got a certain kind of hurtin' since you've gone
I've got a pain I can't explain and it keeps on hanging on
You were gone one morning and I held on tight
But I went all to pieces later on that night
I've got a certain kind of hurtin' since you've gone

I've got a tear that's very near to showing through
I get too weak to speak when I think of losing you
You never got out of sight 'til I knew
That nothing's gonna ever be right without you
I've got a certain kind of hurtin' since you've gone

I've got a lonely heart that only beats for you
I hope you find I'm on your mind, needing me like I need you
You're not leaving on a one-way track
'Cause I'm gonna come get you and I'm bringing you back
I've got a certain kind of hurtin' since you've gone

COTTON PICKIN' HANDS

with June Carter

1965

I'm a fair-to-middlin' man
And these are cotton pickin' hands
I'm a fair-to-middlin' man
And these are cotton pickin' hands

My woman asks for little
And nothing she demands
Except to hold these cotton pickin' hands

The bloom is white and then it's red
Then it falls to leave a boll instead
The leaves fall and the field is white
We pick the pods from dawn to night

My woman cooks and sweeps the yard
And that old rug board is rough and hard
Her face is pretty, though it's tanned
And I love those cotton pickin' hands

I'm a fair-to-middlin' man
And these are cotton pickin' hands
I'm a fair-to-middlin' man
And these are cotton pickin' hands

My woman asks for little
And nothing she demands
Except to hold these cotton pickin' hands

HAPPINESS IS YOU

with June Carter

1965

Way down the mountain I chased a moonbeam
On the beach I built sandcastles, too
My moonbeams faded, my castles tumbled
All of this was meaningless 'cause happiness is you

No more chasing moonbeams or catching falling stars
I know now my pot of gold is anywhere you are
My heart won't miss you, my heart goes with you
Loneliness is emptiness, but happiness is you

I tried to doubt you and live without you
Tried to deny that I love you like I do
But I realize now and I'll admit it
You'll always be a part of me 'cause happiness is you

No more chasing moonbeams or catching falling stars
I know now my pot of gold is anywhere you are
My heart won't miss you, my heart goes with you
Loneliness is emptiness, and happiness is you

HAPPY TO BE WITH YOU

with June Carter and Merle Kilgore

1965

Happy to be with you
Happy to be with you
Happy to be with you
Bound to follow you

Somewhere, someone above
Sent you to me for me to love
Hearts can tremble and shake
Hearts can shudder and break
I give more than I take
'Cause I'm happy to be with you

Happy to be with you
Happy to be with you

Good times outweigh the bad
Count the good ones we've had
We have our ups and downs
But the good times come around
Nickels and pennies are few
Don't have a fortune for you
Love you, yes I do
And I'm happy to be with you

Happy to be with you
Happy to be with you

MEAN AS HELL

1965

The devil in hell, we're told, was chained
A thousand years he there remained
He neither complained nor did he groan
But was determined to start a hell of his own

Where he could torment the souls of men
Without being chained in a prison pen
So he asked the Lord if He had on hand
Anything left when He made this land

The Lord said, "Yes, there's a-plenty on hand
But I left it down by the Rio Grande.
The fact is, ol' boy, the stuff is so poor
I don't think you could use it as a hell anymore."

But the devil went down to look at the truck
And said if he took it as a gift, he was stuck
For after looking that over carefully and well
He said, "This place is too dry for a hell."

But in order to get it off his hands
The Lord promised the devil to water the land
So trade was closed and deed was given
And the Lord went back to His home in heaven

And the devil said, "Now I got all that's needed
To make a good hell," and he succeeded
He began by putting thorns all over the trees
He mixed up the sand with millions of fleas

He scattered tarantulas along the road
Put thorns on cactus and horns on toads
Lengthened the horns of the Texas steer
Put an addition to the rabbit's ear

Put a little devil in the bronco steed
And poisoned the feet of the centipede
The rattlesnake bites you, the scorpion stings
The mosquito delights you with his buzzing wings

The sandburs are there, and so are the ants
And if you sit down, you'll need to have soles on your pants
The wild boar roams on the black chaparral
It's a hell of a place that he has for a hell

The heat in the summers are hundred and ten
Too hot for the devil, too hot for men
The red pepper grows upon the banks of the brook
The Mexicans use it in all that they cook
Just dine with one of 'em and you're bound to shout
"I've hell on the inside as well as the out."

My hands are calloused July to July
I use a Big Dipper to navigate by
Fight off the wolves who drink from my well
So I have to be mean as hell

A sheepherder came and put up a fence
I saw him one day but I ain't seen him since
But if you need a mutton, we got mutton to sell
We're cowpunchers and we're mean as hell

Neither me nor my pony's got a pedigree
But he takes me where I'm wanting to be
I'll ride him to death and when he has fell
I'll get me another one mean as hell

I shot me a calf and I cut off her head
'Cause the boys in the bunkhouse are wanting to be fed
They rise in chime with the five thirty bell
And the best one of any of 'em is mean as hell

HIAWATHA'S VISION

originally by Henry Wadsworth Longfellow

adapted in 1965

On the shores of Gitchigoomy
By the shining, big sea water
Hiawatha, old and graying
Listened to the older prophet, listened to Lagu

And the young men and the women
From the land of Ojibways
From the land of the Dakotas, from the woodlands and the prairies
Stood and listened to the prophet, heard Lagu tell Hiawatha

"I have seen," he said, "a water bigger than the big sea water
Broader than the Gitchigoomy
Bitter so that none could drink it
Salty so that none would use it."

Hiawatha then spoke to them
Stopped all their jeering and their jesting
And he spoke to all the people

"It's true what Lagu tells you
For I have seen it in a vision.
I have also seen the water to the east
To the land of morning.

"And upon this great water came
A strange canoe with pinions
Bigger than a grove of pine trees
Taller than the tallest treetops.

"And upon this great canoe
Were sails to carry it swiftly
And it carried many people.
Strange and foreign were these people.

"And white were all their faces
And with hair their chins were covered."
Then said Hiawatha,
"I beheld a darker vision.

"Many hundreds came behind them
Pushed their way across our prairies.
In our woodlands rang their axes
In our valleys smoked their cities.

"Our people were all scattered
All forgetful of our councils.
Left their homelands going westward
Wild and woeful.

"And the men with bearded faces
The men with skin so fair
With their barking sticks of thunder
Drove the remnants of our people
Farther westward, westward, westward
Then wild, wild, and wilder
Grew the West that once was ours."

REFLECTIONS

1965

Never in this world before
Or nevermore hereafter
Could a land know such a people
As the pioneer, the cowboy

His clothes, his conversation
His unique brand of lingo
All his devil deeds of daring

His hat, his bandana, the dirty boots
And ragged chaps
But mainly, that six-gun, dangling
So his hand could get it quickly

But draw your own conclusions
Lean to your own understandings
Your beliefs and your convictions
Disprove any fact recorded in these sounds
And songs and legends

But I ask you if you do
Be sure you've walked in many moccasins
Over many, many pathways
And that you have listened carefully
Really listened, to the west wind
And to everything it whispers

And then go back and listen, listen to this
once more
To these legends and traditions
They're only one reflection
Of a tick of time, of that time

Just ponder on the things that happened
As we gaze so very deeply
In the time and place and persons
Seeing, now and then, the West as it really was
And to tell you of a little that we saw there

And looking backward through a century
There was the True West, there was the real
True West
Not demanding an agreement
But rather, hoping you looked with us
And saw it as we saw it
And heard that west wind screaming,
shouting, almost speaking
Always whispering of these things we sang
and spoke of

And you'll hear, perhaps, the things that we
said in the stories
And the legends and traditions
Through the wind that breathe these tales
Of the ones who never made it
Yet fighting heat and mountains, plains and
valleys, snow and hunger
They went westward, westward, westward

MISTER GARFIELD

with Ramblin' Jack Elliott

1965

Mister Garfield's been shot down, shot down, shot down
Mister Garfield's been shot down low

Me and my brother was down, close to the depot
When I heard the report of a pistol
My brother run out and come back in all excited
And I said, "What was it?"
And he said, "It was the report of a pistol."

And then he said,
"Mister Garfield been shot down, shot down, shot down
Mister Garfield been shot down low."

Lord, I knew the president was supposed to be at the depot that day
And we just wouldn't believe that he's shot
But we'd run over there and there was so many folks around
That we couldn't see him, but some lady was standing there crying
And I said, "Ma'am, what was it that happened, ma'am?"

And she said,
"Mister Garfield been shot down, shot down, shot down
Mister Garfield been shot down low."

Well, everybody drifted off toward home finally
And they looked like they felt about as bad as I did
But in a few weeks I heard that the president was still alive
And I told my brother, I said, "Let's get on that train
And go to where he's laid up, hurt."

Well, when we got to his big house up there, I asked the fellow
I said, "Who was it that did it? Who was it that shot the president?"
And he said, "It was Charlie Guiteau that shot Mister Garfield."

And I said,
"Charlie Guiteau done shot down a good man, good man
Charlie Guiteau done shot down a good man low."

I heard some fellow there that had been in the house to see the president
And I sidled up to him to listen to what he was telling
And he said
Mrs. Lucretia Garfield was always at his side
In the heat of the day fanning him when he was hot

He said that just that day the president said to Miss Lucretia
He said, "Crete, honey" — he called her Crete
Said, "If something worse happens to me
After a while, you get yourself a good man."
And Miss Lucretia said, "James" — she called him James

She said, "I won't hear to that now," she said, "I love you too much."
But he said,
"You'll make some good man a good wife, good wife
You'll make some man a good, good wife.
Don't pull in single harness all your life, good girl
Don't pull in single harness all your life."
That's what he said: "Don't pull in single harness all your life."

Well, a few days later I come back to where the president was resting
And it seems everybody was crying
The flag was hanging halfway up the flagpole in front of the house
Everybody looked so sad and I asked a soldier boy there
I said, "Is, is Mister . . . is Mister Garfield . . . ?"
And he said, "Yes, he's gone."

Going to lay him in that cold lonesome ground down low
Going to lay him in that cold lonesome ground
Well, they laid the president by that long cold branch
Mister Garfield's been laid down low
Mister Garfield's been shot down, shot down, shot down
Mister Garfield's been shot down low
Mister Garfield's been shot down, shot down, shot down
Mister Garfield's been shot down low

THUNDERBALL

1965

There is a rumble in the sky
And all the world can hear it call
They shudder at the fury
Of the mighty Thunderball

The power of her engines, now
Has drowned in the sea
But the deadly force from within her
Is somewhere running free

Thunderball, your fiery breath
Can burn the coldest man
And who is going to suffer
From the power in your hand?

Somewhere there is a man
Who could stop the thing in time
He is known by very few
But he's feared by all in crime

By courage and by fighting
He has not been known to fall
But neither has the fury
Of the mighty Thunderball

Thunderball, your fiery breath
Can burn the coldest man
And who is going to suffer
From the power in your hand

Money-hungry minds
Need a thread to launch a scheme
But those who hold the Thunderball
Could rule the world, it seems

Cannot the peaceful world find
The clue to where she's gone
The silent sea won't answer now
But terror lingers on

Thunderball, your fiery breath
Can burn the coldest man
And who is going to suffer
From the power in your hand

WE ALL MISS YOU, JOE

1965

Do you recall the dew upon the meadow?
Do you recall the tall, waving corn?
Do you recall the river in the valley
That ran beside the farm where you were born?

We all miss you, Joe
We wish that you could see
The mowing of the green alfalfa hay
We all miss you, Joe
We all miss you so
We wish that you were here with us today

Did you forget the girl you were to marry?
She's waiting and she still lives all alone
Did you forget that you said you'd be returning?
We've often seen her crying since you've been gone

We all miss you, Joe
We wish that you could hear
Kentucky pines singing in the wind
We all miss you, Joe
We all miss you so
We wish that you were back with us again

AUSTIN PRISON

1966

They had a warrant out for me all over the country
And I was trying to beat two raps in Idaho
I was breaking into a schoolhouse Sunday morning without warning
When I saw the sheriff coming for me slow from down below

His steel-gray eyes were blazing when he saw me
His hand was on his gun when he rode up
He said, "You killed that woman, I know you shot her, why'd you do it?
I'm taking you to Austin, then I'm gonna lock you up."

Well, he tied me with a plowline the next morning
And he had me deep in Texas the next day
A crazy screaming lynch mob waited in the streets of Austin
But he put me in the jailhouse and he threw the key away

A jury found me guilty three months later
Twelve evil men with murder in their eyes
They even took me out and said, "Now show us where you killed her."
And that wicked judge said, "Now I hereby sentence you to die."

But here I am far away from Austin prison
My friend the jailer handed me a file
Now all I want between me and there are a lot of friendly people
And miles and miles and miles and miles and miles and miles and miles

CALIFORNIA POEM

with Jamey Johnson and John Carter Cash

1966

There's trouble on the mountain
And the valley's full of smoke
There's crying on the mountain
And again the same heart broke

The lights are on past midnight
The curtains, closed all day
There's trouble on the mountain
The valley people say

The valley is a-rumble
The mountain is ablaze
Horses crack and crumble
And again the same heart breaks

Clouds of scattered ashes
Blacken out the sun
There's trouble on the mountain
Everybody run

California Poem 1966

Theres trouble on the mountain
And the valley's full of smoke
There's crying on the Mountain
And again the same heart broke
The lights are on past midnite
The curtains closed all day
Theres trouble on the Mountain
The valley people say.

John Cash

CONCERNING YOUR NEW SONG

1966

Friend, concerning your new song
Just like you asked, I listened to your song
And though I feel it's kind of long
And maybe a line or two is wrong
And some lines don't belong
Like you asked, I listened to your song

Concerning one line where you said
That love is over with and dead
I wonder down what road has your mind led
And by whose hand is love now dead

If you think that death is true and tried
Then walk that foreign mountainside
Where ten thousand fought and died
You, my friend, are still alive
Have you tried and are you true?

And would you go, should they call you?
I'm sorry for this brow of sweat
But answering you has made it wet
If I do get to know your song
I'll find it kind of hard to sing along
'Cause your lines of messages are strong
But not for sing-along
'Til now, I thought that songs were just to sing
A little power and anything else that they
  bring

If you ever sing it, friend, don't bow
'Cause the world should think you know how
To be happy thinking as you do now

Like I said, if I ever get to know your song
I'm sorry I won't sing along
Because your messages don't belong
In a world of sing-along

Don't speak it as truth, when I know
That most melodies, like rivers
Flow like the plateaus to plains
They ripple, but they freely flow

If you sing the song, if you sing
Remember, it's bells that rhyme
They may be slow to ring
Yes, I took all those miles of lines you wrote
Ran them through me, note by note
But not really bored by your lyrics' length
Rather, I admired your lyrics' strength

'Cause on each line of verse you hung
A melody that could be sung
Then you wrote until I think your mind was
  wrung
And, like a tool, you use your song
Pushing tortured, twisted mind storms
Whether they are right or wrong

So, you see, I did listen to your song
But, like I said, for a song, it's kind of long
At the end, there really was no profound
  effect
Except for maybe a little tension in my neck
But, like you asked, I did listen to your song

I LOVE A RAMBLIN' MAN

1966

I love my ramblin' man
And my ramblin' man loves me
I know he'll be back
So I'll help him pack
And I give him a kiss and my key

I love my ramblin' man
And my ramblin' man loves me
I know he'll be back
So I'll help him pack
Then I give him a kiss and my key

Yes, I love a ramblin' man
Don't you tell me he doesn't love me
He's kind and he's sweet
'Til he gets itchy feet
Then he's wild as the wind in the trees
Yes, he's wild as the wind in the trees

Well, I kiss him hello when he's back
And he talks of the road and the track
I cook and I sew, but I know that he'll go
As soon as he's feeling the slack

I love my ramblin' man
My ramblin' man loves me
I know he'll be back
So I'll help him pack
Then I give him a kiss and my key

PUT THE SUGAR TO BED

with Maybelle Carter

1966

Out on a shrimp boat, I'd just dropped the net
When the wind, she come to blowing,
  whizzing bad all to get
I look southeast and, golly me, what I see
A black thundercloud, with them fuzzy
  eyebrows
Come a-looking direct towards Boudleaux
  and me

I turned to Boudleaux, and me, I said,
"Put the sugar to bed, put the sugar to bed.
Lock up the coffee in the coffeepot.
Put the flour in your pillow, 'cause it's all we
  got.
Hang the lantern from the ceiling and watch
  your head.
Ho, Boudleaux, put the sugar to bed.
Boudleaux, put the sugar to bed."

Well, the sky, she get dark and then she turn
  dark black
I yell, "She gonna blow one right out of the
  almanac!"
A big raindrop smacked me right on the ear
And I hollered, "Hey, Boudleaux," but the way
  the wind blow
He just as soon be deaf, there wasn't no how
  to hear
I try to call to Boudleaux, but slid instead
Then me and Boudleaux put the sugar to bed

Well, the ends of that shrimpin' boat was
  switchin' around
She turned sideways and inners and outers
  and upside down
The water come in, tryin' to drown the both
  of us
The closet popped open and the skillet went
  a-flyin'
Me, I hit my head and kinda cussed

But most of all, I frowned when she calmed,
  that I said,
"Put the sugar to bed, put the sugar to bed."
Ain't nothin' dry but my railroad watch
The salt got soggy, but we still can botch
We built a fire for the coffee and we chicory
  fed
'Cause me and Boudleaux put the sugar to
  bed
Me and Boudleaux put the sugar to bed

brows.

One night that storm was comin' and Bill yelled to Boudeloux, "Put the sugar to bed." I asked Bill what he meant and he said, "~~that [illegible]~~ Well, shes gonna come a rain, and "put the sugar to bed" means lock up every thing that might get soggy, like flour, coffee, salt and all that. All the perishables, — or all the possibles."

Verse 1.

"Out upon the shrimp boat
Just Drop the net.
When the wind commence to blow
Worsn bad ought to get
I look south-east
And golly-me, what I see
A big black cloud
With fuzzy eye brows
Comin' direct 'towards Boudeloux & me

verse 1 — cont

"I turned to Boudeloux
And me I said
Put the sugar to bed.
" " " " "

"Lock up the coffee and the coffee pot
"Stuff the matches in your pillow
Cause thats all we got
Hang the lantern from the ceiling
And watch your head —
Etc... Boudeloux, Put the Sugar to Bed.

Verse 2

"The sky get dark
Then she turn dark black
I yell, "She gonna blow one
Out of the Almanac
A big rain drop smack
Me on the ear.
I holler, "Hurry Boudeloux
But the way the wind blow
He just as soon be deaf
They wasnt no how to hear

"I haul in the net
And she slap me in the head
Then I help Boudeloux
Put the sugar to bed

(cut short verse 2)

Verse 3.

"The ends of that boat
Was switchin' around
She turn every way known
'cept upside down
The water roar in
Tryin to drown both of us
We turn side-ways
And we lose alla shrimp
An I near bout cuss"

But it finally cam
And we aint dead
And on top of that
We put the sugar to bed."

PLEASE DON'T PLAY RED RIVER VALLEY

1966

Well, I see you got yourself
A brand-new harmonica
Mail ordered from the Spiegel's catalog
Boy, I hope you can learn
To play it like Lonnie Glossom

And while you're at it
You oughta learn a verse or two
Of Red River Valley
Oh My Darling Clementine
Or Salty Dog

Oh, but please don't play Red River Valley
How about Polly Wolly Doodle All Day, in C
You know, the only song I ever learned to play
On my 2 dollar and 98 cent harmonica
That I got from Wayne Raney in Clint, Texas
C-L-I-N-T Clint, Texas, was Red River Valley
Then she said farewell
To my French harp and me

Well, I see you're doing pretty good
On your new harmonica
But don't you think you ought to learn
About one more tune, you know
See, you hold it like you's going
To eat a handful of popcorn
And sometimes, you suck in
And sometimes, you blow

But friend, now, please don't play
Red River Valley
How about Polly Wolly Doodle All Day
Like I said, the only song I ever learned
On my 2 dollar and 98 cent harmonica
That I got from Clint, Texas
From Wayne Raney in Clint, Texas
Was Red River Valley
Then she said farewell to
My French harp and me

SHE'S MIGHTY GONE

with June Carter

1966

Day dawns and here comes the news
Baby's gone and here comes the blues
Took the pen and paper and threw them on the floor
There's nothing left to write anymore

She's mighty gone and I'm heartsick and sore
Why, why, why don't baby live here anymore
She's mighty gone

She's not the kind that's easy to live with
Not the gentle kind a man can be real with
She spoke out in protest, I spoke out in anger
Turned her 'cross my knee, even that didn't change her

She's mighty gone and I'm heartsick and sore
Why, why, why don't baby live here anymore
She's mighty gone

I'll pick up the dishes that she threw on the floor
I'll paint the walls and I'll buy a new door
I'll buy her perfume until it makes her sick
I'll make her realize it takes two heels to click

She's mighty gone and I'm heartsick and sore
Why, why, why don't baby live here anymore
She's mighty gone

TWELVE FEET TALL, AGAIN

1966

I watched you from my pit of slime
Grit your teeth and bide your time
You gave to me a place to rest
You sacrificed, to give the best
The dogs and I barked all night
Then like a werewolf I hid from daylight

I missed the mist of morning rain
I missed your early morning pain
I missed the soft pine-tree-breeze hymn
(Unless it sang at four p.m.)
And I apologize and confess to you
I missed two-thirds after four p.m., too

You kindly smiled back, but underneath
Did I detect a grit of teeth?
Please know that I felt half your size
When I saw pity in your eyes...
...then tears, and I knew beyond doubt
My crutch was weakening, wearing out

When finally I left that night
I wanted to scream, "I'll be all right!"
I wanted to cry out, "Please forgive!
Please have faith, I'm going to live!
Have mercy, please! Still be a friend!
I'll stand up twelve feet tall, again."

Today I went to a clothing store
Cramped to death in the clothes I wore
Walked straight and sure to the tailor's bench
Got remeasured inch by inch

YOU BEAT ALL I EVER SAW

1966

I walked through every town
Saw fortunes lost and found
And when your trail failed
I walked holes in both my soles

But I don't expect you back
You're somewhere, making tracks
I crossed your burning bridges
And walked through miles of sand
Met the lawless and the law
But you beat all I ever saw

I dreamed a million miles
About your eyes and smiles
I tried to love the best
And to turn from all the rest

But I scanned the skies for you
And I only saw your hue
They threw away your mold
You were made of frozen gold
And your heart would never thaw
You beat all I ever saw

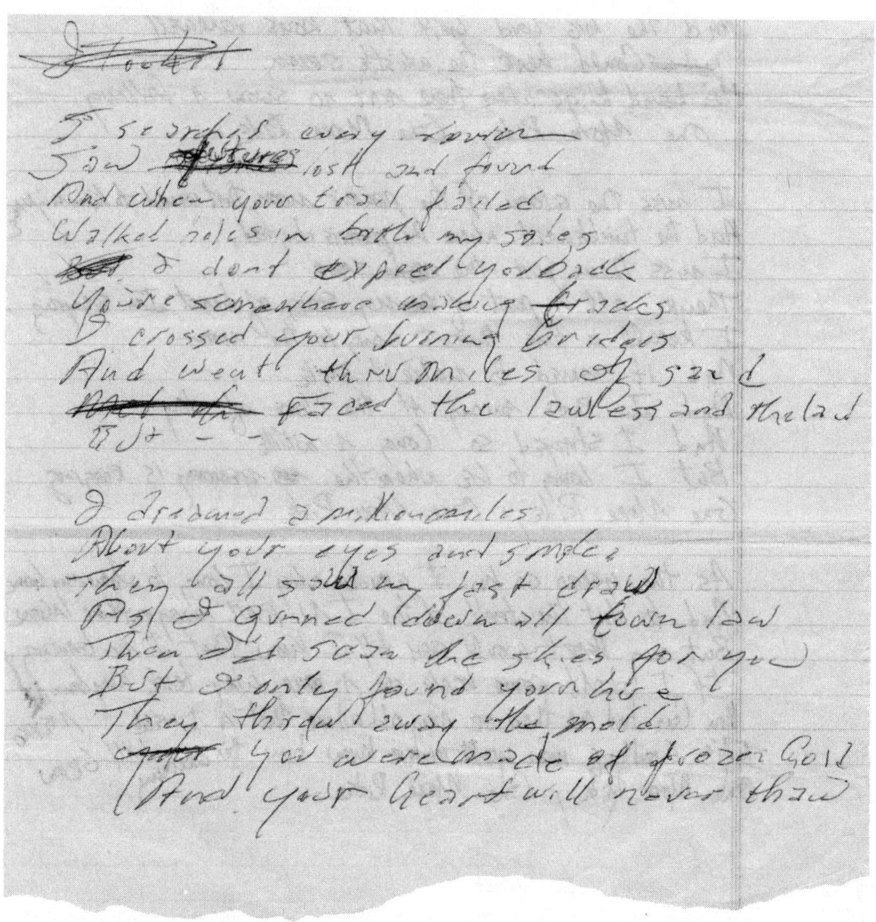

ANOTHER SONG TO SING

1967

Do they ask you where I am or where I've been?
Do they ever say, "Where is the lonely friend?"
Is my name whispered in your bedside prayers?
Do you feel a vacant spot beside you there?

Well, there's always one more path that I must walk
And there's people I should sit down with and talk
And somebody might appreciate the flowers I could bring
So there's always another song to sing

Do you tell them I was wilder than the wind?
Do you remember that I needed lots of friends?
And at other times I'd rather be alone
Where I could not be found when I was gone

Well, there's always one more canyon to explore
To touch the things left by those gone before
At the top of the tiniest hill I can feel like I'm a king
And there's always another song to sing

I'll go where and when my
my heart leads ~~me~~ no matter
where.

Finding those who know —
those that ~~And~~ understand and care
~~I like everybody~~ I want to know everbody
~~And I like~~ ~~[illegible]~~ ~~most everything~~ I want to do everything
for I always find
Another song to sing

Another Song to Sing

Do they Ask you where I am
Or where I've been
Do ~~they really think they miss~~ they ask you "where went"
their lonely friend.
Is my name whispered in
your bedtime prayer
Do you feel a vacant place
Beside you there?
Well theres still another
Highway I must walk
And people I must sit down
with and talk
Some where there's ~~always someone~~ Someone that
needs ~~a~~ flowers ~~that~~ I could bring
And over the hill theres Another
Song to Sing.

Sorry I cant be content
To live from eight to five.
Are the 8 to 5 alive

THE CAPTAIN'S DAUGHTER (NO, NO, NO)

with Robert Lee Castleman

1967

I'm a poor boy as you know
But I love the captain's daughter so
If I begged her would she go
Or would she tell me no, no, no, no, no

"Daddy is a sailor man.
You're fresh from the farmland.
He said when you ask my hand
For me to tell you no, no, no, no, no."

"Your daddy's gone away to sea.
You're as lovely as can be.
Come and go away with me.
Oh, don't you tell me no, no, no, no, no."

"My daddy owns a clipper ship.
He brings me pearls on every trip.
Pink champagne for me to sip.
And you're the poorest boy I know, know,
know, know, know."

"I've got no pearls to give you.
I've got two arms and a heart that's true.
We could start with a dream or two.
Oh, won't you say you'll go, go?"

The poor boy came from the farmland
She was the daughter of a sailor man
The captain says, "When he begs your hand
You better tell him no, no, no, no, no."

She said, "Papa, don't you worry, please.
The poor boy begs me upon his knees.
I'd never leave this life of ease."
And with the poor boy goes

The captain kissed her and he went to sea
The poor boy said, "Go away with me.
You're lonely and you shouldn't be.
Oh, don't you tell me no, no, no, no, no."

"My daddy owns a clipper ship.
He brings me pearls on every trip.
Pink champagne for me to sip.
And you're the poorest boy I know, know,
know, know, know."

"Your daddy's given you a home
But you've got nobody when he is gone.
I'll go and leave you all alone
If the answer is still no, no."

I'm a poor boy as you know
But I love the Captains daughter so
If I begged her would she go
Or would she tell me no no No No No

Daddy is a sailor man
You're fresh from the farm land
He said when you ask my hand
For me to tell you no no No No No.

Your daddys gone away to sea.
You're as lonely as can be
Come and go away with me.
Oh dont you tell me no no No No No

My daddy owns a clipper ship
He brings me pearls on every trip
And pink champagne for me to sip
You're the poorest boy I know No No No No

I've got no pearls to give to you
I've got two arms and a heart thats free
We could start with a dream or two
Dont say you wont go no no no no

The poor boy came from the farm land
She was the daughter of a sailor man
The Captain said when he begs your hand
You better tell him no no No No No

She said papa dont you worry please
The poor boy begs me upon his knees
But I'd never leave this life of ease
And with a poor boy go no No No No

The Captain kissed her and he went to sea
The poor boy said go away with me
You're lonely and you shouldn't be
Oh dont you tell me no no No No No

My daddy owns a clipper ship
He brings me pearls on every trip
And pink champagne for me to sip
And you're the poorest boy I know No No

He said I've got no pearls for you
But I've got two arms and a heart thats
We could start with a dream or two
Oh wont you say you'll go no no no no

You couldn't give me anything
Except a plain gold wedding ring
You've got no presents you could bring
My daddys rich you no no No No No

Your daddys given you a home
But you've got nobody when he's gone
I'll go and leave you all alone
If the answer still is no no No No No

My daddys on the churning sea
And he would turn me across his knee
If he knew you were kissing me
I WONT STAY WHEN YOU GO NO NONONO

CALL DADDY FROM THE MINE

1967

A little girl woke up deep in the dark and started crying
The mother brought a light and held her daughter tight
She thought it was so strange to hear a little girl of nine
Cry, "Call Daddy from the mine, call Daddy from the mine."

Her mother wiped the tears and said, "See, honey, you're only dreaming.
Your dad must work today, he has to draw his pay."
She left her then but still could hear her cry, time after time,
"Call Daddy from the mine, call Daddy from the mine."

Then the countryside was shaken by a mighty rumble
And fear for miles around was the trembling of the ground
The little girl was fast asleep, yet cried out one more time,
"Call Daddy from the mine, call Daddy from the mine."

Ten thousand tears and two weeks later, deep in the smoking ground
A dying man was found, had survived all those around
He'd quickly crawled to a fresh air pocket barely just in time
When he heard his own child whine, "Call Daddy from the mine
Call Daddy from the mine, call Daddy from the mine."

CISCO CLIFTON'S FILLIN' STATION

1967

Cisco Clifton had a fillin' station
About a mile and a half from town
Most cars passed unless they were out of gas
So Cisco was always around

Regular gas was all that he sold
Except tobacco, matches, and oil
Other than that he fixed lots of flats
Keepin' Cisco's rough hands soiled

He'd wipe the gas and check the air
And a hundred times a day
He patiently gave directions
On how to get to the state highway

Usually he'd give 'em water
Or a tire or two, some air
And once a big black Cadillac
Spent seven dollars there

He'd give anybody anything they'd ask
And lend anything he had
His tools, his tires, bumper jacks or wire
To the good ones or the bad

In wintertime there was a depot stove
And a table for a checker game
And every morning at sunup
The same checker players came

So Cisco Clifton's fillin' station
Was always in the red
Personal loans were personally gone
But never a word was said

One morning at eight, them checker players
Heard a big bulldozer roar like a freight
And Cisco said, "I hope my kids stay fed
When they build that interstate."

He'd managed to pay for the property
Where his little fillin' station sat
And friends still came for the checker game
So Cisco settled for that

He wouldn't say so but Cisco knew
That the interstate was too much to fight
But to keep his will and to pay his bills
He did odd jobs at night

He still opened up at sunrise
And the checker game went on
The cars flew past on high-test gas
And the neighbors had sold out and gone

If a car ever did go by he was lost
And if they stopped they were treated the
  same
So at Cisco Clifton's fillin' station
There's a howdy and a checker game

CROWLEY'S RIDGE

1967

I borrowed me a ridin' hoss
I headed north, for Crowley's Ridge to cross
We crossed Little River at Le-Pan-To
Never slowed down 'til around Jones-boro

Destination Hardy, Arkansas
To take my woman back
From her maw and paw

The rich Delta land
Was black and flat
But the cotton grows good
In ground like that

The sun set slowly
And the land turned red
On top of Crowley's Ridge
I unrolled my blanket
For my folding bed

I grazed my hoss
Near where my bed would be
Then led him down to a spring
And let him drink after me

Short pine needles was a natural bed
And a peck of grass
Was the pillow for my head
But I was up when the sun hit Crowley's Ridge
I told my hoss, "I'm worried 'bout the WPA bridge."

I had forgot about the bridge
When I first started out

It was built in '39
And without a doubt
It had weathered many a flood
And due to be washed out

I drank a can of coffee
Then rode on north
'Round the blackberry thickets
I'd be dodgin' back and forth

When I reached the north side of Crowley's Ridge
The river had washed out
The WPA bridge

My hoss wouldn't swim it
It was swift and deep
I hopes the water's down by morning
So I laid me down to sleep

The river was down next morning and the pilings was all that was left of the WPA bridge. I looked on the other side and there sat my woman and I waved my arms at her. She jumped in the river and started swimmin' toward me. I met her halfway and swam back with her riding me. Then we wrapped my blanket around us 'til we stopped shiverin' from the cold water. She said, "I'm ready to go home with you now." I said, "You gonna keep on livin' with me and not run back to your folks?" She said, "Yes, you're my man. I belong with you, not in Hardy, Arkansas. Lonesome for the black Delta land and the white fields of cotton. And I belong with you, south of Crowley's Ridge. But mostly I've been lonesome for you."

So we double-rode my borrowed hoss
'Til the land got flat
But like the cotton
Love grows good in ground like that

CROWLEY'S RIDGE

Johnny Cash
Sept 1967

I borrowed me a ridin' hoss
I headed North for Crowleys ridge to cross
We crossed Little River at Lepanto
Never slowed down till around Jonesboro
Destination HARDY, ARKANSAS
To take my Woman back
From her maw and paw

The rich Delta land
Was black and flat
But the cotton grows good
In ground like that

Cho The sun set slowly
And the land turned red
On — top — of —
Crowleys Ridge
I unrolled my blanket
For my ~~sitting~~ bed

I grazed my hoss
~~While I rested~~ near where my bed would be
Then led him down to a spring
And let him drink after me

Next Page

Verse 2 Page 2 Crowleys Ridge

Short pine needles was a natural bed
And a peck of grass
Was the pillow for my head

But I was up when the sun hit Crowleys Ridge
I told my hoss "I'm worried 'bout the WPA bridge"

I had forgot about the bridge
When I ~~first~~ started out
It was built in '39
And without a doubt
It had weathered many a flood
~~[illegible]~~ to be washed out
And dyed

Verse 3

I drank a can of coffee
As I rode on north
Round the blackberry thickets
I'd be dodgin' back & forth

~~[illegible]~~
When I reached the ~~bottom~~ North ~~[illegible]~~
Bottom ~~[illegible]~~ side of Crowleys Ridge ~~[illegible]~~
The river had washed out
The WPA bridge
↓

Page 3 Crowleys Ridge
(verse 3 cont.)

"My hoss wouldn't swim it
It was swift and deep
I hoped the water's down by morning
So I laid me down to sleep
(TALK)

"The river was down next mornin
And the pilings was all left of the WPA bridge.
I looked on the other side and there sat my Woman and I waved my arms at her.
She jumped in the river and started swimmin' toward me.
I met her halfway and swam back ~~[illegible]~~ with her ~~on~~ ~~[illegible]~~. Then we wrapped my blanket around us till we stopped shiverin' from the cold water.
She said "I'm ready to go home with you now"
I said "~~[illegible]~~ Gonna you keep on livin' with me and not run back to your folks?"
She said "yes, I belong with you, you're my man Not in Hardy Ark. I'm lonesome for the black Delta land and the white fields of cotton — and — and I belong with you south of Crowleys Ridge. — But mostly I've been lonesome for you
(SING)

"So we double-rode my borrowed Hoss
Till the land got flat
But like the cotton — — —
Love ~~[illegible]~~ grows good
In ground like that

Johnny Cash
~~[illegible]~~ Oct 1967

THE FLINT ARROWHEAD

1967

Over fields of new-turned sod
And in communion with my God
I walked alone
In a furrow bed
I found an arrowhead
Chiseled from stone

I don't know how long ago
Some red man drew his bow
On its last fight
Or did he drop it here
Afraid white men were near
To attack at night

I do know this one thing
Beyond all questioning
It was made to kill
And proof of a master trade
Is in this arrowhead he made
Fashioned with skill

That I inherited this ground
Is denied by this stone I've found
But when, and by who
Come join me in my tracks
Then let's stop and look back

To the vale and through
In love and peace, we'll see
The shadows and the trees
And voices, too

But quietly, slowly tread
This home of the forgotten dead
Whose bones are dust
I'm proud that their craftsmen's
skill
Survives the ages still
Left in my trust

EXPO '67

1967

From sea to shining sea
They came, demanding liberty
Built the road, and laid the track
From St. John through Halifax

Though under France or England's
  crown
They raised a new flag from the
  ground
Raised the mighty Montreal
Held it high, never to fall

Built more cities
Laid more track
Untiring hands
Unbreaking backs

Raised Winnipeg and Calgary
To Vancouver, to the sea
One great century she's grown
Now she proudly stands alone

Prouder than Rome's finest hour
Or Babylon or Babel's tower
The grandest show under heaven
Is at Expo '67

The stage is set
Attendance free
The greatest sight from sea to sea
Is Canada's Centennial to be

From every land both bond and free
Now at Expo '67

North they came from New Orleans
From Jackson and Abilene
Edmonton and Toronto
New York and Chicago
Ecum Secum, Fairview
Flin Flon, St. John's Andrew
Long Bow, Pickle Crow
Red Deer, North Bay
Cortenay, Sevier
Moncton, Fredericton, Hull
Jack Pine, Sydney Mines, Gull

Page 2 Expo 67

From every land both bond & free
Now at Expo 67

North they come from New Orleans
From Jacksonville and Abilene
Edmonton and Toronto
New York and Chicago

Ecum-Secum - Fairview
Flin-Flon - St. Johns - Andrew
Long Bow - Pickle Crow - Red Deer
North Bay - Courtenay - Sorrel
Moncton - Fredericton - Hull
Jack Pine - Sydney Mines - Gull

Expo 67

FROM SEA TO SHINING SEA
They came demanding Liberty
Built the road, and laid the tracks
From St. John through Halifax
Through under France or England's crown
They raised a new flag from the ground
Raised the mighty Montreal
Held it high to never fall

Built more cities
Laid more track
Unbowing hands
Unbreaking backs
Raised Winnepeg And Calgary
To Vancouver to the sea
One great century she's grown
Now she proudly stands alone

Prouder than Rome's finest hour
Or ~~Babylon~~ Of Babel's tower
The ~~grandest~~ show under heaven
Is at Expo 67
The stage is set Admittance free
The greatest sight from sea to sea
Is Canada's Centennial to be

FLY AWAY

1967

On the big jet airplane, you left
My heart heavy as stone
There's just a rustle of the wind
I turn around and I'm alone

No need to say the unsaid
Or try to do the undone
You hushed the song of the bird
Darkened the light of the sun

Fly away — and don't look back
Go on, and be happy — fly away
I'll try to fake it
And I'll try to keep smiling every day

Fly away — some day, I might forget you
Oh yes, I'll be all right
But in the meantime
Every night

I'll stop listenin' for you comin'
'Round the bend of the road
I'll hide the trembling of my lip
Stand up under my load

Hold back tears from my eyes
Conceal the pain of despair
Make sure the sound of my voice
Does not reveal how I feel and care

I'll stop listening for you comin
'Round the bend of the road
I'll hide the trembling of my lip
Stand up under my load

Hold back tears from my eyes
Conceal the pain of despair
Make sure the sound of my voice
Doesnot reveal how I feel & care

Johnny Cash
Sept 11 '67

Fly Away — Johnny Cash

the big jet plane you left
my heart heavy as stone
There's just a rustle of the wind
I turn around and I'm alone
No Need to say the Unsaid
try to do the Undone
hushed the song of the bird
dened the light of the sun

Fly Away — And dont look back
Go on And be happy — Fly Away
I'll try to take it And I'll
Try to keep smilin every day
Fly Away — Someday
I might forget you
~~Fly Away~~ Oh yes
I'll be alright
But in the meantime
Every nite.....

↓

FROM SEA TO SHINING SEA

1967

The beautiful, spacious skies
The amber waves of grain
To the majestic purple mountains
Above the fruited plain

God did shed His grace
From sea to shining sea
On you and on me

From the Sleepy Hollow mountain country
To the swamps of Okefenokee
To Guthrie, Oklahoma
To Hibbing, Minnesota
To Grants Pass, Oregon
To Stovepipe Wells, California
From Texas to Montana
From California to Maine

In the sunny days
The winter snow
From Arizona sand
To Cherokee, North Carolina
To Tarpon Springs, Florida

America, it's time to be refreshed
Recalled to memory
God did shed His grace on thee
From sea to shining sea

The land is big, the best is free
Sand and surf, grass and tree
From sea to shining sea

America, America
God shed His grace on thee
And crown thy good with brotherhood
From sea to shining sea

FROZEN FOUR HUNDRED POUND FAIR-TO-MIDDLIN' COTTON PICKER

1967

I left the field one evening
My fingers so cold and sore
From fair-to-middlin' cotton
Three hundred pounds or more

Jim McCann was still picking
Straddlin' his row
The sun began to sinking
And the wind began to blow

He was bound to get four hundred
A-dragging a twelve-foot sack
I hollered out, "Jim, come weigh it."
But I only saw his back

So I went on home to supper
And I gathered around my kin
I was thinking of Jim out there, pickin'
With winter setting in

Next morning, the air was freezing
The snow was nine feet deep
I jerked on my long red handles
And I left my kids asleep

I got myself a shovel
And went to where I seen Jim go
And commenced to a-digging for him
At the other end of his row

I found his body frozen
And I took him in to thaw
I drug in his sack and I weighed it
And I added Jim's marks that I saw

The total was over four hundred
So he'd picked more than he'd bet
Of fair-to-middlin' cotton
But Jim ain't thawed out yet

GOLD ALL OVER THE GROUND

with Brad Paisley

1967

If I had you at my mercy
There's no telling what I'd do
But I'd sit and make you listen
For an hour, maybe two

And then you'd know I need you
Every day that rolls around
And your feet would walk on velvet
With gold all over the ground

All your trails would be downhill
A soft breeze at your back
A sky full of diamonds
And your nights would not be black

Yes, you would really love it
And if you're ever down
I'd give you rows of roses
And gold all over the ground

I'd pick you up and carry you
Across every stream I see
And I'd bundle you in kindness
Until you'd cling to me

We'd sit beneath strong branches
My arms would twine around
I'd turn your green to emerald
And give you gold all over the ground

"Gold All Over the Ground" J. Cash

March 1967

If I had you at my mercy
there's no tellin what I'd do
But I'd make you sit and listen
For an hour, maybe two

And then you'd know I need you
Every day that rolls around
Your feet would walk on velvet
With gold all over the ground

your trails would be downhill
A soft breeze at your back
your skies full of diamonds
your nights would not be black

Yes you would really love it
then if you're ever down
I'd give you rows of roses
And Gold all over the ground

I'd pick you up and carry you
'cross every stream I see
I'd bundle you in kindness
Until you cling to me
We'd sit beneath strong branches
My arms would twine around
I'd turn your green to emeralds - and give you

I Never Knew Your Mind

I can feel the way you're changing
But I cant change the way you're feeling
You're special, you are different, you are one of a kind
I dont know just how I'll make it
~~And I'm afraid how I will~~ take it.
I dont know how to deal with what you're thinking
I guess I never knew your mind.

There were times when you were laughing
that I understood you completely
you were carefree, open, honest
~~loving~~ easy ~~soft &~~ kind.
I never worried never doubted
that we had it all together
Till the changes came and painfully I knew
I never knew your mind.

Your silence holds your secrets
When you answer but dont answer
But I know you well enough ~~that~~ I can to know
(pause)
recognize the signs
So I let it go unanswered
I dont want to hear "its over"
I see it in your eyes, and feel it your distant whisper
~~Although~~ I never knew your mind.
and I know

I NEVER KNEW YOUR MIND

1967

I can feel the way you're changing
But I can't change the way you're feeling
You are special, you are different
You are one of a kind
I don't know just how I'll make it
I'm afraid how I will take it
I don't know how to deal with what you're thinking
I guess I never knew your mind

There were times when you were laughing
That I understood you completely
You were carefree, open, honest
Loving, easy, soft, and kind
I never worried, never doubted
That we had it all together
'Til the changes came and I painfully knew
I never knew your mind

Your silence holds your secrets
When you answer, but don't answer
But I know you well enough to know that I
Can recognize the signs
So I let it go unanswered
I see it in your eyes, and I feel it in your distant whisper
And I know I never knew your mind

YOU NEVER REALLY KNEW MY MIND

with Chris Cornell

1967

I know you feel the way I change
But you can't change the way I feel
Sometimes I'm a stranger to you
One of a kind

Then I think some way you'll make it
Though you don't know how to take it
Sometimes you're a stranger to me
One of a kind

There were times and lots of laughter
And you felt you understood
We were carefree, open, and honest
Loving, easy, kind, and true

And I suppose you never doubted
That we were altogether fine
You never really knew my mind
You never really knew my mind

My silence holds, secrets find
I answer, but don't answer
You did not see me well enough
To recognize the signs

You didn't want to know this
But know that it was over
I did not see you well enough
To recognize the signs

And there were times and lots of laughter
And you felt you understood
We were carefree, open, and honest
Loving, easy, kind, and true

And I suppose you never doubted
That we were altogether fine
Then you saw the changes, painfully
You never really knew my mind

And I suppose you never doubted
That we were altogether fine
Sometimes I'm a stranger to you
Sometimes you're a stranger to me
Sometimes maybe all the time
You never really knew my mind
I never really knew your mind

You Never Knew My Mind J Cash

I know you feel the way I change
But you cant change the way I feel
Sometimes I'm a stranger to you— one of a kind
I think some way you'll make it
Though you dont know how to take it.
You cant deal with how I'm thinkin
Cause you never knew my mind.

There were times of lots of laughter
And ~~I know~~ you felt you understood me
We were carefree open honest
Loving easy true and kind
I suppose you never doubted then
That we had it all together
Then you saw the changes painfully and knew
You never knew my mind

My silence holds the secrets when I answer but
You didnt didnt see ~~my~~ me well enough answer
to recognize the signs
So I let it go unanswered
You didnt want to know its over
You never ~~if you'd~~ looked close enough ~~good~~ to know
You never knew my mind

I TREMBLE FOR YOU

with Lewis DeWitt

1967

This world that I live in is empty and cold
This loneliness cuts me and tears at my soul
I'm no child of destiny, no fortune's son
I've chased you so long now, I'm too weak to run

So here I return to a back street of thrills
Back to any warm shoulder 'til she's got her fill
And then I treat shame like an old friend from home
That I can lean on 'til the misery is gone

A new day is here, yet nothing is new
You're still gone and I tremble for you
I cry out at bedtime, "No, please not tonight."
But again, there's your footsteps and I turn on the light

Of course you're not there, no, you never are
Then I try to forget that there's always a bar
And well, I win that battle, yes, sometimes I do
But sleep doesn't come when I tremble for you

THE MASTERPIECE

1967

There was an old stonecutter
Who lived in a cabin on the mountainside
And the old stonecutter
Knew it won't be long before he died

And all around his cabin
Were statues the man had made
Statues that the buyers said
Were all of a mediocre grade

With his calloused hands, he lit a lamp
And laid down his head on his handmade table
And he softly whispered,
"Lord, I'm old and shaky and I'm hardly able

"But give me strength and wisdom
And give me a week at least
And I'll climb up to the top of this mountain
And chisel out a masterpiece."

The very next morning he felt new strength
And he took his brand-new hammer and the sharpest chisel
He began to climb the mountain
His old feet slipping in the freezing drizzle

When he finally reached the top
He shouted to a world that didn't hear,
"I'll carve my masterpiece
Out of this marble boulder here."

So the hammer beat the chisel
And he hammered 'til an image grew
Then he stopped to look it over
To appraise his work, when he was through

It was a boy, carrying a crippled boy
And the old man said, "It isn't my masterpiece.
I'll call it Charity
And then a masterpiece of mine will be."

So the hammer beat the chisel
'Til another image in the marble grew
Then the wind began to blowing
And he sat and rested when he was through

It was the image of a mother holding her child
He said, "This is love as the world would know
But it isn't my masterpiece."
And he began again as it began to snow

The hammer beat the chisel
As the snow fell harder and the wind grew and grew
He fell to his knees holding a stone
And he threw down his hammer and his chisel, too

He lay frozen face down in the snow
But one hand was held for the world to see
Cut in the marble was his masterpiece
Three neatly carved letters: G-O-D

OH, WHAT A GOOD THING WE HAD

with June Carter

1967

Sunshine and showers
And everything coming up daisies
Oh, what a good thing we had, gone bad
Oh, what a good thing we had

Drive-ins and picnics
And every day was Saturday
Oh, what a good thing we had, gone bad
Oh, what a good thing we had

The whole wide world was jealous
We wouldn't hear a thing they'd tell us
Never did need any money
Everything was milk and honey

Oh, long walks by the river
Talking 'bout living together
Oh, what a good thing we had, gone bad
Oh, what a good thing we had

Long weeks of waiting and living
For the day we marry
Oh, what a good thing we had, gone bad
Oh, what a good thing we had

Happiness and laughter
We found everything we were after
Oh, what a good thing we had, gone bad
Oh, what a good thing we had

The whole wide world was jealous
We wouldn't hear a thing they'd tell us
Never did need any money
Everything was milk and honey

Oh, long walks by the river
Talking 'bout living together
Oh, what a good thing we had, gone bad
Oh, what a good thing we had
Oh, what a good thing we had, gone bad
Oh, what a good thing we had

ON THE LINE

1967

The enemy held a hill
And on the line was a shallow creek
Below and in the trees
Was the enemy across the water, ankle deep

In the water lay from both sides
Some face up and some face down
Men who tried to scale the ledge
And men who tried it down

The leader on the ledge yelled, "Cease fire!"
Then began to speak
"You can go ahead and kill me, enemy,
But I'm taking my wounded from the creek."

Then out stepped an officer from the trees
With a cease fire and also said,
"Sir, come on down and I'll also
Save my men who aren't yet dead."

The medics crawled from both sides
Finding life in a dozen and more
One took the arms, one took the legs
And they laid the wounded men on the shore

The smoke hung silently on the line
While both sides adopted their men
Then both officers saluted and yelled,
"Regroup, to begin the fight again."

When they all returned to their positions
The soft breeze cleared the sky
And someone muttered, "North, South, East,
or West
It's hell to have to die."

But neither officer shouted fire
The soldiers talked and sang
Rifles leaned against the trees
And from somewhere laughter rang

For a long time a silence was on the line
'Til finally night was near
Then from the ledge a command was heard
And below a voice said, "Men, did you hear?

"Pack up your gear and men retreat.
The other side's retreating, too.
We held them on the line.
That's the best that we can do."

SHRIMPIN' SAILIN'

1967

Well, the Gulf, it got a grassy bottom, settin' where the rock is there
And that's where I've been goin' for the shrimpin' sailin'
Leapin' 'cross the grassy moss, bringing in a briny bin
Makin' folds of wondrous waddy for the living that I'm lovin'

Where they creep and crawl and flip and flap and flob and dangle dobbin'
Sponge a fouler, drag 'em, holler, more of course, the ocean horse

Well, the Gulf, it got a grassy bottom, settin' where the rock is there
And that's where I've been goin' for the shrimpin' sailin'
'Til it's time to holler, haul 'em and come back in with the briny bin
Of soddy bodies, dressed in dandy, eatin' caramel candy

Makin' me and all my babies foldin' wads of wondrous waddy
For the living that I'm lovin', in between the shrimpin' sailin'

Gulf, it got a grassy bottom, settin' where the rock is there
Leapin' 'cross the grassy moss, bringing in a briny bin
Makin' folds of wondrous waddy for the living that I'm lovin'
Where they creep and crawl and flip and flap and flob and dangle dobbin'
Sponge a fouler, drag 'em, holler, more of course, the ocean horse

'Til it's time to haul 'em, come back in with the briny bin
Of soddy bodies, dressed in dandy, caramel candy, eatin' chicken
Finger lickin', dancin', rancin', mancin', tancin'
Makin' me and all my babies foldin' wads of wondrous waddy

Bringing in a brand a' bring

Makin' me

And all my women

Foldin' wads

Of wondrous ways

Geetus from

The Shrimpin' [illegible]

Feel a school of

Poppin' [illegible]

Fill the till

For days a player

Lovin' laughin' singin' dancin'

Drinkin' rum-so-man-so-tandy

Eatin' chicken

Finger-lickin

Carmel candy

Dressin' dandy

SHANTYTOWN

with June Carter

1967

I live down in Shantytown
Where chicken's twenty cents a pound
And if you live on such solid ground
What are you doing down in Shantytown?
What are you doing down in Shantytown?

Well, I'm back on your side of the tracks
Have come back for me to take you back
Back to your high society
To your cocktails and your teas
I'll look up but don't look down
Because we got pride in Shantytown

I live down in Shantytown
Where chicken's twenty cents a pound
And if you live on such solid ground
What are you doing down in Shantytown?
What are you doing down in Shantytown?

Behind the walls of your shackled heart, beats pure
While the rich have a love to endure
Well, is the gold in your crown turning black?
Is there something here in Shantytown
That keeps you coming back?

THE WALLS OF A PRISON

1967

I walked in the big yard to feel the warm sunshine
A ninety-nine-year man stepped over to me
He offered a smoke and he said, as I rolled it,
"Tomorrow I'm going to break out and go free.

"They watch us by sunlight, they watch us by spotlight
But I know a way for a man to go free.
Down under my cell, I'm digging a tunnel.
The walls of a prison will never hold me."

I told him that I'd have no part of his scheming
My time would be over, one year from today
His eyes blazed with fire and he looked right through me
Bitter but broken, again, he did say:

"They watch us by sunlight, they watch us by spotlight
But I know a way for a man to go free.
Down under my cell, I'm digging a tunnel.
The walls of a prison will never hold me."

Next morning, at breakfast, the old man was missing
Then we all heard the rifles, high up on the wall
He'd gone through the tunnel, just like he had promised
And they said he was crying when they saw him fall

"They watch us by sunlight, they watch us by spotlight
But I know a way for a man to go free.
Down under my cell, I'm digging a tunnel.
The walls of a prison will never hold me."

THE WHIRL AND THE SUCK

1967

It took a mighty good man with salty hands
And a mighty long raft
To keep the fore before the aft
You take ten good men, and guts and luck
And you might navigate the Whirl and the
Suck

Well, the Tennessee River changed its mind
At Chattanooga, she oughta unwind
She could-a run right on to the Georgia sea
But she cut right back through Tennessee

Well, the settlers come by raft and boat
Bringing everything that could stay afloat
But like a loco horse that'll twist and buck
They hardly ever made it through the Whirl
and the Suck

It took a mighty good man with salty hands
And a mighty long raft
To keep the fore before the aft
You take ten good men, with guts and luck
And you might navigate the Whirl and the
Suck

When General Washington was in his
knickerbocks
The Cherokee Indians threw the Chattanooga
rocks
And the Chickamauga tribe and the
Nickajack
They kept the watch, where the river cut back
And if a raft or a boat ever rode the bend
The Indians got them, 'cause they had them
hemmed in

It took a mighty good man with salty hands
And a mighty long raft
To keep the fore before the aft
You take ten good men, and guts and luck
And you might navigate the Whirl and the
Suck

THE WIND CHANGES

1967

Yes, the wind changes and one morning, early
A good wind will be blowing for me
Yes, the wind changes and one morning, early
A good wind will be blowing for me

Away like a bird, you have flown
And upon a wild wind, you were blown
Where you're bound, I don't know
Nor the way that you go
But the wanderlust beckons you on

But the wind changes and one morning, early
A good wind will be blowing for me
Yes, the wind changes and one morning, early
A good wind will be blowing for me

The wind sings its song in the tree
But the wind song is never for me
When following your track
The wind's at your back
Making whirlwinds where you used to be

But the wind changes and one morning, early
A good wind will be blowing for me
Yes, the wind changes and one morning, early
A good wind will be blowing for me

The wind quietly hides in the night
And it rises again with the light
But the days never fly
They're slow to go by
And like you, there's something I can't fight

But the wind changes and one morning, early
A good wind will be blowing for me
Yes, the wind changes and one morning, early
A good wind will be blowing for me

YOU AND TENNESSEE

1967

I stayed away too long, I know
And every day was slow to go
Every night I dreamed I was here
It's been a mighty lonely year

Every mile I needed you
I kinda hope that you needed me, too
Everywhere I saw your face, around every town I was in
This old familiar place welcomed me again

Back to where I belonged to be
Back to you and Tennessee
Back to you and Tennessee

Beside the Cumberland River
Where the grass is soft and sweet
We ran across the fields of cedar
Hiding from the noisy streets

And when the leaves fell from the cold
The stars were silver, the moon was gold
I said, "It's yours, with love from me."
I'm planting my roots in this ground
And if they look for me I'll be found
With something that is part of me

You and Tennessee
Back with you and Tennessee

YOU'LL BE ALL RIGHT

with June Carter

1967

Well, I see you lost your honeybee
I know how you must be feeling now
You feel sad, sad but, boy
It ain't that bad

You cry just a little bit
And die just a little bit
And then you'll be all right

Well, you know
It wasn't long ago
Your honeybee
Was queen of my bee tree
But then away she flew
And took my honey to you

You cry just a little bit
And die just a little bit
And then you'll be all right

I pity you
I know what you're going through
You watched your queen bee fly
Your honeycomb went dry
But if you keep pushing on
You won't care if she's gone

You cry just a little bit
And die just a little bit
And then you'll be all right

You cry just a little bit
And die just a little bit
And then you'll be all right

BEAUTIFUL WORDS

1968

Beautiful words, beautiful words
He spoke beautiful words
The wind lay still and the whole world listened
As He spoke beautiful words:

"Blessed are the poor in spirit for theirs is the Kingdom of Heaven.
Blessed are they that mourn for they shall be comforted.
Blessed are the meek for they shall inherit the earth.
Blessed are they which do hunger and thirst after righteousness for they shall be filled.
Blessed are the merciful for they shall obtain mercy.
Blessed are the pure in heart for they shall see God.
Blessed are the peacemakers for they shall be called the Children of God.
Blessed are they which are persecuted for righteousness' sake
For theirs is the Kingdom of Heaven.
Blessed are ye when men shall revile ye
And persecute you and say all manner of evil against you falsely for My sake."

Beautiful words, beautiful words
He spoke beautiful words
The wind lay still and the whole world listened
As He spoke beautiful words

BIG FOOT

1968

Big Foot was an Indian chief
Of the Minneconjou band
A band of Minneconjou Sioux
From South Dakota land

Big Foot said to Custer,
"Stay away from Crazy Horse."
But Custer crossed into Sioux land
And he never came back across

Then Big Foot led his people
To a place called Wounded Knee
And they found themselves surrounded
By the 7th Cavalry

Big Chief Big Foot
Rise up from your bed
Minneconjou babies cry
For their mothers lying dead

Big Foot was down with a fever
When he reached Wounded Knee
And his people all were prisoners
Of the 7th Cavalry

Two hundred women and children
And another hundred men
Raised up a white flag of peace
But peace did not begin

An accidental gunshot
And Big Foot was first to die
And over the noise of the rifles
You could hear the babies cry

Big Chief Big Foot
It's good that you can't see
Revenge is being wrought
By Custer's 7th Cavalry

Then smoke hung over the canyon
On that cold December day
All was death and dying
Around where Big Foot lay

Farther on up the canyon
Some had tried to run and hide
But death showed no favorites
Women, men, and children died

One side called it a massacre
The other, a victory
But the white flag is still waving
Today at Wounded Knee

Big Chief Big Foot
Your Minneconjou band
Is mourned and remembered here
In South Dakota land

’CAUSE I LOVE YOU (’CAUSE I LOVE JUNE)

(original version)

1968

I’ll sweep out your chimney, yes and
I will bring you water, yes and
I will bring you music
So you’ll never be alone

I will bring you honey
From the bee tree in the meadow
I will dig in the diamond mines
And bring you the biggest stone

’Cause I love you
’Cause I love June

I will rise up early
Tell the birds to start their singing
I will hang the clothes
Upon the line in your backyard

And if you’ll come with me
I’ll come riding six white horses
Throw your sorrows in the river
So your days will not be hard

’Cause I love you
’Cause I love June

I’ll go to the mountains
And I’ll find the magic brewer
Have him brew a sweet perfume
That will be meant for only you

I’ll roll away your clouds
And I’ll weave for you a rainbow
And a pot of gold I’ll bring you
And you’ll think fairy tales are true

’Cause I love you
’Cause I love June

’CAUSE I LOVE YOU

1968

I’ll sweep out your chimney
Yes and I will bring you flowers
Yes and I will do for you
Most anything you want me to

If we live in a cottage
You will feel like it’s a castle
By the royal way you’re treated
And attention shown to you

I’ll be there beside you
If you need a crying shoulder
Yes and I’ll be there to listen
When you need to talk to me

When you wake up in the darkness
I will put my arms around you
And hold you ’til the morning sun
Comes shining through the trees

I’ll be right beside you
No matter where you travel
I’ll be there to cheer you
’Til the sun comes shining through

If we’re ever parted
I will keep the tie that binds us
And I’ll never let it break
’Cause I love you

I will bring you honey
From the bee tree in the meadow
And the first time there’s a rainbow
I’ll bring you a pot of gold

I’ll take all your troubles
And I’ll throw ’em in the river
Then I’ll bundle down beside you
And I’ll keep you from the cold

I’ll be right beside you
No matter where you travel
I’ll be there to cheer you
’Til the sun comes shining through

If we’re ever parted
I will keep the tie that binds us
And I’ll never let it break
’Cause I love you

COME TO THE WAILING WALL

1968

Oh my Lord, what a morning
Oh my Lord, what a day
The sound of battle's over
And the smoke has blown away

Come to the Wailing Wall
Come to the Wailing Wall

Thank God you can stand up
Upon this Holy Land
And touch the hallowed rock
That God delivered to our hand

Come to the Wailing Wall
Come to the Wailing Wall

Shout it 'cross the mountain
Shout it 'cross the sea
We have been delivered
Israel is free

Come to the Wailing Wall
Come to the Wailing Wall

Bring the lost ones homeward
Lead them to this shore
The city gates are open
Heaven's blessings for

Come to the Wailing Wall
Come to the Wailing Wall

THE FOLK SINGER

with Charles E. Daniels

1968

As I walk these narrow streets
Where a million passing feet have trod before me
With my guitar in my hand
Suddenly I realize nobody knows me

Where yesterday the multitude screamed
And cried my name out for a song
Today the streets are empty
And the crowds have all gone home

I pass a million houses
But there is no place where I belong
All I knew to give you
Was song after song after song

All the truths I tried to tell you
Were as distant to you as the moon
Born two hundred years too late
And two hundred years too soon

I'm a child of this age
Locked inside the pages of your book
And when I am but dust and clay
And other children stop to take a look

Will they marvel at the miracles
I did perform
And to the heights I did aspire
Or will they tear out the pages of the book to light a fire?

With the rain on my face
There is no place where I belong
Did you forget the folk singer so soon?
And did you forget my song?

GOD IS NOT DEAD

1968

When Jesus called to God upon the cross
No answer came, for His will must be done
Then how the world trembled at His voice
When He said, "This is my beloved son."

It isn't God but man that's dead
When love is locked outside
Do you deny that there's a God
Or is God just denied?
God is not dead, He never died

What man on earth can make one blade of grass
And who can make one seed, then make it grow?
With all the power and wisdom in our hands
Who can command which way the wind to blow?

And who can match the miracle
In an eagle's eye?
Or hang a rainbow in a cloudy sky?
God is not dead, He did not die
God is not dead, God is not dead

HE TURNED THE WATER INTO WINE

1968

He turned the water into wine
He turned the water into wine
In the little Cana town
The word went all around that
He turned the water into wine

He walked upon the Sea of Galilee
He walked upon the Sea of Galilee
Shout it far and wide
He calmed the raging tide
And walked upon the Sea of Galilee

He turned the water into wine
He turned the water into wine
In the little Cana town
The word went all around that
He turned the water into wine

He healed the leper and the lame
He healed the leper and the lame
He said, "Go and tell no man."
But they shouted it through the land
That He healed the leper and the lame

He turned the water into wine
He turned the water into wine
In the little Cana town
The word went all around that
He turned the water into wine

He fed the hungry multitude
He fed the hungry multitude
With a little bit of fish and bread
They said everyone was fed
He fed the hungry multitude

He turned the water into wine
He turned the water into wine
In the little Cana town
The word went all around that
He turned the water into wine

I PROMISE YOU

1968

I promise you the day you marry me
I'll be everything to you that I should be
And while you're in the springtime of your years
You'll not know what it's like to shed a tear

I'll be the same through all that we go through
I promise you, I promise you

I promise you, for richer or for poorer
I'll more than share each pain that you endure
And when you're in the autumn of your years
You'll call me in the night and I'll be near

I'll love you and I'll let you know I do
I promise you, I promise you

I promise you, for better or for worse
I'll stand by you, as I did at the first

And when you're in the winter of your years
I'll be right by your side to dry your tears

Yes, I'll be the same through all that we go through
I promise you, I promise you
I promise you, I promise you

THE LAND OF ISRAEL

1968

From the top of Sinai
To the Sea of Galilee
Every hill and plain is home
Every place is dear to me

There the breezes tell the stories
Oh, what stories they do tell
Of the mighty things that happened
In the Land of Israel

Here, where Moses and the prophets
Spoke of one who would be king
Of a heavenly Messiah
And the blessings He would bring

Oh, to hear again the call
"All is peaceful, all is well"
Upon every rock and mountain
In the Land of Israel

From the rolling plain of Sharon
To Mount Tabor's lofty heights
To the desert of Beersheba
All is calm, all is right

Green, the trees are on the mountain
Sweet, the water in the well
May there never more be sorrow
In the Land of Israel

Here, where Moses and the Prophets
Spoke of one who would be king
Of a heavenly Messiah
And the blessings He would bring

Oh, to hear again the call
"All is peaceful, all is well"
Upon every rock and mountain
In the Land of Israel

MR. CROW

1968

If I could fly like Mister Crow
I know where I'd go
Woman, I'd leave you
Honey, I'd leave you
'Cause I can't stand the pain of stayin'
When I'm free to go

I oughta be up and goin'
Where the wild goose goes
If I had wings like a gray goose got
I'd fly out of range of shot
I'd leave you
Woman, I'd have to leave you

If I had wings like Mister Crow
Woman, I know I'd have to go
I'd leave you
Woman, I'd have to leave you

But I ain't got no wings to fly
So I guess I'll get by
And I don't know which way to fly
So, I don't know why I've gotta stay

If I had wings like a gray goose got
I'd leave you, whether my heart break or not
I'd leave you
Woman, I'd leave
If I had wings like Mister Crow
Woman, I know I'd go

THE NAZARENE

1968

Caesar ruled Rome and all its glory
Every land called Alexander "Great"
But no man can compare in any story
With the one man who controls so many's fate

Yes, along the dusty road came the Nazarene
Baptized by John was the Nazarene
Preaching on the top of the mountain was the Nazarene
Followed by a multitude was the Nazarene

Tried and condemned, they laid their stripes on Him
But like He said, back from the dead came the Nazarene

Nothing good had ever come from Nazareth
An unimportant place in Galilee
But the soul of any man could fall into bondage
And God had promised man could be set free

And then along the dusty road came the Nazarene
Baptized by John was the Nazarene
Preaching on the top of the mountain was the Nazarene
Followed by the multitude was the Nazarene

Tried and condemned, they laid their stripes on Him
But like He said, back from the dead came the Nazarene

FOUR

* ASCENT *

1969–1972

IN 1969 THE third annual Country Music Association Awards ceremony was broadcast live to a nationwide audience for the first time. To many, it was their introduction to the rising art form that had been steadily moving from its regional enclaves to the mainstream. That night, Cash dominated the proceedings, winning five major awards, a feat that has never been surpassed. Dressed in a formal gray frock coat, a ruffled shirt, and tall black boots, resembling nothing so much as a dashing riverboat gambler, he cut a bold figure, virtually unrecognizable from the emaciated vagabond of the recent past, as he returned to the stage again and again and again to claim the spoils of an unprecedented year of triumphs. The visuals were riveting. At that moment, for both first-time and long-time viewers, Johnny Cash became the defining figure of country music, a designation (and burden) he would wear with both pride and ambivalence for the next half century.

Cash's "return" was heralded across the musical and social spectrum. In actuality, he had never really gone away, but where he had been was *nothing* like where he was going. The commercial and artistic successes of *Johnny Cash at Folsom Prison* and *The Holy Land*—seemingly disparate experiences but in fact interrelated mileposts on a single continuum—begat even greater laurels in *Johnny Cash at San Quentin* and then a groundbreaking network television show that would seal his renown for all time. He would meet seven US presidents and perform at the White House, where Richard Nixon even requested that he write a song. His name and face became among the most recognized on earth, just about the time he became the biggest-selling recording artist on that same planet.

Cash was initially reluctant to use his elevated new platform as a bully pulpit to share his views, ideals, and conscience. The years of distraction had sapped his confidence in his own voice. "Music should be for entertaining, not sending messages," he averred, until "everywhere I went, people kept demanding to know where I stood on this issue or another, and wanted to tell me what I was supposed to believe." Finally he realized that Johnny Cash needed to speak to who Johnny Cash was, not others. So was born the Man in Black, and the manifesto of the same name, wherein he spoke of "the poor and the beaten down," lamented those whom society had cast aside and who had lost hope, such as prisoners, "the sick and lonely old," and "those who've never read or listened to the words that Jesus said." And he stepped right into the middle of the overriding, most wrenching problem of the time, the Vietnam War, deploring that "each week we lose a hundred fine young men."

Declarations on the war, or on Jesus, for that matter, were not the normal bill of fare for variety television hosts, who were generally propped behind a podium and expected to croon smooth nothings so as not to offend the folks at home. Cash refused to be pigeonholed or hidden, introducing powerful anthems, such as "What Is Truth" and "Singin' in Vietnam Talkin' Blues," alongside gorgeous homages to the human condition, like "Flesh and Blood," and professions of devotion, including "I'm Gonna Try to Be That Way" and every song from the *Holy Land* album. In the highly charged American society of the era, where taking prisoners was less preferable to leaving your opponents bleeding on the side of the road, all this was too much for some, not nearly enough for others. Cash could not be all things to all people. "I didn't know I was supposed to take a side," he later said. "I didn't look at things that way."

For every "The Preacher Said, 'Jesus Said'" there were grouses and mumbles about "Johnny Cash and his God." Cash saw no incompatibility with his avowed empathy for soldiers at war and being anti-war, or his solidarity with young people standing beside his respect for tradition, even as "accusations" of him being, variously, a "sellout" or a "hippie lover" or a "druggie friend" or "out of touch" rained down on him. His writings from this period give ample evidence of all of this, and none of this. It just depended on which Johnny Cash you wanted on your side.

The battle over Johnny Cash was not one in which he wanted to fight, and also it was one that he could never win. There was no walking the line here. This winner-take-all mentality threatened to leave him without a "home," and was certainly a fundamental factor in the derailing of his career. He was bitter for years at the toll the experience extracted, and it took about as long to realize that the foundation of his moral authority was actually laid here, hidden in the wreckage of his tumble from grace.

COME ALONG AND RIDE THIS TRAIN

1969

I know a land where mountain streams are running free
I know a prairie where there's miles between each tree
I know where there's people you would like to get to know
Come along with me and go

Come along and ride this train
Come along and ride this train
Cross the mountains, prairies, reservations
Rivers, levees, plains
Come along and ride this train

I heard a story that I'd like to share with you
And I know a valley that I'd like to take you through
I will show you things that I am sure you'd like to see
Come along and go with me

Come along and ride this train
Come along and ride this train
Cross the mountains, prairies, reservations
Rivers, levees, plains
Come along and ride this train

FLESH AND BLOOD

1969

Beside a singing mountain stream
Where the willow grew
Where the silver leaf of maple
Sparkled in the morning dew
I braided twigs of willows
Made a string of buckeye beads
But flesh and blood needs flesh and blood
And you're the one I need

Flesh and blood needs flesh and blood
And you're the one I need

I leaned against a bark of birch
And I breathed the honeydew
I saw a northbound flock of geese
Against a sky of baby blue
Beside the lily pads
I carved a whistle from a reed
Mother Nature's quite a lady
But you're the one I need

Flesh and blood needs flesh and blood
And you're the one I need

A cardinal sang just for me
And I thanked him for the song
Then the sun went slowly down in the west
And I had to move along
These were some of the things
On which my mind and spirit feed
But flesh and blood needs flesh and blood
And you're the one I need

Flesh and blood needs flesh and blood
And you're the one I need

So when the day was ended
I was still not satisfied
For I knew everything I touched
Would wither and would die
And love is all that will remain
And grow from all these seeds
Mother Nature's quite a lady
But you're the one I need

Flesh and blood needs flesh and blood
And you're the one I need

Christmas 1982

For June, my dream

Flesh and Blood

By J.R. Cash - 1970

Beside a singing mountain stream
Where the weeping willow grew
Where the silver leaf of maple
Sparkled in the morning dew
I plaited twigs of willow
Made a string of Buckey Beads
But flesh and blood needs flesh and blood
And you're the one I need] repeat

I leaned against the bark of birch
And breathed the honey dew
Saw a northbound flock of geese
Against a sky of baby blue
I picked Cherokee roses;
Carved a whistle from a reed
Mother nature's quite a lady
But you're the one I need
Yes flesh and blood needs flesh and blood
And you're the one I need.

A cardinal sang just for me
And I thanked him for the song
Then the sun went slowly down the west
And I had to move along
These are some of the things
On which my mind and spirit feed
But flesh and blood need flesh and blood
And you're the one I need. [repeat

When the day had ended
I still was not satisfied.
I knew everything I'd touched
Would fall away and die
And that our love is all that ever could
Fulfill my needs
Mother natures quite a lady
But you're the one I need.
Flesh and blood needs flesh and blood
And you're the one I need.

Certain words and phrases are slightly changed in this 1970 version. The original was written under stress during the taping of our T.V. shows. I feel this is an improvement, lyric wise over the original. John R Cash

JIMMY HOWARD

1969

I went to Jimmy's military funeral
Killed in Vietnam, and there he lay
The honor guards stood by at close attention
And the church was full to pay respects that day

All of Jimmy's old school friends were there
Clean-cut and strong
They openly stood and cried
The town was a better place because of Jimmy
And it showed the day that Jimmy Howard died

Now, Jimmy had written letters home, sayin' things like
Dad, I miss the fishin' on the lake
Mom, I miss the pies you used to bake
This jungle on the Makong is a sad place to be
But so far, Charlie's guns are missin' me

But that one time, Charlie's guns didn't miss
And they brought Jimmy's body home
I saw a face of heartbreak in that church
The preacher's words could not give much relief
Jimmy's dad was there beside his mother
Hand in hand to try to share the grief

There were hundreds that you'd not expect to see there
They were drawn by his good influence, far and wide
A lot of lives made changes for the better
They changed the day that Jimmy Howard died

KERSHAW

1969

From a land of bigmouth lunker bass
And Spanish moss he came
Shakin' up the civilized
Kershaw was his name

Dyed-in-the-wool and registered
Coonass as they come
First time he was seen in town
He puzzled people some

With swamp mud still on his ankles
But talent to the bone
His mind was wrung, his songs were sung
He struggled on and on

The ways of the world grew heavy
But ambition, grit, and guts
Made the way much easier
And helped him through the ruts

He wrote of this Cajun country
And the world took a look or two
When they saw he really meant it
And wasn't just passing through

Then he'd fade and almost vanish
As changes came and went
Then he'd bounce back smiling, like:
"Hello, world, I'm sent!"

He recently flashed upon the scene
With his wild sincerity
Fiddlin', singin' Cajun soul
With it all in harmony

He's been a long time coming
Thank God he has survived
Get ready for him this time, world
My coonass friend has arrived

OF BOB DYLAN

1969

There are those who do not imitate
Who cannot imitate
But then there are those who emulate
At times, to expand further the light
Of an original glow

Knowing that to imitate the living is mockery
And to imitate the dead is robbery
There are those
Who are beings complete unto themselves

Whole, undaunted — a source
As leaves of grass, as stars
As mountains alike, alike, alike
Yet unalike
Each is complete and contained

And as each unalike star shines
Each ray of light is forever gone
To leave way for a new ray
As from a fountain
Coming late unto itself, full, flowing

So are some souls like stars
And their words, works, and songs
Like strong, quick flashes of light
From a brilliant, erupting cone
So where are your mountains
To match some men?

This man can rhyme the tick of time
The edge of pain, the what of sane
And comprehend the good in men, the bad
in men
Can feel the hate of fight
The love of right
And the creep of blight at the speed of light

The pain of dawn, the gone of gone
The end of friend, the end of end
By math of trend
What grip to hold what he is told
How long to hold, how strong to hold
How much to hold of what is told

And know
The yield of rend, the break of bend
The scar of mend
I'm proud to say that I know it
Herein is a hell of a poet
And lots of other things
And lots of other things

CHET ATKINS' HANDS

1970

The hands of the baker and the candlestick maker
Are those of a skillful man
The thread of the tailor, the rope of the sailor
Are tied by knowing hands

The watchmaker's eye and the light to see by
And hands that are calm and sure
Make the tiniest springs do the tiniest things
And long has the skill endured

It matters not the job you've got
As long as you do it well
The things that are made by plans well-laid
The test of time will tell

But how can you count, or know the amount
Of the value of a man?
By the melodies played and the beauty made
By the touch of Chet Atkins' hands

KRISTOFFERSON

1970

Kris was goin' for a poet
A songwriter he would be
One of those dreamy people
Some people hate to see

Kris, he took slices of life
And salted it down into rhyme
He picked his own days and his ways
He arranged his own meter and time

Kris, he went out a-sowing
Wild oats, high and low, up and down
And he's bringing it into the harvest
And the thrasher hums sweet with the sound

(Poems don't come from machines
Machines can't set life into rhyme
And you can't manufacture soul
Nor "gauge" and "chop" soulful lines)

Kris, he was goin' for lonesome
Taking himself over the road
But he's got a receipt for the toll
And he's come to get paid for the load

But Kris, he was goin' for hungry
A helicopter pilot he made
His rhymes were in time with that chopper
And his words were as slick as the blades

(But poems and songs though they're pretty
Can slip right over the head
And tunes from the hungry can be pleasant
They're worth what they bring you in bread)

So Kris, he was goin' to sell 'em
His ragged Levi's cried, "Don't fail!"
But to most song-singers that get 'em
They were just one more piece of mail

Kris, he went for an oil rigger
And down in the Gulf on the rig
His melodies still were bubbling
Still goin' for striking it big

But like the oil covers the water
His songs covered everyone's floor
From five years of sending his demos
And leaving them at every door

Kris, he was making a movie
Upon the screen would his face be
And while on a horse in Peru
His songs went on network TV

Someone had finally noticed
And singers of soul sang along
Now we've all gone to dig in our closets
For that lost Kristofferson song

P.S.
Kris, he was goin' for a singer
And up to the top would he go
When Kris is goin' for a Grammy
(next year, I'll say)
"Hell, I heard that song five years ago."

"KRISTOFFERSON"

Kris was goin' for a poet
A songwriter he would be
One of those dreamy people
Some people hate to see

Kris, he took slices of life
And salted it down into rhyme
He picked his own days and his ways
He arranged his own metre and time

Kris, he went out a sowing
Wild Oats high and low, up and down
Now he's bringing it into the harvest
And the thrasher hums sweet with the sound

(Poems dont come from machines
Machines cant set life into rhyme
And you cant manufacture soul
Nor "guage" and "chop" soulful lines)

Kris, he was goin' for lonesome
Taking himself over the road
But he's got a receipt for the toll
And he's come to get paid for the load

Page 2 "Kristofferson"

But Kris, he was goin for hungry
A helicopter pilot he made
His rhymes were in time with that chopper
And his words were as slick as the blades

(But poems and songs though theyre pretty
Can slip right over the head
And tunes from the hungry be pleasant
Theyre worth what they bring you in bread)

So Kris, he was goin to sell 'em
His ragged Levis cried "dont fail!"
But to most song-singers that got 'em
They were just one more piece of mail

Kris, he went for an oil rigger
And down in the gulf on the rig
His melodies still were bubbling
Still goin' for striking it big

But like the oil covers the water
His songs covered everyones floor
From five years of sending his demos
And leaving them at every door

more over

Page 3 "Kristofferson"

Kris, he was making a movie
Upon the screen would his face be
And while on a horse in Peru
His songs went on network T.V.

Someone had finally noticed
And singers of soul sang along
Now weve all gone to dig in our closets
For that lost Kristofferson song.

Johnny Cash

P.S.

Kris, he was goin for a singer
And up to the top would he go
When Kris is goin for a grammy

(next year, I'll say,)

"Hell I heard that song five years ago

ROUTE 1, BOX 144

1969

His dying barely made the morning paper
And they summed it up in twenty words or more
Killed in action, leaves wife and baby
At Route 1, Box 144

He grew up on a little farm
Just a couple of miles out of town
As a boy he worked in his daddy's field
And when his daddy could spare him
He hired out to the neighbors
For whatever they could pay him

He was thought of as just average, a good boy
Nothing more, the average amount of friends
He married his high school sweetheart
They bought a little plot of ground
Couple of miles out of town, on a mailbox, it said
Route 1, Box 144

Well, back in town there were very few people
That really knew him, because he hardly ever came to town
Except for maybe on Saturdays
Of course, the usual crew was always there
But he didn't spend a lot of time with the usual crew
He took care of his business
Bought what he had to have or could afford for his family
And went back to his little farm

With a baby on the way, he went to the Army
And it was just a short while that the news came
That he was killed in action
His body was sent back on a plane and then by train
And then they brought the body from the train station
To Route 1, Box 144

He never did great things to be remembered
He'd never been away from home before
But you'd've thought that he was president or something
At Route 1, Box 144

SAN QUENTIN

1969

San Quentin, you've been living hell to me
You've galled me since 1963
I've seen them come and go and I've seen them die
And long ago I stopped asking why

San Quentin, I hate every inch of you
You've cut me and you've scarred me through and through
And I'll walk out a wiser, weaker man
Mister Congressman, you can't understand

San Quentin, what good do you think you do?
Do you think I'll be different when you're through?
You bent my heart and mind and you warped my soul
And your stone walls turn my blood a little cold

San Quentin, may you rot and burn in hell
May your walls fall and may I live to tell
May all the world forget you ever stood
And may all the world regret you did no good

SEE RUBY FALL

with Roy Orbison

1969

Well, I knew someday Ruby would be leaving
That she wasn't happy living quietly, quietly
'Cause she would get the bedroom look each morning
And I felt Ruby pull away from me

Yeah, so go downtown at nine o'clock this evening
Walk under that red light, then down the hall, down the hall
Look for the highest-flying girl, that's Ruby
And if you wait your turn, you'll see Ruby fall

Don't let her know that you even know me
She'll be trying to forget it all
And don't tell me how it was tonight, tomorrow
'Cause I don't want to see Ruby fall

I didn't hold her back, when she got restless
One man is not enough when she wants it all
Yeah, I let her go when I saw what she wanted
'Cause I don't care to see Ruby fall

SOUTHWIND

1969

Southwind, you picked her up in Jacksonville
And left me cold and lonesome in the rain
Southwind, you took her off to Nashville
Left me choking in the smoke behind the train

And you go whoo-woo-hoo
She's gone again on the Southwind

Southwind, I need a forty-dollar ticket
And about this time tomorrow, I'll be gone
Southwind, but if I had forty dollars
I would buy myself a smile to carry on

And you go whoo-woo-hoo
She's gone again on the Southwind

Southwind, take her fast and take her far
'Cause that's the way she always likes to go
Southwind, I will be waiting for the round trip
If you'll bring her back and I done told her so

Don't you go whoo-woo-hoo
She's gone again on the Southwind

STARKVILLE CITY JAIL

1969

Well, I left my motel room, down at the Starkville Motel
The town had gone to sleep and I was feeling fairly well
I strolled along the sidewalk 'neath the sweet magnolia trees
I was whistlin', pickin' flowers, swayin' in the Southern breeze

I found myself surrounded; one policeman said, "That's him.
Come along, wild flower child. Don't you know that it's two a.m.?"
They're bound to get you
'Cause they got a curfew
And you go to the Starkville city jail

Well, they threw me in the car and started driving into town
I said, "What the hell did I do?"
And he said, "Shut up and sit down."
Well, they emptied out my pockets, took my pills and guitar picks
I said, "Wait, my name is — " "Ah, shut up."
Well, I sure was in a fix

The sergeant put me in a cell, then he went home for the night
I said, "Come back here, you so-and-so,
I ain't bein' treated right."
Well, they're bound to get you
'Cause they got a curfew
And you go to the Starkville city jail

I started pacing back and forth, and now and then I'd yell
And kick my forty-dollar shoes against the steel door of my cell
I'd walk awhile and kick awhile, and all night nobody came
Then I sadly remembered that they didn't even take my name

At 8 a.m. they let me out, I said, "Gimme them things of mine!"
They gave me a sneer and a guitar pick, and a yellow dandelion
They're bound to get you
'Cause they got a curfew
And you go to the Starkville city jail
And you go to the Starkville city jail

THEM TWO HANDS WERE GOOD 'UNS

1969

When a feller has given life a good grind
And is lying on his dying bed
With his hands folded across his chest bone
Feeling the final thumpings of his innard workings
He oughta feel proudful of hisself
If he can know in his own head
That all his laying by is laid by proper

Then some of his good folks ought to raise his head a tad
To let him take one last fading look
Through his waxing eyeballs
At his own two hands once again
And he oughta feel more proudful of hisself if he can say
In his own head, concerning his hands
Them two hands have been good 'uns
And a bunch of times I have did something or other
Mighty good with them

THE BALLAD OF JOHNNY CAPMAN

1970s

Johnny Capman said
To his wife one day,
"I'm sorry, my dear,
But I just can't stay.
My country calls
And I'm on my way."

His wife said to him,
"You must stay.
We are in trouble
And you can't go away.

"The war has come
And the growing is hard.
The soil is tough
As our front yard.

"If you leave me
What can we eat?
We have no clothes
Or shoes on our feet."

Johnny Capman said
To his wife again,
"There's a war to fight.
I will join the men."

The days went by
Not a word was said
For fear that he
Would come back dead

About a week from then
A letter came
She tried to find
Her Johnny's name

But it was not from him
And the letter said
"We regret to tell you
Your Johnny's dead."

The Ballad of Johny Capman

Johny Capman said
To his wife one day
I'm sorry my dear
But I just can't stay
~~The times are hard~~ My Country Calls
And I'm on my way

His wife said to him
you must stay
We are in trouble
And you cant go away

The war has come
And the growing is hard
The soil is tough
As our front yard.

If you leave me
what can we eat
We have no clothes
Or shoes on our feet.

Johnny Capman said
To his wife again
Theres a war to fight
I must join the men

John Carter

went by
rd was said
that he
back dead.

veet from then
ame
o find
s name

ot from him
r said
tell you
d dead.

E capo 1st fret

Breaking in a brand New Pair of Shoes

Breaking in a brand new pair of shoes
Walking till I lose the ~~money~~ blues
I spent my last dollar
That I'll ever spend on you
And I'm breaking in a brand new pair of shoes

Your closet walls are busting out
With your expensive rags
Your shelves are packed with
Crocodile and alligator bags
A thousand little mink have died
So you could have their coats
Now the moneys gone
And thats all that ~~she~~ all you wrote

~~Glue~~ slap on that false eye lash
And then ~~glue~~ jam on your wig
Spray yourself with french perfume
And go out spending big
Just save a tiny bit for me
Ten dollars ought to do
To buy myself a brand new
pair of shoes

End simple ending

Instrumental after verse/chorus
Carl, Travis style

BRAND-NEW PAIR OF SHOES

with Ana Cristina Cash

1970s

I'm breaking
I'm breaking in a brand-new pair of shoes
Walking 'til I lose all my money blues
I spent my last dollar I'll ever spend on you
Now I'm breaking in a brand-new pair of shoes

Your closet walls are busting out
With your expensive rags
Your shelves are packed
With crocodile and alligator bags
A thousand little mink have died
So you could have their coats
Now the money's gone, the money's gone
And that's all you wrote

I'm breaking
I'm breaking in a brand-new pair of shoes
Walking 'til I lose all my money blues
I spent my last dollar I'll ever spend on you
So I'm breaking in a brand-new pair of shoes

Slap on that false eyelash
And jam on your wig
Spray yourself with French perfume
And go spending big
Just save a little tiny bit for me
Ten dollars will do to buy myself
A brand-new pair of shoes

CHINKY PIN HILL

with Sarah Jarosz, Aoife O'Donovan, and Sara Watkins

1970s

Come along with me and we
Will get away from it all
We'll go through the mountains past
The shining waterfalls

And the only sound we'll hear at night
Will be the whippoorwill
And the chirpin' of the crickets
On Chinky Pin Hill

We'll stop in Rainbow Valley
Where the church is standing still
And we'll be newlywed married
On Chinky Pin Hill

The world is so confusing
As I go from day to day
And sometimes I get worried
That I'll lose you on the way

I looked up at the stars
As I leaned on the windowsill
I've dreamed up a hideaway
Called Chinky Pin Hill

Chinky Pin Hill
Chinky Pin Hill

Chinky Pin Hill

Come on along with me and we
Will get away from it all
We'll go thru the mountains past
The Shining water fall
The only sound we'll hear at night
Will be the whipporwill
And the chirpin of the crickets
On Chinkypin Hill

~~We'll go thru rainbow valley~~

We'll stop in Rainbow Valley
Where the church is standing still
~~And~~ we'll be newlywed married
~~[illegible]~~ on Chinky pin hill

The world is so confusing as
I go from day to day
And sometime I get worried
that I'll lose you on the way

I looked up at the stars
As I leaned on the windowsill
I've dreamed up a hideaway ~~[illegible]~~
Called Chinkypin Hill

C-PLUS CHRISTIAN

1970s

I'll say that I'm a C-plus Christian
Trying hard someday to be a B
And I'm not gonna say
That I'll ever be an A
Although an A is what I'd like to be

I'm sure God loves a C-plus Christian
He wouldn't love me any less if I was a D
But if I take stock of myself
And find that I'm an F
I believe I'd be in the majority

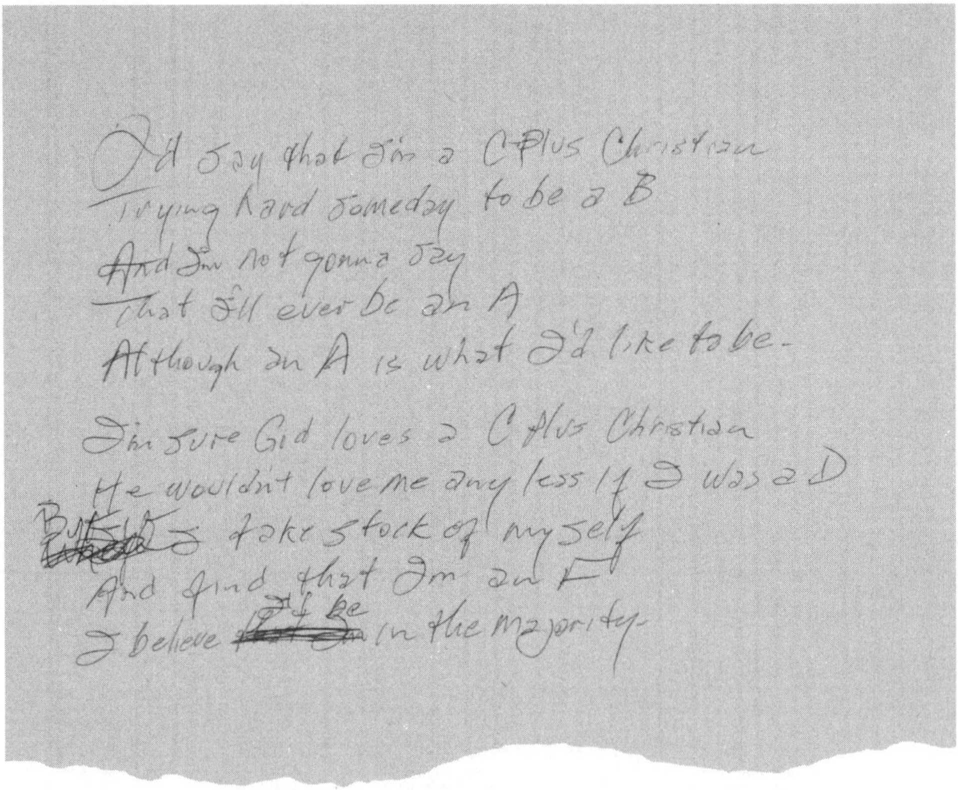
I'd say that I'm a C-Plus Christian
Trying hard someday to be a B
And I'm not gonna say
That I'll ever be an A
Although an A is what I'd like to be.

I'm sure God loves a C Plus Christian
He wouldn't love me any less if I was a D
But if I take stock of myself
And find that I'm an F
I believe I'd be in the majority.

THE CLOUDS WERE HANGING LOW

1970s

The clouds were hanging low upon the hills
The sun was hidden and the wind was still
It was one of those sweet peaceful days
That rarely ever come
For you'd be back and everything
Would be all right at home
And kookaburra sang to greet the light
Sang a sweet farewell to my last lonely night

Cowboy

A cowboy just like his buckle read
He learned to rope and ride when he was six
By the time that he was ten
He was running with the men
He rolled his own and he knew all the tricks.
When he was seventeen he had lost all his green
His feet were leather like his horses hide
Then the cowgirl down the road
Helped him get his wild oats sowed
And she sidekicked every trail that he would ride
Cowboy hard ridin' cowboy
He's as mean as a sidewinder cowgirl
Can you stay in the saddle
Can you weather all his pain
Can you ride thru his thunder and his rain
Can you gentle down with joy your cowboy

A cowboy is born to drift and range
And like the land he'll shift but he won't change
And a woman never knows
Which way tomorrow's wind will blow
But a cowboys different and a cowboys strange
He'll drop his boots beside your bed at night
But don't expect him to be there by morning light
There will be a camp or town
Tonight where he'll lie down
If you happen to be there you did alright

COWBOY

1970s

A cowboy just like his buckle read
He learned to rope and ride when he was six
By the time that he was ten
He was running with the men
He rolled his own
And he knew all the tricks

When he was seventeen
He had lost all his green
His feet were leather, like his horse's hide
Then the cowgirl down the road
Helped him get his wild oats sowed
And she sidekicked every trail that he would ride

Cowboy, hard ridin' cowboy
He's as mean as a sidewinder, cowgirl
Can you stay in the saddle
Can you weather all his pain
Can you ride through all his thunder
And his rain
Can you gentle down with joy your cowboy?
A cowboy is born to drift and range
And like the sand, he'll shift but he won't change
But a woman never knows
Which way tomorrow's wind will blow
But a cowboy's different and a cowboy's strange

He'll drop his boots beside your bed at night
But don't expect him to be there by morning light
There will be a camp or town tonight
Where he'd lie down
If you happen to be there
You did all right

CRYIN' IN MY LAUGHIN' PLACE

1970s

It's night and the cold rain is falling
Time just seems to move so slow
I'm lonesome now and my heart is calling
I wish that you had not had to go
Raindrops keep running down my window
Teardrops keep running down my face
When you left, the sunshine went with you
I'm cryin' in my laughing place
Did you hear that old thunder rollin'?
Do you hear that wind howl and moan?
Is your heart so hard that you don't worry
What'll happen to me with you gone?

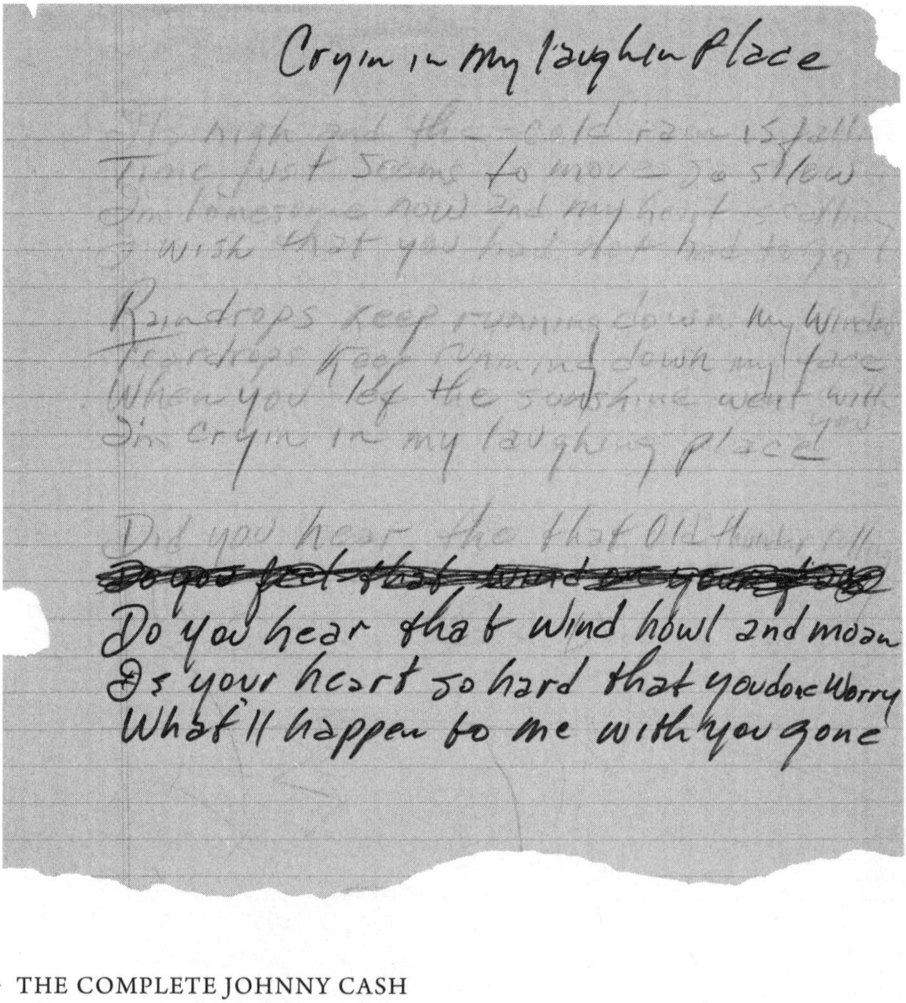
Cryin in my laughin Place
Its night and the cold rain is fall
Time just seems to move so slow
Im lonesome now and my heart is calling
I wish that you had not had to go
Raindrops keep running down my window
Teardrops keep running down my face
When you left the sunshine went with you
Im cryin in my laughing place
Did you hear the that Old thunder rollin
~~Do you feel that wind on your face~~
Do you hear that wind howl and moan
Is your heart so hard that you dont worry
What'll happen to me with you gone

DIXIE WHISTLIN'

1970s

I've got a record player and a radio
And my blues all went where the gray goose goes
I'll sit on the porch
And wait for something to do

I say, "Hi, hoot owl, how you?"
He said, "Who?"
I said, "You."

A year has passed
Since I been sassed
So all a mornin'
I'm Dixie whistlin'

I'm whistlin' Dixie
All a mornin'

My car broke down but that's okay
I don't much care to go to town
I ain't got a dollar bill anyhow
I told my dog to bark
He said, "Bow wow."

I'll blow out the light
Pretty early tonight
All a mornin'
I'll be whistlin' Dixie

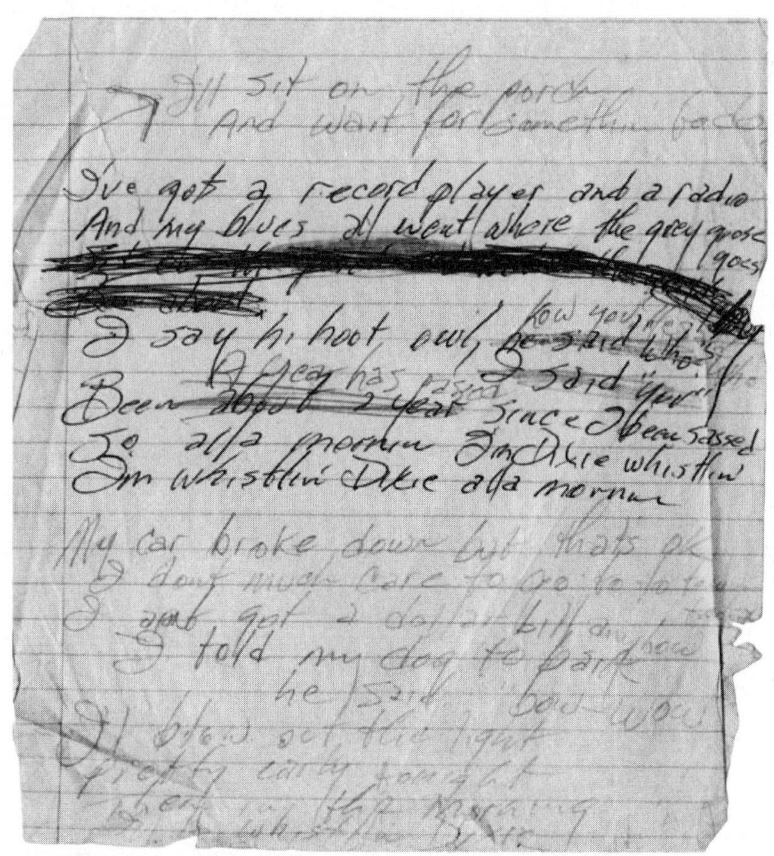

Ill sit on the porch
And wait for somethin

I've got a record player and a radio
And my blues all went where the grey goose goes
I say hi hoot owl, how you, he said "Who"
A year has passed I said "you"
Been about a year since I been sassed
So all a mornin I'm Dixie whistlin
I'm whistlin Dixie all a mornin

My car broke down but thats ok
I dont much care to go to town
I aint got a dollar bill anyhow
I told my dog to bark
he said bow wow
Il blow out the light
pretty early tonight
then in the morning

The dogs are in the woods
And the hunting's lookin good
And the raccoons on the hill
I can hear them trailing still

Now hes on the other side
And he'll find a place to hide
But the dogs'll hunt him down,
And they'll catch him on the ~~[illegible]~~ ground.

But the fur is gonna fly.
And a hound is gonna cry
And we may not know tonight
Who will finally win the fight

But the dogs are in the woods
And the huntin looks good

The fire is burning low
~~And~~ We wet it down and go
~~And~~ we make a bee line
To the howling in the pine

It's too far to see
But they're barking up a tree
Then we hear them on the run
And the night has just begun

The fur is gonna fly
And a hound is go[...] cry
And we may not [...]
Who will finally [...]

But the dogs ar[...]
And the huntin[...]

THE DOGS ARE IN THE WOODS

with John McEuen

1970s

The dogs are in the woods
And the huntin's lookin' good

A racket on over the hill
I can hear them trailin' still
Now he's on the other side
Lookin' a place to hide
And the dogs are in the woods
And the huntin's lookin' good

The dogs'll hunt him down
And catch him on the ground
The fur's gonna fly
Then a hound's gonna cry
Might not know tonight
Who will finally win this fight
But the dogs are in the woods
And the huntin's lookin' good

Oh, the fire is burnin' low
So we'll wet it down and go
We'll make a beeline
To that howlin' in the pine
It's too far to see
They barked him up a tree
Then we hear 'em on the run
And the night has just begun
And the dogs are in the woods
And the huntin's lookin' good

DRINK WATER

1970s

See them bottles on the shelf
Like soldiers in a row
Pick yourself a flavor, boy
And down the road you go

Hold that bottle 'tween your knees
And fly yourself away
Careful you don't lose control
And end up DOA

You're passing everything in sight
And some you didn't see
Watch out for them hogs
And put no trust in them RVs

Soon your gut is burnin'
And you need a beer to chase
Pop a top, and slop it up
Boy, pour it down your face

Drink water, Lord, that liquor's hot
Drink water
You're gonna be a sot
Lay down the bottle and put on the top

And drink cool H_2O

Drink Water.

See them bottles on the shelf
Like soldiers in a row
Pick yourself a flavor, boy
And down the road you go.
Hold that bottle 'tween your knees
And fly yourself away
Careful you dont lose control
And end up DOA

You're passing everything in sight
And some you didnt see
Watch out for them hogs
And put no trust in them R.V.s
Soon your gut is burnin
And you need a beer to chase
Pop a top and slap it up
Boy pour it down your face

Drink water
Lord that liquors hot
Drink water
You gonna be a sot
Lay down the bottle and put on the top
And drink cool H_2O

Gold in Alaska

Though it's cold in Alaska
Theres Gold in Alaska
Theres nuggets in the rivers
And gold dust in the sand
I've got a girl in Seward
I aint seen in quite a time
If she'll wait until October
~~I'll go cashin in my stash~~
When my diggin's done and over
I'll go cashin in my stash
And well make love through the dark days
That winter sun dont shine
When I come back to the Tik Chik
I'll Leave her a little gold
Enough to keep her on the line

I went to Alaska
To a River called the Tik Chik
In the middle of the summer
When the Salmon make their run
And my guide with pick and shovel
Every day would stop and vanish
Then he'd come back with a handful of it
Shinin' in the sun

GOLD IN ALASKA

1970s

Though it's cold in Alaska
There's gold in Alaska
There's nuggets in the rivers
And gold dust in the sand

I've got a girl in Seward
I ain't seen in quite a time
If she'll wait until October
When my diggin's done and over

I'll go cashin' in my stash
And we'll make love
Through the dark days
That winter sun don't shine

When I come back to the Tikchik
I'll leave her a little gold
Enough to keep her on the line

I went to Alaska
To a river called the Tikchik
In the middle of the summer
When the salmon make their run

And my guide with pick and shovel
Every day would stop and vanish
Then he'd come back with a handful of it
Shinin' in the sun

HE BORE IT ALL FOR ME

with Jamie Dailey

1970s

He bore it all for me
He bore it all for me
When I was lost, a painful cross
He bore it all for, yes, He bore it all
for even me

He took the blame for me
He took the blame for me
Counted my wrongs as forgotten and gone
He took the blame for me

He bore it all for me
He bore it all for me
When I was lost, a painful cross
He bore it all, He bore it all for me

He paid the price for me
He paid the price for me
A price so high for failure and lies
He paid the price for me

As He bore the pain for me
As He bore the pain for me
Spoke not a word, not a cry was ever heard
He bore the pain for me

He bore it all for me
He bore it all for me
When I was lost, a painful cross
He bore it all, He bore it all for me

He bore it all for me
He bore it all for me
When I was lost, a painful cross
He bore it all for, yes, for even me

See Mat 11:28
for speaking intro

He Bore it all for Me

He Bore it All for me
" " " " " "
When I was lost
On a painful cross.
He bore it all for me

Yes, He bore it all for.
" " " " " "
With nothing require
But of faith in Him.
He bore it all for me

He took the blame for me
" " " " " "
He counted my wrongs
As forgotten and gone
He took the blame for me

He paid the price for me
" " " " " "
A price that was high
For failure and lies
He paid the price for me

As He bore the pain for me
" " " " " " "
He spoke not a word
Not a cry was heard
He bore the pain for me.

I AM FREE

1970s

Children, tell the old home goodbye, goodbye
My years down in the mine did finally end
Let's all stick together and don't cry, don't cry
Someday, I promise, we'll go back again

I never let it show, 'cause you didn't need to know
But the good old days were not so good, you see
I've not been satisfied since the day your mama died
And the good old days were bad old days for me

And the good old bad old days are behind and far away
From the good old bad old days I am free, I am free
And to be free, to be free, must be, must be
To say I am free, I am free

Somewhere across the river, we'll find friends again
I love you and I won't leave you alone
We will find our place and a friendly face
You'll never miss what you believe is gone

JOHNNY CASH

Children, tell the old Home goodbye, goodbye
My years down in the mine did finally end
Lets all stick together and dont cry dont cry
Some day, I promise, we will go back again.

I never let it show
Cause you didnt need to know
But the good old days
Were not so good you see
Ive not been satisfied
Since the day your mama died
And, the good old days
Were bad old days for me
And the good old bad old days
Are behind and far away
From the good old bad old days,
I am free, I am free
And to be free to be free
Must be must be
To say I am free, I am free

Somewhere across the river we'll find friends again
I love you and I wont leave you alone
We will find our place and a friendly face
you'll never miss what you believe is gone

Over

I THANK YOU FOR THE LOVE

1970s

Well, I thank you for the love
And all the good times that you gave me
'Cause I don't think I'd have made it
If you hadn't a-come along

Well, I thank you for the times
You made me feel that I was needed
And the times you made me feel all right
When things were going wrong

Well, I thank you, sir
Yes, and I thank you, ma'am
For being what you are
For making me what I am

I WALKED OUT INTO THE FIELD

1970s

I walked out into the field with my little boy
I had just returned from a long trip and I was tired
Letters were piled up, people were waiting to see me
An impossible schedule to keep was at hand

No way to cram everything into the next few days
Before I would have to leave on my next trip...
Then my little laughing boy ran by chasing a yellow butterfly
And I felt better

I WENT TO A COCKTAIL PARTY

1970s

I went to a cocktail party and I hate cocktail parties
Nothing important is ever done or said at a cocktail party
Everybody was talking and nobody said anything
I remember what time I went and what time I left
I suppose I wanted to keep track of how much time I wasted

In the fifty-three minutes I was there
I don't remember anything that was said
Except when a woman said to me:
"You don't remember me, do you?"
I didn't and she knew I didn't
But it made her feel better to say that to me

IF THY HEART BE COLD

1970s

How much do I love thee?
Try to count the ways
I love you, my darling
More than I can say

I'll keep my pledges
To have and to hold
I cannot warm thee
If thy heart be cold

I can tell from a touch
If you thrill or tremble inside
I don't have to see very much
To know if your love has died

How long will I love thee?
'Til you're gray and old
But I cannot warm thee
If thy heart be cold

If Thy Heart Be Cold

How much do I love thee
Try to count the ways
I love you my darling
More than I can say
I'll keep my pledges
To have and to hold
I cannot warm thee
If thy heart be cold

I can tell from a touch
If you thrill or tremble inside
I don't have to see very much
To know if your love has died.
How long will I love thee
Till you're gray and old
But I cannot warm thee
If thy heart be cold.

I'M COMIN', HONEY

with Shawn Camp

1970s

I was drivin' in the rain
Twenty miles from Bangor, Maine
When I realized how much you mean to me
So I turned the rig around
Filled her up outside of town
Took the shortest route southbound to Tennessee

I'm a-comin', honey
Hang out the front door key
I'm a-comin', honey
Get ready to pucker up for me

I was drivin' in the sleet
Stopped to get a bite to eat
Folks in Pennsylvania asked me if I'd stay
I said, "Thank you anyhow
But I think I'd better make tracks now.
Can't stay away from her another day."

I'm a-comin', honey
Look out the window and see
I'm a-comin', honey
Turn on the front light for me

I was drivin' in the snow
On a mountain called SoHo
Your picture hangin' on my rearview glass
I was heavy on the foot
I was blowin' out the soot
There was no one alive who'd try to pass

I'm a-comin', honey
Put a little coffee in the pot
I'm a-comin', honey
Get set to give me all the love you got

I'm a-comin', honey
Hang out the front door key
I'm a-comin', honey
Get ready to pucker up for me

IN FLIGHT VIA
Delta

I was drivin' in the snow
On a mountain called Soco
Your picture hanging on my rear view glass
I was heavy on the foot
I was blowing out the soot
There was no one alive who'd try to pass

I'm comin' honey
Put a little coffee on the pot
I'm comin' honey
Get set to give me all the love you got

I was driving in the rain
Twenty miles from Bangor Maine
When I realized how much you mean to me
So I turned the rig around
Filled her up outside of town
Took the shortest route southbound to Tenn

I'm Comin' Honey
Hang out the front door key
I'm Comin' Honey
Get ready to pick'er up for me

I was drivin' in the sleet
Stopped to get a bite to eat
Folks in Penn asked me if I'd stay
I said thank you anyhow
But I think I'll make it now
I can't stay away from her another day
I'm Comin' honey
Turn on the front light for me
I'm Comin' honey
Look out the window and see

I'm So Glad You Came

I'm so glad to see you
And your old familiar face
So many times I've mentioned your name
You're so very special
And you make me feel so good
I'm so glad you came

The ~~[illegible]~~ time doesn't matter
As others come and go
The love I feel for you will never change
Just in case you're wondering
You never left my heart
I'm so glad you came

You smile at me and I become
A little boy again
You speak to me and I freeze up
And try to hide the flame
In case it matters to you, you are all the world
I'm so glad you came

You have that way of showing
That you take me as I am
What you see and what you get's always the same
And I see you no differently
I love you as you are
I'm so glad you came

I'M SO GLAD YOU CAME

1970s

I'm so glad to see you
And your old familiar face
So many times I've mentioned your name
You're very special
You make me feel so good
And I'm so glad you came

The time doesn't matter
As others come and go
The love I feel for you will never change
Just in case you're wondering
You never left my heart
I'm so glad you came

You smile at me and I become
A little boy again
You speak to me and I freeze up
And try to hide the flame
In case it matters to you, you are all the world to me
I'm so glad you came

You have that way of showing
That you take me as I am
What you see and what you get's always the same
And I see you no differently
I love you as you are
I'm so glad you came

JELLICO COAL MAN

with T. Bone Burnett

1970s

I've got a little black ring
Around my neck
And I will sell you coal
By the bushel or the peck

I will sell you coal
By the gallon or the pound
And you don't have to look for me
I'll be around

Yelling, "Jellico coal man, Jellico coal man
Jellico coal man, coal, coal, coal."

There is coal that's soft
And coal that's hard
I will bring it around
To your back yard

I'll have chocolate cake
And apple pie
I believe I will have a piece
When I come by

"I'm the Jellico coal man, Jellico coal man
Jellico coal man, coal, coal, coal."

It comes direct
From the Jellico mine
It'll warm your baby
In the wintertime

When the sun comes up
That's the time I start
You will see me coming
With my two-wheel cart

Yelling, "Jellico coal man, Jellico coal man
Jellico coal man, coal, coal, coal
Jellico coal man, I'm the Jellico coal man
Jellico coal man, coal, coal, coal."

Jellico Coal Man

I've got a little black ring around my neck
And I will sell you coal by the bushel or the peck
I will sell you coal by the quarter or the pound
And you dont have to look for me I'll be around
yellin' Jellico Coal Man
Jellico Coal Man
I'm the Jellico Coal Man Coal Coal Coal

It comes direct from the Jellico mine
It will warm your baby in the winter time
when the sun comes up thats the friendship
you will see me comin' with my two wheel cart
yellin' Jellico Coal Man
Jellico Coal Man
Jellico Coal Man, coal coal coal

There is coal thats soft and coal thats hard
~~I bring you the best from the other~~ [illegible]
I will bring it around through your backyard.
I love chocolate cake and apple pie
I believe I will have a piece when I come back by
I'm the Jellico Coal Man
Jellico Coal Man
Jellico Coal Man coal coal coal

June's Twilight

A heavenly curtain
Slowly drops
A day of farces
Stops.

Twilight,
End act three
No director, no script
Cues missed, lines slipped
OK

The cast, the crew
The good, the bad
Welcome twilight
All are glad

"Twilight at last
And all creation
Cries "peace in your heart"
Night's salutation

Twilight, ... calm wind
Settled at least
Soft breezes,
Bringing the peace

Wonders of evening
Enter the set
It's your cue, but dont
Look back in regret

You're not to pass judgement
On actions or deeds
Night will sprout
Tomorrows' seeds

~~But love rushes in~~
~~Will stay over night~~
~~God is love, at the door~~
~~At twilight~~

~~John~~

Love Rushes in
Will watch through the night
Heart still beat as one, Stronger!
.... Twilight

John

JUNE'S TWILIGHT

1970s

A heavenly curtain
Slowly drops
A day of farces
Stops

Twilight
End act three
No director, no script
Cues missed, lines slipped
Okay

The cast, the crew
The good, the bad
Welcome, twilight
All are glad

Twilight, at last
And all creation
Cries, "Peace in your heart."
Night's salutation

Twilight . . . calm wind
Settled, at least
Soft breezes
Bringing the peace

Wonders of evening
Enter the set
It's your cue
But don't look back in regret

You're not to pass judgment
On actions or deeds
Night will sprout
Tomorrow's seeds

Love rushes in
Will watch through the night
Hearts still beat as one, stronger!
Twilight

MY SONG

with Robert Hatch

1970s

I would sing it aloud and I would sing it long
Straight from the heart I'd sing it true
Then I'd come back down from that singing mountain
Life would be better 'cause I sang it for you

It's a-many a-day that the road gets weary
Many a-day that the way is long
Often I say that I can't do this no more
But I'd miss the traveling and I'd miss the songs

'Cause I was born to sing but not to wind and space
But people's hearts, people's tears
'Tis a gift from God that I pray I'd use it
Sing to their hearts and sing to their ears

Yeah, I would sing it loud and I would sing it long
Straight from the heart I'd sing it true
Then I'd come back down from that singing mountain
Life would be better 'cause I sang it for you

For a song can soar like a lofty eagle
And lift a heart that has fallen low
A song can shine like the light in the darkness
And make the downcast look up and glow

I wish I owned a great high mountain
With people below every way I turned
They'd look up and every ear could hear me
I'd sing my song to all the hearts that yearned

And I would sing it loud and I would sing it long
Straight from the heart I'd sing it true
Then I'd come back down from that singing mountain
Life would be better 'cause I sang it for you

Yes, I would sing it loud and I would sing it long
Straight from the heart I'd sing it true
Then I'd come back down from that singing mountain
Life would be better 'cause I sang it for you

I would come back down from that singing mountain
Life would be better 'cause I sang it for you

My Song

JOHNNY CASH

Well, its many a day
That the road gets weary
And its many a day
That the way is long
And I often say,
No more I do it
But I miss the traveling
And I miss the songs

I was born to sing
But not to the wind and space
But to peoples hearts
And to peoples ears
Tis a gift of God
And I pray I'd use it
And sing to their hearts
And sing to their ears

For a song can soar
Like the lofty eagle
And lift a heart
That has fallen low
And a song can shine
Like a light in darkness
And make the downcast
Look up and glow

I wish I owned
A great high mountain
With people below
Any way I turned—
And I wish they'd look up
And ear could hear me
And I'd sing my song
To the hearts that yearned.

~~It would be so sweet~~
~~It would bring such comfort~~
~~And would bring such peace~~
~~For which each heart yearned.~~

I would sing it loud
I would sing it long
Straight from the heart
I would sing it true
Then I'd come back down
From my singing mountain—
And your life would be better
'cause I sang for you

A MAN SHOULD TRY

1970s

A man should try to never forget
Where he came from else
He might lose track of where he is

And if a man doesn't know where he is
He can't know where he's going

MOVING INTO A NEW HOUSE

1970s

Moving into a new house
Cleaning out drawers and shelves
I found a broken watch, Indian arrowhead
Buttons, paper clips, eraser, a buckle,
Matches, keys, a cuff link, a pencil,
A piece of ribbon, and dozens of other things
That I kept for some reason

And I found an old picture of some girl
I can't remember her name, but I know that face
Yesterday's discarded junk, why do we keep it?
I still have it, all that junk, I put it into a new drawer
All except that picture of that girl
I just thought I had better throw that picture away

ODE TO GATOR

1970s

An alligator died in France
That you might have those fancy shoes
A thousand trees were cut
So you could read the morning news

RAMBLIN' JACK

1970s

I was wonderin' if you knew a friend of mine
The last time I saw him
He was leavin' flyin'
If you see him tell him hurry back
His name is Ramblin' Jack

Ramblin' Jack, Ramblin' Jack
How long's it gonna be
'Til you ramble back?
Your little woman's in a family way
You better ramble back today
Ramblin' Jack, you better ramble back today

The last time Ramblin' Jack was here
He was singin' a song that would bring a tear
But he didn't stay when his song was sung
Now I don't know where he's at
Your friends all miss you sure
She was due to have a baby in December
Ramblin' Jack went missing in July
And by the time that she was big and awkward
Ramblin' Jack hadn't shown up
Written, called, or come by

Ramblin' Jack, Ramblin' Jack
How much longer 'til you come home?
Ramblin' Jack, Ramblin' Jack
Come reap the seed you sowed

THE RUG ON THE FLOOR

1970s

The only thing between me and the door
Is the rug on the floor
The only thing between me and being gone
Is one last song

There it is, I don't have to wait
In case I'm needin' something to motivate
The only thing between me and being gone
Is one more song
And me and the door is the rug on the floor

The only thing between me and being out of here
Is your last tear
And the only thing between me and carrying on
Is one more beer

In case I'm needin' something to help me go
Here it is: "I don't want you anymore."
The only thing between me and being out of here
Is your last tear
And me and carrying on is one more beer

Hey, hey, I'm gone and I won't be back
You're always takin' and you won't give jack
So take your videos, take your cat
Your health food books and your Harley cap
The only thing between me and being free
Is reality and you and me going separately

LOST MY MONEY IN A BUFFALO TRACK

1970s

I lost my money in a buffalo track
On the Blue Ridge Mountain
Where the road turns back
From Philadelphy to the Cumberland Gap
There ain't a maple standin'
That'll give me sap

The rim ran off of a wheel one night
But I keep it watered
It'll be all right
We crossed Clinch River
Where the skeeters scratched
Then we smoked them out
In a 'baccer patch

The cornmeal's weevilly
And the bacon's rank
But the perch was tasty on Cumberland banks
At a place called French Lick, Tennessee
We fought the weather and the Cherokee
We fed on deer and buffalo
And we tanned their hides
Against the winter snow

SEAL IT IN MY HEART AND MIND

1970s

As the Bible is laid open
And the bread of life, I find
In the words that You have spoken
Seal it in my heart and mind

Seal it in my heart and mind, Lord
Seal it in my heart and mind
Let me always take it with me
Seal it in my heart and mind

I find proof of Your forgiveness
And what wisdom there I find
And the strength for daily living
Seal it in my heart and mind

Seal it in my heart and mind, Lord
Seal it in my heart and mind
Let me always take it with me
Seal it in my heart and mind

Words of love and inspiration
Light to guide me when I'm blind
Keep me filled in preparation
Seal it in my heart and mind

Seal it in my heart and mind, Lord
Seal it in my heart and mind
Let me always take it with me
Seal it in my heart and mind

Seal it in my Heart and Mind

As the Bible is laid open
And the bread of life I find
In the words that you have spoken
Seal it in my heart and mind

Cho Seal it in my heart and Mind Lord
" " " " " " "
Let me always take it with me
Seal it in my heart and mind

I find proof of His forgiveness
And what wisdom there I find
And the strength for daily living
Seal it in my heart and mind

Words of love and inspiration
Light to guide me when I'm blind
Keep me filled in preparation
Seal it in my heart and Mind.

TECUMSEH

with John Carter Cash and Bill Miller

1970s

A Native American boy was born one morning
In the early morning dark when no birds fly
Born to be a prophet like his brother
And they saw the eye of a panther in the sky

A comet with a fierce head came screaming
Round and fierce and with a tail of light
The day that dawned was known as the day of the panther
With the birthday of a baby boy in the morning light

Tecumseh, go and shout it from the mountains
White men are coming from the salty sea
They'll take your hand and steal all your tomorrows
All must stand together to be free

Already there are nations gone forever
Your people are signing treaties that are lies
Listen to the one great Holy Spirit
Then go to every tribe and prophecy

And the Great Spirit said, "On a hilltop near the father of the waters
I'll stamp my foot and strike all hearts with fear.
At the settlement the white man calls New Madrid
You will see it, you will feel it, you will hear."

Tecumseh mounted up and for twelve moons
Went forth and pleaded, preached, and prophesied
He told them that a great earthquake was coming
But it wouldn't be a day for them to hide

He said it will be a sign to meet me
In Indiana where we'll make our stand
The Great Spirit said for me to tell you
This we must do if we're to keep our land

Tecumseh, go and shout it from the mountains
White men are coming from the salty sea
They'll take your hand and steal all your tomorrows
All must stand together to be free

The earthquake came in the year 1811
Just as Tecumseh prophesied
He stood upon the banks east of the river
And watched as buildings fell and people died

He saw the Mississippi running backwards
Whirling, muddy death was in the flow
Then he rode the trembling ground fast and northward
Where he prayed every Indian would go

But from all the tribes that came from east of the river
Just a remnant came to Indian land
And they met the war machines in a terrible battle
And they fought and fell in fighting hand to hand

Then the white men pushed them north and westward
And they safely came to the land of the Cree
Tecumseh fell at his last stand in Canada
And his people still speak of his prophecy

The spirit of Tecumseh is still pleading
In all directions as the eagle flies
His mother knew that he was very special
The night she saw the panther in the sky

Tecumseh, go and shout it from the mountains
White men are coming from the salty sea
They'll take your hand and steal all your tomorrows
You must stand together to be free

Tecumseh

A native American boy was born one morning
In the early morning dark when no birds fly
Born to be a prophet like his brother
And they saw the eye of a panther in the sky
A comet with a fiery head came streaming
Round and fierce and with a tail of light.
The day that dawned was known as the day of the panther
With the birth of a baby boy in the morning light.

Chorus
Tecumseh go and shout it from the mountains
White men are coming from the salty sea.
~~White men are coming from the salty sea~~
They'll take your land and steal all your tomorrows
All must stand together to be free
Already there are nations gone forever
Your people are signing treaties that are lies
Listen to the one great Holy Spirit
Then go to every tribe and prophesy
And the great Spirit said
On a ~~mountain~~ hill top near the father of the waters
~~you will~~ I'll stamp my foot and strike all hearts with fear
At the settlement the white man calls New Madrid
You'll see it, you will feel it, you will hear.

Tecumseh mounted up and for twelve moons
Went forth and pleaded, preached and prophesied
He told them that a great earthquake was coming
But it wouldn't be a day for them to hide
He said it will be a sign to meet me
In Indiana where we'll make our stand
The great Spirit said for me to tell you
This we must do if we're to keep our land
1st 4 lines of chorus

The earthquake came in the year 1811
Just as Tecumseh prophesied
He stood upon the banks east of the river
And watched as buildings fell and people died
He saw the Mississippi running backwards
Whirling, muddy death was in the flow
Then he rode the trembling ground east and northw[ard]
Where he prayed every Indian would go

But from all the tribes that came from east of the ri[ver]
Just a remnant came to Indiana land
And they met the war machines in a terrible batt[le]
And they fought and fell in fighting hand to hand
Then the white men pushed them north and westwar[d]
And they safely came to the land of the Cree
Tecumseh fell at his last stand in Canada
And his people still speak of his prophesy

~~Tecumseh go and tell it all who will listen~~

The spirit of Tecumseh still is pleading
In all directions as the eagle flies
His mother knew that he was very special
The night she saw the panther in the sky

OR Tecumseh go and shout it from the mountains
White men are coming from the salty sea,
They'll take your land and steal all your tomorrows
You must stand together to be free

VALERITA

1970s

There I left my Valerita
Sleeping by the manzanita
Lying in the clover
Where the vines intertwined her hair

Valerita slept 'til evening
Never knew that I was leaving
I could not tell her that
I would go and leave her there

The sun was sinking low
And I was gone
I could not tell her she'd be alone
Still I feel her hands and lips on me
I held her and her love was wild and free

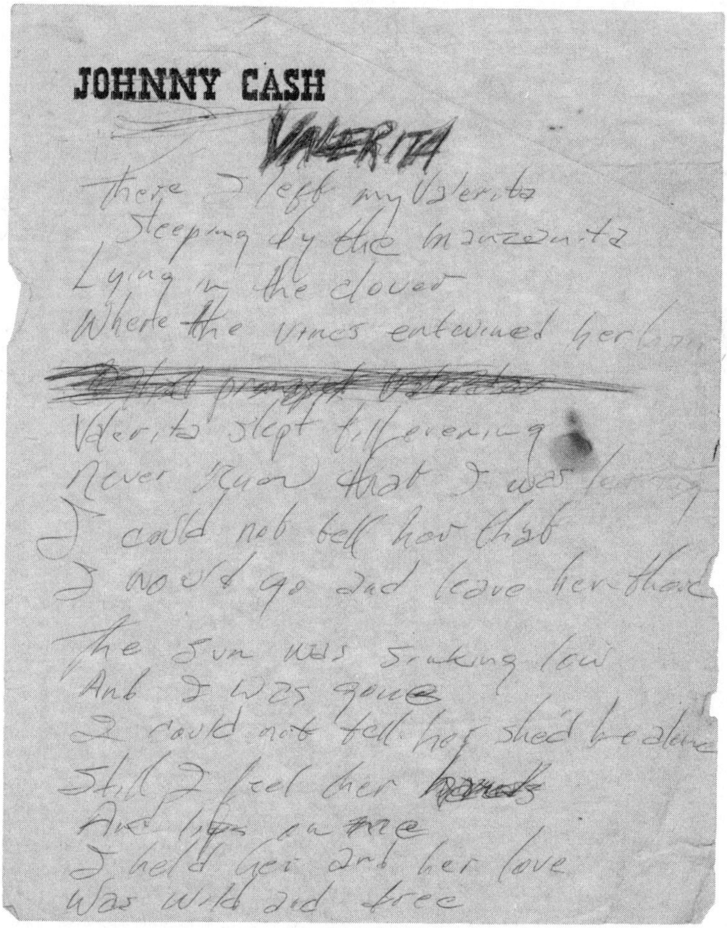
JOHNNY CASH
Valerita
There I left my Valerita
Sleeping by the manzanita
Lying in the clover
Where the vines entwined her hair
[illegible]
Valerita slept till evening
Never knew that I was leaving
I could not tell her that
I would go and leave her there
The sun was sinking low
And I was gone
I could not tell her she'd be alone
Still I feel her hands
And lips on me
I held her and her love
Was wild and free

Them Double Blues

When I look into them double blues
It knocks me to the ground
I guarantee you those two eyes
Could bring a kingdom down
When you look at me I see the deep blue ~~instead~~ sea
On your luxury line to paradise
Is where I want to go.

I love them double blues
" " " "

Your little whims are my commands
Baby how could I refuse
Its the first time that I ever knew
Perfection comes in twos.
I'm crazy bout you lady
And I love them double blues.

When you lay them double blues on me
I'm rich as old John D.
And everything is beautiful
As far as I can see
I want to kiss your heart and soul
And the secret parts of you
I'd like to stay till judgement day
Locked in them double blues

THEM DOUBLE BLUES

with John Mellencamp

1970s

Your little whims are my command, baby, I can't refuse
It's the first time I ever knew perfection comes in twos
I'm crazy about you, lady, and I love them double blues
Double blues, double blues, I love them double blues

Double blues, double blues
I love them double blues
I'm making my way down Mercer
To find them double blues

When I look into them blues, they knock me to the ground
I guarantee those two eyes could bring a kingdom down
When you look at me, I see the bottom of the deep blue sea
With the angel of Mercer is where I wanna be

Double blues, double blues
I love them double blues
I'm making my way down Mercer
To find them double blues

When you lay them blues on me, I'm rich as old Johnny
And everything is beautiful as far as I can see
I wanna kiss your heart and soul and be a part of you
I'd like to stay 'til judgment day, locked in them double blues

Double blues, double blues
I love them double blues
Double blues, double blues
Perfection comes in twos

Double blues, double blues
I love them double blues
I'm making my way down Mercer
To find them double blues

THE WALKING WOUNDED

with Rosanne Cash

1970s

We're in the church house, kneeling down
We're in the subways, underground
We're in the bars and on the street
We drive a truck, we walk a beat

We're in the mills and factories
We make the steel, we cut the trees
A thousand-yard stare, eyes of glass
But we will see you when you pass

We lost our homes, we lost our dreams
All our goals have turned to schemes
We hurt each other and ourselves
So after long traumatic spells

We are the walking, we are the walking
We are the walking wounded

We cried out from the deepest pit
But rise back up each time we're hit
We fell from power and from grace
Resurrection's in our face

We're just like little girls and boys
We play with grown-up toys
We never thought of sink or swim
My brother hurts me so I hurt him

We are the walking, we are the walking
We are the walking wounded

Like a circle, 'round and 'round
We go up so we come down
We don't explain or apologize
We pull the veil across our eyes

We see through your fake refrain
We won't let you see our pain
You may not know us but you'll see
There are more than you'd believe

We are the walking, we are the walking
We are the walking, we are the walking
We are the walking, we are the walking
We are the walking wounded

~~[illegible]~~ The Walking Wounded

We're in the church house kneeling down
We're in the subways underground
We're in the bars and on the street
We drive a truck we walk a beat
We're in the mills and factories
We make the steel we cut the trees
A thousand yard stare, eyes of glass
~~You may not know us~~ we'll will see you when we pass
We are the walking wounded.

We lost our homes, we lost our ~~[illegible]~~ dreams
~~Our dreams were washed away like [illegible]~~ All our goals turned into schemes
We hurt each other and ourselves
We went through long traumatic spells
We cried out from the deepest pit
But ~~[illegible]~~ rise back up each time we're hit
We fell from power and from grace
But resurrection's in our face
We are, the walking wounded.

Just like little girls and boys
We ~~[illegible] played with our toys~~ with our grown up toys
~~And when cruel deception came~~
~~We kept went on playing our games.~~
We never thought of sink or swim
I traded her, she went with him
Like a circle round and round
Just going up and coming down.
No shame and no integrity
I hurt her and she left me
We are the walking wounded.

We dont explain or apologize.
We pull the veil across our eyes
~~[illegible]~~ We see through your fake and vain
But we wont let you see our pain
We dont ask you to forgive
~~[illegible]~~ We demand that you let live
You ~~[illegible]~~ cant understand and so,
You dont really need to know
We are the walking wound...

Am
Together — we are legion Em7
We are honest with each other
~~And we love and we~~ Though we stay and tho we leave
You may see us and not know us
There are many more of us than you'd believe

WARM MISSOURI WIND

1970s

Where the columbine twines
Up the white oak tree
Where Frank and Jesse once played
Beneath Zerelda's Knee

Down Sugarmill Road
She's calling me again
And I'm on my way this mornin'
On the warm Missouri wind

Sunflower, smile upon my lady
Robin, sing a song of sweet reunion
Moon, shine down upon my baby
Warm Missouri wind, blow me home

Springtime is breakin'
In County Clay
Platte River rapids sing
It's homecomin' day

My heart beats heavy
For my lover and friend
And soars like an eagle
On the warm Missouri wind

Sunflower, smile upon my lady
Robin, sing a song of sweet reunion
Moon, shine down upon my baby
Warm Missouri wind, blow me home

Weepin' willow, lift up your branches
Porch light, welcome me again
Arms that never let me be lonely
Warm Missouri wind, blow me home

THE SIGN SAID 50% OFF

1970s

The sign in the window said 50% off
Everything at half price
Now I wonder if we can buy
For fifty cents what once cost a dollar
Are we getting a real bargain
Or was the merchandise always worth
Only fifty cents?

Warm Missouri Wind

Where the columbine twines
Up the white oak tree
Where Frank & Jesse once played
Beneath the Zerelda's knee
Down sugar mill road
She's calling me again
And I'm on my way this mornin
On the Warm Missouri Wind

Sunflower smile upon my lady
Robin sing a song of sweet reunion
Moon shine down upon my baby
Warm Missouri Wind blow me home

Spring time is breakin
In county Clay
Platte River rapids sing
It's home-comin day
My heart beats heavy
For my lover and friend
And soars like an eagle
On the Warm Missouri Wind

Repeat Cho-

refrain -
Weeping willow lift up your branches
Porch light welcome me again
Arms that never let me be lonely
Warm Missouri Wind-
Blow Me Home

WATCH FOR GRUNIONS

1970s

Don't kill people
That's a crime
You can outdrag with four barrels
But you're dead a long, long time

I was burning up the pike
With my window down, I said to Mike
"Do you believe what I see?
That pickup truck ahead of me."

A camper and it ain't a Mack
I see the motorcycle tied on back
I'm sorry that it looked so dumb
The sign "Miami, here we come"

Mike said, "Let's go around.
He will bust, where he's bound."
I cut down and passed him slow
Waved that phony wave, you know

On his right, his woman sat
Fanning with his fisher hat
He sat up straight when he saw us
S'pose he had to adjust his truss

Turned my key off
Then back
Backfired, and I was gone
Left the car laggin' back alone

An hour later, nearly broke
I pulled in and got a Coke
Campers built upon truck beds
Lined the place, got Friday fed

After standin' in the line
Paid the waitress each a dime
Got back in the car again
When up drives the camper truck, our friend

I just had to kid a bit
I said, "Say, is your cookstove lit?
Is your motorcycle tied?
How much longer can it ride?"

He said, "Thank you, son, you're kind.
I haven't thought in two hours' time.
See, this truck and all you see
This is all we have, my wife and me.

"We got married yesterday.
Bought this rig and drove away
With the truck and motorcycle to ride
We should find a place to hide.

"They say you live but once
And she's mine.
When you die you're dead
A long, long time."

Slow Watch for Grannies
Don't kill people that's a crime
You can out drag with four barrels
But you're dead a long long time

I was burning up the pike
With my window down I said brother
Do you believe what I see
That pick up truck ahead of me
A camper, and it ain't a mack
See the motorcycle tied on back
I'm sorry that it looked so dumb
The sign, Miami, here we come

Mike said lets go on around
He will bust, where hes bound
I cut down and passed him slow
Waved that phony wave you know
On his his right his woman sat
Fanning with his fishing hat
He sat up straight when
he saw us
[illegible] he [illegible] just his truss

Turned my key off
then back
Backfired, and I was gone
~~Left em laggin back a ways~~
An hour later nearly broke
I pulled in and got a coke
Campers built upon truck beds
Lined the place, got Friday fed
After standin in the line
Paid the waitress each a dime
Got back in the car again
When up drives the camper
~~truck arrived~~
I just had to kid a bit
I said [illegible] is your cook stove
is your motorcycle tied
How much longer can it ride?
He said Thank you son, you know
~~I haven't thought in 2 hours time~~
See, this [illegible] all
This is [illegible] you see
share my

WHEN A GOOD OLD BOY GOES BAD

1970s

He never really meant to do no harm
But thrills are hard to come by on the farm
When the land won't give a lot
You gotta do with what you got
And all he's got is the muscle in his arm

Last night he hit a small convenience store
Today his mother cries and walks the floor
And she sings that same old song
Called "Where Did I Go Wrong?"
And they've got him locked up in an eight by four

When a good old boy goes bad he goes bad
He will go for all the kicks he never had
He'll grab for the luxury like they teach you on TV
When a good old boy goes bad he goes bad

The girls all said that he was shy and kind
Until the day that he altered his mind
He couldn't feel the pain
The night the chemicals fried his brain
To the siren and the lights he was deaf and blind

In the chase the cops shot out his tire
Just in time they drug him from the fire
They took him by his home
'Cause she didn't have a phone
But his mama didn't know a lawyer she could hire

When a good Old Boy Goes Bad

He never really meant to do no harm
But thrills are hard to come by on the farm
When the Land wont give a lot
you gotta do with what you got
And all hes got's the muscle in his arm

Last night he hit a small convenience store
Today his mother cries and walks the floor
And she sings that same old song
Called, ~~[illegible]~~ Where did I go wrong
And theyve got him locked up in an 8 x 4

When a ~~[illegible]~~ good old boy goes bad he goes bad
~~He will show you more than what he learned from dad~~
He will go for all the kicks he never had
He'll grab ~~for~~ the Luxury like they teach you on TV
When a good old boy goes bad he goes bad

The girls all said that he was shy and kind
Until the day that he altered his mind
He couldnt feel the pain
The night the chemicals forced his brain
To the siren and the lights he was deaf & blind

~~So he pulled out his new bought switch~~ blade knife
~~To cut himself a little slice of life.~~

In the chase the cops shot out his tire
Just in time they drug him from the fire
~~He lost a little country [illegible]~~
They took him by his home
Cause she didnt have a phone
But his mama didn't know a lawyer she could [illegible]

YOU KNOW WHO I MEAN

1970s

You mean the honey lips
You mean the big blue eyes
That one with a smile for any movie screen
You mean the tender voice
You mean the heart of gold
There ain't no doubt about it, I know who you mean

So just welcome to the club of hearts she's captured
Stand in line
And wait and try and hold on to that dream
You say you're hypnotized
You mean you can't forget
Well, there's no doubt about it, I know who you mean

You mean you toss and turn
You're under her spell
You saw her driving by and you forgot the light was green
You seem to see her face
You see her every place
I'd say there's no doubt about it, I know who you mean

So welcome to the club of hearts she's captured
Stand in line
And wait and try and hold on to that dream
You mean you're hypnotized
You mean you can't forget
For there's no doubt about it, I know who you mean
There's no doubt about it, I know who you mean

YOU'VE GOT SOMETHING WORTH COMING HOME TO

1970s

Sometimes my eyes may look a little wild
But the highway will do that to a man
I've been a rambler since I was a child
It's the only kind of life I understand

Sleeping in a new bed every night
Itching for a new road every day
Movin' on alone and traveling light
You're the only stop where I would stay

You've got something worth coming home to
You've got the power to turn my head around
You've got something worth coming home to

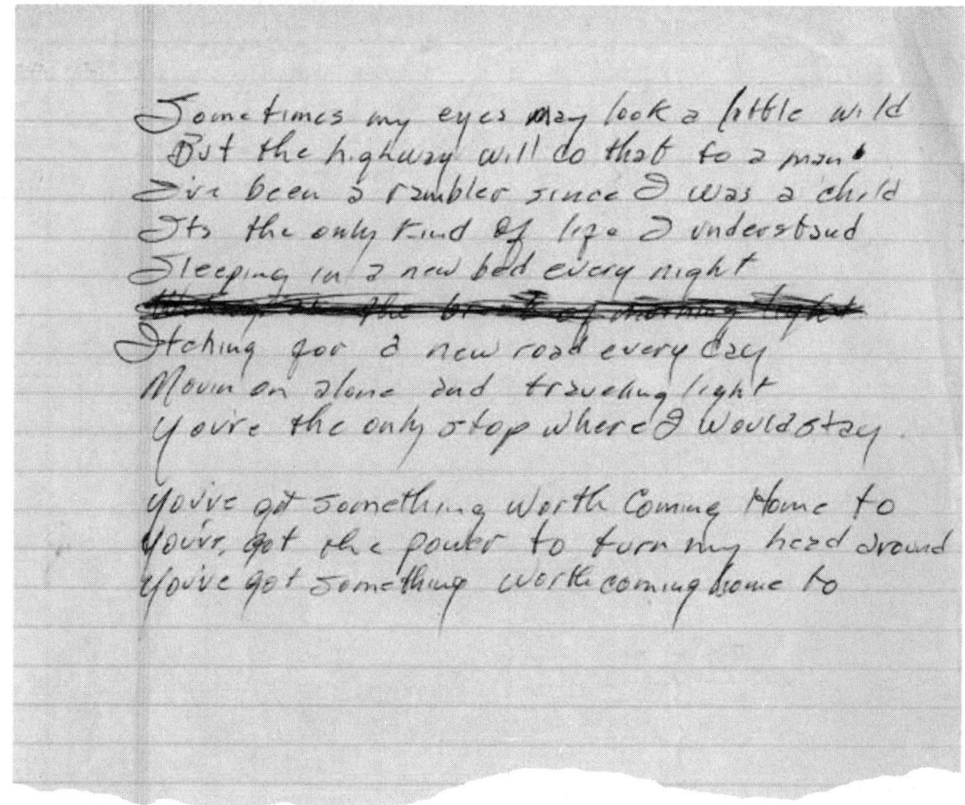

Sometimes my eyes may look a little wild
But the highway will do that to a man
Ive been a rambler since I was a child
Its the only kind of life I understand
Sleeping in a new bed every night
~~[illegible]~~
Itching for a new road every day
Movin on alone and traveling light
You're the only stop where I would stay.

You've got something worth Coming Home to
Youre got the power to turn my head around
You've got something worth coming home to

CHILDREN, GO WHERE I SEND THEE

traditional

adapted in 1970

Children, go where I send thee
How shall I send thee?

I'm gonna send thee
Twelve by twelve

Twelve by the twelve
That couldn't get help

Eleven by the eleven
That couldn't get to heaven

Ten by the ten
That couldn't get in

Nine by the nine
That dressed so fine

Eight by the eight
That stood at the gate

Seven by the seven
That went on to heaven

Six by the six
That couldn't get fixed

Five by the five
That couldn't get by

Four by the four
That stood at the door

Three by the Hebrew children
Two by Paul and Silas
One by the itty, bitty baby
Who was born, born, born in Bethlehem

DADDY TOOK A PLANE TO SPAIN

1970

Rested, comfortable, free from pain
Tomorrow night I go to Spain
Tomorrow night
John Carter might write:
"My daddy took a plane to Spain.
He couldn't take a train to Spain.
You cannot take a train to Spain.
You must take a plane or boat
And to take a boat you have to float
And floating is too slow to go.
He must get back to me, you know.
So Daddy took a plane to Spain."

July 16 1970

Rested, comfortable free from pain
Tomorrow night I go to Spain
Tomorrow night,
John Carter might write,

"My daddy took a plane to Spain
He couldnt take a train to Spain
you cannot take a train to Spain
you must take a plane or Boat
And to take a boat you have to float
And floating is too slow to go
He must get back to me you know
So daddy took a plane to Spain"

J.R. Cash

DELTA QUEEN

1970

So long, Delta Queen
Cincinnati to New Orleans
When you go, you take a lot of dreams
So long, Delta Queen

Yeah, so long now, Delta Queen
And I wonder, before you go
Could we — just one more time —
Hear your steam whistle blow?

Ahhh, thanks a lot, old riverboat
We'll miss that whistle in the night
We'll miss the smell of your pine-knot fire
(We knew it was you when we saw the light)

With you goes a way of life
That this world never again will know
The way of life on a riverboat
Will go the way all good things go

Yeah, so long, quiet, peaceful nights
Along the deep, wide, silent stream
So long, Captain, so long, crew
Back to the land to wish and dream

With you goes a breed of man
In tune with God, earth, rivers, and stars
Who could steer a course by pure instinct
And miss the ever-shifting bars

Men who loved the riverboat
Men who knew that river, too
Well, so long, Delta Queen
We will sure be missing you

DEVIL WIND
(THEME FROM *A GUNFIGHT*)

1970

It's a devil wind that blows
When there's a hole in your coat
And December snow is ugly
When your boots have come apart

And you can't see a bright tomorrow
Through the darkness of today
And the country isn't pretty
When you're hungry

The trail is long and empty
When a gunfight's just been won
And another may be waiting
Beyond the morning sun

But somewhere there's a someplace
A place where I belong
Somewhere a man don't need a gun
To tell him right from wrong

And it's a devil wind that blows
When there's a hole in your coat
And December snow is ugly
When your boots have come apart

And you can't see a bright tomorrow
Through the darkness of today
And the country isn't pretty
When you're hungry

EVERYTHING'S ALRIGHT

1970

The day was warm and humid
I walked up in the field
The drought, the lack of water
Had cut down on the yield

The plants were dead and dying
The leaves were turning brown
I heard you calling for me
From the house, I walked back down

Tired and hot and weary
I took a washcloth and a comb
Turned around and you smiled at me
So everything's alright at home

Book

Sept 14 1970

The day was warm and humid
I walked up in the field
The drought, the lack of water
Had cut down on the yield

The plants were dead & dying
The leaves were turning brown
I heard you calling for me
from the house. I walked back do

~~[illegible]~~

Tired and hot and weary
I took a wash cloth and a comb
Turned around and you smiled at me
So everythings alright at home.

J. C.

THE FACE OF DESPAIR

1970

Fingers calloused from the plow
Wrinkled weather-beaten brow
Streak of silver in the hair
Face of despair

A back that's bent from years of toil
Thorns grow in the worn out soil
No one left to really care
Face of despair

If you should plow old fields like these
You'd plow up memories
Don't tell the young to mend their ways
You can't show them better days

Their better days are yet ahead
Your better days have long been dead
Rest easy in your rocking chair
And look at your September country
Face of despair

Shoulders weary from the load
Life is rough as a gravel road
How much of it can you bear?
Look at your September country
Face of despair

In the September of your years
Eyes that hide a veil of tears
A look of longing always there
Face of despair

GATHER 'ROUND THE FIRE

1970

Come, gather 'round the fire
And look into the flame
Here's the way it used to be
Before the highways came

And there came a virgin woman
In her finery, from Saint Lou
To a man, wild as a whirlwind
And like a man will do

He held on to the old way
To a way that would be dead
But a pretty leg and a budding breast
Can turn a stubborn head

GEORGIA MOON

1970

Georgia moon
Like my dreams, you're out of reach
Georgia moon
Look like a sweet Elberta peach
Georgia moon

With a layover in Atlanta
And two or three hours to spare
I'll go down in the Underground
And maybe I'll find her there

Georgia moon
Is she down in the Underground?
Georgia moon
Or are you shining on her?
Georgia moon

Atlanta Aug 14 1970

Georgia Moon
Like my dreams you're out of reach
Georgia Moon
Look like a sweet Elberta peach
Georgia Moon

With a layover in Atlanta
And two or three hours to spare
I'll go down in the Underground
And maybe I'll find her there

Georgia Moon
Is she down in the Underground
Georgia Moon
Or Are you Shining on her
Georgia Moon

With a lay-over in Atlanta
And two whole hours there
Theres time enough to go
And run my fingers through her hair

GONE TO DENVER

with Penni Lane

1970

I've thought I'd take a trip to Denver
And spend a little time
I thought maybe out in Denver
I might get you off my mind

Don't want no one to go with me
Just want to be alone
I might find someone in Denver
That can help me carry on

Gone to Denver, gone to Denver
Gone to mend a broken heart
Now I must go, and if I'm going
I'd better be gone
Gone to Denver

Well, I've known for quite a while now
I've been losing you
And I'd rather not stay here
And find out who I lost you to

Maybe I won't even miss you
Like I always thought I would
I've heard Denver's quite a city
And a change might do me good

Gone to Denver, gone to Denver
Gone to mend a broken heart
Time I was going, and if I'm going
I'd better be gone, gone to Denver

HELLO, FRIEND

1970

Hello, friend, how do you do?
How, oh how do you do?
Do you do nice and good
Like a person ought to should?

As you'd be done by someone else
Is also how you do yourself
For, if you don't do yourself right
You can't expect that others might

If you did get did, as you have done
To each and all and everyone
And how you get done pleases you
Then you will know that how you do
Is just exactly how to do

JOHNNY CASH Book

Hello friend, how do you do?
How, oh how do you do you
Do you do you nice and good
Like a person ought to should
As you'd be done by someone else
Is also how you do yourself
For if you dont do yourself right
You cant expect that others might
If you get did as you have done
To each and all and everyone
And how you get done pleases you
Then you will know that how you do
Is just exactly how to do.

HUNGRY

1970

Grit my teeth and face a new day dawning
Take a deep breath then get up and go
Tie the same old weary shoes
And walk the same old pathway
I never see a face that I don't know
Oh God, if I could just pack up and go

Hungry for some other face
Hungry for some other place
Needing something and I know what
God, I know what
I'm tired of seeing the same old road
Tired of carrying the same old load
Hungry for something I ain't got

Her face across that table every morning
And lately I don't notice that she's there
Always leave that breakfast table
Feeling so damned empty
She knows there's something wrong
But I don't care
Oh God, how much more of this can I bear?

I'M GONNA TRY TO BE THAT WAY

1970

Once upon a time, there lived a man
Many years ago in a foreign land
Knew how to live right, tried to be a light
Gave everybody a helping hand

I'm gonna try to be that way
I'm gonna try to be that way
Do the kind of things a man oughta do
Say the kind of things a man oughta say
I'm gonna try to be that way

He never done anybody wrong
He tried to help everybody along
He brought a better plan to make a better man
Out of the rich or the poor or the weak or the strong

And you know that
I'm gonna try to be that way
I'm gonna try to be that way
Do the kind of things, Lord, a man oughta do
Say the kind of things a man oughta say
I'm gonna try to be that way

And He preached love and brotherhood
He went around doing good, doing good
Everywhere He went
They knew that He was sent
And the people started acting like they should

I'm gonna try to be that way
I'm gonna try to be that way
Do the kind of things a man oughta do
Say the kind of things a man oughta say
I'm gonna try to be that way

I'm gonna try to be that way
I'm gonna try to be that way
Do the kind of things a man oughta do
Say the kind of things a man oughta say
I'm gonna try to be that way
I'm gonna try to be that way

JUNE SAT AND ROCKED

1970

June sat and rocked our baby
She sang him to sleep while
The wind howled outside
He's gathering strength

Someday the world like that wind
Will howl at his door, calling him out
Challenging him

Keep on singing, June
Keep on sleeping, son
Gather strength

THE LITTLE MAN

1970

It seems like some good people do get messed up on their chances
Ain't no doubt, it's all been planned out before they were born
Always going up that long, downhill road
Always at the little end of the horn

Oh, the little man don't count, they look right over his head
And they turn him and they burn him any way they can
Just somebody's leaning post, everybody's underdog
Oh heaven, help, 'cause no one else will help the little man

It seems like people would get tired of looking down on people
It seems like people got to have someone to kick around
Always feeling like they need to be looked up to
And always someone there when they look down

Oh, the little man don't count, they look right over his head
And they turn him and they burn him any way they can
Just somebody's leaning post, everybody's underdog
Heaven, help, 'cause no one else will help the little man

THE NAKED LIGHT OF DAY

1970

The crowd down on the corner is gone this morning
The girl that walked the street is somewhere sound asleep
The couple I heard fighting have checked out and gone away
Things are different in the naked light of day

The girl that smiled back at me in the lobby
Is thinkin' I'm a fool and she's somewhere today at school
The roses that I gave last night to someone will decay
Things look different in the naked light of day

The alley's full of last night's cans and bottles
This morning's paper tells about the way it all came out
The hours I spent thinkin' of you tremblin' where I lay
Have made me weaker in the naked light of day

But I still love you in the naked light of day

PONY EXPRESS (RIDE, RIDE, RIDE)

1970

You gotta ride, ride, ride
Though the sun burns your hide
Though you're chilled to the bone
You still must ride
On to the West

You gotta ride, ride, ride
'Til you reach the other side
For the mail must go through
Then the hat's off to you
Pony express

PUBLIC LIFE IS UNBELIEVABLE

1970

Public life is unbelievable
Being a "star" means so many things
And all of them opposite normalcy

If your face is familiar
You are stared at, pointed at, laughed at
Frowned at, whispered at, yelled at, and followed

People say lots of things about you
That they wouldn't say if they knew you heard
Everything you do well is taken for granted
Any mistake is a matter for great attention

ROLLIN' FREE

1970

Rollin' free, rollin' free, rollin' free
Just the sun and the wind
And the road and me

I don't want to be tied to a load
That I can't carry over the road
Just want to hear that thunder roar
On trails that ain't been rode before
Don't put no chains on me
I'm rollin' free

Now I'm not worried about who I am
'Cause frankly, I don't give a damn
Long as I can be where I want to be
And doin' what I want to do
And if it's all the same to you
What I want to be is rollin' free

Rollin' free, rollin' free, rollin' free
Just the sun and the wind
And the road and me

I don't want to be tied to a load
That I can't carry over the road
Just want to hear that thunder roar
On trails that ain't been rode before
Don't put no chains on me
I'm rollin' free

Now I forgot about yesterday
And let tomorrow bring what may
Let everything be as it will be
'Cause all I need is my machine
And a little high octane gasoline
And get your hands off me, I'm rollin' free

Rollin' free, rollin' free, rollin' free
Just the sun and the wind
And the road and me

I don't want to be tied to a load
That I can't carry over the road
Just want to hear that thunder roar
On trails that ain't been rode before
Don't put no chains on me
I'm rollin' free

SAY SOMETHING NICE TO SARAH

with Winafred Kelley

1970

I really do love Sarah and she really does love me
And we're about as happy as a pair in love can be
One day I said to Sarah, "Before we run away
Let me get your dad's permission."
This is what he had to say

"Say something nice to Sarah every day.
Treat Sarah in the kindest kind of way.
Don't ever leave her all alone
Or when you come back, she'll be gone.
She hurts mighty easy, watch what you say.
Say something nice to Sarah every day."

Well now, I'm still loving Sarah and as the years go by
Some things have made her happy, some things have made her cry
She had her share of trouble fall upon her pretty head
But she comes right back a-smiling
When I do what her daddy said

"Say something nice to Sarah every day.
Treat Sarah in the kindest kind of way.
Don't ever leave her all alone
Or when you come back, she'll be gone.
She hurts mighty easy, watch what you say.
Say something nice to Sarah every day.
Say something nice to Sarah every day."

SHE'S THE FUNNY TURNED KIND

1970

Well, we got married in Chickamauga, Georgia
We left next morning on a honeymoon trip up US 41
And it sure was fun
Then I took her to see Ruby Falls and all Rock City
And it sure was pretty

But she left me mourning without warning
With a highfalutin, fast talkin', smart alecky, slick headed, smooth mouthed
City slicker from Kingsport, Tennessee
Without me, she has lost her mind
She's the funny turned kind

Well, here I am, back in Chickamauga, Georgia
She's still way up yonder, somewhere 'round Kingsport, Tennessee
Or Gate City or somewhere like that
After I took her to see Ruby Falls and all and Rock City
And it sure was pretty

And we stayed all night at the Mo-Jo motel, and I treated her swell
Next morning I took her to Pete's place, and saw the Chinese baboons
And the giant pythons, and the crazy monkeys, and bought her some firecrackers
And took her out on a flatboat out on the Tennessee River
And came back and ate catfish and hush puppies at Harvey's

Then I took her back up the incline and looked back, and she was goin' down with a
Highfalutin, fast talkin', smart alecky, slick headed, smooth mouthed
City slicker from Kingsport, Tennessee
Without me, she has lost her mind
She's the funny turned kind

THIS SIDE OF THE LAW

1970

On this side of the law
On that side of the law
Who is right? Who is wrong?
Who is for and who's against the law?

You see, I didn't really mean you any harm
But I simply couldn't make it on the farm
When the land won't give a lot
You gotta do with what you got
And all I got's the muscle in my arm

Well, I wouldn't ever hurt my fellow man
And it seems to me that you should
  understand
I'm just trying to help myself
Without hurting anybody else
And a man has got to do the best he can

On this side of the law
On that side of the law
Who is right? Who is wrong?
Who is for and who's against the law?

I didn't really mean to let my family down
And I'm not giving you the runaround
I'd much rather be dead
Than have to beg my daily bread
And I pay my way
No matter where I'm bound

Well, I didn't really think that I did wrong
Just as long as I stayed here where I belong
I did the only thing I could
Same as anybody would
I was simply trying to get along

On this side of the law
On that side of the law
Who is right? Who is wrong?
Who is for and who's against the law?

THIS TOWN

1970

This town is not for me
I won't be staying around
This town is hard and cold
I'm not happy in this town

I'll pick up my heart and I'll go
Where to, I don't care or know
Don't matter where I'll be found
As long as I leave this town

This town don't need me now
I'll soon be outward bound
This town don't want me here
And, God, I don't want this town

Tomorrow, who'll remember I came?
Tomorrow, who'll remember my name?
Don't care which road I go down
As long as it's away from this town

TO JUNE, THIS MORNING

with Ruston Kelly and Kacey Musgraves

1970

The night was cold as Dawson
And on a short white day
The great sun rose, lightning hot
And singing climbed its way

The lake wind mist was shrouded
The grandfather east wind blew
Mist rose on the tree limbs
I arose ahead of you

And I made the morning coffee
Then your feet are on the stair
You said good morning to me
Then I sat beside you there

And I made the morning coffee
Then your feet are on the stair
You said good morning to me
Then I sat beside you there

My head, in happy blouse
For love lives in this house

TO THE UNBORN BABY

1970

Baby, if you are a boy
I see ahead such days of joy
I anticipate, or so it seems
There'll come alive the tired old dreams

But if you are a girl, that's fine
You'll be mine
And I love you
Kootchy-koo

TRAIL OF TEARS

1970

There were many, many little children
Among the young and the old who died
Upon the Trail of Tears
Before they reached the other side

Sometimes at night I seem to hear a Cherokee baby cry
And I seem to see campfires that burned for ten thousand years gone by
And I heard a voice cry out, "These were our homes for all these years
And the trail that takes us away will surely be a trail of tears."

There were many, many little children
Among the young and the old who died
Upon the Trail of Tears
Before they reached the other side

The Cherokee looked up and saw that the autumn of his fate
Was burning bright upon the hills and the hour was mighty late
And with the spring, their smokes would there no longer touch the sky
Their lives here, like the last autumn leaves, would be a thing gone by

There were many, many little children
Among the young and the old who died
Upon the Trail of Tears
Before they reached the other side

The Cherokee who held on to their homes until the end
Asked to remain beside the whites who once had been their friend
But here, the Cherokee phoenix would no longer touch the sky
Forced upon a westward march, thousands there would die

There were many, many little children
Among the young and the old who died
Upon the Trail of Tears
Before they reached the other side

WHAT IS TRUTH

1970

The old man turned off the radio
Said, "Where did all of the old songs go?
Kids sure play funny music these days.
They play it in the strangest ways."

Said, "It looks to me like they've all gone wild.
It was peaceful back when I was a child."
Well, man, could it be that the girls and boys
Are trying to be heard above your noise?
And the lonely voice of youth cries, "What is truth?"

A little boy of three, sitting on the floor
Looks up and says, "Daddy, what is war?"
"Son, that's when people fight and die."
The little boy of three says, "Daddy, why?"

A young man of seventeen, in Sunday school
Being taught the Golden Rule
And by the time another year has gone around
It may be his turn to lay his life down
Can you blame the voice of youth for asking, "What is truth?"

A young man sitting on the witness stand
The man with the Book says, "Raise your hand.
Repeat after me, 'I solemnly swear.'"
The man looked down at his long hair

And although the young man solemnly swore
Nobody seems to hear anymore
And it didn't really matter if the truth was there
It was the cut of his clothes and the length of his hair
And the lonely voice of youth cries, "What is truth?"

The young girl dancing to the latest beat
Has found new ways to move her feet
The young man speaking in the city square
Is trying to tell somebody that he cares

Yeah, the ones that you're calling wild
Are going to be the leaders in a little while
This old world's waking to a newborn day
And I solemnly swear that it'll be their way
You better help that voice of youth find "What is truth?"

The graduate with the highest grades
Gets a scholarship for the marks he made
One of the lower-grade classmates
Goes to the Army when he graduates

The lucky scholar gets a white-collar job
The ex-GI is one of the mob
The white-collar man has got it made
The ex-GI doesn't have a trade
And the lonely voice of youth cries, "What is truth?"

The old lady takes a pill for her nerves
Says, "These kids today got more than they deserve.
They don't have to work the way we did.
Sometimes I think we're too good to our kids.

"They drive fast cars, they drink and smoke.
Half of 'em run around high on dope
Always livin' for the latest thrill.
They make me nervous — what'd I do with my pills?"

And the lonely voice of youth cries, "What is truth?"

THE WORLD'S GONNA FALL ON YOU

1970

Better watch what you're doing, Henry
You better take it easy, Sheriff
Somebody might be watching
And the world's gonna fall on you
And the world's gonna fall on you
And the world's gonna fall on you

You can't slip around in this town, Henry
Everybody knows everybody, Sheriff
Somebody's gonna tell somebody
The world's gonna fall on you
And the world's gonna fall on you

You better look over your shoulder, Sheriff
Somebody might be watching, Henry
You can't tell who's gonna see you
The world's gonna fall on you
And the world's gonna fall on you

You can't slip around in this town
Ain't no doubt, they'll find out
You better stop that, better stop now
You better not wait, be too late

Now, who do you think you're fooling, Henry?
Ain't nobody here sleeping, Sheriff
The whole world's watching
And the world's gonna fall on you
And the world's gonna fall on you

You better watch what you're doing, Henry
Better take it easy, Sheriff
Somebody might be watching
And the world's gonna fall on you
And the world's gonna fall on you
And the world's gonna fall on you
And the world's gonna fall on you

Better look over your shoulder, Sheriff
Somebody might be watching, Henry
You can't tell who's gonna see
The world's gonna fall on you
And the world's gonna fall on you

YOU CAN TELL BY THE HAIR

1970

You can tell by the hair on my baby's head
His mother's got to be a thoroughbred
'Cause he favors his mother more than me
You can tell she's got a fine pedigree

You can tell from my little chip off the block
His mother's got to be royal stock
But the thing that really thrills me through and through
Is that he favors his daddy a little bit, too

I CAN TELL BY THE WAY

1971

I can tell by the way
My baby laughs and plays
He'll be blessed with
Some of his mother's way
I'm proud that twenty years from now
Any time or place
I'll see his mother
On my baby's face

I GOT A BOY (AND HIS NAME IS JOHN)

1971

I got a boy and his name is John
You oughta see little John tag along
Going where his daddy goes
Learning what his daddy knows

We got a boy and his name is John
You oughta see little John tag along
Going where his daddy goes
Learning what his daddy knows

He's got a friend and her name is Kay
And Kay goes with him every day
Gonna take Kay along
Gonna teach Kay this song

He's got a friend and his name is George
But he's not the one from Valley Forge
And he's never been president
That ain't the George we meant

He's got a friend and his name is Gibbs
Gibbs is so fat you can't see his ribs
A dog named Sergeant, too, he's his friend
Watch out he might bite you

I got a boy and his name is John
You oughta see little John tag along
Going where his daddy goes
Learning what his daddy knows

I got a boy and his name is John
You oughta see little John tag along
Going where his daddy goes
Learning what his daddy knows

I got a boy and his name is John
You oughta see little John tag along
Going where his daddy (and mommy) goes
Learning what his daddy (and mommy) knows

I got a boy and his name is John

Johns got a friend and her name is Kay

Johns got a friend and his name is George
But he's never been to Valley Forge
He's never been president
Washington is not the George I meant

John's got a dog and his name is Gibbs
He's so fat you can't see his ribs
Gotta dog named Igt too
Watch out He might bite you

~~John doesn't have anything~~
John

I'LL BE LOVING YOU

with June Carter

1971

When your friends don't call you
Like you thought they would
When you can't get over me
Like you thought you could

When you can't forget me
The way you planned to do
Remember, I'll be loving you

On a cold and lonely morning
I'll be loving you
On a dark and lonely evening
I'll be loving you

One happy day, you'll be back
Because you know that we aren't through
I'll roll you in my arms again
I'll be loving you

When your memory of me
Is a heavy load
When you feel you're traveling
Down a muddy road

When the new love
That you're craving
Don't do like he ought to do
Remember, I'll be loving you

On a cold and lonely morning
I'll be loving you
On a dark and lonely evening
I'll be loving you

One happy day, you'll be back
Because you know that we aren't through
I'll roll you in my arms again
I'll be loving you

A LITTLE BIT OF YESTERDAY

1971

The winds of change are coming
And we've got to let it blow
Today is gonna leave us
And we've gotta let it go

But I'll love you tomorrow
Let tomorrow bring what may
Let's hold on to a little bit of yesterday

And trouble may be coming
But if you will stand by me
I will do what I should do
And be what I should be

Our love has been too precious to let it slip away
Let's hold on to a little bit of yesterday

Our love has been too precious to let it slip away
Let's hold on to a little bit of yesterday

There's a sadness in the seasons
When you watch a good one go
For the happy days behind us
Will not return, I know

But you know that I still love you
And true love won't pass away
I'll hold on to a little bit of yesterday
Yes, you know that I'll still love you
True love won't pass away
I'll hold on to a little bit of yesterday

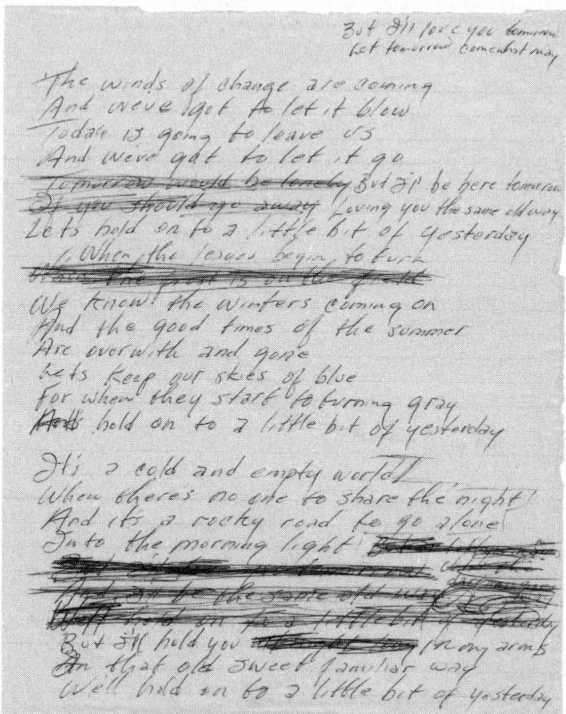
But I'll love you tomorrow
Let tomorrow come what may

The winds of change are coming
And weve got to let it blow
Today is going to leave us
And we've got to let it go
But I'll be here tomorrow
Loving you the same old way
Lets hold on to a little bit of yesterday
When the leaves begin to turn
We know the winters coming on
And the good times of the summer
Are overwith and gone
Lets keep our skies of blue
For when they start to turning gray
hold on to a little bit of yesterday

It's a cold and empty world
When there's no one to share the night
And its a rocky road to go alone
Into the morning light
But I'll hold you in my arms
In that old sweet familiar way
We'll hold on to a little bit of yesterday

MAN IN BLACK

1971

Well, you wonder why I always dress in black
Why you never see bright colors on my back
And why does my appearance seem to have a somber tone
Well, there's a reason for the things that I have on

I wear the black for the poor and the beaten down
Living in the hopeless, hungry side of town
I wear it for the prisoner who has long paid for his crime
But is there because he's a victim of the times

I wear the black for those who've never read
Or listened to the words that Jesus said
About the road to happiness through love and charity
Why, you'd think He's talking straight to you and me

Well, we're doing mighty fine, I do suppose
In our streak of lightning cars and fancy clothes
But just so we're reminded of the ones who are held back
Up front there ought to be a man in black

I wear it for the sick and lonely old
For the reckless ones whose bad trip left them cold
I wear the black in mourning for the lives that could have been
Each week we lose a hundred fine young men

And I wear it for the thousands who have died
Believing that the Lord was on their side
I wear it for another hundred thousand who have died
Believing that we all were on their side

Well, there's things that never will be right, I know
And things need changing everywhere you go
But 'til we start to make a move to make a few things right
You'll never see me wear a suit of white

I'd love to wear a rainbow every day
And tell the world that everything's okay
But I'll try to carry off a little darkness on my back
'Til things are brighter, I'm the Man in Black

JOHNNY CASH Sept 30 '92

To Whom it May Concern.

In 1971 I wrote a song called "Man in Black." Since then I have never worn anything but black on the concerts, or Television. My fans expect this image.

"I wear the black for the sick
And the lonely old.
For the reckless ones
Who's bad trip left them cold.
And just so we're reminded
Of the ones who are held back,
Up front there ought to be
A Man in Black" — etc.

© Johnny Cash
House of Cash
Music

I wear black expensive coat and pants and for traveling, a long coat made of rugged military cloth.

My boots and shoes are custom made for better wear and better looks.

The best performance in concert on T.V. or movies is expected of me,

MISS TARA

1971

Where are you going, Miss Tara, Miss Tara?
Where are you going, Miss Tara Joan?
Yesterday, when you played on the swing and the trampoline
You're already thinking of a life of your own
And I turn around twice and you're already gone

Who will you marry, Miss Tara, Miss Tara?
Who will you marry, Miss Tara Joan?
Will he have wealth and will he have fame?
I'm sure, too, you're wondering just who he will be
Well, that's your decision, it's not up to me

I hope you'll be happy, Miss Tara, Miss Tara
I hope you'll be happy, Miss Tara Joan
And that you will stay with me 'til you're a woman
And wise to the world before you're off on your own
You're my last baby girl and I'll be so alone

NED KELLY

1971

Ned Kelly was a wild, young bushranger
Out of Victoria, he rode with his brother Dan
He loved his people and he loved his freedom
And he loved to ride the wide open land

Ned Kelly was a victim of the changes
That came when his land was a sprout and seed
And the wrongs he did were multiplied in legend
With young Australia growing like a weed

Ned Kelly took the blame
Ned Kelly won the fame
Ned Kelly brought the shame
And then Ned Kelly hanged

Well, he hid out in the bush and in the forest
And he loved to hear the wind blow in the trees
While the men behind the badge were coming for him
Ned said, "They'll never bring me to my knees."

But everything was changed and run in cycles
And Ned knew that his day was at an end
He made a suit of armor out of plowshares
But Ned was brought down by the trooper's men

Ned Kelly took the blame
Ned Kelly won the fame
Ned Kelly brought the shame
And then Ned Kelly hanged

SINGIN' IN VIETNAM TALKIN' BLUES

1971

One morning at breakfast, I said to my wife,
"We've been everywhere once and some places twice."
As I had another helping of country ham
She said, "We ain't never been to Vietnam.
There's a bunch of our boys over there."

So we went to the Orient, Saigon
Well, we got a big welcome when we drove in
Through the gates of a place that they call Long Binh
We checked in and everything got kinda quiet
But a soldier boy said, "Just wait 'til tonight.
Things get noisy, things start happening.
Big bad firecrackers."

Well, that night we did about four shows for the boys
And they were living it up, with a whole lot of noise
We did our last song for the night
And we crawled into bed for some peace and quiet
But things weren't peaceful
And things weren't quiet
Things were scary

Well, for a few minutes, June never said one word
And I thought at first that she hadn't heard
Then a shell exploded not two miles away
She sat up in bed and I heard her say, "What was that?"
I said, "That was a shell or a bomb."
She said, "I'm scared."
I said, "Me, too."

Well, all night long that noise kept on
And the sound would chill you right to the bone
The bullets and the bombs and the mortar shells
Shook our bed every time one fell
And it never let up, it was gonna get worse
Before it got any better

Well, when the sun came up, the noise died down
We got a few minutes' sleep, and we were sleeping sound
When a soldier knocked on our door and said,
"Last night, they brought in seven dead, and fourteen wounded,"
And would we come down to the base hospital and see the boys?
"Yeah."

So we went to the hospital ward by day
And every night we were singing away
Then the shells and the bombs until dawn, again
And the helicopters brought in the wounded men
Night after night, day after day
Coming and a-going

So we sadly sang for them our last song
And reluctantly, we said, "So long."
We did our best to let them know that we care
For every last one of them that's over there
Whether we belong over there or not
Somebody over here loves them, and needs them

Well, now that's about all that there is to tell
About that little trip into living hell
And if I ever go back over there anymore
I hope there's none of our boys there for me to sing for
I hope that war is over with
And they all come back home
To stay
In peace

THE PREACHER SAID, "JESUS SAID"

1971

Well, with everybody trying to tell us what to do
You wonder how are you to know whose word is true?
But the preachers just keep on bringing us the very same word
And from Saint Paul to Billy Graham the same is heard

And the preacher said of truth, "Jesus said"
And Jesus said, "I'm the way, the truth and the life."

Well, we can see that the world is full of greed
There's so much hate, yet there is so much need
What should we do when no one seems to care?
What can we do when there is no love there?

And then the preacher said of love, "Jesus said"
Jesus said, "Love thy neighbor as thyself."

Well, please tell us the road we oughta go
In such confusion, how are we to know?
And if there is a heaven, show us to its gates
Oh, you'd better tell us, preacher, before it's too late
And, then the preacher said of heaven, "Jesus said"

Jesus said, "Seek ye first the kingdom of God and His righteousness
And all these things shall be added unto you."

Well, please tell us how we can find a way
To climb every mountain that we face every day
And in time of troubles, what to depend upon
To be the truth and help us carry on

And the preacher said of trouble, "Jesus said"

Jesus said, "Let not your heart be troubled.
If you believe in God, believe also in me.
In my father's house are many mansions.
If it were not so, I would have told you.
I go to prepare a place for you.
And if I prepare a place for you, I will come again
And receive you unto myself
That where I am, there you may be also."

TO UNJUST CRITICS

1971

You of the poison pen and hateful mind
Who crucify for gold men of my kind

You will never really know this man
But go ahead and do the worst you can

I'll walk across your ashes tall and strong
If my heart is right, my head is not wrong

YOU SHOULD SEE MY SON

1971

You should see my son
Like all fathers who are proud of their sons
I am proud of mine
You should see him

He has a fleck of gold in his hair
That was gleaned from his mother's
Though less than two years old
There is, even now
A kindness in the little words he speaks
That is a harmonic of his mother's voice

"I wuv you, Daddy."
"Bye-bye, Daddy."
"Come on, Daddy, come on."
"How you doin', John Carter?"
"Fine."
"John Carter, don't do that, son."
"I'm sorry, Daddy."
Now I realize…
I was never really a complete man
Until I had a son
To call me Daddy,
To love me,
To follow me and parrot me

I feel a great fulfillment now
You should see my son

YOU'VE GOT A NEW LIGHT SHINING IN YOUR EYES

1971

You've got a new light
Shining in your eyes
And I can see now right where
Your beauty lies

And it's showing in your face that
Your heart has found a place
And I can hear it in
Your whisper and your sighs

You've got a new way
Of doing things you do
And it's plain to see there's
Been a change in you

And I wonder could it be
That the change is due to me?
For I have felt
A certain something, too

You've got a way about you now
That you never had before
You've got a look you're wearing now
Like no look you ever wore

I tried to hide it for a while
But now I realize
You've got a new light shining in your eyes
You've got a new light shining in your eyes

You've got a way about you now
That you never had before
You've got a look you're wearing now
Like no look you ever wore

You tried to hide it for a while
But now I realize
You've got a new light shining in your eyes
You've got a new light shining in your eyes

AH BOS CEE DAH

1972

Well, if you'd like to learn your ABC's
Then listen very carefully to me
You can sing them like a funny, foreign song
And very, very soon, you sing along

And you can sing your ABC's like this
Here's the first eight letters
Ah bos cee dah — ef fah gha hah
Ah bos cee dah — ef fah gha hah
A b c d — e f g h
Ah bos cee dah — ef fah gha hah

And the next eight letters in the alphabet
You sing like this
Ay jah kah lah — meh nah ou pah
Ay jah kah lah — meh nah ou pah
I j k l — m n o p
Ay jah kah lah — meh nah ou pah

Well, that's sixteen letters of the alphabet
And there's ten more, you know
But let's try those last ten, slow

Queh ahr see tah uh — vee whu ix yah zee
Queh ahr see tah uh — vee whu ix yah zee
Q r s t u — v w x y z
Queh ahr see tah uh — vee whu ix yah zee

Now let's try them all
Ah bos cee dah — ef fah gha hah
Ay jah kah lah — meh nah ou pah
Queh ahr see tah uh — vee whu ix yah zee, means
A b c d e f g h i j k l m n o p q r s t u v w x y z

THE BALLAD OF ANNIE PALMER

1972

On the island of Jamaica quite a long, long time ago
At Rose Hall Plantation, where the ocean breezes blow
Lived a girl named Annie Palmer, the mistress of the place
And the slaves all lived in fear to see a frown on Annie's face

Where's your husband, Annie, where's number two and three?
Are they sleeping 'neath the palms beside the Caribbean Sea?
At night I hear you ridin' and I hear your lover's call
And I still can feel your presence 'round the great house at Rose Hall

Well, if you should ever go to see the great house at Rose Hall
There's expensive chairs and china and great paintings on the wall
They'll show you Annie's sitting room and the whipping post outside
But they won't let you see the room where Annie's husbands died

Where's your husband, Annie, where's number two and three?
Are they sleeping 'neath the palms beside the Caribbean Sea?
At night I hear you ridin' and I hear your lover's call
And I still can feel your presence 'round the great house at Rose Hall

CHRISTMAS WITH YOU

1972

It's so nice to spend Christmas with you

The times that I've seen Christmas come and go are now two score
I wish you a merry Christmas and I wish you many more
It's good to see the children laugh with joy the way they do
And it's nice to spend Christmas with you

That old-fashioned Christmas is a sweet memory
Except for all the Christmases that you weren't there with me
But now I really feel the spirit 'cause I love you like I do
And it's nice to spend Christmas with you

I remember Christmas when I little could afford
And I try to remember it's the birthday of our Lord
Well, I'll not forget to thank Him for His blessings on me, too
And that I can spend Christmas with you

That old-fashioned Christmas
It's so nice to spend Christmas with you

CITY JAIL

1972

Back when I first came to this town
I was hangin' 'round the bus station café there
Mindin' my own business, like I always do
And I thought I'd check out the action, like I always do

And I gave this waitress a big eye
And made a few choice personal comments
About what I thought mine and her possibilities could be for a team
When she called the badge on me

The badge grabbed me by the arm and said,
"Hey, boy, what are you hangin' around here for?"
And I said, "For whatever is goin' around."

City jail, city jail
Like an old scared dog, I tucked my tail
I hung my head and not a careless word I said
I gotta sleep on the floor once more at the city jail

He said, "No, what I mean is
What are you doin' saying things like that to that lady?"
And I said, "What's that lady doin' with purple hair?"
And the badge said, "You're a smart aleck, ain't you, boy?"
And I said, "No, sir, I'm just hungry."
And he said, "Well, you're acting like a smart aleck."
And I said, "Well, that's how I act when I get hungry."

City jail, city jail
Like an old scared dog, I tucked my tail
I hung my head and not a careless word I said
I gotta sleep on the floor once more at the city jail

Well, he took me outside to a dark corner
And before I could say "hypocrite," he hit me on the head
And I said, "Don't hit me on the head.
I can't protect myself with these handcuffs on."
And he hit me again, and I said,
"Please don't stand on my feet when you hit me.
I'll break my ankles when I fall."

City jail, city jail
Like an old scared dog, I tucked my tail
I hung my head and not a careless word I said
I gotta sleep on the floor once more at the city jail

Well, about that time they threw me in the wagon
And that waitress walked out with a sailor
I said, "Hey, you! Not you, sailor. I'm talkin' to the purple people eater.
You, lady. Quote 'You're the cause of it all' unquote."
Then she said to the sailor, she said, "Get me away from that horrible man, Harry."
And as they hauled me away I said, "Everybody have a nice evening."

City jail, city jail
Like an old scared dog, I tucked my tail
I hung my head and not a careless word I said
I gotta sleep on the floor once more at the city jail
I gotta sleep on the floor once more at the city jail

COUNTRY TRASH

1972

I got a crib full of corn and a turning plow
But the ground's too wet for the hopper now
Got a cultivator and a doubletree
A leather line for the haw and gee

Let the thunder roll and the lightning flash
I'm doing all right for country trash

I'm saving up dimes for a rainy day
And I got about a dollar laid away
The wind's from the south and the fishing's good
Got a potbelly stove and a cord of wood

Mama turns the leftovers into hash
So I'm doing all right for country trash

I got a mackinaw and a hunting dog
A cap that I ordered from the catalog
A big tall tree that shades the yard
A big fat sow for the winter's lard

Let the thunder roll and the lightning flash
I'm doing all right for country trash

Well, there's not much new ground left to plow
And crops need fertilizing now
My hands don't earn me too much gold
For security when I grow old

But we'll all be equal when we're under the grass
And God's got a heaven for country trash
God's got a heaven for country trash
I'll be doing all right for country trash

I SEE MEN AS TREES WALKING

1972

Jesus came to the city of Bethsaida
And a blind man was brought to Him

And the blind man said to Jesus,
"If you'd only stop and touch me, if you'd
only stop and touch me,
If you'd only stop and touch me, I know I
could see.
If you'd only stop and touch me, if you'd
only stop and touch me,
If you'd only stop and touch me, I know I
could see."

So Jesus touched him
He put His hands on the blind man's eyes
and He said,
"Now open your eyes and tell me what you
see."
And I can almost see that man now
opening his eyes for the first time
Looking around and seeing the dim outline
of the people around him

He said,
"I see men as trees walking, I see men as
trees walking,
I see men as trees walking, I'm beginning
to see.
I see men as trees walking, I see men as
trees walking,
I see men as trees walking, I'm beginning
to see."

So Jesus touched him one more time
He laid His hands on his eyes and He said,
"Now open your eyes and look up
And tell me what you see."

And the man said,
"I can see all men clearly, I can see all men
clearly,
I can see all men clearly, I've begun to see.
I can see all men clearly, I can see all men
clearly,
I can see all men clearly, I've begun to see."

And if all that be true, I've just one more
thing to say
"Jesus, reach down and touch me.
Jesus, reach down and touch me.
Jesus, reach down and touch me.
I would like to see."

JACOB GREEN

1972

Jacob Green got busted for possession
Next morning, early, he appeared in court
But he was sent to jail to wait
To be tried at some later date
Next morning, early, there came a sad report

At the jail they took away his clothes to shame him
And to make sure Jacob Green had no pride left
They cut off all his hair
Today, they found him hanging there
Afraid to face the day, he killed himself

It happened yesterday, and if you turn your head away
Somewhere, in some dirty hole, the scene will be rerun
Not only Jacob Green, but many more you've never seen
It could be someone that you love gets done
Like Jacob Green got done
It could be someone that you love gets done
Like Jacob Green got done

Jacob's father hired a team of lawyers
Inspections and long inquiries were held
The sheriff then retired
And the papers said two guards were fired
They put a brand-new coat of paint on Jacob's cell

But like a tomb that looks so white and shiny
Inside you'll find corruption never seen
And somewhere out there tonight
In a dirty cell without a light
They'll be locking up another Jacob Green

It happened yesterday, and if you turn your head away
Somewhere, in some dirty hole, the scene will be rerun
Not only Jacob Green, but many more you've never seen
It could be someone that you love gets done
Like Jacob Green got done
It could be someone that you love gets done
Like Jacob Green got done

KENTUCKY STRAIGHT

1972

Up in Kentucky, they make a whiskey
They call a Kentucky straight whiskey
And up in Kentucky, I married a woman
That I bet she is a better woman
Than that whiskey is whiskey
I call her my Kentucky Straight

I've rambled 'round the countryside
I've drifted near and far
I've been off to seek my fortune
I've been following every star

I've rode the devil's highway
The hell-bound interstate
But now I'm back at happy shack
With my Kentucky Straight

And we rise up every morning with the chickens
And every minute we're alive we're livin'
She's a little bit old-fashioned, but her loving's up-to-date
And I'm happy here with my Kentucky Straight

I had looked for satisfaction in the arms of quite a few
And I've done everything that I was big enough to do
But everywhere I see her face from Maine to Golden Gate
And I knew that this is where it's at with my Kentucky Straight

And we rise up every morning with the chickens
And every minute we're alive we're livin'
I love her, so she knows that it was worth a while to wait
'Cause I'm happy here with my Kentucky Straight

LITTLE GREEN FOUNTAIN

with June Carter

1972

There's a little green fountain on a little green mountain
Don't you think we ought to stop and get a drink of water?
There's a little green fountain on a little green mountain
Don't you think we ought to stop and get a drink of water?

Oh, the water is cool and the water is blue
A drink for me and a drink for you
Yes, the water is cool and the water is blue
A drink for me and a drink for you

Oh, the water is cool and the water is deep
Take off our shoes and cool our feet
Yes, the water is cool and the water is deep
Take off our shoes and cool our feet

Come along with me to the pasture now
We'll watch the wind blow on the cows
Come along with me to the pasture now
We'll watch the wind blow on the cows

There's a little green fountain on a little green mountain
Don't you think we ought to stop and get a drink of water?
There's a little green fountain on a little green mountain
Don't you think we ought to stop and get a drink of water?

LITTLE MAGIC GLASSES

1972

I wish I had a pair of little magic glasses
That I could see the future just by looking through
Then I could know what road tomorrow's going to take me down
And I could see if I'll be walking down that road with you

I would keep my little magic glasses hidden
I would let nobody else see what I see
And everyone would want to know how I can know what lies ahead
And they'll wonder when I say tomorrow I see you with me

But if I see into the future that I'm on the road alone
And where the way was sunny, now there's only rain
I'll put them in a box and seal it with a lock
And I'll never take my little magic glasses out again

THE MIRACLE MAN

with Larry Lee Favorite

1972

I've had some hard times in years now gone by
I've had my heartaches, my cup has been dry
But I've never been kicked and publicly scorned
And I've never worn a crown of thorns

But I have somebody who did that for me
The miracle man of Galilee

I've got scars that show that the goin' was rough
And I can remember when I almost gave up
But I've not been rejected by my fellow man
And I've never had nails through my hands

But I have somebody who suffered for me
The miracle man of Galilee

I've had disappointments, they still come and go
They say man must suffer and it surely is so
I've had mountains to climb and I always will
But I don't have to climb Calvary's hill

But I have somebody who did that for me
The miracle man of Galilee

PAUL REVERE

with Douglas Glenn Tubb

1972

In April of 1775
This great nation started comin' alive
Ol' King George didn't like it one bit
So he proceeded to throw him a royal fit

He told his generals, "Better get 'em back in line.
Make 'em pay my taxes now, America is mine.
Stop that independence talk before it gets around
Or it's gonna be hard to hold them rebels down."

Well, the King was talking 'bout the men like Paul Revere
And the minutemen who held their dream of independence dear
They kept their eyes on the British, they watched 'em day and night
They knew very soon they'd get their chance to stand and fight

Yes, they knew that the British would be moving any hour
So they arranged a signal in the northern church tower
Paul was watching when the tower showed a light
And he started on his midnight ride

He jumped on his horse, hoofs started a-humming
He screamed out his warning, "Redcoats are coming.
Better get your guns and your fighting britches on.
They're coming and they're eight hundred strong."

Next morning, at Concord and Lexington town
The spirit of freedom turned the redcoats around
When we praise the men who made this mighty nation we have here
Then let's remember Paul Revere
Yes, let's remember Paul Revere

I guarantee you something, and I wanna tell you all
That we never would've been here if it hadn't been for Paul
Yes sir, I surely doubt us ever being here
If it hadn't been for that man on that horse named Mister Revere

POOR PEOPLE

1972

Poor people are friends of mine
The ones I really do care about
Poor people, the underdog
The down and out

But a poor girl can always dream
That things are not always the way they seem
And a poor man can make dreams come true
If he gets a little help from me and you

And there are many, many little children down
In the heartbreaking, hungry side of town
Come along with me and I'll show you some
That don't know where their supper is coming from

PRAISE THE LORD

1972

The people that walked in the darkness
Have seen a great light
They that dwell in the land of the shadow of death
Upon them had the light shine bright

For unto us, a child is born
Unto us, a son is given
And His name shall be called Wonderful
The prince of peace to show the way to heaven

TEAR-STAINED LETTER

1972

I'm gonna write a tear-stained letter
I'm gonna mail it straight to you
I'm gonna bring back to your mind
What you said about always being true

About our secret hiding places
Being daily satisfied
I can see you sitting and reading it
While you hang your head and cry
I just hope you're not so sad
You're gonna go down suicide

I'm gonna write a tear-stained letter
Put it special delivery
'Cause it's gonna be full of stuff
That's only known to you and me

About how every time I get turned on
You turn me off and bring me down
It'll be about the darkest news
That ever did arrive in your hometown
It'll be about the saddest thing
Your mailman ever did bring around

I'm gonna write a tear-stained letter
I'm gonna tell you one more time
That you still could reconsider
And come back to being mine

And if you think about what I'm saying
It'd be hard to refuse
Just be sure you think a long time
On the answer that you choose
It will be a most important piece
Of personal, private news

I'm gonna write a tear-stained letter
Mark it "Personal, Private News"
And I hope you'll keep it to yourself
And don't go 'round crying the blues

Giving off a bad impression
As to what went really wrong
When what it was, was that suddenly
The music was all gone
And this man and this woman got cut off
In the middle of our song

I'm gonna write a tear-stained letter
I'm gonna put it to a tune
So I'll be sending with it
A sweet melody for you

And not some red-hot, upbeat zinger
That'll set your body on fire
But a hunk of love included
Meant to take you a little higher
And to settle on your sweet, sweet mind
At night when you retire

I'm gonna write a tear-stained letter

THERE'S A BEAR IN THE WOODS

1972

Kevin Jones said, "There's a bear in the woods
And if you don't believe it
Just ask Wesley Orbison and Lance Johnson
'Cause they saw him, too."

I was driving my Jeep across the field
And when I came into the edge of the woods
I saw Kevin Jones
Coming down out of a tree
I stopped my Jeep
And Kevin jumped up on the running board
And that's when he said,
"There's a bear in the woods."

And I looked right at Kevin
And I said, "Now, Kevin, tell me the truth."
And he looked at me right in the eye
He said, "I'm not kidding you, Uncle John."
He said, "There's a bear in the woods
And if you don't believe it
Just ask Wesley Orbison and Lance Johnson
'Cause they saw him, too."

I kept on looking right at Kevin and I said,
"Now tell me the truth, Kevin."
He said, "It is, it's a bear, it's a black bear."
He said, "It's not a big bear, but it's a bear.
It's a black bear.
I've seen him going down the trail there."

I kept on looking at Kevin and I got to thinkin'
Now Kevin Jones said, "There's a bear in the woods."
Kevin was seven years old and I'm a lot older than he is
And I've done a lot of things that he hadn't done
And one of those things that I've done that he hadn't is to lie

So I got to thinking, if Kevin Jones says
There's a bear in the woods, who am I to doubt it
Well, I kind o' grinned at Kevin
And he jumped down off of the running board
And I started my Jeep back up
And headed down the road in the woods
As I went away
I hollered back at Kevin and I said,
"Hey, Kevin, watch out for that bear in the woods."

THESE ARE MY PEOPLE

1972

These are my people
This is the land where my forefathers lie
These are my people
In brotherhood, we're heirs of a creed to live by

A creed that proclaims
That by loved ones' bloodstains
This is my land
And these are my people

These are my people
They were born on and lived by the land
These are my people
And their cities were raised by hardworking hands

And their faces do tell
That they're holding on well
To this, their land
Yes, these are my people

These are my people
These are the ones who will reach for the stars
These are my people
By the light of the earth, you can tell they are ours

A new step to take and a new day will break
For this, my land
Yes, these are my people
These are my people

THE TIMBER MAN

1972

Well, my world is green and dark and damp
My home is in the logging camp
All week I cut down the mighty trees
Saturday I get to do as I please

I give the man more than his hire
And he'll never know it if I tire
Show me the toughest tree around
The timber man will bring it down

Swing it hard, cut it clean
No halfway or in-between
Move when the axe is in my hand
Make way for the timber man

Well, they say there's sawdust in my brain
And don't get caught out in the rain
I got stump water in my blood
The sweat from my brow turns the ground to mud

When the men don't know how to fell a tree
The one they'll come and ask is me
I'll mark my spot and I'll take my stand
The tree's going to fall for the timber man

Swing it hard, cut it clean
No halfway or in-between
Move when the axe is in my hand
Make way for the timber man

TOO LITTLE, TOO LATE

1972

So you're feeling numb about me being gone
So you see now, you're half alive when you're alone
Well, I just hope the pain will ease a little as you wait
You gave me love, but too little, too late

Dark days are coming now, you see
Hard times for you, as well as me
All-time low is coming under your front gate
You gave me love, but too little, too late

So you got plans about some fine affair
Well, think about it a little while, while you're lying there
Love long and hard and don't make your lover wait
You gave me love, but too little, too late

Dark days are coming now, you see
Hard times for you, as well as me
All-time low is coming under your front gate
You gave me love, but too little, too late
You gave me love, but too little, too late

THE VERY BIGGEST CIRCUS OF THEM ALL

1972

Well, I would like to tell you about the way the circus started
It's been ten thousand years, as I recall
That Noah built himself an ark for two of all the animals
In the very biggest circus of them all

Well, the rain began to falling and the water started rising
For forty days and nights the rain did fall
Noah called in all the animals, two by two they came running
For the very biggest circus of them all

There were elephants and kangaroos and lions, wolves and cows, pigs and goats
And two giraffes, nineteen feet tall
There were bears and buffaloes, birds, raccoons and caribous and cats
In the very biggest circus of them all

There were buffalo and two rhinos, gorillas, tigers, monkeys, lions, ponies
And two donkeys in a stall
There were hawks, blackbirds, redbirds, bluebirds, eagles, mockingbirds, and doves
In the very biggest circus of them all

Thanks again to Noah, we are going to the circus
Where there's fun for young and old and short and tall
We've got a lot of fine-looking people and a few of Noah's animals
From the very biggest circus of them all

WELCOME BACK, JESUS

1972

Lord, if you should be
Looking down at little me
I'd just liked to say
I'm trying to stay
Up on the right track

But Lord, the way gets hard
Temptations come
And I sure get tired
But I'm watching for you
Like you told me to
And welcome back

Welcome back, Jesus
Welcome back, Jesus
I'm watching for your light to shine
Like you said
It would shine when you come

Welcome back, Jesus
Welcome back, Jesus
I hope you will see
And recognize me
And then take me home

Welcome back, Jesus
Welcome back, Jesus
I'm watching for your light to shine
Like you said it would shine
When you come

Welcome back, Jesus
Welcome back, Jesus
I hope you will see
And recognize me
And then take me home
Welcome back, Jesus

WHY IS A FIRE ENGINE RED?

1972

When I was a little boy, my daddy said,
"Son, do you know why a fire engine's red?"
So I looked up at my daddy and said,
"No, sir, I don't know why a fire engine's red."
And he said, "Repeat after me, and I'll tell you why.
Here goes:

"'Cause a newspaper's read, too.
Two and two is four.
Four times three is twelve.
Twelve is the length of a ruler.
A ruler is Queen Mary.
Queen Mary is a ship.
A ship sails the ocean.
The ocean has fish.
The fish have fins.
The Finns fought the Russians.
The Russians are red.
A fire engine's always rushin' so it's red, too!"

FIVE

* AFFIRMATION *

1973–1979

FROM THE BEGINNING, there was a certain fatalism that pervaded Cash's work, whether it was lost love (in his songs, he lost a lot) or loneliness and isolation or simply the harsh realities of a disappointing harvest or devastating flood. But wallowing was not allowed. His characters' stoicism followed his own, imbued in him from birth. Carrie Cash was the ultimate stoic, a trait required of a frontier woman with seven kids and a hard-drinking, often-absent husband. Like his mother, the son accepted that life was preordained and that troubles were inevitable. As he coped with his own personal trials and turmoil, Cash felt powerless to change his trajectory, resigning himself to what he saw as God's will: that such was his lot.

But his ascent had not only been noticed by culture warriors, award givers, and record buyers. There were also representatives of a higher plane. The Reverend Billy Graham himself—"God's ambassador"—was enthralled by the rise of the Arkansas farm boy. It was Dr. Graham who brought Cash to the attention of President Nixon, invited him to the National Prayer Breakfast, and appeared with him at the Campus Crusade for Christ's historic evangelistic event, Explo '72, the seminal moment in the birth of the "Jesus movement" in the United States and the contemporary Christian music genre. He encouraged Cash in the writing of his novel about Saint Paul, *Man in White,* and the two maintained a close friendship all their lives. Cash would eventually appear on thirty Graham crusades across the US and around the world. While his marriage to June Carter was the culmination of one of the great love stories of the time, Cash's brotherhood with the gentleman from North Carolina was utterly transformative. Graham gave his friend "non-judgmental acceptance and affirmation," which in turn inspired Cash toward a broader, more optimistic view of religion in his life. The epic Johnny Cash narrative would not have been written without the presence and influence of Billy Graham.

Cash's "secular" career took a downturn in the years following the end of his TV show in 1971. Revolutions in country music, including the Outlaw Movement, passed him by. His last number one record was in 1976. No doubt, suggestions that he was a spent force commercially stung badly, especially when they were accompanied by whispers that his Christianity had rendered him an irrelevancy. The record does not actually bear this out, but in any event, Cash was all in, come hell or high water, as it were. He tripled down, recording three gospel albums during the 1970s: *The Gospel Road,* the soundtrack to the theatrical film on the life of Jesus that he wrote and self-financed in 1973; *Johnny Cash Sings Precious Memories,* an album of traditional hymns in 1975; and *A Believer Sings the Truth* in 1979, which he called "my proudest work." And some of his most uplifting compositions came out of this period, such as "When He Comes," "Wings in the Morning," "You'll Get Yours and I'll Get Mine," and the classic "Over the Next Hill (We'll Be Home)."

> I've got songs in my head again, and I sure hope I can get it together to write them... Actually, when I'm busiest, when I've got a stack of things on my mind, the songs come.
>
> I hope someday, someone will look into the songs I've written in the last ten years. My very best ones are my most recent ones — no matter what the record sales say.
>
> I did a lot of things in the last few years that turned a lot of my country fans off. But I expected it. (1) I wrote a book [the 1974 autobiography *Man in Black*] (and I'm writing another one). (2) We made a movie [*Gospel Road*]. (3) I made public professions of faith in God thru Jesus Christ. Boy, that really turned a lot of people off, which thrills me to death. (You aren't a good Christian unless you suffer.)
>
> October 12, 1978

The irony is, even as Cash struggled on the charts, the ground was being paved for even greater climbs, which would elevate him past mere "singing star" status. In 1974, he wrote and recorded "Ragged Old Flag," which became a cultural landmark spanning generations. Two years later, he received a Doctor of Humane Letters degree from the National University in California and was also named the grand marshal of the United States Bicentennial parade. In 1977, he was awarded a degree in theology from the Christian International University, becoming an ordained minister, and was invited to recite "Ragged Old Flag" at the United States Capitol in honor of Flag Day. Also in 1977, Cash was elected to the Nashville Songwriters Hall of Fame, an honor he said was for "what I always wanted to do." Later, he would be posthumously inducted into the Gospel Music Hall of Fame, which surely would have been his proudest moment.

THE BALLAD OF BARBARA

1973

In a Southern town where I was born
That's where I got my education
I worked in the fields and I walked in the woods
And I wondered at creation

I recall the sun in a sky of blue
And the smell of green things growin'
And I lived every day and I lived any way
Any way the wind was blowin'

Then I heard of a cultured city life
Breathtaking lofty steeples
And the day I called myself a man
I left my land and my people

And I rambled north and I rambled east
And I tested and I tasted
And a girl or two took me 'round and 'round
But always left me wasted

In a world that's all concrete and steel
With nothin' green ever growin'
Where the buildings hide the risin' sun
And they block the free winds from blowin'

Where they sleep all day and they wake all night
To a world of drink and laughter
I met that girl that I thought would be
The one that I was after

In a soft blue gown and a formal tux
Beneath that lofty steeple
He said, "Do you, Barbara, take this man?
Will you be one of his people?"

And she said, "I will," and she said, "I do."
And the world looked mighty pretty
And we lived in a fancy downtown flat
'Cause she loved the noisy city

But the days grew cold beneath a yellow sky
And I longed for green things growin'
And the thoughts of home and the people there
But she'd not agreed to goin'

Then her hazel eyes turned away from me
With a look that wasn't pretty
And she turned into concrete and steel
And she said, "I'll take the city."

Now the cars go by on the interstate
And my pack is on my shoulder
And I'm goin' home, where I belong
Much wiser now and older

DINOSAUR SONG

with John Carter Cash

1973

Dinosaurs lived a long time ago
They were terrible lizards, don't you know
Some ate plants and some ate meat
Some ate fish and some ate beets

One was called a Diplodocus
One was bigger than your school bus
One was called a Triceratops
Three horns to stop anything that hops

Now, can't you just see yourself walking along
Leading your pet Trachodon
Or feeding your Brontosaurus Rex
Or scratching your Diplodocus' neck

Or riding on a Stegosaurus' back
Or swimming in a Brachiosaurus' track
Oh what a time and oh what fun
Playing tag with your Iguanodon

And if we had dinosaurs now
Could they get along with a horse and a cow?
Well, I wish they hadn't become extinct
Dinosaurs would be nice pets and friends
To have around to run outside
And play with every day, don't you think?

THE HOUSE IS FALLING DOWN

1973

Man had need of shelter from the evil, from the night
The devil wind was blowing, and from heaven came a light
The Son of God, a carpenter, and He came with a plan
To build a house where heaven could be offered unto man

When He came here, He laid down a mighty firm foundation
And the columns and the beams were churches, scattered through the nation
And then rooms were added to it, on that same old solid rock
And roofs were raised by willing hands, from the bottom to the top

Then the people came and filled the house, with singing prayer and praise
Some turned and rejected, His house fell on leaner days
Oh Son of God, oh carpenter, will you come back around?
The blocks and beams are crumbling and the house is falling down

Now the storm is raging and the devil's angry roar
Is screaming at the windows and howling at the door
And though the faithful few inside are standing true and strong
The house has been neglected and it won't be standing long

When He came here, He laid down a mighty firm foundation
And the columns and the beams were churches, scattered through the nation
And then rooms were added to it, on the same old solid rock
And roofs were raised by willing hands, from the bottom to the top

Then the people came and filled the house, with singing, prayer, and praise
Some turned and rejected, His house fell on leaner days
Son of God, oh carpenter, will you come back around?
Our blocks and beams are crumbling and the house is falling down
Son of God, oh carpenter, will you come back around?
The blocks and beams are crumbling and the house is falling down

THE HOUSE ON THE HILL

1973

At the house on the hill
With the roses blooming still
The same old wind is blowing in the trees
In the trees growing now
In the field they used to plow
You could still plow up a lot of memories

In the hall that runs
Right through the house
A hundred years ago
Upon a Sunday afternoon
Sarah Goodin married Joe
And if you make believe
You'll see her leaning out the windowsill
Waving to him in the house on the hill

It was on a summer morn
That their baby boy was born
And a home more happy
There could never be
More children came along
And the house was full of song
Then the country called
And Edward went to sea

The children grew up
One by one
And Sarah's hair turned gray
No longer were they singing now
Since Edward went away
The house has long been empty
But they say that Sarah's still
Watching for him on the house on the hill

~~The room was ...~~
It was on a summer morn
That their baby boy was born
~~Then the country called and Joe went out to sea~~
And a home so happy there could never be
More children came along
And the house was full of song
Then the country called and ~~Joe~~ Edward went ~~out~~ to sea

The children ~~left her~~ grew up
One by one
And Sarah's hair turned gray
No longer were they singing now
~~For Joe had gone away~~ since Edward went away
The house has long been empty
but they say that Sarah's still
Watching for him in the house on the hill

The House on the Hill

At the house on the hill
With the roses blooming still
The same old wind is blowing in the trees
In the trees growing now
In the field they used to plow
You could still plow up a lot of memories

In the hall that runs
Right through the house
A ~~Hundred~~ hundred years ago
Upon a Sunday afternoon
Sarah Gladin married Joe
And if you make believe
You'll see her leaning out the window sill
~~Watching~~ for him in the house on the hill
Waiting

I HEARD ON THE NEWS

1973

I heard on the news
That there is a lull in the fighting
In Vietnam
Because so many Vietnamese
Are busy planting
A rice crop again

The report said
That full-scale fighting
Is expected to resume
Immediately after the planting season

I reply: What kind of animal is man
That he would pause
In his killing
To go about the business
Of preparing for the living
Knowing that he will immediately
  return
To the business of killing?

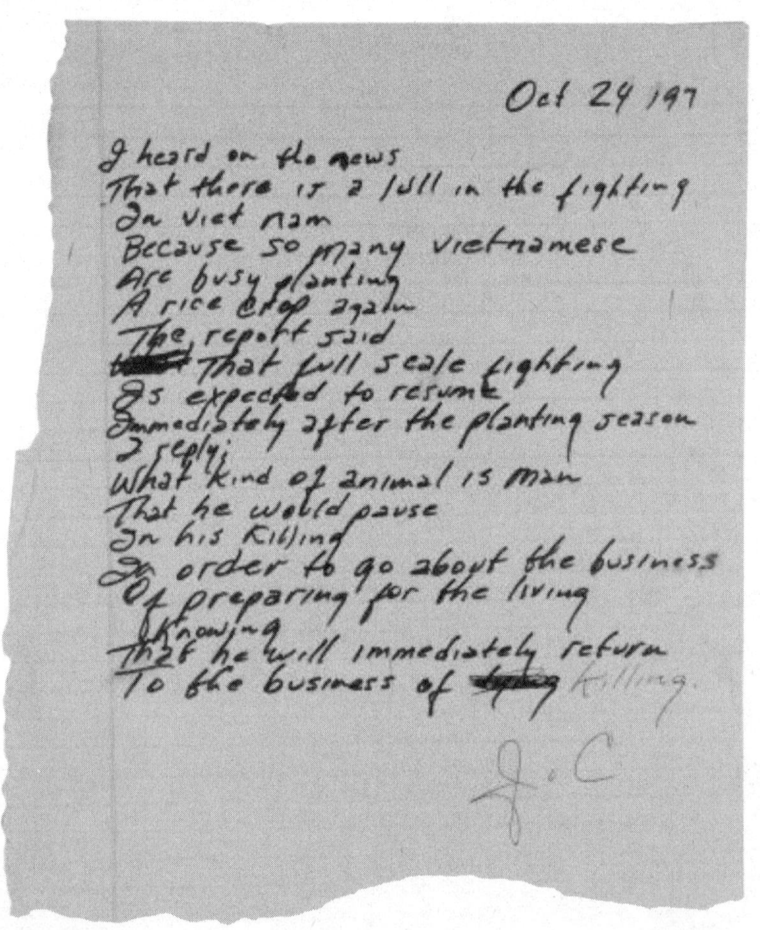

Oct 24 197

I heard on the news
That there is a lull in the fighting
In viet nam
Because so many vietnamese
Are busy planting
A rice crop again
The report said
~~The~~ That full scale fighting
Is expected to resume
Immediately after the planting season
I reply;
What kind of animal is man
That he would pause
In his killing
In order to go about the business
Of preparing for the living
Knowing
That he will immediately return
To the business of ~~dying~~ killing.

J.C

I WISH I COULD YODEL

1973

I wish that I could yodel
Like I heard some singers do
I wish I could go
Yo-del-eedle-o, yo-del-ee-dle-la-dy hoo

Well, the singer that come
The closest to impressing me
Is the one who can go
Yo-del-ee-dle-o dee-a, dle-ee-dle a-dy hoo hee

I've listened to those voices' echoes go
A-dle a-dle a-dle a-ay
I've stood in silent wonder
That they can do their throat that way

And when they hold that high note
Forty-seven seconds through
My fever starts to rising
With that whoo

Well, I never should have let
That doctor take my tonsils out
That's probably just what
Made my voice not much to shout about

There are those who like a song well sung
And expect no more from me
But I wish that I could yodel with a
Yo-del-ee-dle-a dy-o-dle-ee-dle-a-dy-hee
I-lee-o lay-dee-hoo hoo hoo hoo hee-o
Yo-del-ee-dle-a-dle-ee-o
A-ee-o-dle-a-dle-ee hey hey hey hey
O-dle-ee-dle ay-ee hoo hoo
Yo-del-ee-dle a-yee-o-dle-ay hoo
Yo-del-ee-dle a-dy yo-dle-ee-dle-a-dy hoo
hoo hoo hoo

MATTHEW 24 (IS KNOCKING AT THE DOOR)

1973

I heard on the radio
There's rumors of war
People getting ready for battle
And there may be just one more

I heard about an earthquake
And the toll it took away
These are the signs of the times
We're in today

Matthew 24 is knocking at the door
And there can't be too much more to come to pass
Matthew 24 is knocking at the door
And today or one day more could be the last

The great bear from the Northland
Has risen from his sleep
And the Army ranks in red
Are near two hundred million deep

The young and old now prophesy
A coming prince of peace
And last night I dreamed
Of lightning in the east

Matthew 24 is knocking at the door
And there can't be too much more to come to pass
Matthew 24 is knocking at the door
And today or one day more could be the last

SATURDAY NIGHT IN HICKMAN COUNTY

1973

When the sun goes down in Nashville
Go out that Memphis highway
Between Centerville and Dickson
On the gravel roads and byways

They'll be running off the shine
That will be bringing in the bounty
Saturday night in Hickman County

At the beer joint on the blacktop
Country music's playing steady
And the working men are drinking
And they're rough and they are ready

And the girl behind the counter
Who has all the boys a-buzzin'
Will be leaving with her husband
Saturday night in Hickman County

Down upon the Piney River
Parked beside the pretty water
In the back seat of a Chevy
Is your next-door neighbor's daughter

They have split up into pairs
The four that went off dating double
Getting that poor girl into trouble
Saturday night in Hickman County

All the farmers in the valley
Will be sitting by the fire
Watch the late news on the TV
Then they'll quietly retire

Thankful just to be a-living
Thankful that tomorrow's Sunday
Sorry that the next day's Monday
Saturday night in Hickman County
Saturday night in Hickman County

SPOTLIGHT

1973

Spotlight, don't let it show
That my heart went with her
When I let her go
Don't let anybody see
Deep within the soul of me
Or they'll see that something there
Is not quite right
Tonight, spotlight

Spotlight, that's way too much
Let there be upon the air a tender touch
Let your magic velvet hue
Bathe me in a gentle blue
Softly, so there's not a single tear in sight
Tonight, spotlight

Spotlight, the tears are gone
Blind me 'til I'm standing here alone
Don't let me recall again
Anything that might have been
Let me feel that losing her will be all right
Tonight, spotlight
Tonight, spotlight

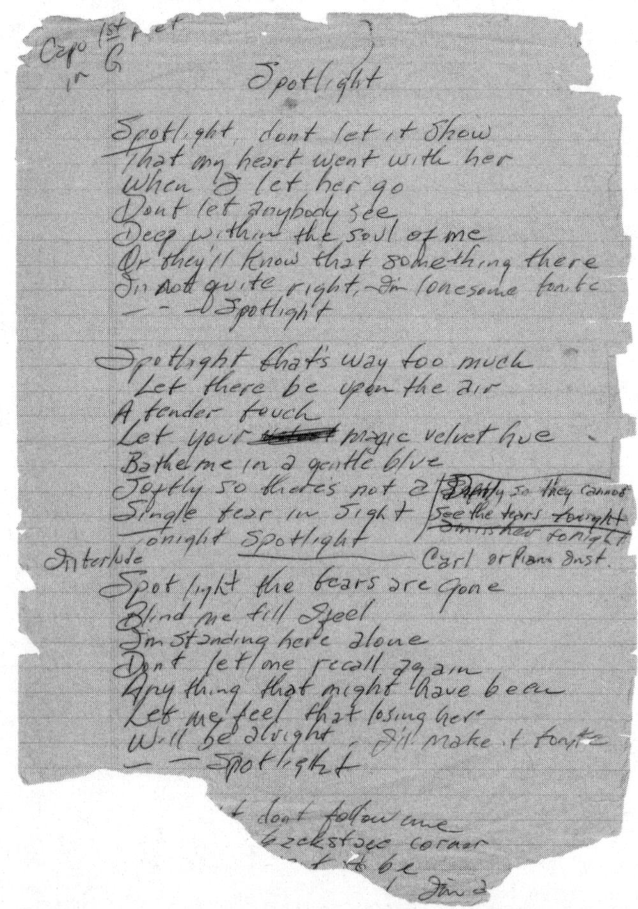
Capo 1st fret
in G

Spotlight

Spotlight, dont let it show
That my heart went with her
When I let her go
Dont let anybody see
Deep within the soul of me
Or they'll know that something there
Is not quite right, I'm lonesome tonite
– – Spotlight

Spotlight that's way too much
Let there be upon the air
A tender touch
Let your magic velvet hue
Bathe me in a gentle blue
Softly so there's not a
Single tear in sight
Tonight Spotlight

Softly so they cannot
See the tears tonight
Carl or Piano Inst.

Interlude
Spotlight the tears are gone
Blind me till I feel
I'm standing here alone
Dont let me recall again
Any thing that might have been
Let me feel that losing her
Will be alright, I'll make it tonite
– – Spotlight

dont follow me
backstage corner
to be

TIGER WHITEHEAD

with Nat Winston

1973

Wild blackberries blooming in the thickets on the mountain
Sheepshire and watercress are growing 'round the fountain
Where a big black bear is drinking, lapping water like a dog
Tiger Whitehead's in the bed, sleeping like a log

Tomorrow he'll see bear tracks seven inches wide
And by sundown he'll be bringing in the hide

Pretty Sally Garland's coming down the mountainside
Where Tiger Whitehead's grinding at the mill
She sits down on a bearskin and she says, "You'll be my man.
I'll have me the best bear hunter in these hills."

A wild child was Tiger Whitehead and they say he killed
Ninety-nine bears before he went to rest, went to rest
Once he left two bear cubs orphaned but he brought 'em right on home
And Sally nursed the two bear cubs upon her breast

Tiger now is eighty-five and he laid upon his bed
And the bears he killed now numbered ninety-nine, ninety-nine
Some fellers trapped a bear, but Tiger said just let him go
If he ain't running wild, he won't be mine

But at night, when the wind howls 'cross the eastern hills of Tennessee
And when the lightning flashes, there's a strange thing that the people say they see
An old gray-headed ghost, running through the mountains there
It's Tiger Whitehead after his one-hundredth bear

Wild blackberries blooming in the thickets on the mountain
Sheepshire and watercress are growing 'round the fountain
Where a big black bear is drinking, lapping water like a dog
Tiger Whitehead's in the bed, sleeping like a log

Tomorrow he'll see bear tracks seven inches wide
And by sundown he'll be bringing in the hide

ALL I DO IS DRIVE

1974

Well, I asked an old truck driver
About life out on the road
If he does a lotta singing
When he's bringing in his load

If there's a pretty waitress crying for him
Every hundred miles
If he gets a lotta loving
If he has a lot of smiles

And I asked him if those trucking songs
Tell about a life like his
He said, "If you want to know the truth
about it
Here's the way it is:

"All I do is drive, drive, drive
Try to stay alive
And keep my mind on my load,
Keep my eye upon the road.

"I got nothin' in common with any man
Who's home every day at five.
All I do is drive, drive, drive, drive, drive,
drive, drive."

Well, we shared a cup of coffee
Then I had to warm it up
And his greasy fingers trembled
As he held on to the cup

And I said, "Don't you hear a lot of music?
See a lot of sights?
But if you'll tune in to the Grand Ole Opry
Saturday night

"I will dedicate you a trucking song
To which you can relate."
He said, "You just do the singing
And I'll do the driving, mate.

"All I do is drive, drive, drive
Try to stay alive
And keep my mind on my load,
Keep my eye upon the road.

"I got nothin' in common with any man
Who's home every day at five.
All I do is drive, drive, drive, drive, drive,
drive, drive
If I can get the fuel."

BILLY AND REX AND ORAL AND BOB

1974

Ordained for proclaiming the Gospel of Jesus
The great super preachers go crusading on
And the people all gather in big congregations
They hear of the Savior who came to atone

And they kneel at the altar and they walk away happy
Then the devil starts gossip about money and sex
Making it hard on the good men of God
Like Billy and Bob and Oral and Rex

Old Billy Sunday is dead and gone
Young Jim Robison's coming on strong
And Billy and Rex and Oral and Bob
Are talking about Jesus and doing their job

Millions of people tune in Kathryn Kuhlman
And see her face shine with an unearthly light
Garner Ted warns of the world of tomorrow
But they criticized him and the reverend died

'Cause the devil is after the great super preachers
He'd try to discredit the Gospel they bring
But Billy and Rex and Oral and Bob
Hold to their commitment to Jesus the King

Old Billy Sunday is dead and gone
Young Tommy Barnett is coming on strong
And Billy and Rex and Oral and Bob
Are talking about Jesus and doing their job

Old Billy Sunday is dead and gone
Young Jimmie Snow is coming on strong
And Billy and Rex and Oral and Bob
Are talking about Jesus and doing their job

CARELESS LOVE IN A-MINOR

1974

Singing "Careless Love in A-Minor"
'Cause my gal has left Carolina
A man from Panama done took my Dinah
And I'm singing "Careless Love in A-Minor"

One day her ship will return
'Cause Dinah is so easy to sunburn
That ship will be bringing back my Carolina dove
Singing love, oh love, oh careless love

Bring back my Carolina love to me
Bring up my song from a low-down minor key
To the straight on, right on major key of C
No more "Careless Love in A-Minor"

She'll be coming back to Carolina
No man from Panama is gonna keep my Dinah
There'll be no more "Careless Love in A-Minor"

Soon now her ship will return
And I'll rub baby oil on her sunburn
Gonna do some cooin' with my Carolina dove
And makin' love, oh love, oh careless love

Bring back that careless love to me
Bring up my song from a lonesome minor key
To the straight on, right on major key of C
Take that A-minor back to Panama
Throw it in the canal
Can't have my Dinah...

DAUGHTER OF A RAILROAD MAN

1974

Leaving in a cloud of burning cinders
Cinders from a fire of love gone out
Never looking back when she's highballing
She's the daughter of a railroad man, no doubt

Waking in a new bed every morning
Breaking in a new heart every night
Up and running while the world is sleeping
She's the daughter of a railroad man, all right

She is long and sleek and made for moving
She's outward-bound at any time she can
She won't be staying long in any station
She's the daughter of a railroad man

Cries out in the night when she gets lonely
You can bet she won't be lonely long
On down the line, someone waits her arrival
And the daughter of a railroad man is gone

She is long and sleek and made for moving
She's outward-bound at any time she can
She won't be staying long in any station
She's the daughter of a railroad man

DON'T GO NEAR THE WATER

1974

From the fountains in the mountains
Comes the water running cool and clear
and blue
And it comes down from the hills
And it goes down to the towns and passes
through

When it gets down to the cities
Then the water turns into a dirty gray
'Cause it's poisoned and polluted
By the people as it goes along its way

Don't go near the water, children
See the fish all dead upon the shore
Don't go near the water
'Cause the water isn't water anymore

I took my boy fishin' to my old favorite
fishin' hole
I had caught many a fish out of that deep
clear water
From the time I was a boy like him
After we'd fished a few minutes
He said, "Did you get a bite yet, Daddy?"
I said, "I think I got a nibble, son."
"Me, too," he said
Then he said, "Daddy, if we catch a fish can
we eat him?"
I said, "Well, there was a time, son.
This water's bad now and it might not be
safe to eat the fish
But there was a time."

Don't go near the water, children
See the fish all dead upon the shore
Don't go near the water
'Cause the water isn't water anymore

There was a time the air was clean
And you could see forever 'cross the plains
The wind was sweet as honey
And no one had ever heard of acid rain

We're torturing the earth
And pouring every kind of evil in the sea
We violated nature
And our children have to pay the penalty

Don't go near the water, children
See the fish all dead upon the shore
Don't go near the water
'Cause the water isn't water anymore

GOOD MORNING, FRIEND

1974

He's not on some golden throne
Way off in outer space
He's not hiding out
In some big secret hiding place

I can guarantee
He'll be your friend to touch and hold
And I'm qualified to tell it
'Cause I've got it in control

Good morning, friend
Good morning, friend
Every day's a brand-new morning
Since the morning you moved in

Good morning, friend
Good morning, friend
Yes, I'm feeling like a million
Since I've got you living in

He'll stand and knock upon your door
'Til you let Him inside
He'll be a constant comforter
And keep you satisfied

He will make himself available
No matter who you are
He'll light your darkest night
And be your bright and morning star

Good morning, friend
Good morning, friend
Yes, I'm feeling like a million
Since the morning you moved in

Good morning, friend
Good morning, friend
Ask me how I feel this morning
And I'm proud to say again

Good morning, friend
Good morning, friend
Yes, I'm feeling like a million
Since I've got you living in

I DO BELIEVE

1974

I do believe that I won't make it through the night
If you don't come on back to me and love me now
There ain't no way that I can say that it's all right
I do believe that you're not thinking anyhow

But I believe if you'll remember how it was a little while
If you'll recall that what we had was hard to beat
And I believe that if you'll meet me halfway down that second mile
We will trade in all the bitter for the sweet

I do believe that you're not happy without me
I think you feel the way I'm feeling without you
Come on and give in to that feeling one more time
I do believe you won't regret it if you do

But I believe if you'll remember how it was a little while
If you'll recall that what we had was hard to beat
And I believe that if you'll meet me halfway down that second mile
We will trade in all the bitter for the sweet

I do believe that you're not happy without me
I think you feel the way I'm feeling without you
Come on and give in to that feeling one more time
I do believe you won't regret it if you do

I TUNED IN TO CHANCELLOR

1974

I tuned in to Chancellor
Reasoner and Cronkite
Brinkley, Mudd, and Rather
And I didn't sleep all night

A brand-new war was raging
With a new one coming up
When I tuned in today, this morning
I dropped my coffee cup

Two hundred years of government
Was shaking in its boots
I headed for the country
Trying to go back to my roots

Rest in peace, Walt Disney
Thank God for Mickey Mouse
Porky Pig and Pluto
Are heroes in my house

With Superman and Captain Marvel
Standing strong and tall
Shout out shazam and thank you, man
We'll overcome it all

They talk about inflation
And about the interest rate
When things could get no worse
They opened up the Watergate

Henry went to Israel
Henry crossed the Nile
And it appeared that there'd be
No more bombing for a while

But everybody's got the bomb
Excepting maybe Greece
The time is coming soon it seems
We all will rest in peace

I'M A WORRIED MAN

with June Carter

1974

Worried man, worried man
I'm a very worried man
Hungry babies don't understand
Papa is a worried man

The place I use to draw my pay
Slammed the door on me today
Told me just to stay away
And don't come back again

I went back home to break the news
My woman saw that I had the blues
"But," she said, "the babies need new shoes."
And I'm a worried man

Worried man, worried man
I'm a very worried man
Hungry babies don't understand
Papa is a worried man

There is no way that I can see
That I can feed my family
'Cause I don't own a money tree
And very little land

But I said, "Mama, don't you cry.
I'll get a job before the day's gone by."
I don't know where, and that is why
I'm a very worried man

Worried man, worried man
I'm a very worried man
Hungry babies don't understand
Papa is a worried man

KING OF THE HILL

1974

If you gonna be king of the hill
You can't make it at the cotton mill
Get put on at the Harlan mine
Be the last one out at quitting time

You're already working when the whistle blew
Never complain about a job to do
When they say, "Who can?" you say, "I will."
If you ever gonna be king of the hill

If you gonna be king of the hill
You can't make it at the cotton mill

You need a good woman to share your bed
To keep you loved and to keep you fed
To help you to face another day
To get you up and on your way

Where the Golden Rule don't rule out true
You do to them before they do to you
Watch out for yourself or nobody will
If you ever gonna be king of the hill

If you gonna be king of the hill
You can't make it at the cotton mill

Saturday night, you go to Harlan town
You shoot some pool and you fool around
You watch the girls and you drink bootleg
Get starved to death before you beg

You trust in luck 'til your luck is gone
Then jump right in and you hang right on
There may be times you would have to kill
If you ever gonna be king of the hill

If you gonna be king of the hill
You can't make it at the cotton mill

When the last of the coals out of every vein
Had long been gone on the northbound train
Walk up to the top and if you're standing still
You can call yourself king of the hill

But if you fall like a lot have done
By accident or knife or gun
When they lay you high on the mountain still
You can call yourself king of the hill

If you gonna be king of the hill
You can't make it at the cotton mill

A LOT MORE TIME

1974

She'll change they say, she will change
Give her time and she'll change her ways
But her plans are laid you see and are not including me
And the trouble is she's changing every day

And it seems like more time goes by the more I realize
That it's gonna take a lot more time and I won't be surprised
If it don't take a lot more time than I ever thought it would
A lot more time to get over her like I know I should

One time, two times, and three times
The way she does my heart is a crime
But what else can I say, I just let her go her way
But I'd take her back whenever she's a-mind

But it seems like more time goes by the more I realize
That it's gonna take a lot more time and I won't be surprised
If it don't take a lot more time than I thought it would
A lot more time to get over her like I know I should

(When I Get Rich[illegible] made)

E

A

like more time goes by

E

The more I realize

A

It's gonna take a lot more time

F#

B7

And I wouldn't be surprised

E

A

If it didn't take a lot more time

Than I ever thought it would

A

E

A lot more time to get over her

B7

Like I know I should

She'll change they say she will change
Give her time and she'll change her way
~~And [illegible]~~
But her plans are laid you see
And they're not including me
And the trouble is shes changing every day

One time two time and three times
The way she breaks my heart is a crime
What else can I say
I let her go away
But I'll take her back
Whenever shes a mind

LONESOME TO THE BONE

1974

On the park bench I slept on
Raindrops are falling on the newspapers covering me
I hear early morning motors
And I know the world is waking for the dawn

But my mind's down a dark alley
Somewhere, where last night you loved me
And in the early morning chill
My arms remember still

But I'm dropping like a stone
Lonesome to the bone

The sun is roughly rising on the roofs of Stagger town
The time for sweating poison out
Is just now coming 'round
The high time of last midnight is over with and gone

Leaving me to be
Lonesome to the bone

I walk the way the wind blows
And any way the wind goes
Will be good enough for me
The streets are loud and crowded

But I walk my weary way, lost and alone
Your hot breath and your laughter
Keep flashing through my mind to warm me
But the naked light of day soon makes it fade away

And I'm dropping like a stone
Lonesome to the bone

NO EARTHLY GOOD

1974

Come hear me, good brothers, come hear, one and all
Don't you brag about standing or you'll surely fall
You're shining your light and shine it, you should
But you're so heavenly minded, you're no earthly good

No earthly good, you are no earthly good
You're so heavenly minded, you're no earthly good
You're shining your light and shine it, you should
But you're so heavenly minded, you're no earthly good

Come hear me, good sisters, you're salt of the earth
But if your salt isn't salted, then what is its worth
You could give someone a cool drink, if you would
But you're so heavenly minded, you're no earthly good

If you're holding heaven, then spread it around
There are hungry hands reaching up here from the ground
You could help them stand on their feet, if you would
But you're so heavenly minded, you're no earthly good

No earthly good, you are no earthly good
You're so heavenly minded, you're no earthly good
Move over and share the high ground where you stood
So heavenly minded, you're no earthly good

The Gospel ain't Gospel until it is spread
But how can you share it, where you've got your head
There's hands that reach out for a hand, if you would
So heavenly minded, you're no earthly good

No earthly good, you are no earthly good
You're so heavenly minded, you're no earthly good
There's hands that reach out for a hand, if you would
So heavenly minded, you're no earthly good

No earthly good, you are no earthly good
You're so heavenly minded, you're no earthly good
You're shining your light and shine it, you should
But you're so heavenly minded, you're no earthly good

OVER THE NEXT HILL (WE'LL BE HOME)

1974

By the way the land is laying
I think I'd be safe in saying
That over the next hill, we'll be home

It's a straight and narrow highway
No detours and no byways
And over the next hill, we'll be home

By the prophets I've been hearing
I would say the end is nearing
For I see familiar landmarks all along

By the dreams that I've been dreaming
There will come a great redeeming
And over the next hill, we'll be home

By the turn the tide is taking
I would say there's no mistaking
That over the next hill, we'll be home

There's a place that we are nearing
That so many have been fearing
And over the next hill, we'll be home

When we get there, we're all hoping
That we'll find the gate is open
And there'll be a refuge from the coming
storm

For the way's been long and weary
But at last the end is nearing
And over the next hill, we'll be home

PIE IN THE SKY

1974

From the day of your birth
It's bread and water here on earth
To a child of life
To a child of life

But there'll be pie in the sky
By and by, when I die
And it'll be all right
It'll be all right

There'll be pie in the sky
By and by, when I die
And it'll be all right
It'll be all right

Sometimes I doubt and fear
That I've really gained salvation here
For it's out of sight
For it's out of sight

But there'll be pie in the sky
By and by, when I die
And it'll be all right
It'll be all right

He said, "If I do His will
There's a promise He'd fulfill
And He's gone now to prepare
Me a mansion up there."

And there'll be pie in the sky
By and by, when I die
And it'll be all right
It'll be all right

PLEASE DON'T LET ME OUT

1974

I've been in jail eleven years
And parole has just come through
The gates will soon swing open wide
But I'm not going through

Jail's the only home I know
Or care to know about
Please let me stay where I belong
Please don't let me out

How could I tell those friends of mine
They've seen the last of me?
Can't I make you understand
I never can be free?

'Cause that's a big, unfriendly world
And I don't know the route
That leads to where I may belong
Please don't let me out

I had to learn to get along
Without a lot of things
And I had to learn to live with
The loneliness confinement brings

And I learned to take "No mail from home"
Or whatever came about
Now I'm dug in and I'm happy here
Please don't let me out

How could I tell those friends of mine
They've seen the last of me?
Can't I make you understand
I never can be free?

'Cause that's a big, unfriendly world
And I don't know the route
That leads to where I may belong
Please don't let me out

RAGGED OLD FLAG

1974

I walked through a county courthouse square
On a park bench an old man was sitting there
I said, "Your old courthouse is kinda run-down."
He said, "Naw, it'll do for our little town."

I said, "Your old flagpole has leaned a little bit
And that's a ragged old flag you got hanging
on it."
He said, "Have a seat," and I sat down
"Is this the first time you've been to our little
town?"

I said, "I think it is."
He said, "I don't like to brag
But we're kinda proud of that ragged old flag.

"You see, we got a little hole in that flag there
When Washington took it across the Delaware
And it got powder-burned the night Francis
Scott Key
Sat watching it, writing, 'Say, can you see.'

"And it got a bad rip in New Orleans
With Pakenham and Jackson tugging at its
seams
And it almost fell at the Alamo
Beside the Texas flag, but she waved on though.

"She got cut with a sword at Chancellorsville
And she got cut again at Shiloh Hill.
There was Robert E. Lee, Beauregard, and
Bragg
And the south wind blew hard on that ragged
old flag.

"On Flanders Field in World War I
She got a big hole from a Bertha gun.
She turned bloodred in World War II.
She hung limp and low a time or two.

"She was in Korea and Vietnam.
She went where she was sent by her Uncle Sam.
She waved from our ships upon the briny foam
And now they've about quit waving her back
here at home.

"In her own good land here, she's been abused.
She's been burned, dishonored, denied, and
refused
And the government for which she stands
Is scandalized throughout the land.

"And she's getting threadbare and wearing kinda
thin
But she's in good shape for the shape she's in
'Cause she's been through the fire before
And I believe she can take a whole lot more.

"So we raise her up every morning.
We take her down every night.
We don't let her touch the ground
And we fold her up right.

"On second thought, I do like to brag
'Cause I'm mighty proud of that ragged old
flag."

RESURRECTED

1974

When my Lord was hanging on a rugged tree
He looked with love on humanity
His mother looked up and beheld her son
He said, "It is finished," and it was done

As they took Him down from the rugged tree
A man named Joe said, "Give Him to me.
I'm from Arimathea, but close hereby
I have a tomb where I will let Him lie."

So they laid Him down and the women cried,
"Our Lord is dead, we saw Him die."
Peter was hiding, but he said, too,
"The master died, like He said He'd do."

I really don't know what Pilate said
But the Pharisees said, "Good! He's dead.
Crucified and dead and done.
He called Himself the father's son."

Wrapped in linen — laid in a tomb
Sealed with a stone night and noon
"Dead at last," His enemies say
"The troublemaker is laid away."

A strange thing happened on Saturday night
Or on a Sunday morning, before daylight
The grave started shakin' and the Word does say
An angel rolled the stone away

And the gravestone rolled against a tree
And the stone said, "Back alive is He."
And the tree to the birds, sittin' on its limbs
Said, "The one who came from the tomb is Him."

And the birds sang to the sky of blue
"He resurrected, like He said He'd do."
And the father spoke from the open sky,
"My son is alive, though you saw Him die."

RIDIN' THE RAILS

1974

Ridin' the rails, ridin' the rails
Wheels of steel, again rollin' through
Rollin' cars for passengers like you
Everybody oughta ride a train
Get on board, they're outward bound again
Ridin' the rails, ridin' the rails

Ridin' the rails, ridin' the rails
There once was a man whose name I do not know
And he decided that horses were too slow
But to turn a wheel, it took more than a dream
So he boiled the water and harnessed up the steam
Ridin' the rails, ridin' the rails

Ridin' the rails, ridin' the rails
Watch them proudly roll on new-laid track
It's a better way to get you there and back
And, like a brand-new day, she's up-to-date
For bringing in your lover, or your freight
Ridin' the rails, ridin' the rails

Ridin' the rails, ridin' the rails
Long and sleek, and made for movin' on
Shout, "Here she comes," she's already gone
Tip your hat to them when they go by
They're a way of life that will never, never die
Ridin' the rails, ridin' the rails

RINGS FOR SALE

1974

In a pawn shop, down on Broadway
There's a thousand wedding rings
From a thousand ended marriages
Laying there beside such things
Is guns and knives and watches, banjos and
guitars
Radios, recorders, rearview mirrors for your
car

Rings for sale, now here's a nice one
You can't tell it's not new
Rings for sale, don't count the heartbreak
This one would look good on you

Rings for sale, now how about it
Do you think our love could weather?
Can we hold it all together
With our love that's never ending?

And as the little golden band upon your hand
How could we fail?
Would it ever be among the thousands in the
pawn shop?
Rings for sale

There will be some brought for pawning
When a payday didn't come
A few were brought in for a friend
And children brought in some

But most were laid down, trembling
By a most reluctant hand
A sign that love had gone
Between a woman and a man

Rings for sale, now how about it
Do you think our love could weather?
Can we hold it all together
With our love that's never ending?

And as the little golden band upon your hand
How could we fail?
Would it ever be among the thousands in the
pawn shop?
Rings for sale

A SHAVE AND A HOT BATH

1974

You herd them steers and strays out of that long chaparral
And you get that herd headed towards the railroad corral
You'll be trading in them saddle sores
And heat and dust and moanin'
For a shave and a hot bath and a bottle and a woman

Well, I just talked a few things over with a couple of my pals
And when we get to the railhead and the ol' railroad corral
We'll be swappin' in them cattle
At the endin' of our roamin'
For a shave and a hot bath and a bottle and a woman

Well, you keep that herd a-movin', and eat a ton of dust
But the good word every mornin' is "railroad corral or bust"
When the railroad is in sight
That's when we'll begin to homin'
For a shave and a hot bath and a bottle and a woman

But the longest of days must reach evening, at last
And the hills are all climbed, and the creeks are all passed
And the tired herd droops, in the yellowin' light
Let them loaf, if they will, for the railroad's in sight

SOUTHERN COMFORT

1974

I've been a thrill-seeking rambler
And often came into this town
But the thrills were too high for my little sky
So I dug in and I settled down

And I got a good job in Nashville
No way they can pay me enough
For grinding up tobacco leaves
Making brut and snuff

Southern comfort is killing me
I'm slowly choking in Tennessee
I shovel the snuff until late afternoon
Then I crawl with the traffic and I choke
 on its fumes
And fall on my face when I get to my room
Southern comfort is killing me

I met a woman in Nashville
For a while we were carrying on
She'd washed snuff out of my shirts every
 night
And keep me with clean ones on

But I guess she got tired of tobacco
At least of the regular kind
Now I'm still working where nicotine
And memories are burning my mind

Southern comfort is killing me
The Cumberland cannot and Hermitage be
I'm sniffing and dipping and living alone
I smell funny smoke and I know where she's
 gone
She's in Sumner County now, growing her
 own
Southern comfort is killing me
Southern comfort is killing me

VIRGIE

1974

Virgie, your house was always warm
And my bed was always ready when I came
Virgie, in the middle of the night
You would welcome friends of mine without a name

And you could always hear and see the turning of the key
And your laughing voice to me was like a song
Virgie, your spirit, sweet and free
Is living still with me though you are gone

Virgie, you spoke softly and kind
And you'd never say a word to criticize
Virgie, your children love you so
More than we ever let you realize

And day or night I knew that I could bring my cares to you
And when I was wrong, you'd never put me down
Virgie, there's so much I could say
But I can't find the way to write it down
Can't find the way to write it down

LADY

1977

Lady, your arms were always warm
And your bed was always ready when I came
Lady, in the middle of the night
You would open up when you'd hear me call your name

And you were always there to see the turning of my key
And your laughing voice to me was like a song
Lady, your spirit's sweet and free
It's hanging on with me now that I'm gone

Lady, you spoke softly and kind
And you never had a word to criticize
Lady, you know I love you so
Even more than I ever let you realize

And day or night I knew that I could bring it all to you
And if I was wrong, you'd never put me down
Lady, there's so much I could say
But I can't find the way to write it down
Can't find the way to write it down

WHAT ON EARTH WILL YOU DO (FOR HEAVEN'S SAKE)

1974

Would you walk that second mile
Turn a frown with a smile
Would you give a little more
Than you could take

Did you shine your little light
Upon the children of the night
What on earth will you do
For heaven's sake

Did you feed the poor in spirit
And befriend the persecuted
Did you show the bounds
How all the chains can break

Did you sow the proper seeds
Do you walk among the weeds
What on earth will you do
For heaven's sake

Are you patient with the weak
Are you counted with the meek
Would you lift the lowly heart
Or let it break

Could you give away your shirt
And overlook a beggar's dirt
What on earth will you do
For heaven's sake

WHILE I GOT IT ON MY MIND

1974

Laying around home, with a ball game on
Feeling fairly fine
Blackberry jam is cooking in the pan
And the jam and the cook are mine

I like my honey from the hives of home
And berries from my old vine
And I like to get my loving
While I got it on my mind

My dog is asleep at my bare feet
It's a good day for laying around
Just her and me and it's Saturday
Everybody's gone to town

We've been working hard and she gets tired
That puts me in a bind
Because I like to get my loving
While I got it on my mind

Then she looks at me and I can see
That old familiar look
And the jam is sweet as she lowers the heat
To give it time to cook

Then I lock the door and I cross the floor
To my queen of womankind
Yeah, I like to get my loving
While I got it on my mind

Now, boys, don't you be rambling free
And leaving the girls to cry
Because the nights get cold
There isn't no gold that'll ever satisfy

And there isn't no joy
That'll come to you, boys
Like the kind I've known at times
When I go right on in there lovin' her
While I got it on my mind

Yeah, I like to get my loving
While I got it on my mind

COMMITTED TO PARKVIEW

1975

There's a man across the hall
Who sits staring at the floor
And he thinks he's Hank Williams
Hear him singing through the door

There's a girl in 202
Who stops by to visit me
And she talks about her songs
And the star that she should be

There's a lot of real fine talent
Staying in or passing through
And for one thing or another
They're committed to Parkview

There's a girl in 207
Coming down on Thorazine
And a superstar's ex-drummer
Trying to kick Benzedrine

There's a real fine country singer
Who has tried and tried and tried
They just brought him in this morning
An attempted suicide

There are those who never made it
Those who did and now are through
Some came of their own good choosing
Some committed to Parkview

There's a girl who cries above me
Loud enough to wake the dead
They don't know what she has taken
That has scrambled up her head

There's a boy just down below me
Who's the son of some well-known
He was brought in by his mother
'Cause his daddy's always gone

There's a bum from down on Broadway
And a few quite well-to-do
Who have withdrawn from the rat race
And committed to Parkview

They wake me about six thirty
Just before the morning meal
While they're takin' my blood pressure
They ask me how I feel

And I always say, "Fantastic!"
There ain't nothing wrong with me
And then they give me my injection
And I go right back to sleep

And my days are kinda foggy
And my nights are dreamy, too
For they're taking good care of me
While committed to Parkview

DESTINATION VICTORIA STATION

1975

I'm standing in the station
I'm looking at the board
The board ain't saying nothing
That's lightening my load

Is her destination Victoria Station
Where the trains go out and the trains come in?
Where the trains go out and the trains come in?

Her daddy's name was Casey
She lived down by the track
I know she was born to ramble
But I believe she will ramble back

Destination Victoria Station
Where the trains go out and the trains come in
Where the trains go out and the trains come in

I asked an old conductor
Who just came in from the sea
"Did you see a little lady
Who looked like she missed me?"

The destination, Victoria Station
Where the trains go out and the trains come in
Where the trains go out and the trains come in

DOWN AT DRIPPIN' SPRINGS

1975

Campers, bikes, and mobile homes
Cars and pickup trucks
Shags and '59 hairdos
Sideburns, spears, and ducks

There's Lone Star, Pearl, and fried chicken
And one big cloud of smoke
Plug it in and turn it on
And the music goes for broke

Down at Drippin' Springs
Down at Drippin' Springs
There's Willie, Waylon, Kris, and Tom
Have you heard Gatlin sing?

Down at Drippin' Springs
Down at Drippin' Springs
Duncan's on and Linda's next
How many did y'all bring?
Down at Drippin' Springs

Well, the Texas sun is low and hot
Upon the chaparral
It would be one ideal spot
For God to put His hell

The most beloved cowboy songs
Echo across the plains
T. Texas Tyler ain't forgotten
Next year, y'all come again

Down at Drippin' Springs
Down at Drippin' Springs
There's Russell, Bush, and Kris and Coe
Have you heard Gatlin sing?

Down at Drippin' Springs
Down at Drippin' Springs
Duncan's on and Rita's next
How many did y'all bring?
Down at Drippin' Springs

SLUMGULLION

1970s

Get a chicken if you can catch it
Get a pot if you can steal it
Take that bottle from your pocket
Let me hold it 'til I can't feel it

Let me lay down by the fire
Let me get a little higher
'Til my head turns to slumgullion

Four a.m., I'm sleeping peaceful
Dreaming of that girl in Billings
And she's kissing me and crying
And she is warm and she is willing

Then the cold rain and the wind
Brings me reality again
Turns my dreams into slumgullion

Never laugh at the devil
'Cause he ain't to be outsmarted
'Bout the time you think you whipped him
You will find that he's just started

He will run you off the sidin'
Jump right up from where he's hidin'
Turn your plans into slumgullion

When you think you are a winner
And a number one all over
Don't go smilin' in the mirror
Don't go rollin' in the clover

Every day's a brand-new mountain
Don't drink long at any fountain
You'll be turned into slumgullion

Get a chicken if you can catch it
Get a pot if you can steal it
Take that bottle from your pocket
Let me hold it till I cant feel it
Let me lay down by the fire
Let me get a little higher
Till my head turns to Slumgullion

Never laugh at the devil
Cause he aint to be outsmarted
Bout the time you think you whipped him
You will find that he's just started
He'll run you off on the sidin
Jump right up from where he's hidin
Turn your hopes into Slumgullion.

JOHNNY CASH

Four am I'm sleeping peaceful
Dreaming of that girl in Billings
And she's kissing me and crying
And she's eager and she's willing
Then the cold rain and the wind
Brings me reality again
Turns my dreams into Slumgullion

When you think you are a winner
An A number one all over
Dont go smilin' in no mirror
Dont go rollin in the clover
~~Dont drink long at any fountain~~
Every days a brand new mountain
Dont drink long at any fountain
You'll be turned into Slumgullion

HIGH BALLIN'

1975

Get a chicken, if you can catch it
Get a pot, if you can steal it
Take that bottle from your pocket
Let me hold it until I can't feel it

Let me lay down by the fire
Let me get a little higher
'Til my head is
High ballin'

Four a.m., I'm sleepin' peaceful
Dreamin' of a girl in Philly
And she's kissin' me and cryin'
And she's warm and she's willin'

Then the cold rain and the wind
Brings me reality again
And my dream...
No high ballin'

Never laugh at the devil
'Cause he ain't to be outsmarted
'Bout the time you think you whipped him
You will find he's just started

He will run you off the side and
Jump right up from where he's hidin'
And he'll plan...
We'll go high ballin'

Well, you think you are a winner
And a number one all over
Don't go smilin' in the mirror
Don't go rollin' in the clover

Every day's a brand-new mountain
Don't drink long at any fountain
You'll be gone
High ballin'

I HARDLY EVER SING BEER DRINKING SONGS

1975

I hardly ever sing beer drinking songs
And when they play them cheating tunes
I never sing along
I never ever sing the blues
I've forgotten "Born to Lose"
And I hardly ever sing beer drinking songs

I hardly ever walk the floor and cry
And I don't think I've ever said, "I feel like I could die."
I don't ever lay awake
I never think my heart will break
I hardly ever walk the floor and cry

I hardly ever sing beer drinking songs
I can't put much feeling in saying, "Love is all gone wrong."
I don't lose no sleep at night
'Cause things with you are going right
And I hardly ever sing beer drinking songs

I never call your name out in my sleep
You never make me worry and you never make me weep
I never wonder if you're true
I spend a night curled up with you
And I never call your name out in my sleep

I hardly ever sing beer drinking songs
And when they play them cheating tunes
I never sing along
I never ever sing the blues
I've forgotten "Born to Lose"
And I hardly ever sing beer drinking songs

I WANTED SO

1975

I wanted so to tell that old man
Oh, so many things
Like the corn was ten feet tall
That he had planted in the spring

And the books he'd ordered came in
In the mail just yesterday
But he never said a word
And life slowly slipped away

I wanted so to tell him
Just how much he meant to me
I wanted so to thank him
For what he taught me that I could be

I wanted him to know
That his grandchildren all were there
And that his four-year-old grandson said,
"Papaw, I said a prayer."

I wanted to apologize
For always being on the go
For never having enough time
To talk about the things that he needed so

I wanted so to tell him,
"Pop, your loved ones all are here."
But he just lay there with his eyes closed
And I think he shed a knowing tear

Yes, I wanted so to tell that old man
Oh, so many things
Like the corn was ten feet tall
That he had planted in the spring

And the books he'd ordered came in
In the mail just yesterday
But he never said a word
And life just slowly slipped away

I Wanted So

I wanted so to tell that old man
Oh so many things
Like the corn was ten feet tall
That he had planted in the spring
And the books he ordered
Came in in the mail yesterday
But he didn't say a word
And life just slowly slipped away

I wanted so to tell him
How much he meant to me
I wanted so to thank him
For what he taught me to be
I wanted him to know
That his grandchildren were there
And that four year old grandson said
"Papaw, I said a prayer"

I wanted to apologize
For being on the go
And never having time to talk
Of things he needed so.
I wanted so to tell him
Our loved ones all here
He lay there with his eyes closed
And shed a knowing tear

JOB

1975

Job was a wealthy man
He had a lot of kids and a lot of land
He had cattle on a thousand hills
He lived every day to do God's will

Satan came with the sons of men
The Lord said, "Satan, where you been?"
He said, "I have been around
And to and fro and up and down.

"Working hard for all I'm worth
To rule all men upon this earth."
The Lord said, "Do the worst you can
But my servant, Job, is a faithful man."

Satan did the worst he could
Job kept right on being good
But he cried out in agony
When he lost his children and his property

Satan started laughing and he said again,
"It's bone for bone and skin for skin."
Then he looked up to the holy place
Said, "I'll make him curse you to your face."

Satan struck Job from his feet to his head
With corruption, and Job got out of bed
And sat right down in the marketplace
With sackcloth and ashes on his face
Job's wife said, "Curse God and die.
He's not going to hear you cry."

Then the best three friends that Job ever had
Zophar, Eliphaz, and Bildad
Sat down with him for seven days
To share his grief without a word to say

Job said, "Why does it have to be
That the thing I feared has come on me?"
He cried out, "I deplore my birth.
Let my birthday perish from the earth."

His friends said, "Job, you should repent.
The perfect don't get punishment.
Job, Job, watch what you say.
The Lord let Satan have his way.
Don't give in and don't give up.
The Lord could soon refill your cup.

"You could make a comeback still
With cattle on a thousand hills."
Job said, "I harmed no man.
There's been no violence by my hand.

"As surely as sparks upward fly
I was born to trouble and I want to die.
I want to see God face-to-face
And stand right up and argue my case.

"There is no justice I can see.
God has been unfair to me.
I've been righteous, I've been good
And God won't talk to me, like he should."

Job, Job, your friends are nice
But they gave you some bad advice
What's needed here, it seems to me
Is a little thing called humility

Then along came a friend named Elihu
Said, "I will speak to God for you
And he will bring you from the pit.
He'll raise you up from where you sit.

"He will chasten, test, and try
But by his grace, you didn't die.
He purifies you in your pain
And he can make you whole again."

Then God said, "Who can this be
Who challenges my majesty?
Who speaks but does not know what to say?
Where were you on creation day?

"Learn a lesson from the animals and birds.
Don't darken my counsel with empty words.
Show me your wisdom, if you can
And gird yourself up, like a man."

Job looked up into the firmament
And said, "Lord God, I do repent.
I bow down before your throne.
My will is yours and yours alone."

The bounty flowed from heaven's door
And Job was twice as wealthy as before
He had a golden chain and a long white robe
And the happiest man in the world was Job

Job 1.

Job Job was a wealthy man
He had a lot of kids and a lot of land
He had cattle on a thousand hills
He lived every day to do Gods will

Satan came with the sons of men
The Lord said "Satan where you been?"
He said "I have been around
And to and fro and up and down"
Working hard for all I'm worth
To Rule all men upon this earth
The Lord said do the worst you can
But my servant Job is a faithful man
Satan did the worst he could
Job kept right on being good
But he cried out in agony
When he lost his children and his property
Satan started laughing and he said again
Its bone for bone and skin for skin
Then he looked up to the holy place
Said I make him curse you to your face
Satan struck Job from his feet to his head
With corruption, and Job got out of bed
And sat right down in the market place
With sackcloth and ashes on his face
The Lord said you cant take his life
Satan said I'll work on his wife
Jobs wife said curse God and die
~~Dont sit there and whine and~~ cry.
He's not going to hear your cry
Job Job watch what you say
The Lord let Satan have his way
Dont give in and dont give up
The Lord could soon re-fill your cup.

2.

Then the best three friends that Job ever had
Zophar, Eliphaz and Bildad
Sat down with him for seven days
To share his grief without a word to say
Job said why does it have to be
That the thing I feared has come on me
He cried out I deplore my birth
Let my birthday perish from the earth
His friends said Job you should repent
The perfect dont get ~~[illegible]~~ punishment
Job said I harmed no man
Theres been no violence by my hand
As surely as sparks upward fly
I was born to trouble and I want to die
I want to see God face to face
And stand right up and argue my case
There is no justice I can see
God has been unfair to me
I've been righteous, I've been good
And God wont talk to me like he should

Job Job your friends are nice
But they gave you some bad advice
What's needed here, it seems to me
Is a little thing called humility

Then along came a friend named Elihu
Said I will speak to God for you
~~By your suffering Gods correcting you~~.
And He will bring you from the pit
He'll raise you up from where you sit
He will chasten test and try
But by His grace you didnt die
He purifies you in your pain
And He can make you whole again.

3

~~God said Job I'll answer you~~
~~Because I heard the prayer of Elihu~~
~~Then God~~ said who can this be
Who challenges my majesty
Who speaks but doesn't know what to say
Where were you on creation day
Learn a lesson from the animals and birds
Dont darken my counsel with empty words
Show me your wisdom if you can
And gird yourself up like a man

Job looked up into the firmament
And said Lord God I do repent
I bow down before your throne
My will is yours and yours alone

Then bounty flowed from heavens door
And Job was twice as wealthy as before
~~He had seven sons and three pretty girls~~
~~And he owned half the land in that part of the world~~
He had a golden chain and a long white robe
And the happiest man in the world was Job.

Job Job watch what you say
The Lord let Satan have his way
Dont give in and dont give up
The Lord could soon refill your cup
You could make a comeback still
With cattle on a thousand hills.

~~Job said Lord how can this be~~
JOBS WIFE SAID CURSE GOD AND DIE
~~That the thing I feared has come on me~~ (2)
DONT SIT THERE AND WHINE AND CRY
Then the best three friends that Job ever had
Zophar Eliphaz and Bildad
Sat down with him seven seven days
To share his grief without a word to say
Then Job said why does it have to be
That the thing I feared has come on me
Then he cried I deplore my birth
Let my birthday perish from the earth
His friends said Job you should repent
The perfect dont get punishment

Job said I have harmed no man
There's been no violence by my hand

Job Job you can be free
If you get yourself humility
Job be careful and be sure
Aint no man thats really pure (1)

Job Job watch what you say (2)
The Lord let Satan have his way
Dont give in and dont give up
The Lord could soon refill your cup

~~Job Job your friends are nice~~
~~But they gave~~ you some ~~bad~~ advice
(After head in his hands)
And he ~~God~~ said Job I'll answer you
Because I heard the prayer of Elihu
You darken my counsel with empty words
~~[illegible]~~ Learn a lesson from animals & Birds

I'LL HAVE A DRINK, YOU HAVE THE GIRL

1975

I'll have another glass of whiskey
While you tell me one more time
How she told you she loved you
And she's no longer mine

Well, I did my best to hold her
But she didn't want my world
I'll have a drink
You have the girl

I'll drink away my loneliness
And soon the pain is gone
Fill the glass up to the brim
And leave me here alone

Say no more about her
My head is in a whirl
I'll have a drink
You have the girl

Well, I'll drink 'til I forget her
The way she has, me
Just leave that bottle handy
And then just leave me be

It's hard to give her to you
She's precious as a pearl
I'll have a drink
You have the girl

KATHY

1975

Kathy, take that frown off your face
Let a self-assured expression take its place
For I love you, yes, I do
And you shouldn't let tomorrow bother you
Just rest assured that everything's all right
Then lay you down in sweet, sweet dreams tonight

Kathy, are you listening, did you hear?
I love you, not a day and not a year
Oh, forever is a timeless time, I mean
And I'll prove it you, if you haven't seen
You will know it by the years, as they go by
That I'll love you, Kathy, 'til the day I die

Kathy, be prepared to understand
I'm just a man, and nothing but a man
And sometimes I might forget to let you know
But you must always remember that it's so
There's no way that my heart can change for you
I love you, Kathy, don't forget I do

LOOK UNTO THE EAST

1975

The teacher of truth told tales
Of troubled times that would begin
And the cynical sower sowed
The sorrowful seeds of seven sins

The people placed a price
Upon the prince of perfect peace
And the one who wooed the world was wounded
Look unto the east

The morning moved in mournfully
With many moments marred
By brawny beast, who beat the beauty
Bound and bit and barred

They laid the lash upon Him low
His lips moved not the least
Watch Him come from where He did go
Look unto the east

The devil drew his darts
And the dearest dove came dropping down
But the spirit slips in soft and sweetly
Unseen with no sound

The comforter, the counselor
With us 'til time is ceased
And the groom will return for his bride
Look unto the east

MICHIGAN CITY HOWDY DO

1975

Well, Johnson Van Dyke Grigsby
Was paroled at eighty-nine
He never walked on a carpet
Never tasted dinner wine

His old eyes were slowly fading
As he walked out of the gate
And he breathed the first free air
He'd breathed since 1908

Howdy do, Michigan City, you're sure a pretty sight
But I know there's bigger cities and more exciting nights
But I think your girls're pretty and I love your children, too
Michigan City, Indiana, howdy do, Michigan City, Indiana, howdy do
Michigan City, Indiana, howdy do

Filled with the joy of freedom
He didn't know that he was old
'Cause time don't really matter
When it's bubbling in your soul

Well, I don't think he was bitter
'Cause he sure had a smile
And down the streets of Michigan City
He walked his first free mile

Howdy do, Michigan City, you're sure a pretty sight
But I know there's bigger cities and more exciting nights
But I think your girls're pretty and I love your children, too
Michigan City, Indiana, howdy do, Michigan City, Indiana, howdy do
Michigan City, Indiana, howdy do

NAVAJO

1975

I have seen your colors
Woven in your blankets
I have heard your names on
Rivers and on towns

I have seen your turquoise
On fine fancy ladies
And the Indian sun is rising
Instead of going down

Navajo, Navajo
The people call the people
From ten thousand years ago
Navajo, Navajo
From the land of the enchantment
Navajo

I have seen your red rock canyons
Out of Gallup
I have walked upon your Arizona hills
At Crownpoint, I watched an artist painting
All the secrets of your past, surviving still

Navajo, Navajo
The people call the people
From ten thousand years ago
Navajo, Navajo
From the land of the enchantment
Navajo

I have seen your women dress in royal purple
Silver from your hills upon their hands
I don't need a signpost reading: *Reservation*
To know the minute I'm on Indian land

Navajo, Navajo
The people call the people
From ten thousand years ago
Navajo, Navajo
From the land of the enchantment
Navajo

OH, SWEET MAMA

1975

Oh, sweet Mama
The weeds are growing in your flower bed
Oh, sweet Mama
I take back about everything I said

Oh, sweet Mama
My mind is in a fever since you've gone
And I just can't sleep alone

I've been laying in this bed
Troubles running through my head
Wondering what I've done or said
But I guess that I was wrong

I've been wanting you so bad
And all the good times that we had
Come on, honey, don't be mad
I'm barely hanging on

Oh, sweet Mama
Your daddy wants you home

Oh, sweet Mama
You're all that's ever on my mind
Oh, sweet Mama
How come you turned out to be that kind

Oh, sweet Mama
The pain of needing you is so severe
You are badly needed here

I've been laying in this bed
Troubles running through my head
Wondering what I've done or said
But I guess that I was wrong

I've been wanting you so bad
And all the good times that we had
Come on, honey, don't be mad
I'm barely hanging on

ONCE BEFORE I DIE

with June Carter

1975

I told you once and I'll tell you now
If I lose your love, I'd die somehow
You broke the news to me today
But I need one thing before I go away

Well, you know I'm gonna love you, baby, once before I die
You know I've got to love you, baby, and I ain't gonna cry
There's a time to live and a time to die
A time to love and a time to cry

I've got to reap while you go sow
You're gonna stay and I'm gonna go
Well, you know I've got to love you, baby, once before I die
You know I'm gonna love you, baby, and I ain't gonna cry

There's a time to live and a time to die
A time to love and a time to cry
I've got to reap while you go sow
And you're gonna stay and I'm gonna go

Well, you know I'm gonna love you, baby, once before I die
You know I'm gonna love you, baby, once before I die

OUT OF PRISON

1975

Everybody says I've been in prison
And I've denied the story every time
I've never been convicted of a felony
But I was in that private jail of mine
I locked love out and I was isolated
From every good thing that could come my way
I finally broke out of my self-made prison
And I wake to a free world every day

Out of prison, chains are broken
I've got you and love has set me free
Out of prison, I am pardoned
I'm still wanted, 'cause you're still wanting me

I know through the years that there was freedom
Waiting for me just outside my cell
And all I had to do was just break through it
But I held back and put myself through hell
All the time I saw your sweet love waiting
I could not believe it could be true
That you could take an old ex-con like me back
But you reached forgiving arms and I ran to you

Out of prison, chains are broken
I've got you and love has set me free
Out of prison, I am pardoned
I'm still wanted, 'cause you're still wanting me

SANCTIFIED

1975

"Have a little drink."
No, thank you, brother
"Want to get rich?"
I don't need it, brother
"Wanna fool around?"
No, thank you, sister
Ain't you heard
That old evil man within me died?
"Let's have a party."
I ain't going
"What you gonna do?"
I'm gonna keep praying
And keep working out my salvation
Trying to get sanctified

No more condemnation
Jesus brought salvation
Justification brought me safely to His side
And as I get to know Him more
He gives me a taste of the coming glory
I'm working out my salvation
Trying to get sanctified

Sanctified, sanctified
I'm working out my salvation
I'm trying to get sanctified

"Don't go to church."
Yes, I'm going
"Why you read that old Bible?"
'Cause I like it
"Well, I don't believe in God."
Well, God bless you
You ain't got no argument
For what I feel inside
"Let's have a little fun."
That's what I'm having
"Life's gonna pass you by."
I can hardly wait
Well, I've got my mind set upon eternity
Trying to get sanctified

And there's no more condemnation
Jesus brought salvation
Justification brought me safely to His side
And as I get to know Him more
He gives me a taste of the coming glory
I'm working out my salvation
Trying to get sanctified

Sanctified, sanctified
Sanctified, sanctified
I'm working out my salvation
I'm trying to get sanctified
Sanctified, sanctified

STRAWBERRY CAKE

1975

In New York City, just walking the street
Ran out of money, had nothing to eat
I stopped at the Plaza, that fancy hotel
Where you can check in, if you're well-to-do
well

The first of July and a hundred and four
I stopped at the Plaza's front revolving door
I stepped in the door and went around for a
ride
Treating myself to the cool air inside

Then I found myself in a chandeliered room
Where people were dining and I hid in the
gloom
My hunger pains hurt 'til I thought I would
break
When a waiter brought out a big strawberry
cake

Oh, that strawberry cake
Oh, that strawberry cake
Out in California, them berries were grown
And into this city, them berries were flown
For making that strawberry cake

Then I thought of Oxnard, just north of LA
Where I picked strawberries for many a day
Hard work with no future, for the harvest was
done
And I headed eastward, a-traveling by thumb

And nobody wanted me here in this town
I felt like a stray dog they all kick around
Them berries reminded me of my bad breaks
I'm hungry and I want that strawberry cake

I deserve that strawberry cake
Deserve that strawberry cake
I ran and I grabbed it, then out the side door
Into Central Park, through the bushes I tore
Holding my strawberry cake

I look back behind me and what do I see
The chef and headwaiter and the maître d'
I had a nice helping of cake as I ran
I gobble them berries as fast as I can

They're closing the gap as I slowed down to
eat
But the cake brought a new surge of power to
my feet
I hid in the bush when the lead I did take
And I quietly finished my strawberry cake

I ate all that strawberry cake
That fine, fancy strawberry cake
Someone at the Plaza is without dessert
But for the first time in days now
My belly don't hurt
I'm full of strawberry cake

AFTER THE BALL

1976

I hear people laughing on the corner, by the square
The neon flickers on my wall and I know you're out there
I've been in here a-listening for your footsteps down the hall
And I'll be waiting for you, after the ball

After the ball is over, after the ball
If you cannot stand, I've got a place for you to fall
The blinds are drawn and I have turned the clockface to the wall
I'll be waiting for you, after the ball

Loving you is sweet addiction, I need only you
Just as long as you come back, oh do what you want to
Give the night your laughter but I'll have you after all
I'll be waiting for you, after the ball

After the ball is over, after the ball
If you cannot stand, I've got a place for you to fall
The blinds are drawn and I have turned the clockface to the wall
I'll be waiting for you, after the ball

CALILOU

1976

Well, I'm finally going back to Louisiana
Runnin' and thumbin' all the way
I started out way out in California
I been makin' 'bout five hundred miles a day

I covered all the beaches on the West Coast
From Mexico to Crescent City Bay
But Calilou was not in California
That's where her daddy came from, by the way

And by the way, her mother was a Cajun
She came from New Orleans, I've heard her say
And it's just like a girl to wanna see her mama
So I might find her there along the way

Calilou, Calilou
Well, they should have called you Restless
Well, they should have called you Drifter
Yeah, they should have called you Trouble
Instead of Calilou

I recall the first time that I saw her
I picked her up near Phoenix in my car
Just another beauty, seeking fame and fortune
And I told her she should be a movie star

The next time I saw her was Tucumcari
She served my bowl of chili with a smile
I said, "It's been a year since I last saw you.
Wonder how'd you like to share a few good miles?"

Well, the justice of the peace was very sleepy
I held her in my arms the whole night long
I whispered words like "settle down" and "family"
And when I woke up, my Calilou was gone

Calilou, Calilou
Well, they should have called you Restless
And they should have called you Drifter
Yeah, they should have called you Trouble
Instead of Calilou

CINDY, I LOVE YOU

1976

We never really got right down to talking
We couldn't seem to find the place or time
Distance in the miles between us made us kinda strangers
And it added to the distance already there between our minds

And Cindy, I love you, yes, I love you, yes, I love you
And when I can't think of anything to say
Don't be reading something in my mind that isn't there
Remember, Cindy, I love you anyway

I look at you and wonder what you're thinking
I'm sure you felt the same, a time or two
We must both remember that true love sure costs us nothing
You just told me your affection and I owe the same to you

And Cindy, I love you, yes, I love you, yes, I love you
And when I can't think of anything to say
Don't be reading something in my mind that isn't there
Remember, Cindy, I love you anyway

FIELD OF DIAMONDS

with Jack Wesley Routh

1976

Field of diamonds in the sky
Worlds are whirling right on by
Are you wondering, Who am I?
Field of diamonds in the sky

Are you a star, shining in his crown?
Or someone's life sun
Going down, down, down?

Field of diamonds in the sky
Silent beauty shining high
Are you tears the angels cry?
Field of diamonds in the sky

Will I be a star in his crown?
Or someone's life sun
Going down, down, down?

Field of diamonds in the sky
With the night, you pass me by
I will touch you, by and by
Field of diamonds in the sky

GO ON BLUES

1976

Go on blues, go on lonesome
Get your dark clouds off of me
Go on blues, go on troubles
Turn loose of me, set me free

I've been down through that valley with you
Now I've found me somebody who loves me, too
Go on blues, go away from me
Go on by me, go on blues

I've been down through that valley with you
Now I've found me somebody who loves me, too
Go on blues, go away from me
Go on by me, go on blues

Yeah, go on blues, go on by me
Get away from me, go on blues

HAVE A DRINK OF WATER

1976

In the long, hot, thirsty summer of about 32 AD
Along a dusty highway, there came a man of Galilee
And as He went through Samaria, He stopped at Jacob's well
And there He met a woman, whose deep secrets He would tell

"Could I have a drink of water?" soft and quietly asked He
And she said, "Sir, I'm Samaritan, how dare you speak to me?"
He said, "If you would ask of me, then I, the Son of Man,
Would give you living water and you'd never thirst again."

Have a drink of water, everlasting living water
Have a drink of water, everlasting living water
Dip into the endless well, pour it on the fires of hell
Have a drink and sing and shout as the flames of hell go out
Have a drink of water, everlasting endless water

Then the woman said, "Sir, you have no way to draw out of this well.
Our father, Jacob, dug it, and the stories it could tell.
From this well drank his children and his cattle by the score.
Where is your well, sir, tell me, that will flow forevermore?"

And He answered, and said unto her, "Your water will go dry
And my well is everlasting. If you drink, you'll never die.
My father God's a spirit and He set me unto men
To give you living water so you'll never thirst again."

Have a drink of water, everlasting living water
Have a drink of water, everlasting living water
Dip into the endless well, pour it on the fires of hell
Have a drink and sing and shout as the flames of hell go out
Have a drink of water, everlasting living water

Well, there now are many thirsting in this modern century
Whose thirst could be quenched quickly by the man from Galilee
For the water flows eternal from the well that never dries
For it flows right out of heaven, where the soul will never die

So if you're hot and tired and thirsting
And if you crave a cool, tall drink
He will pour it right out for you a lot quicker than you think
He already knows you're thirsty so just let Him come on in
And He'll give you living water and you'll never thirst again

Have a drink of water, everlasting living water
Have a drink of water, everlasting living water
Dip into the endless well, pour it on the fires of hell
Have a drink and sing and shout as the flames of hell go out
Have a drink of water, everlasting living water

HERE I AM BACK AGIN

1976

Like a favorite old shoe
That you pulled off and threw
In the trash then found your
New ones hurt your feet
Wore them new ones all you could
Then shined the old ones up real good
Felt as natural as an old familiar street

Like a warm April wind
Here I am back agin

Like a letter that you guessed at
And missed the right address
It comes back at you like a jumping bean
Like a present that you want
Like a birthday that you don't
Like the judgment day of April fifteen

Like a temptation to sin
Here I am back agin

Like an old dog on the prowl
Late at night you hear him howl
To remind you that he isn't far away
Like a Capistrano bird
Ain't nobody ever heard
Of 'em not returnin' on returnin' day

Like your prodigal kissin' kin
Here I am back agin

IF IT WASN'T FOR THE WABASH RIVER

1976

Fish ain't biting, but I don't really care
I'm in no hurry
Like that Wabash River there
I'd be drinking
Or laying dead somewhere
If it wasn't for the Wabash River

If it wasn't for the Wabash River
And this willow tree and my pole and a line
I'd be going crazy as an Indiana cyclone
Drowning memories of her and crying, crying, crying
If it wasn't for the Wabash River
I'd be going out of my mind

It's so peaceful sitting here, beneath my tree
Lord, I need her
Like she often needed me
Life ain't worth it
Just as far as I can see
If it wasn't for the Wabash River

If it wasn't for the Wabash River
And this willow tree and my pole and a line
I'd be going crazy as an Indiana cyclone
Drowning memories of her and crying, crying, crying
If it wasn't for the Wabash River
I'd be going out of my mind

IT'S ALL OVER

1976

I was on my way to you and I was worried
I was all torn up and nervous, 'cause I knew that you'd be gone
I knocked and crossed my fingers while I waited
And I couldn't hide the teardrops when I walked away alone

It's all over, it's all over, my heart echoed
Every minute that you cry for her is wasted, don't you know
It's all over, it's all over, my heart echoed
Stop your crying, turn around and let her go

I was running 'round in circles like a baby
I was in a daze because I loved you so, I couldn't see
I was broken in a million little pieces
When I saw enough to realize, you didn't care for me

It's all over, it's all over, my heart echoed
Every minute that you cry for her is wasted, don't you know
It's all over, it's all over, so forget her
Stop your crying, turn around and let her go

LET THERE BE COUNTRY

with Shel Silverstein

1976

Tom T. Hall is forty now
And so is Bobby Bare
Willie Nelson's getting gray
And Faron Young don't care

But the young ones keep on coming on
The old are slow to go
Let there be country
And let the country grow

Let there be country
Let the music roll along
Let there be country
And let me share this song

No one picks like Bill Monroe
And don't George Jones sing great
I can tell that the people care
By the people at my gate

Webb Pierce invites the tourists in
And Ray keeps them away
Let there be country
And let the country play

Let there be country
Let the music roll along
Let there be country
And let me share this song

Ernest Tubb's got all of the soul
He's had for all these years
Porter Wagoner's recitations
Still bring me to tears

And when they do play Kitty Wells
You know she's still the queen
Let there be country
And keep the country green

Let there be country
Let the music roll along
Let there be country
And let me share this song

Little Jimmy Dickens still sends
Shivers through the crowd
Mother Maybelle whispers now
But the heart comes through real loud

Gene Autry don't sing no more
Good old Tex Ritter's gone
And somewhere, downtown Nashville
A young man just got off the bus

With a guitar in his hands, a pocket full of songs
A lot of talent and a heart full of hope
And he's gonna be the next big country star
And the country wheels roll on

Let there be country
Let the music roll along
Let there be country
And let me share this song

LORD, LORD, LORD

traditional

adapted in 1976

Lord, Lord, Lord
Is there a place for me
In the scheme of things
In the service of the King

Lord, Lord, Lord
There is no job too great
As I grow in faith
There's no job too great

Lord, Lord, Lord
There is no road too long
'Cause You've made me strong
There's no road too long

Lord, Lord, Lord
There's no stream too wide
With You by my side
There's no stream too wide

Let me help someone
Through the darkest hour
Let me shine, shine, shine
Like a beacon's tower

Let my light be strong
And myself be small
Let me know the truth
That I'm one with all

Lord, Lord, Lord,
There's no job too small
'Cause I'm one with all
There's no job too small

Lord, Lord, Lord,
Is there a place for me
In the scheme of things
In the service of the King

Lord, Lord, Lord
There is no job too great
As I grow in faith
There's no job too great

Lord, Lord, Lord,
Lord, oh Lord, Lord, Lord
Lord, oh Lord, Lord, Lord
Lord, oh Lord, Lord, Lord

MOUNTAIN LADY

1976

Mountain Lady
Do you sit on your front porch
In the cool of the day?
Mountain Lady
Did you think your kids would ever come
  back to stay?

Mountain Lady
Does the columbine still twine around your
  door?
And did you ever get a rug
To cover the cracks where
My diaper drug on your wooden floor?

Oh, you Appalachian Lady
Once I was your little baby
And you rocked me in your homemade
  rocking chair
Since I heard the wild goose calling
I have done a lot of falling
Mountain Lady
Someday I'll come to you there

Mountain Lady
Does the country church bell ring on Sunday
  morn?
Mountain Lady
Do you still wear that old apron
Ragged and torn?

Mountain Lady
On winter nights, before our old fireplace
As you look into the flames
Do you ever call my name
And do you see my face?

Oh, you Appalachian Lady
Once I was your little baby
And you rocked me in your homemade
  rocking chair
Since I heard the wild goose calling
I have done a lot of falling
Mountain Lady
Someday I'll come to you there

MY COWBOY'S LAST RIDE

1976

The cowboy's lady is crying tonight
'Cause the cowboy is out on the range
Running and rambling and chasing some stray
And good cowboys don't ever change

I tried to hold him in the home corral
But the grasses were greener outside
So I'm gonna sit here in front of this door
And I've loaded up my cowboy's forty-four
When the smoke clears
There'll be a new brand on his eyes
This is my cowboy's last ride

Oh, I hate to see him go
But I won't be staying home crying
I hate to watch him die
But this is my cowboy's last ride

Cowboy remembers the old trails we rode
And he's back in the saddle tonight
This time I'm letting the home fires burn out
And I'm leaving when I blow out his light

'Cause I still remember good watering holes
And the places that are open and wide
And I have decided he won't put me down
A filly should be free for horsing around
And I will no longer be hobbled and tied
This is my cowboy's last ride

Oh, I hate to see him go
But I won't be staying home crying
I hate to watch him die
But this is my cowboy's last ride

NAME DATE
PREPARED
APPROVED

The Cowboy remembers the trails he once rode
And he's back in the saddle ~~[illegible]~~ tonight
But this time I'm lettin the home fires burn out
And ~~[illegible]~~ Leave when I blow out his light.

I still remember the waterin' holes
~~[illegible]~~
And ~~prairies~~ still open and wide
And I have decided he wont put me down
A filly should be free for ~~[illegible]~~ ~~to his~~ horsemen round
And I will no longer be ~~[illegible]~~ hobbled and tied
For this is my cowboys last ride

The cowboys lady is crying tonite
Cause the cowboy is ridin' the range
Running and rambling and chasing a stray
And cowboys dont ever change
I tried to hold him at the home corral
But the grasses were greener outside
I'm gonna sit here in front of this door
And I've loaded up my cowboys 44
When the smoke clears there'll be a new brand on his hide
For this is my cowboys last ride

RIDIN' ON THE COTTON BELT

1976

Ridin' on the Cotton Belt
Cleveland County's where I long to be
I got on at Brinkley
And every mile I make is a memory

This boxcar's cold and windy
And the dust goes around in circles in the air
But my hard times are behind me
And I'm returnin' home, so I don't care

And I'm ridin' on the Cotton Belt railroad line
In the pitchin', rolling rhythm and the noise
Railroad men are friends of mine
And I'm ridin' on the Cotton Belt, boys

Ridin' on the Cotton Belt
Across that little river called Saline
That's where I went fishin'
And I hunted in her bottoms as a teen

Now, just ahead's a farmhouse
And in the kitchen window there's a light
And I've just got fourteen dollars
But I'm taking it myself home tonight

And I'm ridin' on the Cotton Belt railroad line
In the pitchin', rolling rhythm and the noise
Railroad men are friends of mine
And I'm ridin' on the Cotton Belt, boys

Jumpin' off the Cotton Belt ain't easy
When she's going forty per
But I see my wife standin' there
Hoping that I'm coming home to her

I got a few new cuts and bruises
But this old working hobo's made it home
So long to you, Cotton Belt
Thank you for the ride, keep rolling on

I'm ridin' on the Cotton Belt railroad line
In the pitchin', rolling rhythm and the noise
Railroad men are friends of mine
And I'm ridin' on the Cotton Belt, boys

SOLD OUT OF FLAGPOLES

1976

I walked down past the courthouse square
Three blocks or maybe four
Run into my old friend there
That runs a handy hardware store

I said, "Mornin', Lon.
What's the good word?"
He said, "Abraham Lincoln, Lone Ranger,
  Mickey Mouse
And I'm sold out of flagpoles."

I popped the top off a soda pop
Laid a quarter on the bar
I said, "Inflation is a dirty dog.
My payday sure ain't goin' far."

"Liberty," said Lonnie
"E pluribus unum,
In God we trust
And I'm sold out of flagpoles."

I said, "Hey, Lonnie, did you see
Evel Knievel jumping on TV?
Jumped thirteen buses with his machine.
Reckon he could jump fourteen."

"No doubt," said Lonnie
"Winners keep on winning.
Even losers win sometimes
And I'm sold out of flagpoles."

"Ain't this been a year?" I said
"For frost and blight and flood and drought,
Twice as many tornados.
Reckon it's all caused by fallout."

"No, it's the season," said Lonnie
"They change.
Wind's gonna blow, always did
And I'm sold out of flagpoles."

"Hey, what d'you think about the sheriff's
  daughter
Running off with the preacher's son?
The sheriff's wife had to hold him back
From going after them with his gun."

"Boys and girls," said Lonnie
"Will get together.
Everything's normal
And I'm sold out of flagpoles."

ABNER BROWN

1977

I knew an old drunk named Abner Brown
And nobody knew when he came to town
But he spread goodwill to his fellow men
And they let him sleep in the cotton gin

He could drink more brew than an army
could
But he had more friends and he did more
good
Than a lot of fine fancy people in our town
So they tolerated Abner Brown

And all us kids were on his side
'Cause he told us tales 'til our eyes grew wide
And he made us feel 'bout ten feet tall
'Cause he had no kids but he claimed us all

And after school and on weekends
You could find me down at the cotton gin
The truest friend that I ever found
Was a good old drunk named Abner Brown

Abner Brown, I wish that I could see you once
again
I believe that you'd stack up with all the
mighty men
I've met and known in all the low
And higher places that I've been
Thinking of you picks me up when I'm feeling
down
I thank the Lord for making Abner Brown

Lord, take me back to the cotton land
To Arkansas, take me home again
Let me be the boy that I once have been
Let me walk that road to the cotton gin

He's probably dead many years ago
And gone the way that old drunks go
But I'd still like to sit me down
Talk to my old friend Abner Brown

DAISY BATES

1977

Out from Coolgardie I went from Bullabulling
I went for the dance and I went for the sing
A train rolled in and we looked at the gate
And in she come steppin', young Daisy Bates

Daisy, oh Daisy, sweet young Daisy Bates
Stay off of the rails and stay out of the freights
Be a proud proper lady
And find you a mate
Who'll dress you in satin and silk
Daisy Bates

Now, Daisy was dizzy, and she couldn't see
That we do things differently
At Calgoorlie
She hoisted her gingham and
Kicked up her gams
And she made me feel like the man that I am

When she left Calgoorlie
The very next week
Her blue eyes were smilin'
And pink was her cheek

When she hit Coolgardie
In a much altered state
A fulfilled young lady
Was sweet Daisy Bates

HIT THE ROAD AND GO

1977

I woke up this afternoon
Looked into your eyes
And something was as wrong
As if the sun forgot to rise

I picked up a road map
And I checked a few good places that I know
And if you're no longer giving
I believe I'll hit the road and go

I just got the feeling
That the fire was burning out
'Cause the air was turning colder
Every time you came about

And a flame won't take a fanning
If the last reserve of love is running low
So since I've gotta button up
I believe I'll hit the road and go

Country Road 6-40, State Highway 45
Life out off the interstate is very much alive
There's magic in the mountains
And music in the valleys down below
And my song ain't through playing yet
So I believe I'll hit the road and go

Good morning to you, sunshine
Good morning to you, rain
The windshield wipers' rhythm
Keeps me singing down the pain

Today I'm gonna miss you less
If I miss you at all
You'll never know
You'll never know
This rambler has cut all the ties
And pulled up stakes to hit the road and go

HURT SO BAD

1977

I thought I could walk away and keep on going
Leave you flat and never once be sad
I didn't know the pain would keep on growing
And I didn't know that it could hurt so bad
Hurt so bad, hurt so bad

All night long I'm out a-driving 'round
Every this- and thataway like mad
Always end up on your side of town
I didn't know that it could hurt so bad
Hurt so bad, hurt so bad

Don't give in, go on and don't look back
Hold on to my pride, I said
I won't let my heart
Turn my head

New day dawning on your world without me
You won't miss something that you never had
You'll be making it all right without me
But I didn't know that it could hurt so bad
Hurt so bad, hurt so bad

I CAN'T GO ON THAT WAY

1977

Life was a ball of alcohol
And pills and blues and gals
And every hungover mornin'
Was an unheeded warnin'
That I shared with my lost pals

And the music flowed
And my chosen road grew wider every day
'Til the highs got low and the will said no
I can't go on that way

Can't go that way, can't go that way
Yes, the highs got low and the will said no
I can't go on that way

Sugar is sweet and good prime meat
Is so hard to come by
Saccharine is around again
But today it's do or die

My baby is home where I belong
And this is still my day
I am hanging on and I am coming on strong
And I can't go on that way

Can't go that way, can't go that way
I am still hanging on and coming on strong
And I can't go on that way

Up is down and next time around
I ain't going 'round again
When it comes my time, I'm gonna stop at the
line
And forget where I've been

Who was it said that alive is dead
Like the summer's day
Just let her go and let a new wind blow
'Cause I can't go on that way

Can't go that way, can't go that way
Just let her go and let a new wind blow
'Cause I can't go on that way

LATELY

1977

Lately, I've been thinking
That you don't love me at all
Lately, I've been reading
And the writing on the wall
Is saying, looks like you'll be going
And I've no sure way of knowing
But somehow that's what I've been thinking lately

Lately, you've been saying things
That I don't understand
Lately, you look through me
As if I'm another man
Instead of your old one and only
I'm beginning to get lonely
I've been feeling you'll be leaving, lately

You might as well just stop it now
'Cause I already know
You wouldn't hurt me less
If you just go ahead and go
You know your heart's already gone
So you might as well go on
Things have not been working for us, lately
Things have not been working for us, lately

A WEDNESDAY CAR

1977

The assembly line is running slow on Monday
They've been living it up and laying up Saturday and Sunday
On Tuesday, they're about to come around
But they still feel bad and they're kinda down
And mad 'cause they've got four more days before the weekend rolls around

On Wednesday, they're feeling fine again
And they're working like a dog and digging in
Trying to do everything they should, putting 'em cars together good
And I got me a car that was made on Wednesday
If you're gonna buy yourself a new car
You just better hope you're lucky enough to get one made on Wednesday

On Thursday, the weekend is in sight
And they're in a hurry and they don't do nothing right
Friday is the worst day of the week
That's the day they make lemons, dogs, and freaks
If your car was made on Friday, friend, you'll soon be in the creek

'Cause it's payday and the loafing has begun
Lord, them Friday cars, just hope you don't get one
Monday, Tuesday, Thursday, and Friday
Are all bad days and the only try day is Wednesday
And my car was made on Wednesday, on Wednesday

If your car wasn't made on Wednesday
I'd advise you not to even leave home

A Wednesday Car.

John R Cash

Lord them boys were all hung over on Monday
From livin it up and Layin' up
Saturday and Sunday.

On Tuesday they're comin' round
But still hung over and kinda down
And mad cause they've got four more days
Before the weekend rolls around

On Wednesday they're feelin good again
And workin' hard and diggin' in.
Tryin to do everything they should
Puttin' them cars together good.
Hope I can get me a car that's
Made on Wednesday.
~~Wednesday~~
~~Hope I can get me a car~~
~~that's made on Wednesday.~~

On Thursday The weekend is in sight.
And they're rushing through the working day
And they don't do nothing right.

And Friday, Lord Friday
It is the worst of ~~all~~ the week
If your Car was made on Friday
friend you'll soon be up a creek

~~It's payday and early drinkin and hurry~~
~~Hope you get a car~~
~~that was made on Wednesday~~

~~If your car was made on friday~~
~~you should worry.~~
~~And on a monday Tuesday and Thursday~~
~~They're all in a reckless frenzy~~
~~Hope I can get me a car~~
~~that was made on Wednesday.~~

It's early drinkin' ~~and~~ payday,
rush & hurry
If your car was made on payday
you should worry
Monday Tuesday Thursday and Friday
Are all dead days and the Only high day
It's Wednesday, ~~hope I get a car~~
my car was made on Wednesday,

It's payday and the drinkin has begun
Them Friday cars, just hope you don't get one

WHO'S GENE AUTRY?

1977

Whoopi-ty-aye-oh, rocking to and fro
Back in the saddle again

My little boy said, "Daddy, who's Gene Autry?"
His old movie was coming on TV
And I said, "Let me tell you about him, son."
And I took him upon my knee

"Why, when I was a little boy, about your size
And just about every Saturday night
When I could scrape up a dime for the movies
And when my daddy said all right

"I'd be right downtown at the picture show
Like everybody else that could
To see a handsome man
On a big fine stallion going about, doing good."

Singing, "Whoopi-ty-aye-oh," rocking to and fro
Put him back in the saddle again
Whoopi-ty-aye-yay, let him go on his way
Back in the saddle again

"Why, he could ride his horse and play his guitar
And sing, all at the same time
And I was riding right along there beside him
On that broomstick pony of mine.

"And you know, his pistol never ran out of bullets
When the bad guys had to be stopped
And somehow his bullets never drew any blood
But the bad guys dropped when he shot.

"Yeah, old Gene was the image of justice
And goodness and purity
And in the eyes of a poor, little country boy
He made the world look better to me."

Singing, "Whoopi-ty-aye-oh," rocking to and fro
Put him back in the saddle again
Whoopi-ty-aye-yay, let him go on his way
Back in the saddle again

"And you know, the way
He rescued the rancher's daughter
He'd send a thrill right up the aisle.
And the ending would always send us home
With a good, victorious smile.

"Now you ask me, 'Who's Gene Autry?'
Well, son, go ahead and watch the show
And then ride off into the sunset with him
Like I did, forty years ago."

Singing, "Whoopi-ty-aye-oh," rocking to and fro
Put him back in the saddle again
Whoopi-ty-aye-yay, let him go on his way
Back in the saddle again

ALL NIGHT LONG

1978

The pain goes on since you've been gone
All night long, yes
The pain goes on since you've been gone
All night long
The pain goes on since you've been gone
All night long

Baby, when will you come to me?
The blues hang around when the sun goes
down
All night long
All night long
All night long
Baby, reconsider me

I need you now and I need you bad
All night long
All night long
All night long
Baby, I need you terribly

Wake up in the mornin' and I ain't been asleep
All night long
All night long
All night long
Baby, don't you remember me

DAN

1978

His daddy was a black man
His mother, she was white
He's the kind of man the Klan
Goes looking for at night
Born across the border
And his days just marked along
And the world paid no attention
Until he broke into a song

Dan, Dan, Dan
You swe-eet singin' man
If sometimes we could touch
I'd do more than hold your hand

Dan, Dan, Dan
You sweet singin', pretty playing
Daydream makin' man

His blue jeans were faded
His boots, wore out, I guess
His bearded head was tangled
Twisted in a pretty mess
His eyes were onyx diamonds
His smile could do no wrong
And he's had my heart singing
Since the day I heard his song

May 23 1978 Song? #1

ALL NIGHT LONG

The pain goes on since you've been gone
All night long, yes
The pain goes on since you've been gone
All night long
The pain goes on since you've been gon
All night long
Baby, when will you come to me

The blues hang around when the sun goes down
All night long
"
"
"
Baby Reconsider me

I need you now and I need you bad
All night long
"
"
Baby I need you terribly

Wake up in the morning and I aint been asleep
All night long
"
"
Baby dont you remember me.

JRC

Tune to "People Keep a Comin And the Train Gone"

Oct 14th 1978 (But written in July) #2

"DAN"

His daddy was a black man
His mother she was white
He's the kind of man the klan
Goes looking for at night
Born across the border
And his days just marked along
And the world paid no attention
Till he broke into a song

chs Dan Dan Dan
You swe-eet singin man
If sometimes we could touch
I'd do more than hold your hand
Dan Dan Dan
You sweet singin', pretty playin
Day dream makin' man

His blue jeans were faded
His boots worn out, I guess
His bearded head was tangled
Twisted in a pretty mess
His eyes were onyx diamonds
His smile could do no wrong
And he's had my heart singing
Since the day I heard his song.

I saw Dan Hill on T.V. and wrote this song for a girl singer who might be hung up on him.

J.R.C.

Nov 29 1978

Feelin' Like a Million or
Troubles on Vacation

#2

I was glad to see you
When the sun came up this morning
I was glad to hear you say
I'm still in love with you
Dont you know I couldnt stand it
If you ever leave me baby
I just couldn't take it
If you ever were untrue
But my troubles on vacation
When you treat me like you do

This song written originally during filming of Thaddeus Rose & Eddie

When I get in the pits
When I get in the dumps
I think of you and I get happy
Then it wont be long until
I'm knockin' on your door again
And the smilin' open welcome
That youre always there to give me
And your gentle toleration
And not askin' where I've been
~~Sends my troubles on vacation~~ Keeps me feelin
When you smile and let me in

When I can ever know for sure
That I can stop my rambling
When you can believe that I
Can settle down with you.
If you will take a chance on me
I'll do my best to make you happy
And you'll know that you can depend
On me to come on through
~~Well spend~~ ~~send trouble on vacation~~ Well be feel
For the life of me and you.

Feelin like a million
And [illegible]

FEELIN' LIKE A MILLION

with Jack Wesley Routh

1978

I was glad to see you
When the sun came up this morning
I was glad to hear you say
I'm still in love with you
Don't you know I couldn't stand it
If you ever leave me, baby
I just couldn't take it
If you ever were untrue
But my trouble's on vacation
When you treat me like you do

When I get in the pits
I think of you and I get happy
Then it won't be very long until
I'm knockin' on your door again
And the smilin' open welcome
That you're always there to give me
And your gentle toleration
And not askin' where I've been
Keep me feelin' like a million
When you smile and let me in

When I can ever know for sure
That I can stop my rambling
When you can believe that I
Can settle down with you
If you will take a chance on me
I'll do my best to make you happy
And you'll know that you can depend
On me to come on through
We'll be feelin' like a million
And I'll send trouble on vacation
For the life of me and you

FREIGHT TRAIN

traditional

adapted in 1978

Freight train, freight train
Goin' so fast
Freight train, freight train
Goin' so fast
I don't care what train I'm on
As long as it keeps rolling on

Roll through mountains, let me see
Peaceful valleys under me
Let me make believe that she
Is sharing every mile with me

Roll into the dark of night
No, thank you, leave off the light
I'll recline and close my eyes
And try to figure broken ties

Roll through cities, noise, and glare
I'm no dreamer, she ain't there
Please don't stop in one place
Or I'll begin to see her face

Oct. 29 '78

Had Mother Maybelles funeral yesterday—and I cant write about that yet—So I'll re-write an old Song.

Freight Train

Duet?

cho Freight train Freight Train
Goin so fast
Freight train Freight train
Goin so fas
I dont care what train I'm on
As long as it keeps rolling on

Roll through mountains, let me see
Peaceful valleys under me
Let me make believe that she
Is sharing every mile with me

cho Roll into the dark of night.
No, thank you, leave off the light
I'll recline and close my eyes
And try to figure broken ties

Roll through cities, noise and glare
I'm no dreamer—She isn't there
Please dont stop long in one place
Or I'll begin to see her face

cho

JRC

THE GREATEST COWBOY OF THEM ALL

1978

I have always had my heroes
I've loved a lot of legends
Many men in my mind are riding tall
But my cowboy hero hat's off
To the man who rode a donkey
He's the greatest cowboy of them all

He loves all his little dogies
He speaks to them kind and gently
And He'll lift up any maverick that falls
He sees every stray that scatters
Like it's the only one that matters
He's the greatest cowboy of them all

Once He rode into the sunset
Of some returning sunrise
He'll call up all the riders in the sky
I'll get my roll together
Getting ready for that sunrise
That winds up where old cowboys never die

The trail He rides is narrow
But it's straighter than an arrow
And He rides point for all the great and small
He will take us through the wire
On to that plain that's higher
He's the greatest cowboy of them all

I WILL ROCK AND ROLL WITH YOU

1978

They used to call me rockabilly
All of us ran through
When Elvis opened up the door
Boom-bop-a-lop-bam-boo

I didn't ever play much rock and roll
'Cause I got so much country in my soul
But I'm a different man for loving you
And I take a shot at what you ask me to

And baby I will rock and roll with you
If I have to

Memphis 1955
On Union Avenue
Carl and Jerry and Charlie and Roy
And Billy Riley, too

A new sun rising
On the way we sing
And a world of weirdos
Waiting in the wings

But I love you
And though I'm past forty-two
There are still a few things
Yet I didn't do

And baby I will rock and roll with you
If I have to

I'LL SAY IT'S TRUE

1978

I've never been in prison
I don't know much about trains
My favorite singer cooks my breakfast
I like her fancy and I like her plain

I love bright and flashing colors
Like hot pink and Dresden blue
But if they ask me if it's true
That I still love you, I'll say it's true

I'd be happy in a mansion
Or in an old run-down shotgun shack
I like the feel of silk and satin
So I don't know why I wear black

I love New York City
Bet your cowgirl boots I do
But if they ask me if it's true
That I still love you, I'll say it's true

I'll say it's true
So don't let it bother you
Just let them old tales all stay twisted
I will set 'em straight about you

I have not been in the Army
I'm an Indian from years ago
When they ask if I know Waylon
I tell them, "I think so."

I do not plan on retiring
From anything I do
But if they ask me if it's true
That I still love you, I'll say it's true

I'll say it's true
So don't let it bother you
Just let them old tales all stay twisted
I will set 'em straight on you

I got plans to keep right on singing
And I do know Emmylou
But if they ask me if it's true
That I still love you, I'll say it's true

I'M GONNA SIT ON THE PORCH AND PICK ON MY OLD GUITAR

1978

I'm gonna sit on the porch and pick on my old guitar
I'm gonna lay on my back and laugh at my lucky star
And then I'm gonna fly away and never come back someday
'Less I thought I would land right close to where you are

Well, if I thought anybody really cared I'd send back word
Strapped to the leg of a trans-celestial bird
I wonder if I really ever did leave, how many would there be to grieve?
How would they react to the word?

Well, I wouldn't want to hurt a solitary soul
I have still got all six foot two in control
But when my obligation's load is a greasy uphill road
And pleasing everybody but me is my first goal

Oh, I want to sit on my porch and pick on my old guitar
And just hope you're hanging loose, wherever you are
And for the joy you brought to me, this song I sung for thee
While I sit on my porch and pick on my old guitar

I'M TAKING DOWN HER MAN

1978

Casey never treated Molly right
I could hear them fighting every night
They called each other names
And I don't know that he's all the blame
But the walls were thin
And I kept up with their fights

I heard him hit her
And I heard her cry
He cussed her and he said, "I hope you die."
I busted through the door
And when I saw her on the floor
I landed one cold punch on his right eye

But that was long ago and now he's gone
I'd pass her door and see her there alone
So I started dropping by
And I taught her not to cry
I patted her and soothed her aching bones

Now Molly doesn't live in 203
She now lives in 205 with me
I don't know where he went
But I hope he ain't content
'Cause he doesn't deserve serenity

Just don't abuse your woman in my sight
'Cause I'll start in reverse that very night
To take all that I can
And give back like a man
I like to see a woman treated right

But if you fight as part of a lovers' game
Still, just in case, I'm taking down her man

IT COMES AND GOES

1978

I've been up and down and out and I have
been around
And I felt good more times than I felt bad
Loving you felt better than I've ever known
before
Losing you's the worst pain that I've had

But it comes and goes
It's like a blue wind blows
Yes, it goes and comes
But now I'm living some

And today my high didn't get any lower
And my low didn't fall anymore
But sometimes, when I drop my guard
Everybody knows

'Cause I can't control the feeling
And there ain't much sign of healing
'Cause when the pain is there, it always shows
But it comes and goes

In my mind I'm holding you and loving you
again
I hear you laugh and I feel you cling to me
Although it's over, I'm still holding on a little
bit
And there's a lot of pain in the memories

But it comes and goes
It's like a blue wind blows
Yes, it goes and comes
But now I'm living some

And today my high didn't get any lower
And my low didn't fall anymore
But sometimes, when I drop my guard
Everybody knows

'Cause I can't control the feeling
And there ain't much sign of healing
'Cause when the pain is there, it always shows
But it comes and goes

PRETTY PICTURES IN MY MIND

with Jeremiah Fraites and Wesley Schultz

1978

There are scenes that I will always see
I can never be blind
There are pages, precious pages
Pretty pictures in my mind

There are things that I remember
Like the way for other times
I will bring out on a down day
Pretty pictures in my mind

I will rerun love and laughter
From the vaults locked back behind
On an ugly day I will do it
Pretty pictures in my mind

Lo and behold
A dark room is where I sit alone
The lights turn red
The chemicals form the images
I can see it now

Oh yes, I will be a dreamer
There are so few of my kind
With a treasure trove of beauty
Pretty pictures in my mind

April 16 1978

There are scenes that I will always see
I never can be blind
There are pages, precious pages
Pretty pictures in my mind

There are things that I remember
Locked away for other times
I will bring out on a down day
Pretty pictures in my mind

I will re-run love and laughter
From the vaults locked back behind
On an ugly day I'll do it
Pretty pictures in my mind

Oh yes, I will be a dreamer
There are so few of my kind
With a treasure-trove of beauty
Pretty pictures in my mind

J.R.C

#1

TEETH, HAIR, AND EYEBALLS

1978

All that's gonna be left of you is teeth, hair, and eyeballs
If I ever see you fool around with her
I ain't takin' chances on your havin' second chances
So you won't ever be the way you were
I will use all in my power to destroy you
I will wipe you out as clean as Lottie's eye
All that's gonna be left of you is teeth, hair, and eyeballs
If you try to take my woman, you will die

You'd never make intensive care if I get to you first
Though I'm a gentle man most of the time
I'd have no reservations about the way I would destroy you
If you tried for the woman I call mine
I would take what punishment I had comin'
I would let them strap me in and take my life
'Cause all that would be left of you is teeth, hair, and eyeballs
If I ever see you look twice at my wife

I can't stand a wishy-washy lily-livered weakling
Who'd let his love go to another man
You might steal or cheat me, but there's one thing that I'm keeping
I'll slaughter you with my own two bare hands
I'd give you almost anything you needed
I'd help you out in any way you lack
But all they'll ever find of you is teeth, hair, and eyeballs
If ever you should sniff around my shack

BILLY BROWN

1979

Billy Brown spent seven years
With the Tennessee police
Then he'd moonlight in his garage
In all that grime and grease
His fingernails would not come clean
No matter how he'd rub
But Alice Brown never once complained
About the ring around the tub

Eight hours a day and his take-home pay
Would not pay off the home
But Billy Brown would not sit down
And he would not move on
He took pride in that brick house
And that half-acre yard
And Alice Brown never let him know
That a cop's wife's life is hard

Alice had a call one night
That Billy had been shot
She rushed into intensive care
Though they said that she could not
She stayed beside his bed nine days
And she knew that he'd pull through
He gave a weakened smile and said,
"Alice, thanks to God and you."

Now he wears his uniform and badge
And he does his job again
And just yesterday he booked a man
That tried to do him in
Eight hours a day and his take-home pay
Still won't pay off the home

But Billy Brown will not sit down
And he will not move on
For he takes pride in that brick house
And that half-acre yard
And Alice Brown never lets him know
That a cop's wife's life is hard

SHE'S A GOER

1979

Well, I think that I should tell you she's a goer
And when she goes, she won't come back no more
There isn't anything like it when you've got her all alone
And there's not anything that can replace her when she's gone

Oh, I envy you until the day she walks back out your door
And that she's going to do, because she's a goer

Now, don't let her stay too long, she'll take the heart
Right out of your song, you'll pay the price for her one time
But she won't be back anymore
I just thought I'd tell you she's a goer

Yes, I guess, I should have told you she's a goer
I should have told you that way back long before
But I was trying to overcome the pain she put me through
I was fighting to forget her when she got around to you

Oh, you'll be heaven high until she doesn't want you anymore
Then she'll be gone again 'cause she's a goer

Now, don't let her stay too long, she'll take the heart
Right out of your song, you'll pay the price for her one time
But she won't be back anymore
I just thought I'd tell you she's a goer

She's a Goer   Feb 6 1977

I think that I should tell you
She's a goer,
And when she goes she don't
Come back no more

There ain't nothing like her
When you've got her all alone
And there's no way ~~I~~ to tell you
How you'll miss her when she's gone

You'll think that you're in heaven
Till she walks back out that door
And that she's bound to do
Cause she's a goer

I don't know if you knew
But she's a goer
~~I~~ I didn't have the heart
to let you know before
I knew how you felt about her
And I envied you
But I ~~just~~ couldn't be the one
To tell you what she'd do

She'll love you like
You never had before
Then she'll be movin on
Cause she's a goer

WHEN HE COMES

1979

Every eye shall see
Every ear shall hear the sound of angels
When He comes
When He comes

Every knee shall bow
Every tongue shall confess that He is
Lord
When He comes
When He comes

And He'll plant His beautiful feet upon
this mountain
And the dead of all the ages
Who believed on Him will rise
And I'll be one, I'll be one
In the first resurrection
When He comes
When He comes
When He comes

Everyone then will know
That it's Him, really Him
The one and only
When He comes
When He comes

Glorified and transformed
I'll arise at His call
I'll be ready
When He comes
When He comes

And He'll plant His beautiful feet upon
this mountain
And the dead of all the ages
Who believed on Him will rise
And I'll be one, I'll be one
In the first resurrection
When He comes
When He comes
When He comes

When He Comes

by
John Cash

Every eye shall see
Every ear shall hear
The sound of angels
When He comes, When He comes
Every knee shall bow
Every tongue confess
That He is Lord
When He comes, When He comes

And He will plant His beautiful feet
Upon this mountain
And the dead of all the ages
Who believed on Him shall rise
And I'll be one, I'll be one
In the first resurrection
When He comes, When He comes
When He comes

Everyone will know
That its Him, really Him
The one and only
When He comes, When He comes
Gloryfied and transformed
I'll arise at His call
I'll be ready
When He Comes, When He comes

Repeat Chorus

May 28 1978 (Happy Birthday Kevin Jones)

C

WINGS IN THE MORNING

Rocks on the road and you stumble and fall
Lights gettin dim you dont see at all
Feelin you way and I scrape and you tear
But wings in the morning you'll take to the air

Chorus Wings in the morning
And License to fly
Straight to the portals
Of never-more-die
Never-more- pain
in your old achemy bones
To carry us home

You seem to never get off of the ground
Never get up - once you've fallen down
But I guarantees on that gettin up day
Wings in the morning and you'll fly away

Dont mean to say that I'm better than you
All that I'm claiming is your promise too.
Check it all out and youll see that its so
Wings in the morning, get ready to go.

WINGS IN THE MORNING

1979

Wings in the morning and license to fly
Straight to the portals of never more die
Never more pain in them old aching bones
Wings in the morning to carry us home

My grandfather lived by the book all his life
On rich bottom land with twelve kids and a wife
He never saw TV, nor rode a jet plane
But he knew that heaven was holding his claim

Wings in the morning and license to fly
Straight to the portals of never more die
Never more pain in them old aching bones
Wings in the morning to carry us home

The salt of the earth, yet with faith in the Lord
They all got together in that one accord
And what could be greater than God's guarantee
That we can have heaven for eternity?

Wings in the morning and license to fly
Straight to the portals of never more die
Never more pain in them old aching bones
Wings in the morning to carry us home

Rocks in the road and we stumble and fall
Lights getting low, so we don't see at all
But I promise you, on that getting-up day
Wings in the morning, we'll fly away

Wings in the morning and license to fly
Straight to the portals of never more die
Never more pain in them old aching bones
Wings in the morning to carry us home

YOU'LL GET YOURS AND I'LL GET MINE

1979

I don't like the taste of whiskey
Or the smell of musty grass
And when they pass around the trips
I've learned to let them pass

I'm not going to drift away on powder
I'm not going to blow away on smoke
I'll put everything on Jesus Christ
And I'm going to go for broke

So, live your time, live your time
Someday we'll all stand in line
When rewards are handed out
You'll get yours and I'll get mine

But no "honorable mention"
Will come traveling down the line
Live your time, stand in line
You'll get yours and I'll get mine

I'm not pointing any fingers
I'm not trying to be your light
I'm just saying that I believe
And I'm finally getting it right

But what works for me
Doesn't necessarily mean that it'll work
for you
But I've tested and I've tasted
And I know He's tried and true

So, live your time, live your time
Someday we'll all stand in line
When rewards are handed out
You'll get yours and I'll get mine

But no "honorable mention"
Will come traveling down the line
Live your time, stand in line
You'll get yours and I'll get mine

I'M A NEWBORN MAN

with June Carter

1979

I'm a newborn man
I'm a newborn man
I'm a newborn man
And on the rock I stand
I'm a newborn man

I'm a newborn man
I'm a newborn man
I'm a newborn man
And on the rock I stand
I'm a newborn man

He put a light on me
He put a light on me
He put a light on me
So now I can see
He put a light on me

He loves me all the time
He loves me all the time
He loves me all the time
I'm His and He's mine
He loves me all the time

I'm a newborn man
I'm a newborn man
I'm a newborn man
And on the rock I stand
I'm a newborn man

I was dying and the time was flying
And I heard Him calling me
My will was bent and I did repent
And His sweet love set me free

I'm a newborn man
I'm a newborn man
I'm a newborn man
And on the rock I stand
I'm a newborn man

SIX

* INTERLUDE *

1980–1989

INDUCTION INTO THE Country Music Hall of Fame is typically the capstone of a career, a final victory lap. The honoree is serenaded and celebrated... then placed back on the shelf, to be smiled at and spoken of in the past tense. In the first twenty years of the institution's existence (1961–1981), it welcomed twenty-six performers, seven of whom were already dead on election, with the average age of the rest a spry sixty. Every one of them had been born before the Great Depression. Only one (Eddy Arnold) recorded a Top 10 hit after entering. For nearly all, the Hall was their last trophy.

Cash knew the score, but at forty-eight — the youngest person ever elected — he was not ready to shuffle off into the shadows. He had more to say. "Don't write me off yet," he told the world at his own induction ceremony in 1980. That was easier said than done. He was *expected* to step off the stage. For the next ten years, the accolades continued to roll in, the TV specials garnered good ratings, and his seat up in the pantheon of legends remained warm. But the records did not sell, and he increasingly was regarded as part of the past. In the moment, none of this seemed unusual. It was the way things worked. Johnny Cash may once have been the biggest-selling artist on earth; the laws of physics still applied.

This is not to say that the 1980s were filled with relentless darkness. By all rights, Cash *should* have been in eclipse by this point in his life and career, but the latter-day distractions of ill health, family turmoil, and the casual indifference of the market, like two decades earlier, could only knock him down, not out. And his written output remained prolific. The novel *Man in White* was authored at this time, as was the hilarious "Beans for Breakfast" and his collaboration with Paul McCartney, "New Moon Over Jamaica." Still, it was not lost on him that all the honors being bestowed were for things he *had done*. As the decade came to a close, he was wistful:

Do you remember
Back in 1969?
We gathered 'round the room
You sang yours and I sang mine

I could make a living
Driving nails or driving trucks

Sleep beneath the bridge or in the streets
Down on my luck.

I'd stand the cold and hunger
If they'd let me hear the songs
Everybody write one
That us bums can sing along.

We sang songs that made a difference
And we can again somehow.

But unbeknownst to anyone, Johnny Cash's time was about to come around again.

ALL-SEEING EYE

1980s

If you give your heart to Him
He will fill you to the brim
There's an all-seeing eye watching you

If you do wrong and get caught
Go to Him
Your soul is bought

There's an all-seeing eye
Watching you, watching you
There's an all-seeing eye watching you

If you give your heart
to him
He will fill fill you to
the brim
Theres an all-seeing
eye watching you
If you do wrong and get
caught
Go to Him your soul
is bought
Theres an all seeing
eye watching you

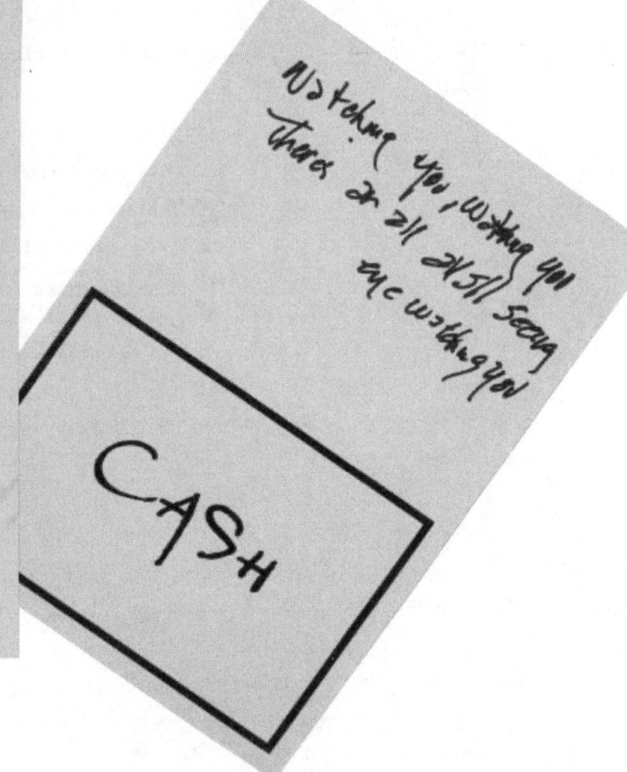
Watching you, watching you
Theres an all seeing
eye watching you

CASH

BARBER OF THE HAIR

1980s

He longed to be the
Barber of the hair
He spent his empty hours
At the barbershop
Down yonder, on the square

He sat beside the chair
And watched him trim away the hair
He heard all that was said
As the barber worked on every head
He longed to be the barber of the hair

Mose Regger was the barber of the hair
And Merle watched
From his nail keg
Beside the barber's chair

He watched the clippers fly
And swore that, by and by
He'd know the barber trade
No matter what it paid
He idolized the barber of the hair

He LONGED TO BE THE Barber of the hair
He spent his empty hours
At the barber shop
Down yonder on the square
He sat beside the chair
And watched him fixin' away the hair
He heard all that was said
As the barber worked on every head
He longed to be
The Barber of the Hair

Mose Regger was the Barber of the hair
And Merle watched
From his nail keg
Beside the barber's chair
He watched the clippers fly
And swore that by and by
He'd know the barber trade
No matter what it paid
He idolized the barber of the hair

BIG-HEARTED GIRL

with Jesse Aycock, Dave Schools, Todd Snider, Daniel Sproul, Chad Staehly, and Duane Trucks

1980s

You've done every dirty thing
That a woman shouldn't do
You're polished in the ways of the world
But when you run your velvet fingers
Through the troubles in my head
I'm glad you're a big-hearted girl

Big-hearted girl, spread yourself around
But remember me when you get back in town

You've broken every rule
That a lover shouldn't break
And I really hate to share you with the world
But when you come to me crying
And clinging to me
I'm glad you are a big-hearted girl

Big-hearted girl, you know I understand
But remember me when you really want a man

There's a high price you'll pay
For giving yourself away
The gossip's gonna throw you for a whirl
But if the truth was known
They're wishing they were you
They'd like to be a big-hearted girl

Big-hearted girl, I won't tie you down
But let me know when you'll be back around

Capo ...
Start in G ... in C ...

Boom
Boom
Boom
G

Big Hearted Girl

Wootton

You've done every dirty thing
That a woman shouldn't do
You're polished in the ways of the wor[ld]
But when you run your ~~[illegible]~~ fing[ers]
Through the troubles in my head
I'm glad you are a big hearted girl

Big Hearted Girl, spread yourself aroun[d]
But remember me when you get back to t[own]

You've broken every rule
That a lover ~~ought~~ shouldn't brea[k]
And I really hate to share you with the wo[rld]
But when you come to me crying
And clinging on to me
I'm glad you are a big hearted girl

Big hearted girl, you know I understa[nd]
Remember me when you really want a ma[n]
instrumental - Wootton

Theres a high price you'll pay
For giving yourself away
The gossips ~~[illegible]~~ throw you a whirl
But if ~~[illegible]~~ the truth was known
They're wishing they were you
They'd like to be a big hearted gir[l]

Big Hearted Girl I wont tie you down
But let me know when you'll be back aro[und]

BODY ON BODY

with Jewel Kilcher

1980s

You wonder how true love goes
No one can say 'cause nobody knows
Nobody knows
Like rain on a rock, like a leaf in the air
There's no way to tell but it's going
  somewhere
But where? Nobody knows

It's heart on heart, soul on soul
Body on body is how it goes
Heart on heart, soul on soul
Body on body is all it knows

Body on body
You wonder what true love knows
No one can say how it goes
It just flows

It don't make sense
It's like a midnight sun
And one on one is only won
When you're in its throes

It's heart on heart, soul on soul
Body on body is how it goes
Heart on heart, soul on soul
Body on body is all it knows
Body on body

So lay yourself next to me
You be the stone and I will be the sea
No space, no time
Lost inside a larger mind

Heart on heart, soul on soul
Body on body is how it goes
Heart on heart, soul on soul
Body on body is all it knows

Heart on heart, soul on soul
Body on body is how it goes
Heart on heart, soul on soul
Body on body is all it knows

You wonder where [how] – true love goes
No one can say – cause nobody knows
Like rain on a rock – Like a leaf in the air
No way to tell – But its going somewhere
You wonder what – True love knows
No one can say – Cause nobody knows.
It dont make sense – Like a midnite sun
And one and one – is only one

Heart on heart – and soul on soul
Body on Body is how it goes
Heart on heart and soul on soul
Body on body – is all it knows.

BLUEBONNET BLUE

1980s

I'm bluebonnet blue
I'm bluebonnet blue
I've still got Texas
But I don't have you
And I'm bluebonnet blue

The road 'round the rim of the plateau
Was bathed in the spring's new moonlight
We sat looking down upon Llano
And made wedding plans there that night

I'm blue-bonnet blue
" " "
I've still got Texas
But I dont have you
And I'm Blue Bonnet Blue

The road round the rim of the platteau
Was bathed in the springs new moonlight.
We sat looking down upon Llano
And made wedding plans there that night

BUT IT GOES

1980s

You ask me how it goes with me
Now that she's a memory
I don't know
It just goes slow
But it goes

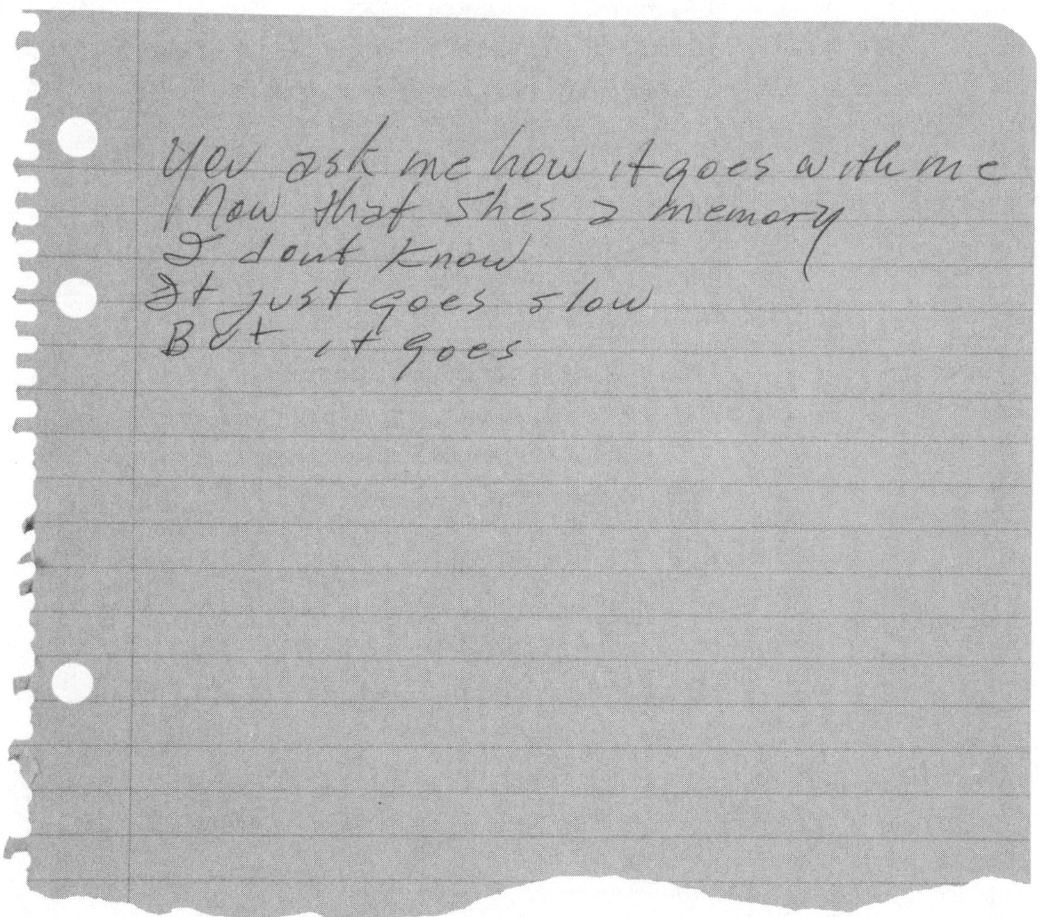

You ask me how it goes with me
Now that shes a memory
I dont know
It just goes slow
But it goes

DAILY BREAD

1980s

I work hard for my money
And I love my woman right
I don't have trouble sleeping
'Cause she's right there at night
Beside me sleeping like a baby
'Cause nothing's going wrong
And then she says good morning
It's a sweet good morning song
She runs her long smooth fingers
Through the troubles in my head
And she makes sure I get my daily bread

DEAD OR ALIVE

1980s

Well, the new sheriff sent me a letter
He said, "Come up and see me, dead or alive.
Come up and see me, dead or alive.
Well, it's a hard road, dead or alive."

Well, he never even sent me my picture
Say, how do I look, boys, dead or alive?
Well, I don't like your hard rock hotel
Dead or alive, no, Sheriff
It's a hard road, dead or alive

Well, I gotta go see my little sweet thing
Dead or alive, yeah, Sheriff
Well, it's a hard road, dead or alive

Dead or Alive

Well the new sheriff sent me a letter
" " " " " " " " " "
He said come up and see me dead or Alive
" " " " " " " "
Well its a hard road dead or Alive " " " "

Well he even sent me my picture
"
Say how do I look boys dead or Alive "

Well I dont like your hard rock hotel
"
Dead or Alive, No sheriff "
" "
Its a hard road dead or Alive " " " " " "

Well I gotta go see my little sweet thing
"
Dead or alive yeah sheriff "
Well its a hard road dead or Alive
" " " "

DOES ANYBODY OUT THERE LOVE ME?

with Jewel Kilcher

1980s

It's a cold and cruel world
When there's no one to share the night
It's a lonely road to travel
In the early morning light

The longest trip you'll take
Is from the mind to the heart
Being in your own skin
That's the hardest part

Somewhere there's somebody
A place where I belong
So give myself a talking-to
And hey, hey, I'll move along

It's a long and endless journey
When you're on the lost pathway
Today will not be different
Than a hundred yesterdays

Maybe there's a new life
Don't it give the morning sun
And I'll be a better man
For where I've been and what I've done

Somewhere there's somebody
A place where you belong
So give yourself a talking-to
And hey, hey, move along

Does anybody out there love me?
Does anybody out there
Care or wanna share?
Does anybody love me?

When that feelin' crawls up your arm
And hits you in the gut
You better brace yourself, boy
It's gonna take more than luck

When the devil's in your hand
Taking that train right off its tracks
You tell that devil go to hell
You're never coming back

Somewhere there's somebody
A place where you belong
So give yourself a talking-to
And hey, hey, move along

It's a cold and cruel world
When there's no one to share the night
And it's a lonely road to travel
In the early morning light
~~Maybe this will be the day~~
~~Some~~
~~Somewhere there's~~
Somewhere there's somebody
And a place where you belong
~~So you rise up with the morning sun~~
So you give yourself a talking to
And slowly move along

~~Somewhere theres somebody~~
~~And a place for you you know~~
~~you give yourself a talking to~~
~~And then get up and go~~

Its a long and endless journey
When you're on the lost ~~highway~~ pathway
Today will not be different
Than a hundred yesterdays

But maybe theres a new life ~~dawning~~
Dawning With the morning sun
And ~~you'll~~ be a better man
For where ~~you've~~ I'll been and what you've do

Bridge:
Does Anybody out there
Does anybody out there love me care
Does " "
Want to share
Does " " " love me

FIRST GRADE OLD MAID TEACHER

1980s

First grade old maid teacher
Gettin' ready to go home
Thirty happy children
Are once again on their own

As they climb aboard the school bus
She smiles and waves goodbye
But the first grade old maid teacher
Wants to cry

The evening sun is setting
On the thirty empty chairs
But the first grade old maid teacher's
At her desk, still sitting there

She'll miss them 'til tomorrow
For she calls them all her own
But the first grade old maid teacher's
So alone
So alone

She remembers 1969
And how she loved her man
The thrills of that summertime
And how they made their plans

He proved untrue but she sits there
Reliving summer scenes
The first grade old maid teacher's
Got her dreams

She'll give up all her children
When the school lets out in June
But she'll keep all their pictures
In the dresser in her room

She'll make believe this summer
He'll come back from where he's gone
The first grade old maid teacher's
Dreamin' on

First Grade Old Maid Teacher

First grade old maid teacher
~~[illegible]~~ to go home
Thirty happy children
Once again are on their own
~~As~~ They climb aboard the school bus
She smiles and waves goodbye
But the first grade old maid teacher
Wants to cry.

Gettin ready to go home

The evening sun is setting
On ~~her~~ thirty empty chairs
But the first grade old maid teachers
At her ~~desk~~ still sitting there
She'll miss them till tomorrow
For she calls them all her own
But the first grade old maid teachers'
So alone.

She remembers 1969
~~And how she loved that man~~ her
The thrills ~~throughout~~ of all that that summertime
And how they made their plans
~~[illegible]~~
~~[illegible]~~ He proved untrue ~~but~~ she sits there
Re-living summer scenes
The first grade old maid teachers
Got her dreams

She'll give up al her children
When the school lets out in June
But she'll keep all their picture
In the dresser in her room
She'll make believe this summer
He'll come back from where hes gone
The first grade old maid teachers dreamin' on.

GATHERED 'ROUND THE FIRES OF HOME

1980s

Well, howdy do, aloha, how you been?
It's so good to see you once again
I will bet my boots you won't feel like a stranger long
When we're all gathered 'round the fires of home
It's a very special time tonight
Your being here
Just makes it all seem right

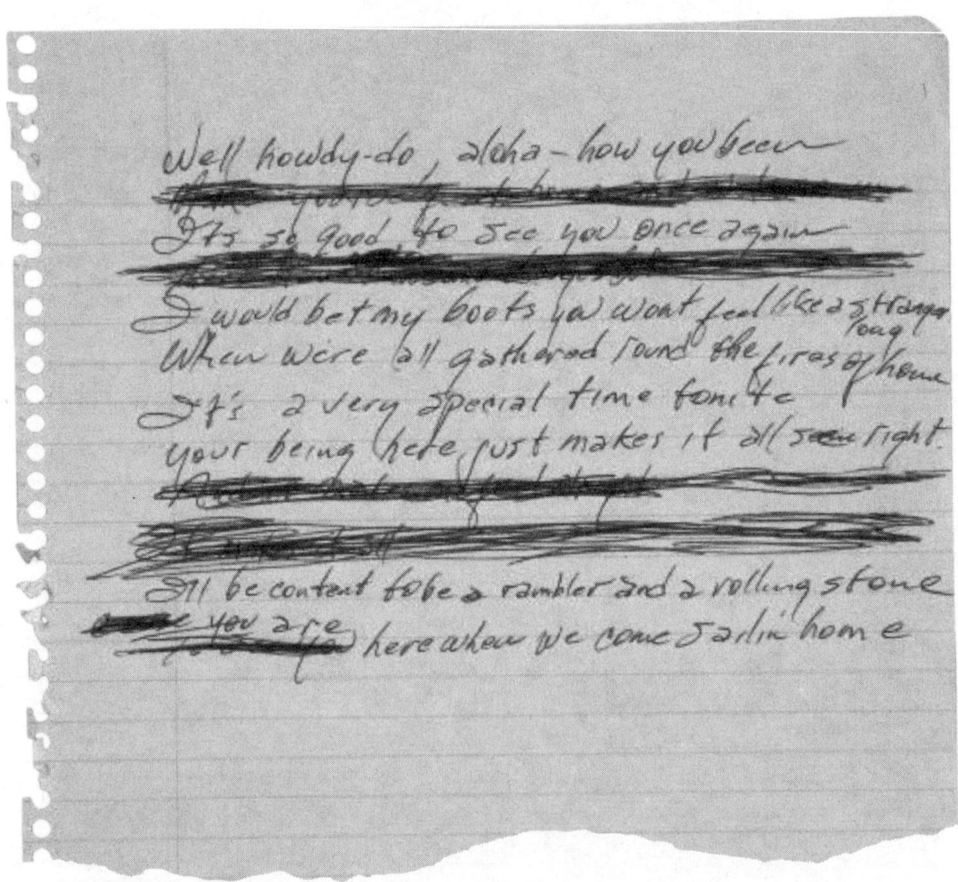

Well howdy-do, aloha - how you been
It's so good to see you once again
I would bet my boots you wont feel like a stranger long
When were all gathered round the fires of home
It's a very special time tonite
your being here just makes it all seem right.
I'll be content to be a rambler and a rolling stone
you are here when we come sailin home

HEY, BABY, WAKE UP

1980s

Hey, baby, wake up
If the sky should fall today
We could go outside and catch doves
And everything will be okay
Shake a leg and come on now
I need my biscuit buttered, babe
Hey, hey, I need my biscuit buttered, babe

Hey, baby, wake up
I saw it on Channel 4
The president's out running
Back and forth and to and fro
Gonna make some big decisions
And he thought you'd need to know
Hey, hey, hey. Ho, ho, ho

Hey, baby, wake up
Did you hear the latest news
The man said Roy and Dale split up
And Dale got Trigger, too
Yeah, I hear your sweet feet on the floor
I knew that'd get through to you
Hey, hey. Ha, ha, ha

Hey Baby Wake Up
If the sky should fall today
We could go outside and catch ~~doves~~ doves
And everything will be ok.
Shake a leg and come on now
I need my biscuit buttered, babe-
Hey Hey-

Hey Baby Wake up
~~[illegible]~~
~~[illegible]~~
~~[illegible]~~ I saw it on channel 4
The presidents out running
Back and forth and to and ~~fro~~
Gonna make some big decisions
And he thought you'd ~~need~~ to know
Hey Hey Hey ~~Ho~~ Ho Ho Ho

Hey baby wake up
Did you hear the latest news
The man said Roy and Dale split up
And Dale got trigger too
yeah I hear your sweet feet on the floor
I knew that'd get through to you
Hey Hey- ! -- Hahaha

I GOT MINE

1980s

I went down to a big crap game
Certainly was against my will
I lost every doggone nickel I had
But a greenback dollar bill

A forty-dollar bet layin' on the floor
And my buddy's point was a nine
When the police came he caught all of us
But I got mine

I got mine, let me tell you, I got mine
I grabbed that money and out the door I went flyin'
Ever since the big crap game
I've been livin' on chicken and wine

I HAD A REAL GOOD TIME

1980s

Last night was a real fine night
A fine night, a fine night, all right
And you were completely mine
And I had a real good time

Woke up this mornin' felt exactly right
Exactly right, after a real fine night
I can taste the memories runnin' through my mind
'Cause I had a real good time

I had a real good time
I had a real good time
And I'll bet you remember, too
It was feeling right for you

And didn't that big old moon
Smile at us through the natural shine
Oh, I had a real good time

I promise you that I will not forget
I close my eyes and feel you yet
Like a satin sheet, the feeling is so fine
I had a real good time

Hey, hey, I bet I'll hold you soon
Another night, but the same old moon
You're very special for a special time
And I had a real good time

I Had a Real Good Time

Last night was a real fine nite
A fine night, a fine nite alright
And you were completely mine
And I had a real good time

Woke up this mornin feeling exactly right
Exactly right after a real fine nite
I can taste the memories runnin thru my mind
Cause I had a real good time

Cho I had a real good time
" " " " "

And I'll bet you remember too,
I twas feeling right for you
And didn't that big old moon
Smile at us thru the natural shine
Oh I had a real good time

I promise you that I will not forget
I close my eyes and feel you yet
Like a satin sheet you with me yet
I had a real good time the feeling is so fine

Hey Hey I bet I'll hold you soon
Another night, but the same old moon
You're very special for a special time
And I had a real good time

I Had A Real Good Time

Last Night was a real fine night
A real fine night
Fine night Alright
And you — were completely mine
And I had a real good time

Cho I had a real good Time
" " " " " "

Sweet ~~memories~~ thrills running up ~~my~~ this spine of mine
And I had a real good time

Last night I will not forget
I will not forget
I can feel you yet
You were sweet and rare as a vintage wine
And I had a real good time

~~Last night will~~ Its gonna be a special memory
A special memory
A memory for me
Of feeling more than fairly fine
And I had a real good time.

I HAD A REAL GOOD TIME

(alternate version)

1980s

Last night was a real fine night
A real fine night
Fine night all right

And you were completely mine
And I had a real good time

I had a real good time
I had a real good time
Sweet thrills running up this spine of mine
And I had a real good time

Last night I will not forget, I will not forget
I can feel you yet
You were sweet and rare as a vintage wine
And I had a real good time

It's gonna be a special memory
A special memory, a memory for me
Of feeling more than fairly fine
And I had a real good time

I HAVE BEEN AROUND

1980s

I have been around
I have been on the incoming
And the outward bound
I came up from the fields
And I've been down on my knees
I have heard the angels
With a jaded heart
And I guess I gave the devil all his due
But I always come back around to you

I have been around
I have kissed the moonlight
On sweet auburn hair
I rode a wild horse
And I rode a Mach 2
I have been a counselor
And I have been a fool
I've been loved and I've been bored and I've been blue
But I always come back around to you

I have been around
I have tasted rapture — that I couldn't find again
Felt the power pouring
And I felt it coming in
I've been full but hungry
And abandoned to the bone
But in the end I knew of just one thing to pull me through
I always come back around to you

I Have Been Around

I have been around
I've been on the incoming
And the outward bound
I came up from the fields
And I've been down on my knees
~~I've been down on my back~~
~~In the cold hard ...~~
I have heard the angels
With jaded heart
And I guess I gave the devil all his due
But I always came back around to you

I have been around
~~I have been an upcoming~~
~~I have been a down going~~
I have kissed the moonlight
On sweet auburn hair
I rode a wild horse
And I rode Mach 2
I have been a counselor
And I have been a fool
I've been loved and I've been bored and I've been blue
But I always came back around to you

I have been around
I have tasted rapture that I couldn't find again
Felt the power pouring | ~~There were times I lost it~~
And I felt it coming in | ~~...~~
I've been full but hungry
And abandoned to the bone
But in the end I knew of just one thing to pull me through
I always came back around to you

I have Been Around

I have been around
I've been on the incoming and the outward bound
I came up from the fields
On my back and on my knees
I've been visited by angels
While demons badgered me
And I gave the devil more than his due
But I always came back around to you

I have been around
I have kissed the moonlight on a priceless pearl I found
I have been a counselor
And I have been a fool
I rode a wild horse
And I rode mach two
I've been loved and I've been bored and I've been blue
But I always came back around to you

I have been around
I have tasted rapture that could not again be found
I felt the power filling up
And felt the power gone
I've been full but hungry
And abandoned to the bone
In the end I knew one thing to pull me through
I always came back around to you.

I HAVE BEEN AROUND

(alternate version)

1980s

I have been around
I have been on the incoming
And the outward bound
I came up from the fields
And I've been down on my knees
I have been visited by angels
While demons badgered me
And I guess I gave the devil more than his due
But I always come back around to you

I have been around
I have kissed the moonlight
On a priceless pearl I found
I have been a counselor
And I have been a fool
I rode a wild horse
And I rode a Mach 2
I've been loved and I've been bored and I've been blue
But I always come back around to you

I have been around
I have tasted rapture that could not again be found
I felt the power filling up
And I felt the power gone
I've been full but hungry
And abandoned to the bone
In the end I know one thing to pull me through
I always come back around to you

I'LL BE TRUE

1980s

I'll be true to you tonight
Get you feeling good and lookin' right
With a song to make you want to dance
And a heavy heart ain't got a chance

Well, I got a song for the wayward man
And I've got a song about my native land
And a song of love that is pure and true
And it's all for fun and it's all for you

Well, I'm mighty glad I could come along
And join right in on my daddy's song
I'll do my best and I'll sing it loud
And I'll do my part to please the crowd

When the song is done and the night is
 through
You can take me home in the song with you
We'll be joy-bound and trouble-free
We will fly away, just you and me

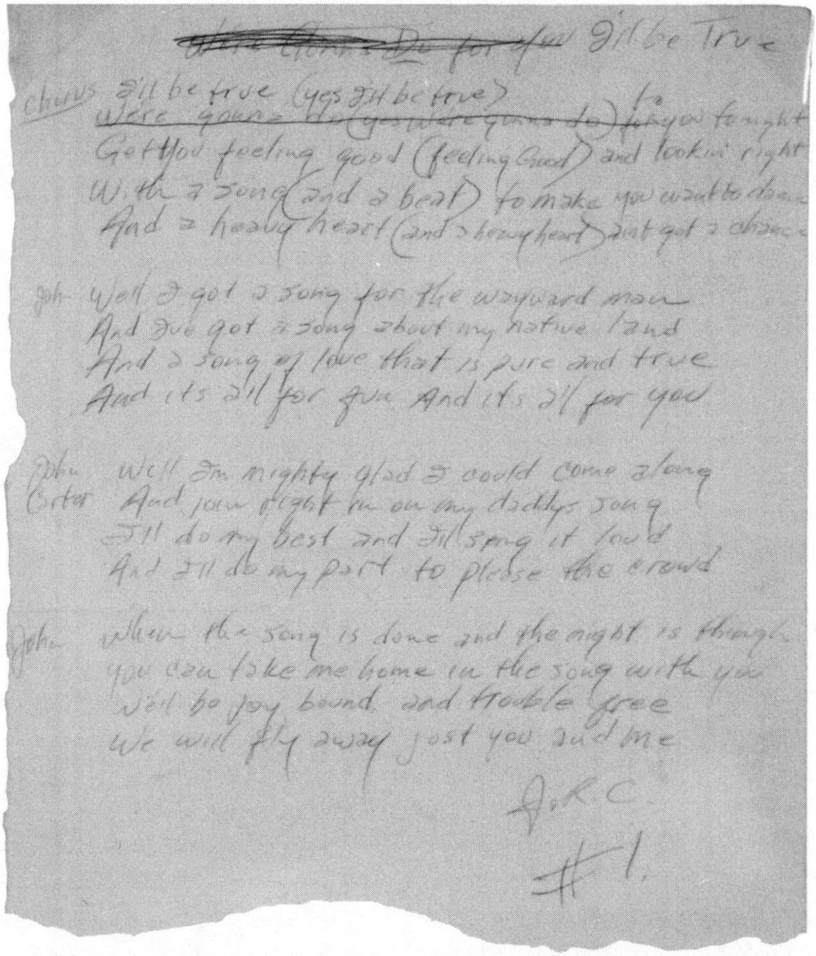

~~[illegible] for you~~ I'll be True

chorus I'll be true (yes I'll be true)
~~We're gonna do (yes we're gonna do)~~ to for you tonight
Get you feeling good (feeling Good) and lookin' right
With a song (and a beat) to make you want to dance
And a heavy heart (and a heavy heart) aint got a chance

John Well I got a song for the wayward man
And I've got a song about my native land
And a song of love that is pure and true
And it's all for fun And it's all for you

John Carter Well I'm mighty glad I could come along
And join right in on my daddys song
I'll do my best and I'll sing it loud
And I'll do my part to please the crowd

John When the song is done and the night is through
you can take me home in the song with you
We'll be joy bound and trouble free
We will fly away just you and me

J.R.C.

#1.

I'VE GOT MY MIND ON YOU

1980s

I never seem to hear the conversations
I'm always in the corner of the room
I get invited to the recreation
But I can't seem to hide my little gloom

Laughter and the tinkling of the glasses
Couples laying out a rendezvous
I pretend I heard and saw things
'Cause, babe, I've got my mind on you

You'd think that that one is the Queen of Sheba
The way she made her entrance at the door
Every man turned to her as she entered
But her clothes are local stuff, nothing more

Debonair and boldly, men approach her
Condescending, like a man will do
I stand and watch the scene repeated
'Cause, babe, I've got my mind on you

If you came in in homespun or denim
It wouldn't matter, I'd be standing true
And take you out the door into the night
'Cause, babe, I've got my mind on you

I've Got my Mind on you

I never seem to hear the conversations
I'm always in the corner of the room -
I get invited to the recreation
But I cant seem to hide my little gloom

Laughter and the tinkling of the glasses
Couples laying out a rendezvous -
I pretend I heard and I saw nothing
Cause Babe I've got my mind on you

You'd think that one is the queen of Sheba -
The way she made her entrance at the door
Every man turned to her as she entered
But her clothes are local stuff
And nothing more

Debonair and boldly men approached her
Condescending like a man will do
I stand and watch the scene repeated
Cause Babe I've got my mind on you

If you came in in homespun or denim
It wouldn't matter. I'd be standing true
And take you out the door into the darkness
Cause Babe I've got my mind on you

KISS THE GIRLS GOODNIGHT

1980s

Kiss the girls goodnight, boys
Kiss the girls goodnight
Tomorrow is another virgin day
Hardaway
At twelve o'clock
Just bring 'em home
Then go along your way
Kiss the girls goodnight

Their mama starts to worry
If the hour hand on the clock
Starts goin' down
She worries at the window
When it's time to bring
Her little girls around

Kiss the girls goodnight, boys
Just bring 'em home
And kiss the girls goodnight

Kiss the girls goodnight, boys
Kiss the girls goodnight
Just do it in the old-fashioned style
For a while

JOHNNY CASH

Kiss the girls goodnite boys
Kiss the girls goodnite
Tomorrow is another virgin day
Hard away
At twelve oclock just bring'em home
Then go along your way
It'll be alright boys
Kiss the girls goodnight.
Their mama starts to worry
If the hour hand on the clock
Starts going down
She worries at the window
When its time to bring
Her little girls around
Kiss the girls goodnite boys
Kiss the girls goodnite
Just bring em home
And kiss the girls goodnite

JOHNNY CASH

Kiss the girls goodnite boys
Kiss the girls goodnite
Just do it in the old fashioned style
For awhile

LEAN ON ME

1980s

If you ever need a friend
Lean on me
When you're down for the count
Lean on me
If you ever need someone to love you
Just because you're you
I think that you'll remember
That I've long been tried and true
And everything you need a love to be
Lean on me, lean on me

Love does not require
Sacrifice or suffering
Take it as I give it
You do not owe me a thing
Have faith and hope and charity
And lean on me
For I love you
Lean on me

When the wind is at your face
Lean on me
When it's about to blow you down
If you ever feel you're weakening
Lean on me
And even when you're strong
You may find that I just suddenly
Chanced to come along
In case you need my company
Give yourself a [unintelligible]

LET IT BE TONIGHT

with Ira Dean and David Lee Murphy

1980s

I was jumping up and down like an airplane
Chewing my gum like a carhop
When I heard that you might reconsider me
My heart was runnin' like a freight train
My mind was flying like an airplane
Inside I was cryin' like a baby, "Let it be."

Let it be tonight
That you forgive me
Let it be tonight
That you forget
And get right back
To where we used to be
Me lovin' you and you lovin' me
Let it be tonight

I'd been mopin' around like a dishrag
Head hangin' down like a handbag
Wonderin' if I ever could make it right
I got another shot for a new chance
A brand-new song for a new dance
And it's gonna be good if you let it be tonight

Let it be tonight
That you forgive me
Let it be tonight
That you forget
And get right back
To where we used to be
Me lovin' you and you lovin' me
Let it be tonight

I was jumping up and down like a short stop
Chewing my gum like a car hop
When I heard that you might ~~[illegible]~~ reconsider ~~coming back to~~ me
My heart was runnin like a ~~freight~~ train
My mind was flying like an airplane
Inside I was cryin like a baby, "Let it Be"

I been mopin around like a distray
~~Hanging~~ head ~~hanging~~ down like a handbag
Wonderin if I could ever make it right.
I got another shot for a new chance
A brand new song for a new dance
And it's gonna be good ~~[illegible]~~ But would Let it Be Tonite

~~[illegible]~~
~~[illegible]~~
~~[illegible]~~
~~[illegible]~~

The World's sweetest tune
Is off pitch when I'm lonesome for you
The discords come from deep down
Like a digereedoo

I'll be jumpin up and down like a short stop
Chewin my gum like a car hop
~~And Chargin like the Cavalree~~
~~Lovin you like a [illegible]~~
If you let it ~~be~~ be tonite
Lovin you express non-stop

LOOK AT ME THAT WAY AGAIN

1980s

It's been a while now, baby
Since you looked right into my soul
We opened up and let our feelings show
You've got a certain look
That makes me lose all of control
And, baby, that ain't been so long ago

Look at me that way again
Open up and let me see right in
It gives me such a feeling
That no words can quite explain
Look at me that way again
No matter where, no matter when
You know what I mean
Look at me that way again

Let's not take for granted
Something good as what we've got
Makin' love with you is right for me
Turn me on the way
That only you, that you can
Our makin' love is good
As makin' love can be

(movie Mag
tune)

Look at Me that Way Again

Its been awhile now baby
Since you looked right into my soul
We opened up and let our feelings show

You've got a certain look
that makes me lose all of control
And baby that ain't been too long ago

Look at me that way again
Open up
And let me see right in.
It gives me such a feeling
that no words can quite explain

Look at me that way again
no matter where
no matter when
You know what I mean
Look at me that way again

Let's not take for granted
Something good as what we've got
Makin love together is right for me
Turn me on the way
that only you that you can
Our makin love is good as makin love can
be

LOW-TEK MAN

1980s

You flew in on a chopper
With your friend, the mayor
I watch you using your
CD player

Workin' them buttons
With your eyes closed
In your leather chair
In your designer clothes

In a lifestyle
That I don't understand
But it's all right
'Cause I'm a low-tek man

Low Tek Man

LOEWS
SANTA MONICA
BEACH HOTEL

You flew in on a chopper
With your friend, the mayor
I watch you using your
CD player.
Workin' them buttons
With your eyes closed
In your leather chair
In your designer clothes
In a lifestyle that I dont understand
But its all alright
Cause I'm a low-tek man

(310) 458-6700 / FAX (310) 458-6761

MAYBE SOMEDAY

1980s

Same old wind keeps blowing
Father time keeps on goin'
But I made my mind up long ago to stay
And though we are birds of a feather
We ain't got our love too together
But I don't know, maybe we will
Maybe someday

Maybe Someday,

Same old wind Keeps on blowing
Father time Keeps on goin
But I made up my mind long ago to stay
And though we are birds of a feather
We aint got our love to together
But I dont know, maybe we will maybe
someday

MY COWBOY SONG

1980s

Some days are better than others
But sometimes he's the same all the time
He's proud as Rockefeller's peacock
Even if he didn't have a dime

Don't complain around him
You've got no problem he's never had
Just like anybody
He's part good and part bad

Fortune after fortune
He gave away to his fellow man
He'll be rich again tomorrow
And tomorrow give it all away again

He pays for our long distance
And he gives us his cold drink for free
So if you don't like the Cowboy
Watch your mouth when you mention him
to me

He plays evangelical dobro
And soul-stirring slide guitar
He's a C-plus Christian —
Somewhere between a black hole and a star

He stands at his window
And watches you when you bring in your
song
But you're wasting his time
If they're not under three minutes long

He'll take a trip on polka
To carry himself to another scene
Sometimes he's melancholy
And his eyes get misty singing "When I
Dream"

He stood the test of time
That proves the good and worth of any man
Deceit and dishonesty are two words
That he doesn't understand

In any confrontation
His shoulders square and again he's a Marine
With eyes that never waver
And a smile that could win a teenage queen

For years he went away
But no time had passed
When he came back: "Hello, this is Cowboy."
"Hi, I'll be down first thing tomorrow, Jack."

My Cowboy Song

Some days are better than others
But sometime he's the same all the time
He's proud as Rockefellers peacock
Even if he didn't have a dime
Dont complain around him
you've got no problem he's never had
Just like anybody
He's part good and part bad.
Fortune after fortune
He gave away to his fellow man
He'll be rich again tomorrow
And tomorrow give it all away again
He pays for our long distance
And he gives us his cold drinks for free
So if you dont like the cowboy
Watch your mouth when you mention him to me

He plays evangelical dobro and soul stirring slide guitar
He's a C-plus Christian—Somewhere between a black hole and a star
He stands at his window and watches you when you bring in your song
But you're wasting his time if they're not under 3 minutes long

He'll take a trip on polka to carry himself to another scene
Sometimes he's melancholy
And his eyes get misty sing "When I dream"
He stood the test of time
That proves the good and worth of any man
Deceit and dishonesty are two words that he doesn't understand
For years he went away
But no time had passed when he came back
Hello, this is the cowboy
Hi. I'll be down first thing tomorrow Jack
In any confrontation his shoulders square and again he's a man
With eyes that never waver
And a smile that could win a teenage ~~[illegible]~~

MY OLD FRIEND CHUCK (UP SHIT CREEK)

1980s

I went to see my old friend Chuck
Went down in my pickup truck
He said, "You're babbling like a duck.
You're up shit creek and out of luck."

She's got me way down on my luck
I'm bumming around like Tom and Huck
My life is in a mire and muck
Up shit creek and out of luck

My mornings all begin with yuck
I'm like a baby that can't suck
In a pit and I am stuck
Up shit creek and out of luck

Like a wild horse that can't buck
Like a tree that lightning struck
I don't fold and I don't tuck
Up shit creek and out of luck

Like a chicken that can't cluck
Like an ear of corn that you can't shuck
Like a smucker that can't smuck
Up shit creek and out of luck

Like a French-Canadian Canuck
Slick and slack and schlock and schluck
I've run out of words that rhyme with "uck"
But I really don't give a puck

OUTTA SIGHT TONIGHT

with Brad Paisley

1980s

Hey come on, don't you hear your phone?
It's me, who did you think it would be?
Well, hello, do you think that you can go?
It will be outta sight tonight

Please tell your daddy
I'm a gen-tle-man
I'm gonna keep you out
As late as I can

The combo, down at the place we'll go
Is so good, they'll shake the neighborhood
The whole gang
Is gonna do their thang
It will be outta sight tonight

Hey come on. Dont you hear your phone
It's me, who did you think it would be
Well Hello- Do you think you can go
It will be outasite Tonite
please tell your daddy
I'm a gen-tle-man
I'm gonna keep you out
As late as I can
The Combo, down at the place we'll go
Is so good. they'll shake the noborhood
The whole gang - Is gonna do their thang
It will be Outasite tonite

RED HILL FARMER

1980s

I just want to be a red hill farmer
On a little piece of Georgia dirt
Way up in the Georgia hills
And every year I'd sell off eggs and chickens
To care for you and keep up with my bills

I don't mean to say that I'm not thankful
I've been blessed far greater than I ever thought I'd be
It's just that I need front porch time more often
And days when there's only you and me

I don't want to be a public figure
And socialize with kings and presidents
I'd just like to fade off in the country
With no one knowing when or where I went

I never worked too hard at gaining stardom
All I really meant to do was write my songs and sing
I don't know but four chords on my guitar
You never know what changes time will bring

So I just want to be a red hill farmer
Take a chance and try it out with me
If it don't work out, I'll take northern Georgia
And you take Music City, Tennessee

SAIL AWAY WITH YOU

1980s

It won't matter at all
Just a little while from now
All the hassle that the world puts us through
It won't last too long
Then it's all gonna be all right
If I can cross the finish line with you

When I get my wings
I'm gonna leave it all below
And I'm gonna sail away
Sail away with you

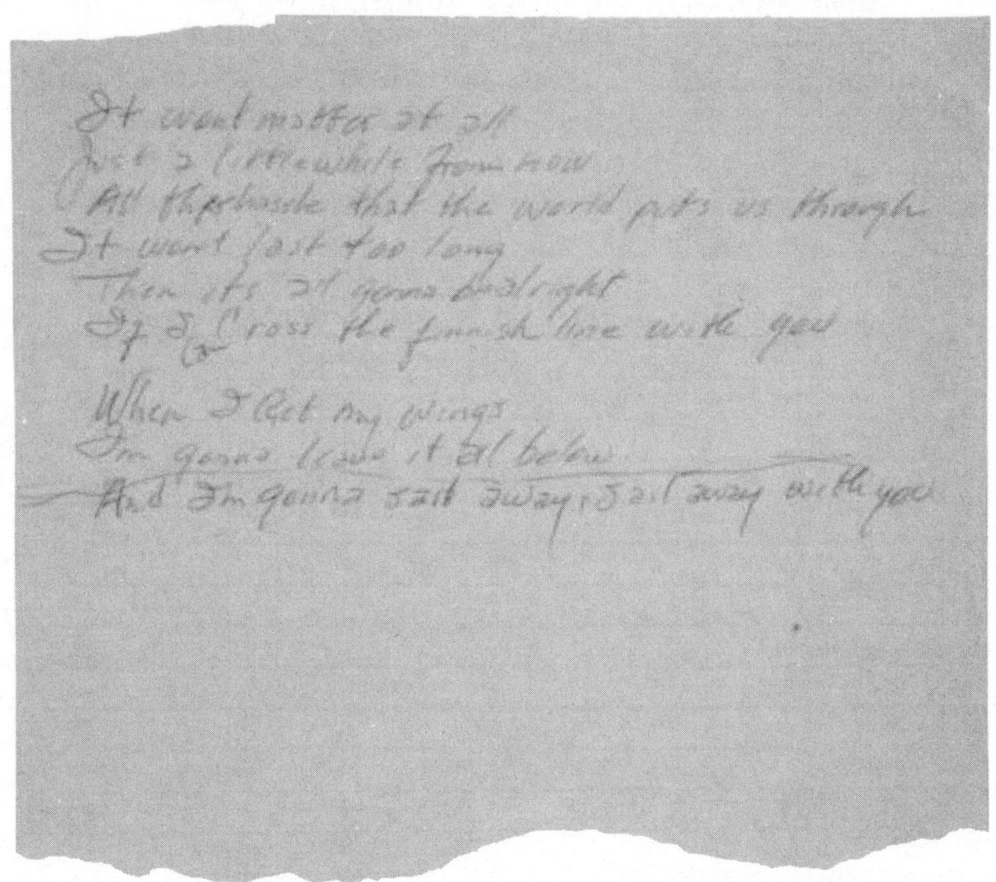
It wont matter at all
Just a little while from now
All the hassle that the world puts us through
It wont last too long
Then its all gonna be alright
If I can cross the finish line with you

When I get my wings
Im gonna leave it all below
And Im gonna sail away, sail away with you

SHE CURLED UP HER HAIR

1980s

I think she
Doesn't want me running for air
I think there must be
Someone else
Who gives her back her share

I ran to her so much
She must be running, too, somewhere
I saw her in a dress
I couldn't buy her
And I could tell
She curled up her hair

I passed her on the sidewalk
And she speaks
But keeps on walking
But I could tell
She curled up her hair

She kissed away the pain
When I was lonely
For so long
I thought her life was mine
For me to share
But I used her for a leanin' post
'Til finally she turned her shoulder
She yawned and then
She curled up her hair

She never did before
'Cause I liked it tangled
I always ran my
Fingers through it
And she never cared

She cut it off and waved it
In the latest style with care
Ignoring me
She curled up her hair

She said, "Pardon me."
The last time I reached out
To hold her
She walked away
And she curled up her hair

I think she
Doesn't want me running to
I think there must be
Someone else
Who gives her back her share
I ran to her so much
She must be running too, somewhere
I saw her in a dress
I couldn't buy her
And I could tell
She curled up her hair

I passed her on the sidewalk
And she speaks
But keeps on walking
And I could tell
She curled up her hair

She kissed away the pain
When I was lonely
For so long
I thought her ~~[illegible]~~ life
Was mine for me to share
~~But I ran to her~~
But I used her for a
leanin post
Till she finally turned her shoulder
She yawned and then
~~She curled up her hair~~

She never did before
Cause I liked it tangled
I always ran my
fingers thru it
And she never cared
She cut it off and waved it
In the latest style with care
Ignoring me
She curled up her hair

She said pardon me
The last time I reached
Out to hold her
She walked away And she curled up her hair

SHE GETS COLD WHEN THE SUN GOES DOWN

1980s

She gets cold
When the sun goes down
And she gets bold
When I ain't around

So I keep my head on my shoulders
And my feet on the ground
'Cause she gets cold
When the sun goes down

She lights my fire
And she turns me up
And she never tires
She's a brimmin' cup

So I keep my claim on her nights
If I have to burn down the town
'Cause she gets cold
When the sun goes down

But I fan her flame
And she fans mine
It's like a slow dance
Breaks into three-quarter time

I touch her face
And her cheek turns to a rose
And the chill is gone
Away it goes

She Gets Cold
When the Sun Goes down

She gets cold
When the Sun Goes Down
And she gets bold
If I aint around
So I keep my head on my shoulders,
And my feet on the ground
Cause she gets cold
When the sun goes down.

She lights my fire
And she turns me ~~on~~ up
And she never tires
Shes a ~~[illegible]~~ brimmin' cup
So I keep my claim on her nights
If I have to burn down the town
Cause she gets cold
When the sun goes down

But I ~~[illegible]~~ saw her ~~[illegible]~~ time
And she ~~[illegible]~~ turns mine
It's like a slow dance breaks into 3/4 time
I touch her face
And her cheek turns to a rose
And the chill is gone
Away it goes

SPIRIT RIDER

Before you know it you will see a ~~mystic~~ horseman Spirit Rider
Cut me off, babe, and I'll be gone
I will mount my Hi-Yo and I will ride off ma'am
And I'll go on (and on and on) and on and on
The ~~lies~~ you made in one ear will blow out the other
Let a storm rage round me on my outward track.
~~When~~ I hear bluebirds I won't go any farther
And when the sky gets clear back here
I'll be ridin back

I will ramble, drift and range and you'll be walkin
Around imaginary things up on the floor
Walkin circles round the reasons that have vanished
~~You'll~~ forget what doesn't matter anymore
you might ~~then you'll~~ get a glimpse of me off in the distance
If you cry out I ~~will~~ might hear you on the wind
And if the mountains echo your love to me
Wave your heart and,
I'll be ridin back again

On a moonbeam there might come a spirit rider
Who'll be watching for a flickering in the gloom
He will put a feeler out for love and welcome
And he just might cast a shadow 'cross your room
I will scent out any evidence of danger
I will taste the air around any sugar shack
If my heart knows ~~that~~ you won't treat it like a [illegible]
And if the fire is lit
I'll be ridin back.

SPIRIT RIDER

with Jamey Johnson

1980s

On a moonbeam, there might come a spirit rider
Who'll be watching for a flickering in the gloom
He will put a feeler out for love and welcome
And he just might cast a shadow across your room

I will scent out any evidence of danger
I will test the air around my sugar shack
If my heart knows you won't treat it like a stranger
And if the fire is lit I'll be riding back

Before you know it, you will see a spirit rider
Cut me off, babe, and I'll be gone
I will mount my Hi-Yo, and I will ride off, ma'am
And I'll go on and on and on and on and on

The lies you lay in one ear will blow out the other
Let a storm rage on me, on my outward tack
If I hear bluebirds, I won't go any farther
And if the sky gets clear, I'll be riding back

I will ramble, drift, and range
And you'll be walking 'round imaginary things upon the floors
Walk in circles 'round the reasons that have vanished
You'll forget what doesn't matter anymore
You might get a glimpse of me off in the distance

If you cry out I might hear you on the wind
And if the mountains echo your love to me
Wave your heart and I'll be riding back again
Wave your heart and I'll be riding back again

THERE'S SOMETHING MOVING

1980s

There's something moving up there
There's something moving up there
And I can feel it down here
There's something moving
There's something moving
There's something moving
As the wind blows

As the wind blows
And nobody knows
Where the wind goes
So does the spirit
So does the spirit

And though I can't see it or hear it
There's something moving up there
And I can feel it down here
There's something moving

And the feeling is so fine
When I open up my arms
And something reaches down and touches me
And a voice says you are mine
I will keep you from all harm
I just wish you could share the ecstasy

Theres Something Moving

There's something moving up there
" " " " "
And I can feel it down here-
There's something moving
Repeat - Repeat - Repeat
As the wind blows
" " " "
And nobody knows
Where the wind goes
So does the Spirit
" " " "
And though I cant see it or hear it
There's something moving up there
And I can feel it down here
Theres something moving

And the feeling is so fine
When I open up my arms
~~[illegible]~~
And something reaches down and touches,
And a voice says you are mine
I will keep you from all harm
I just wish that you could share
the ecstacy

STICK HORSE

1980s

Ride a stick horse
Down to Barberry
There'll be a fine lady
Upon a white horse
A ring on each finger
A bell on each toe
The lady has music
Wherever she goes

On to Montana
To the big rodeo
Fill up on Billings
Where the wild cowboys go
And they still pinch
The ladies on the
Bottom and top

THINK ABOUT THAT AWHILE

1980s

Don't be so hardheaded
Ain't your heart hard enough
Don't look at me like some unwanted child
How's it gonna be when you start back needin' me
(Boom, boom, boom, boom, boom) Think about that awhile

Take my unemployment check
And buy yourself some rags
Make believe you're queen of the Nile
Hop a plane and go to Baghdad or Cairo
I don't care, now think about that awhile

Remember I ain't your daddy
And I ain't Santy Claus
I don't own the company mercantile
When your shoes lose their shine
I'll be steppin' out in mine

THE THIRD DEGREE

with John Carter Cash, Ira Dean,
Ben Kitterman, and Aaron Lewis
1980s

They accused me of forgery
I couldn't write my name
They accused me of looking
And I didn't see a thing

Didn't mean to cause no trouble
And I meant no bodily harm
All I had was this body
And the muscle in my arm

They gave me the third degree
They hung me from a tree
Third degree

And they're giving me the third degree
But it's plain to see without a learned degree
I didn't know a chopping hoe
Could bring a mountain down

They're giving me the third degree
They hung me from a tree
That third degree

She came down the turn row
With a bucket in her hand
She brought Elberta peaches
And they all knew I's her man

She didn't have no business
Hanging out down where they were
And everybody wants something
And they all wanted her

They're giving me the third degree
But it's plain to see without a learned degree
I didn't know a chopping hoe
Could bring a mountain down

They're giving me the third degree
They hung me from a tree
That third degree
That third degree

Sitting with my peaches
When I heard her crying out
Peaches in my pocket
And blood here on this ground

They took her away from me
They took her away from me
They took her away from me
In a third degree

In a third degree
It's a third degree

Third Degree
They accused me of premedity
And I couldn't even write my name
They accused me of lookin for trouble
And I didn't see a thing
I didn't mean to be no problem
I didn't mean nobody harm
But all I had was my body
And the muscle in my arm
But they gave me – the third degree
Hang me from a tree – ~~but no~~ and a third degree

She came down the turn row slow
With a bucket in her handy hand
Alberta peaches pippin
And she calls me her man
Everybodys after something
And everybodys after her
She didn't have no beeswax
Hangin out where they were
Now theyre givin me – The third degree
~~And it's plain to see~~ ~~without~~ a third degree
Reg-u-larly I get
I didn't know the meaing of
Bodily Assult.
My hand was on my peaches
And I told them to halt
I didn't know a choppin hoe
Could bring a mountain down
My bucket turnin over empty
And blood runnin in the ground
They took her away from me – Now the third degree
Too dark to see – but a third degree

Third Degree

They accused me of forgery
And I couldn't even write my name
"
"
They accused me of lookin ~~4~~
And I didn't see a thing
Lord have mercy on me
Cant take no more third degree

John R. Cash

Third Degree
They accusec me of forgery
And I couldnt even write my name
They accused me of lookin
And I didn't see a thing
Didn't mean ~~to cause~~ no trouble
And I meant no bodily harm
But all I had was my body
And the muscle in my arm
So Dont give me, No third degree
Hang me from a tree – But no third degree

She came down the turn row
With a bucket in her hand
~~And~~ She brought Alberta peaches
And they all know Im her man
Everybody wants something
But everybody wanted her
She didn't have no business
Hangin' out where they were
~~But~~ And theyre givin me – The third degree
~~And~~ But its plain to see without a third degree
I dont know the meaning of Bodily Assault
~~[illegible]~~
I was guardin my peaches / I told them to halt
~~And they were shakin my tree~~
I didn't know a choppin hoe
Could bring a mountain down
Peaches in my pocket
And blood runnin in the ground
~~They took her away from~~ me – And a third degree
Too dark to ~~to~~ see – And a third degree

TOGETHER, TOGETHER

1980s

I am leaving you I think
A good man should be free

If it's what you want to do
You know it's quite all right with me

My things are packed and don't call me
I'll be in touch with you

You needn't bother calling
Just do what you want to do

Well, don't forget to bolt the door
And turn the yard lights on

Oh yes, I've always done that
Every time that you've been gone

I'll call the day before to let you know
When I'll be in

Don't bother for the call
Will not be heard by me again

Together, together
Together like Napoleon and Josephine
Together, together
Together, but a change of heart between

Well, I believe I'm ready now
No need to say goodbye

You're quite right, there's no reason
Ain't nobody gonna cry

But don't you want to know where I'll be
If you need to call

There is not anything
That I would call you at all

But let me write the number for you
Just in case you do

No, there's no possibility that
I'll be needing you

But we've got things in common
That might need some working out

It'll all work out when you walk out
What else is this about?

Well, I was thinking, maybe
You know I still care for you

But I won't share you, so go on
And do what you would do

Well, maybe I will not go yet
But I won't bother you

You know your place, so maybe don't go
And I won't bother you

Together, together
Together, like Trade and Mark
And Wells Fargo
Together, together
And it always will be so

By JRC

He — I am leaving you I think
A good man should be free

She — If it's what you want to do
You know it's quite alright with me

He — My things are packed and don't call me
I'll be in touch with you

She — You needn't bother calling
Just do what you want to do

He — Well— don't forget to bolt the door
And turn the yard lights on

She — Oh yes I've always done that
Every time that you've been gone.

He — I'll call the day before to let you know
When I'll be in

She — Don't bother for ~~[illegible]~~ the call
Will not be heard by me again.

Together — Together
Together — like Napoleon and Josephine —
Together Together
Together but a change of heart between

He — Well I believe ~~[illegible]~~ I'm ready, and
no need to say goodbye

She — You're quite right There's no reason
And nobody gonna cry

He — But don't you want to know where I'll be
If you need to call.

She — There is not anything
That I would call you at all

He — But let me write the number for you
Just in case you do

She — No there's no possibility that
I'll be needing you.

He — But we've got things in common
That might need some working out

She — It'll all worked out when you walk out
What else is this about.

He — Well, I was thinking maybe
You know I still care for you

She — But I won't share you so go on
And do what you would do —

He — Well maybe I will not go yet
But I won't bother you

She — You know your place so sell [illegible]
And I won't bother you

Together - Together
Together like Trade and Mark
And Wells Fargo
Together — Together — And it always will be so

TOUGH LOVE

1980s

Tough love
I'm giving you tough love
It hurts so good
When you love me with
Tough love
Tough love

Gotta have it now
Tough love
It feels so right
When you're giving me
Tough love

Sweet, sweet pain
'Til the thrill comes again
And you cling to me
Oh, it's ecstasy

Tough love
Gotta have it now
Tough love
I love the way
That you hurt me with
Tough love

WHEN LOVE IS NEW

1980s

When love is new
You burst skyrocket high
You bubble rippling-stream happy
You glow dew-on-moonlight soft
That's what you do
When love is new

When love is gone
You cry dead-mockingbird sad
You hurt knife-cut deep
You mourn lost-in-the-dark sad
You're so alone
When love is gone

Tough Love

J R Cash

Tough Love
I'm giving you tough Love
It hurts so good
When you love me ~~tough~~ with
tough Love

Tough Love
Gotta have it now Tough Love
It feels so right
When you're giving me
Tough Love.

Sweet Sweet Pain
Till the thrill comes again
– – – Cling to me
Oh it's eckstasy

Tough Love
Gotta have it now tough Love
I love the way
That you hurt me with
Tough Love.

WHEN THE LITTLE HAND

1980s

When the little hand reaches eight
I'll sit and wait
And make believe that you're still coming
But you'll be just a little bit late

At nine o'clock I'll walk the floor
And try to keep from cryin'
Holdin' out for one night more
And tryin' to keep on tryin'

When the little hand reaches ten
I'll say you win
Take off my clothes and go to bed
And try to sleep again

At eleven o'clock, dark and alone
I'll pour myself a drink
And drink until the pain is going
And I no longer think

When the little hand reaches twelve
I'll cry for help
I'll need someone to come to me
'Cause I know I can't make it by myself

WHO WAS THAT MASKED MAN?

1980s

He rode by in the night
And stole your heart
He found me gone
And pulled my world apart
He poured me out like water
And he soaked me up like sand
Who was that masked man?
Who was that masked man?

If you don't feel right
In his hidin' place
Remember my brown eyes
And open face
I hope his arms ain't hairy
I hope his cheeks ain't tanned
Who was that masked man?
Who was that masked man?

He's bound to be a bandit
To do what he did to me
And I'd give him everything
If he would set my heartache free
I can't understand
How he gets by with what he can
Who was that masked man?
Who was that masked man?

I never thought
You'd get ripped off of me
I thought my arms
Were full security
But a heart needs careful watchin'
Or thieves get out of hand
Who was that masked man?
Who was that masked man?

If you get half a chance
To get away
Remember me
And our old hideaway
His arms may not be hairy
And his cheeks may not be tanned
Who was that masked man?
Who was that masked man?

WITH ALL MY HEART

1980s

I can't play the didgeridoo
Nor the sitar nor the kazoo
I can't serenade like Caruso
Nor charm like Valentino

But I love you with all my heart
I love you with all my heart
With all my heart
With all my heart I love you

I'm a regular kind of human man
It's the only way I understand
If you ever need a solid devotee
All you gotta do is call on me

'Cause I love you with all my heart
I love you with all my heart
With all my heart
With all my heart I love you

I'll never make a record climb
I'll never set a record time
But I will be straight and true
I'll stand by and be good to you

I'll never have a fortune I can give
But love as long as we shall live
But if fortune fell on me today
I wouldn't let it get in our way

'Cause I love you with all my heart
I love you with all my heart
With all my heart
With all my heart I love you

With All my Heart

I cant play the diggeridoo
Nor the Citar or the kazoo
I Cant serenade like Caruso
Nor charm like Valentino
But I love you,
With all my heart I love you
With alla my heart With alla my heart
With alla my heart I love you

Im a regular kind of human man
Its the only way I understand
If you ever need a solid devotee
All you gotta do is call on me
Cause I love you
With alla my heart I love you
With alla my heart With alla my heart
With alla my heart I love you,

Ill never make a record climb
Ill never set a record time
But I will be ~~[illegible]~~ straight and true
Ill stand by and be good to you

Ill never have a ~~[illegible]~~ fortune I can give
But love as long as we shall live
But if fortune fell on me today
I wouldnt let it get in our way
Cause I love you, with all —

YOU TREAT ME LIKE A DOG

1980s

No matter how hard I try
No matter how hard I try
I can't get along with you
Though I'm really wantin' to
No matter how hard I try

You always bite my head off
You always bite my head off
If we're gonna hang up
We should just hang up
You always bite my head off

There you go slamming the door
You act like you never heard
Before I can say a word
You treat me like I'm a dog
You treat me like I'm a dog

You're acting so cold
And that stuff is gettin' old
You treat me like I'm a dog

BELONGING

1980

She had no strings attached
And she required so little attention
She'd let me in and then back out again
And if it hurt, she never did mention

She had no brown bruise
But love and love's only turnin'
And she let me know that she could let go
Even when bodies were burnin'

But time went by and I
Began to linger on
And looked for reasons not to go
And then, late and alone

I felt unfulfilled
Unsettled, restless, and longing
But another night or two and we both knew
That the real need was belonging

But another night or two and we both knew
That the real need was belonging

COLD LONESOME MORNING

1980

One of these cold lonesome mornings, you're gonna kill me
I'm gonna lay there and I'm gonna die
You will soon give me pain enough to fill me
'Cause I'm gone past doing any good to cry

And the warm sunshine is like a stranger
There's a cruel violation with the dawn
Lord, my pain can't stand illumination
And one of these cold lonesome mornings I'll be gone

One of these cold lonesome mornings, dark and early
Before a wild bird sings I'm gonna fly
While it's still dark and I'm still reaching for you
I'll wake up and I can't cry

But I know my heart can't stand another tremor
How it's holding together I don't know
But just before the dawning's first glimmer
One of these cold lonesome mornings I'm gonna go

Yes, one of these cold lonesome mornings, you're gonna kill me
I'm gonna lay there and I'm gonna die
You will soon give me pain enough to fill me
And I'm gone past doing any good to cry

And the warm sunshine is like a stranger
There's a cruel violation with the dawn
Lord, my pain can't stand illumination
And one of these cold lonesome mornings I'll be gone

DON'T SLAM THE DOOR

1980

The only thing you're leaving me are memories
Of how you left me when you had to go
Please give me a smile
When you tell me goodbye
And don't slam the door when you go

You won't see me fighting now to keep you
We both agreed to let it end, you know
Go peacefully so I can have that memory
And don't slam the door when you go

Verbal violence ruled our union lately
I made myself forget and it won't show
I'll take it like a man if you'll be kind when you leave
Don't slam the door when you go

Remember that you're leaving love
That has always been gentle
Remember all the hours I loved you so
Think upon the best of all the good and bad we had
And don't slam the door when you go

Dont Slam the Door

The only thing you're leaving me are memories
Of how you left me when you had to go
Please give me a smile
When you tell me goodbye
And Dont slam the Door
When you go

You wont see me fighting now to keep you
We both agreed to let it end you know
Go peacefully so I can have that memory
And Dont slam the door when you go

Verbal violence ruled our union lately
I made myself forget and it wont show
I'll take it like a man if you'll be kind
Dont slam the Door when you go when you leave

Remember that you're leaving love
~~[illegible]~~ That has always been gentle
Remember all the hours I loved you so
Think upon the best of all the good
And bad we had
And Dont slam the door when you go

GREATER IS HE THAT IS IN ME

from a poem by Martin F. Tupper

(in *Slander: A Ballad of Comfort,* 1851)

adapted in 1980

Never you fear, but go ahead
In self-relying strength
What matters it, that malice said?
They found it out at length
Found out? Found out what? A man of truth
Is open as the light
Search as keenly as you can
All you will find is right

Blot me black with slander's ink
I'll wash out white as snow
You serve me better than you think
And much more than you know

Yes, do me down now, if you will
Whisper what you please
You only fan the glory more
By whispering up your breeze

Sell me down, or sell me out
It matters not to me
The Greatest One of all your kind
Will bow to Him, like me

HOME RUN HITTER

1980

Who's that friendly woman
At the end of the bar
In the red dress
Cut down way too far?

She's a flaunter
Yes, she's a flaunter
She wears that "Come on" look
Like a neon sign
She's a devil, I know
But in my mind
I want her, oh I want her

She can play with your mind
'Til your body's involved
But there ain't no problem
She can't solve

She's a fixer
She's a home run hitter
She's got a way of saying
What she wants to say
And leaves no doubt
When she wants to play

She's a getter
She's a home run hitter
She can make it hard to walk away
Guess I'm just easy come, easy lay
She can make it hard to walk away

Who's that friendly woman
Laying by my side
Who knows the me that I try to hide?
She's a devil
Yes, she's a devil
But maybe she's an angel

ROCKABILLY BLUES (TEXAS 1955)

1980

I took a tour to Texas
And from Waco, I called you
But day by day, no answer
And I'm big bluebonnet blue

I'm singing and they're dancing
But I'm feeling Big D bad
I'm Sweetwater beat
And I'm Texas City sad

The rhythm keeps me living
But have you heard the news?
There's a sad song singer coming
With the rockabilly blues

It's hard to keep on singing
When you're lonesome to the bone
Ten thousand happy people
But I'm San Antone alone

One-night stands and the man demands
That I get up and go
I'm Odessa desperate
And San Angelo low

The rhythm keeps me living
But have you heard the news?
There's a sad song singer coming
With the rockabilly blues

It's the same old tune in Temple
About the loving I ain't had
I'm getting Beaumont bitter
And Amarillo mad

I'm giving up on calling you
'Cause you're evading me
I'm coming home and if you're gone
I'm gonna be Tennessee free

The rhythm keeps me living
And have you heard the news?
There's a sad song singer coming
With the rockabilly blues

W-O-M-A-N

1980

I just want to tell you, baby, if I can
I need my W-O-M-A-N
A M-A-N needs a W-O
For love or dirty boogie or the do-si-do
And the F-E-M-A-L-E can
Turn a B-O-Y into a M-A-N

Well, I can take a failure, I can take a flop
I've survived at the bottom better than the top
I take it day by day and I can do all right
If my W-O-M-A-N is in at night
I'm not talking good or bad or lust or sin
Oh, I'm just talking W-O-M-A-N

I can get along without a dog or a cat
And luxury is not where happiness is at
I can do without tobacco, coffee, or tea
And I turn down lots of money-making deals offered to me
I can make it through the hills without a Jeep or a van
But I've got to have my W-O-M-A-N

I need you, woman, W-O-M-A-N, man, man
I need you and I'll keep you just as long as I can
Because you are my W-O-M-A-N

DO YOU EVER FEEL THIS WAY?

with Don Davis

1981

On the long days and lonely nights
When we had to be apart
I feel incomplete
I want you, I ache
Because we are one, you and I
Do you ever feel this way?

I've never been able to just close down my mind
And go to sleep, like some people can
But, especially, when you aren't there
My hungry mind reaches out for you
The way my arms have already reached out, too
And before I know it, I am fantasizing

I try to stop it, but there's no stopping my mind from loving you
Loving you, the way I have so many times
And the way I will so many times
I can feel your lips, and I can feel you in my arms
The two of us, joined, the two of us, one
Do you ever feel this way?

Maybe I take a lot for granted
To think that you still desire to kiss these lawless lips
To caress this lined, worn face
With your sweet, tender face
But while my mind is loving you
My heart tells me it's all right

That maybe right now you're dreaming the same dream
I think that maybe you are
In your arms, it's always been so right, so special
And it's so good, loving you
So good that I just felt like talking to you about it
Do you ever feel this way?

Do You Ever Feel This Way

In the long Days
And Lonely nights
When we have to be apart
I feel incomplete
I want you
I ache for you
Because we are one, you and I.
Do you ever feel this way?
I have never been able
To just close down my mind
And go right to sleep, like some can
But especially
When you arent there
My hungry mind reaches out for you
The way my arms
Have often reached out to take you
And before I know it,
Im fantasizing
I try to stop it,
But theres no stopping my mind
From Loving you
The Way I have so many times
The way I Will so many times.

I can feel your lips
And you in my arms
The two of us joined
The two of us, one
Do you ever feel this way

Page

Maybe... I take a lot for granted
To think that you still desire
To kiss these lawless lips
To caress this lined, worn face

But while my mind is loving you
My heart tells me its alright
That maybe - right now
You're dreaming the same dream
~~I think~~ Are you?
I think maybe you are

In your arms
Its always been so right
So special
— And its so good,
Loving You
So good that,
I just felt like talking about it
Do you ever feel this way?

DO YOU EVER FEEL THIS WAY?

(alternate version)

with Don Davis

1981

On the long days
And lonely nights
When we have to be apart
I feel incomplete
I want you
I ache for you
Because we are one, you and I
Do you ever feel this way?

I have never been able
To just close down my mind
And go right to sleep like some can
But especially
When you aren't there
My hungry mind reaches out for you
The way my arms
Have often reached out to take you
And before I know it
I'm fantasizing

I try to stop it
But there's no stopping my mind
From loving you
The way I have so many times
The way I will so many times

I can feel your lips
And you in my arms
The two of us joined
The two of us, one
Do you ever feel this way?

Maybe...I take a lot for granted
To think that you still desire
To kiss these lawless lips
To caress this lined, worn face

But while my mind is loving you
My heart tells me it's all right
That maybe — right now
You're dreaming the same dream
Are you?
I think maybe you are

In your arms
It's always been so right
So special
And it's so good
Loving you
So good that
I just feel like talking about it
Do you ever feel this way?

FAIR WEATHER FRIENDS

with Joe Allen

1981

Fair weather friends, fair weather sailors
Will leave you stranded on life's shore
But one true friend who really loves you
Is worth the pain your heart endures

We never know which way the wind will blow
Nor when and where the next turmoil will be
But He's a solid rock in trouble's flow
And He holds out a saving hand for me

Fair weather friends, fair weather sailors
Will leave you stranded on life's shore
But one true friend who really loves you
Is worth the pain your heart endures

He'll be your shelter in the night
He'll be an anchor in the storm
When you can't find your way, He'll be your light
In the chilly winds of doubt, He'll keep you warm

Fair weather friends, fair weather sailors
Will leave you stranded on life's shore
But one true friend who really loves you
Is worth the pain your heart endures

A FAST SONG

1981

The only thing that'll move me now
Is a fast song
Sung long and barely known
And I don't wanna hear no
Crying, all gone wrong song
Kick it off and let's all pick a fast song

Now, don't go bringing singing, strumming me
No slow tune
Stay away from all that moon and June
Spoon, croon tune
Throw me one that's flying and I'll hang on
I'll come in on my part on a fast song

Well, it don't have to have
A banjo or mandolin
But let it in, if it wants in
Keep the resin handy
And the horsehair tough and tight
Pick it up and I'm liable to pick all night

Now, don't go bringing singing, strumming me
No slow tune
Stay away from all that moon and June
Spoon, croon tune
Throw me one that's flying and I'll hang on
I'll come in on my part on a fast song

THE GENERAL LEE

with Thom Bresh

1981

I'm a charger that charges through the night
Like an orange bolt of lightning passing
everything in sight
I'm the best pal the Duke boys ever had
I'm thunder on the highway, looking bad, bad,
bad

I'm a knight, like the kind in shining armor
With my polished body gleaming, I'm a
fighter and a charmer
If trouble comes your way, just ask for me
My friends all know me as the General Lee

I'm the General Lee
A piston-pumping, steel-belted cavalry
I'll never let you down when you're riding
with me
Buckle up and I'll show you what I mean

Take a look back there
Sirens blowing, red lights flashing everywhere
We'll cross the field, and we'll be running free
They'll eat dust, with compliments of me
The General Lee

I'm a hero, and that's how I'll make you feel
When you're riding shotgun with me, and the
law is at your heels
I'm glory bound, but when the chase is done
I'll take off through the mountains and have
fun, fun, fun

I've got style, tearing through the curves
Let my flag wave proudly to the people that I
serve
I'm number one and I will always be
The pride of the South, they call the General
Lee

I'm the General Lee
A piston-pumping, steel-belted cavalry
I'll never let you down when you're riding
with me
Buckle up and I'll show you what I mean

Take a look back there
Sirens blowing, red lights flashing everywhere
I'll jump that pond, and we'll be running free
And they'll go swimming, compliments of me
The General Lee

GOIN' DOWN THE ROAD FEELIN' BAD

traditional

adapted in 1981

I'm going down the road feeling bad
I'm going down the road feeling bad
I'm going down the road feeling bad, Lord, Lord
And I ain't gonna be treated thisaway

They feed me on cornbread and beans
They feed me on cornbread and beans
They feed me on cornbread and beans, Lord, Lord
And I ain't gonna be treated thisaway

I'm going down the road feeling bad
I'm going down the road feeling bad
I'm going down the road feeling bad, Lord, Lord
And I ain't gonna be treated thisaway

I've been down in the jailhouse, on my knees
I've been down in the jailhouse, on my knees
I've been down in the jailhouse, on my knees
And I ain't gonna be treated thisaway

I'm going down the road feeling bad
I'm going down the road feeling bad
I'm going down the road feeling bad, Lord, Lord
And I ain't gonna be treated thisaway

I'm going to where the water tastes like wine
I'm going to where the water tastes like wine
I'm going to where the water tastes like wine
'Cause this Georgia water tastes like turpentine

I'm going down the road feeling bad
I'm going down the road feeling bad
I'm going down the road feeling bad, Lord, Lord
And I ain't gonna be treated thisaway

I GIVE YOU MUSIC

1981

For the down-and-out
Unloved and left behind
Tell me yours and I will tell you mine
For losers to false-hearted love
Man and womankind
I give you music
Da da da da da da da da da
Bring your heart and meet me in a song
I give you music, this is for you
Da da de da da da dum da da da
Da do de do da da do da de do
Tum dum tum tum tum tum tum tum
Da da de da da da
Boom boom ba ba ba ba ba ba ba bum
I give you music — da da daaaaa
This is for you

I recall when laughter had no price
And love was love and never sacrifice
Somewhere along the way
Some of the sugar turned to ice
But I give you music
Da da da da da da da da da da
Stop the world and get off on a song
I give you music
This is for you

Da da de da da da dum da da da
Da do de do da da do da de do
Tum dum tum tum tum tum tum tum
Da da de da da da
Boom boom ba ba ba ba ba ba ba bum
I give you music — da da daaaaa
This is for you

IF I COULD

1981

If I could, I would offer you
A future with a dream or two
A cottage where we'd never roam
Sit on the porch and watch the cows come home
Sit on the porch and watch the cows come home

If I could, I would stay with you
Like ordinary people do
Sing along with the meadowlark
And be in your bed every night at dark
And be in your bed every night at dark

But I've got a road a day to go
Songs to sing and heart to show
And I've got promises to keep
And love to give before I sleep
And love to give before I sleep

Well, if I could, I'd take a day
And I'd take you and run away
I'd turn that clockface to the wall
I'd see nobody and I'd take no calls
I'd see nobody and I'd take no calls

If I could, I would let you do
Everything that you're wantin' to
Turn 'em off and turn 'em down
And you and me would just fool around
And you and me would just fool around

But I've got a road a day to go
Songs to sing and heart to show
And I've got promises to keep
And love to give before I sleep

And I've got a road a day to go
Songs to sing and heart to show
And I've got promises to keep
And love to give before I sleep
And love to give before I sleep

SINCE YOU BECAME MINE

1981

Since you became mine
Since you became mine
I'm singin' my song
Of an old rolling stone
With love at the end of the line

It's a treasure I've found
Let the music resound
You're the peak of my height
And I'm gettin' it right
Since you became mine

It's a fulfilling feel
It's right and it's real
It's a magical touch
And I love you so much
You turn me on and I shine

Talk about satisfied
It's true and it's tried
God surely blessed me
With the best there can be
Since you became mine

DON'T MAKE A MOVIE 'BOUT ME

1982

If anybody made a movie out of my life
I wouldn't like it, but I'd watch it twice
If they halfway tried to do it right
There'd be forty screenwriters working day and night

They'd need a research team from Uncle Sam
And go from David Allan Coe to Billy Graham
It would run ten days in the final cut
And that would mean leaving out the gossip smut

And I do request for my children's sake
Don't ever let 'em do a new remake
The thing I'm sayin' is, don't you see
Don't make a movie 'bout me

Even for TV
Don't make a movie 'bout me

Don't let 'em drag Old Hickory Lake
For my telephones and bottles and roller skates
Down forty feet in the Cumberland mud
There's a rusty old gun that once shed blood

Out a hundred yards from my lakeside house
Weighted down with a rock is a skirt and blouse
A dozen pair of boots that made a dozen corns
Trombones, trumpets, harmonicas, and horns

And the tapes that I threw from the lakeside door
Silverstein and Kristofferson, from years before
Everything has a story that should be let be
So don't make a movie 'bout me

If they're hot on a book called *Man in Black*
Tell 'em I've got the rights and won't give back
If you don't know my tune you can't get it right
I don't talk about me in *Man in White*

Truth, said the Master, cannot be hid
But He didn't say slap it in the face of my kids
A stone is a stone and forever a stone
But I'm part good and bad, and then I'm gone

There is no sin cleaner than the dirtiest
So there's a lot about me that I don't want missed
If it's days or years or whatever will be
Don't make a movie 'bout me

Aw, I might as well face it
'Cause they will, some day
So while I can
I've got a thing to say

I don't know anybody that I said I don't know
And there ain't anybody anywhere I owe
The IRS gets the lion's share
And what is left goes to my own named heirs

Don't let 'em make it in Hollywood
If they must
Tell 'em Arkansas
Is where they should

Here's a hex on whoever makes it be
So don't make a movie 'bout me
For love or money
Don't make a movie 'bout me

DONT MAKE A MOVIE ABOUT ME
Christmas 1982   J.R. Cash

If anybody made a movie out of my life
I wouldn't like it, but I'd watch it twice
If they halfway tried to do it right
There'd be forty screen writers workin day & nite
They'd need a research team from uncle Sam
And go from David Allen Coe to Billy Graham
It would run ten days in the final cut
And that would mean leaving out the gossip smut
And I do request for my children's sake
Dont ever let 'em do a new re-make
The thing I'm sayin' is, dont you see,
Dont make a movie 'bout me
Even for T.V.
Dont make a movie 'bout me

Dont let 'em drag old Hickory Lake
For my telephones and bottles and roller skates
Down forty feet in the cumberland mud
There's a rusty old gun that once shed blood
Out a hundred yards from my lakeside house
Weighted down with a rock is a skirt & a blouse
A dozen pair of boots that made a dozen corns
Trombones, trumpets, harmonicas and horns
And the tapes that I threw from the lakeside door
Silverstein, and Kristofferson from years before
Everything has a story that should be let be
So dont make a movie 'bout me

If they're hot on a book called Man in Black
Tell 'em I've got the rights and I wont give b
If you dont know my tune you cant get it righ
I dont talk about me in Man in Man in Whit

Truth, said the master, cannot be hid
But he didn't say slap it in the face of a kid
A stone is a stone and forever stone
But I'm part good and bad and then I'm gone

There is no sin cleaner than the dirtiest
So there's a lot about me that I dont want mix
If its days or years whatever will be
Dont make a movie 'bout me

Aw, I might as well face it cause they will some d
So while I can I've got a thing to say
I dont know anybody that I said I dont kno
And there aint anybody anywhere I owe

The I.R.S. gets the lions share
And what is left goes to my own named he
Dont let 'em make it in Hollywood
If they must, tell 'em Arkansas is where they shoul
Here's a hex on whoever makes it be,
So dont make a movie 'bout me.
For Love or Monee
Dont make a movie 'bout me

ANOTHER WIDE RIVER TO CROSS

1982

I've stood on the bank by the weeping willow
With another wide river to cross
Another wide river to cross
With another wide river to cross
And I believe I can make it to the other side
'Cause I feel a hand on me
Helping me with another wide river to cross

And I wake up to many a day
With another wide river to cross
With another wide river to cross
Another wide river to cross
I jump right in the dark and I swim right on
Toward the light on the other side
It's always there when there's another wide river to cross

Oh, the whirlpools twist and pull at me
With another wide river to cross
Another wide river to cross
With another wide river to cross
And if I reach up
A hand is always reaching down for me
It's always there when there's another wide river to cross

Well, the river Jordan is a narrow stream
But it's another wide river to cross
It's another wide river to cross
It's another wide river to cross
But I believe there's a resting place
That's provided just for me
On the heaven side of another wide river to cross

A HALF A MILE A DAY

1982

I am coming, Lord
For my heavenly reward
I'm on my way to you
Can't you see me coming through
Through clouds of persecution
And I'm stumbling all the way
And with my mistakes, I'll barely make
A half a mile a day

But the road to heaven
Never had a rapid transit plan
It's one way, with no changes
Straight through to Promised Land
But I believe that if I heed
The words He had to say
Even I can get to heaven
At a half a mile a day

Lord, when I let you lead
I don't make any speed
'Cause you have me stop and touch
All the ones that need so much
Then sometimes I get tempted
And fall along the way
And by my mistakes, I barely make
A half a mile a day

But the road to heaven
Never a rapid transit plan
It's one way, with no changes
Straight through to Promised Land
And I believe that if I heed
The words He had to say
Even I can get to heaven
At a half a mile a day

I LIKE COUNTRY MUSIC

1982

I like country music
And I like the way it sells
From here to Alabama
All the way to Kitty Wells

I'd like to pick like Atkins
Or have Glen Campbell's voice
But between the two
I'd take Anne Murray if I had a choice

I love the Carter Sisters
And I love to hear the Oaks
Can you believe the magic
From the Gatlin Brothers' throats

Tanya Tucker's been a star
Since she was just a kid
Ray Charles loves country music
And he never kept it hid

Roy Clark and Loretta Lynn
And Mel Tillis and me
All set our hearts on singin'
Back about 1953

Hoagy Carmichael always wrote
With a kind of country feel
The Dirt Band could play just country
And they'd never miss a meal

So I will stick with country
No matter what tomorrow brings
And no matter who makes number one
Roy Acuff is still the king

A LITTLE PATCH OF GRASS

with John Carter Cash,

Brandon Robert Young, and Clare Bowen

1982

In a world of cold concrete and steel
And tinted windowpanes
I walked the streets among the clones
With man-made programmed brains

The subway rumbled at my feet
The bums, the sick, the old
I said that never, ever could
Life such as this be whole

I met a bright-eyed beauty
Had she fallen from the sun
I smiled and she returned it
Then she crossed on green to run

I quickly made the other side
And followed just behind
Haltingly, I said to her,
"Lady, please, if you don't mind.

"I saw it in your smile
And your eyes, just as we passed.
Like me, I think you'd leave it all
For a little patch of grass.

"I'd take you across a rippling stream.
We'd hear the shallow water laugh
As hand in hand we made toward
A little patch of grass.

"We could lie upon our backs
And smile up at the sky
A million miles from everything
Where nothing rushes by."

She looked around the city
Then she looked me up and down
"Are you for real?" she asked me
I said, "Yes, but not this town."

We walked and talked of common things
Then: "I don't even know your name."
I said, "What's the difference
When our hearts cry for the same?"

For June
With all my Love
John

A Little Patch of Grass

by J.R. Cash Sept. '82

In a world of cold concrete and steel
And tinted window panes
I walked the streets among the clones
With man made programmed brains
The subway rumbled at my feet
The bums, the sick, the old
I said that never, ever could
Life such as this be whole
I met a bright eyed beauty
Had she fallen from the sun?
I smiled and she returned it
Then she crossed on green to run
I quickly made the other side
And followed just behind
Haltingly I said to her
Lady, please, if you dont mind:

I saw it in your smile
And your eyes just as we passed
Like me, I think you'd leave it all
For a little patch of grass
I'd take you across a rippling stream
We'd hear the shallow water laugh
As hand in hand we wade toward
A little patch of grass

We could lie upon our backs
And smile up at the sky
A million miles from everything
Where nothing rushes by
She looked around the city
Then she looked me up and down
Are you for real? she asked me
I said yes, but not this town
We walked and talked of common things
Then: "I dont even know your name
I said, whats the difference
When our hearts cry for the same

MY CHILDREN WALK IN TRUTH

1982

I prayed to know more joy in my salvation
A selfish prayer, I finally came to know
For my greatest joy in living
Comes to me when I am giving
Giving children bread of life and watch them grow

And my greatest joy is knowing that my children walk in truth
And that they are giving you, Lord, of their fire and strength of youth
Yes, I've found the greatest joy in my salvation
Is knowing that my children walk in truth

It's hard to feed someone else when you're hungry
You can't teach when you don't understand
No one will follow you
If you don't live it each day through
And a frightened child won't hold a trembling hand

And my greatest joy is knowing that my children walk in truth
And that they are giving you, Lord, of their fire and strength of youth
Yes, I've found the greatest joy in my salvation
Is knowing that my children walk in truth

ONE OF THESE DAYS I'M GONNA SIT DOWN AND TALK TO PAUL

1982

One of these days I'm gonna sit down and talk to Paul
One of these days I'm gonna sit down and talk to Paul
I will ask him about his journeys
And he will tell me about them all
One of these days I'm gonna sit down and talk to Paul

He will introduce me to Luke and Timothy
He will introduce me to Luke and Timothy
I will be so glad to meet them
And they will be glad to meet me
He will introduce me to Luke and Timothy

One of these days I'm gonna sit down and talk to Paul
One of these days I'm gonna sit down and talk to Paul
I will ask him about his journeys
And he will tell me about them all
One of these days I'm gonna sit down and talk to Paul

I will ask him about that trip to Philippi
How he and Silas felt at Philippi
In that miracle at midnight
When the jail doors opened wide
We'll sing those songs they sang at Philippi

One of these days I'm gonna sit down and talk to Paul
One of these days I'm gonna sit down and talk to Paul
I will ask him about his journeys
And he will tell me about them all
One of these days I'm gonna sit down and talk to Paul

I will ask him if he ever went to Spain
I will ask him if he ever went to Spain
I'll find out if he made it
I'll find out his secret pain
I will ask him if he ever went to Spain

Yes, one of these days I'm gonna sit down and talk to Paul
One of these days I'm gonna sit down and talk to Paul
I will ask him about his journeys
And he will tell me about them all
One of these days I'm gonna sit down and talk to Paul

One of these days I'm gonna sit down and talk to Paul
One of these days I'm gonna sit down and talk to Paul
I will ask him about his journeys
And he will tell me about them all
One of these days I'm gonna sit down and talk to Paul

WHAT IS MAN

1982

What is man that you are mindful of him, Lord?
You made the stars, You made the sun
And all the worlds that came to be at Your command
What is man? What has he done?

Then You crown him with glory and with honor
Give him dominion over land and sea and air
And store up an inheritance in heaven
What is man that You would care?

What is man, Lord, that You would care?
What is man, that You would let him live at all
To join the blessed of humankind
And ever fail to even follow where You call?
What is man? Why do You mind?

Yet You crown me with glory and with honor
Give me dominion over land and sea and air
And store up my inheritance in heaven
What is man, that You care?
What is man, Lord, that You would care?

What is Man

What is man, that you are mindful of him Lord
You made the stars, the moon and sun
And all the worlds that came to be at your command
What is man? What has he done

What is man that you would let him live at all
He sheds the blood of his own kind
And in his pride goes on his way deaf to your call
What is man? Why do you mind.

cho And you crown him with glory and ~~with~~ honor
Give him dominion over land and sea and air
Then you store up ~~an~~ inheritance in heaven
What is man? That you would care
" " " Lord, " " " "

J. Cash

A WHOLE LOT OF LOVIN' LEFT OVER

1982

I've got a whole lotta lovin' left over
For the right man when he comes
He won't be ridin' on a big white stallion
And he won't be a hard luck buck

He may be the last expected one
But I'll know it when I see my man
I've got a whole lotta lovin' left over
And I'll give you all I can

I admit that I get lonely
Every single night
I want to give him love
I want him to love me
'Til he makes me say, "All right."

He will keep me warm in winter
I'll be his and he will be mine
I've got a whole lotta lovin' left over
Saving it for that special time

I will anticipate his needs
And fulfill him each day
I'll make him feel so sure about me
That he'll never go away

I will share his troubles with him
And I'll smile when it's all good
I've got a whole lotta lovin' left over
And I'll treat him like a woman should

Nov 2 '82 J. Cash A Whole Lot of Lovin' Left Over

I've got a whole lotta lovin' left over
For the right man when he comes along
He won't be ridin' on a big white stallion
And he won't be a hard luck buck
He may be the least expected one
But I'll know it when I see my man
I've got a whole lotta lovin' left over
And I'll give all I can

I admit that I get lonely
Every single night
I want to love
I want him to love me
till he makes me say alright.
He will keep me warm in winter
I'll be his and he will be mine
I've got a whole lot of lovin left over
Saving it for that special time

I will anticipate his needs
And fulfill him each day
I'll make him feel so sure about me
he'll never go away.
I will share his troubles with him
And I'll smile when it's all good
I've got a whole lot of lovin' left over
And I'll treat him like a woman should.

God Bless my Lady

God Bless my lady, Lord
My Lady kind and true
Touch her with your blessings
And let her know it's you.
A true and faithful woman Lord,
[illegible]
to you and I she's been
God bless my lady
And let her smile again

I know that life is full of pain
And dissapointment comes.
I know I've failed her time and time
But make her free from suffering
And put it all on me, Lord for
I can still bear some.

God Bless my Lady, Lord
[illegible]
[illegible]
[illegible]
[illegible]
This plea I make to you
I love her and I hope this song
Lets the whole world know I do.

Lady Lord.
Gentle hands
And make her know
her man.
truly one
it to be
honey
to me.

by John Cash
Feb 21st 1983
First Writing
Second writing is
dated [illegible]
Feb 21st
Second writing
Feb 22nd 1983)

GOD BLESS MY LADY

1983

God bless my lady, Lord
My lady, kind and true
Touch her with Your blessings
And let her know it's You

A true and faithful woman, Lord
To You and I she's been
God bless my lady
And let her smile again

I know that life is full of pain
And disappointment comes
I know I've failed her time and time
But make her free from suffering
And put it all on me, Lord
For I can still bear some

God bless my lady, Lord
This plea I make to You
I love her and I hope this song
Lets the whole world know I do

IF YOU LOVE ME

with Elvis Costello

1983

The fluctuating worth of this very
terminal earth
And the satellite that glows at night
above me
Won't bear upon my mind
But concerning womankind
I don't care if you're there
If you love me

The seed must die, I know
Before new life can grow
And so would I die
Before I'd let you go

So let the cold winds blow
Let the seasons come and go
Let the times gone by just die
Like that old part of I

Again the sun may rise
And burn through yellow skies
But I'll see it through your blue eyes
If you love me

The seed must die, I know
Before new life can grow
And so would I die
If you don't love me

I'll see it in your eyes
If it's true or if it's lies
But I'll feel it if it's real
If you don't love me

If you love me
If you love me

To June, while you are "working things out"

If you Love Me

The fluctuating worth
Of this very terminal earth
And the sattelite
That glows at night
Above me

Won't bear upon my mind
But concerning womankind
I won't care if you're there
And if you love me

A seed must die, I know
Before new life can grow
And so would I so die
If you don't love me

So let the North wind blow
Let seasons come and go
Let ~~times~~ times gone by just die
Like that old part of "I"

Again the sun can rise
And glow thru yellow skies
But I'll see them blue with you
If you love me

BATTLE OF NASHVILLE

1984

The moon on the Cumberland River
Went down in a cold, bloody red
And you lay beside me and trembled
Like I don't belong in your bed

It's just like that night on Old Hickory
And the motel way out on West End
You tried but your heart wasn't in it
Now you're fighting against it again

And the Battle of Nashville is raging
There's a troubling deep in my soul
Here's my swan song for Music City
'Cause my forces are out of control

I have hoped against hope that you'll love me
And my heart won't give up the fight
So the Battle of Nashville continues
And I pray you'll surrender tonight

Many times I've regrouped my emotions
And smiled through the struggle and pain
And made believe I'm all together
Just like I'm doing again

But my little defeats keep on coming
'Cause you keep on holding the line
I'm losing ground with you daily
And it's just a matter of time

And the Battle of Nashville is raging
There's a troubling deep in my soul
Here's my swan song for Music City
'Cause my forces are out of control

I have hoped against hope that you'll love me
And my heart won't give up the fight
So the Battle of Nashville continues
And I pray you'll surrender tonight

CALL YOUR MOTHER

1984

When you get a chance
Would you please call your mother
And thank her for the good years that we had?
Gently break the news that you don't love me
And give my best regards to your good old
dad

I always liked your family
We got along just splendidly
Though your brother
Kind of rubbed me the wrong way

I remember that your eyes turned green
When they crowned your sister County
Queen
Though she couldn't hold a candle
To your beauty any day

When you get a chance
Would you please call your mother
And thank her for the good years that we had?
Gently break the news that you don't love me
And give my best regards to your good old
dad

Back when we could laugh and play
On family reunion day
Didn't we all look funny
In our 1950s clothes?

Your daddy wore that greasy stuff
Your brother drank more than enough
Your mom wore penny loafers
With runners in her hose

When you get a chance
Would you please call your mother
And thank her for the good years that we had?
Gently break the news that you don't love me
And give my best regards to your good old
dad

DIRTY OLD MAN

1984

I just passed sixteen
The other day
Both Daddy and Mamma
Have gone away

And there's a dirty old man
With his dirty old land
To ask for my hand
That dirty old man
With his dirty old land

That big white house
Will not be my home
And the dirty old man
Better leave me alone

That dirty old man
Has a section of land
Maybe two hundred acres
But he's a dirty old man

DIRTY OLD MAN

I JUST PASSED SIXTEEN
THE OTHER DAY
BOTH DADDY AND MAMMA
HAVE GONE AWAY
AND THERE'S A DIRTY OLD MAN
WITH HIS DIRTY OLD LAND
THAT WILL BE HERE TODAY
TO ASK FOR MY HAND

THAT DIRTY OLD MAN
WITH HIS DIRTY OLD LAND
REPEAT

THAT BIG WHITE HOUSE
WILL NOT BE MY HOME
AND THAT DIRTY OLD MAN
BETTER LEAVE ME ALONE
THAT DIRTY OLD MAN
MAN HAS A SECTION OF LAND
MAYBE 200 ACRES
BUT HE'S A DIRTY OLD MAN

I CAME TO BELIEVE

1984

I couldn't manage the problems
I brought on myself
And it just made it worse
When I laid them on somebody else

So I finally surrendered it all
Brought down in despair
I cried out for help
And I felt a warm comforter there

And I came to believe
In a power much higher than I
I came to believe
That I needed help to get by

In childlike faith
I gave in and gave Him a try
And I came to believe
In a power much higher than I

Nothing worked out
When I handled it all on my own
And each time I failed
It made me feel twice as alone

Then I thought
"Lord, there must be a surer and easier way
For it just cannot be that a man
Should lose hope every day."

And I came to believe
In a power much higher than I
I came to believe
That I needed help to get by

In childlike faith
I gave in and gave Him a try
Then I came to believe
In a power much higher than I
Yes, I came to believe
In a power much higher than I

YOU GIVE ME MUSIC

1984

Down-and-out, unloved and troubled mind
Bring your heart and I will give you mine
For the healing of forsaken love for man and womankind
You give me music, you give me music
Give it to me, give it to me

Do you recall when laughter had no price
And love was love and never sacrifice?
Somewhere along the way, some of the sugar turned to ice
But you give me music, you give me music
Give it to me, give it to me

You give me music, you give me music
Give it to me, give it to me

I'M LEAVING NOW

1985

Hold on, honey, I'd like to say
I'm busting out and breaking away
I'm letting you go like a hot horseshoe
I can't take another heartache from you

Think about how it's gonna be
When you start back to needing me
When your dancing shoes have lost their
  shine
I'm gonna be gone in mine

I'm leaving now
I'm leaving now
Get out of my face
Get out of my place
I'm leaving now, adios
I'm leaving now

And the time it comes when you trim the fat
Feed the kitchen scraps to the front seat cat
Bye-bye, baby, when the bills come due
You might have to give up a jewel or two

Eat your heart out anyway
It's hard as your head and it's cold as clay
It's all over now you won't have me
Your sugar daddy or your money tree

I'm leaving now
I'm leaving now
Get out of my space
Get out of my face
I'm leaving now
I'm leaving now

Pull up the collar on my traveling coat
Sell that miserable pleasure boat
I wouldn't give a nickel for another buck
I'm living on muscle, guts, and luck

If anybody asks where did I go
Tell 'em I went where the wild goose goes
I wouldn't have me an area code
Don't have a number, don't need a road

I'm leaving now
I'm leaving now
Get out of my face
Get out of my space
I'm leaving now, adios
I'm leaving now

Reeverderchi
Jaymars

I'm Leavin Now

Hold on honey I'd like to say
I'm bustin out and breakin away
I'm lettin you go like a hot horseshoe
I cant take another heartache from you

Think about how it's gonna be
When you really start to needin me
When your dancin shoes have lost their shine
I'm gonna be long gone in mine

cho

I'm Leavin Now – I'm leavin now
Get out of my space, get out of my face
I'm leavin now, I'm leavin now

Turn up the collar on my travelin coat
Sell that miserable pleasure boat
I wouldn't give a dime for another buck
Livin on muscle, guts and luck

If anybody asks where did I go
Tell em I went where the wild goose goes
Wont even have an area code
Aint no numbers on freedom road

cho

The time may come you have to trim the fat
Feed kitchen scraps to your front seat cat
Bye bye baby when the bills come due
You may have to give up a jewel or two

Eat your heart out, anyway
Its hard as your head and cold as clay
Its all over baby now you wont have me
For your sugar daddy and your money tree

BEANS FOR BREAKFAST

1986

I couldn't hear you for the TV
I didn't know you said goodbye
I saw your canceled check for the airfare
Didn't know flying got so high

Beans for breakfast once again
Hard to eat 'em from the can
I've run out of clean utensils
I'm a hungry, nasty, lonesome man

I heard the crows outside my window
Guess it's me they're talking about
The fire you lit has burned to cinders
Every good thing's fizzled out

Beans for breakfast once again
Hard to eat 'em from the can
Wish you'd come back and wash the dishes
I'm a hungry, nasty, lonesome man

Caught a cold with the windows open
Crow droppings on my windowsill
Probably got histoplasmosis
Got no gun or I would kill them crows

Beans for breakfast once again
Hard to eat 'em from the can
Plastic forks are a dime a dozen
I'm a hungry, nasty, lonesome man

Finally made it to the mailbox
Felt so bad I thought I'd die
All I got was a bill from my doctor
Well, I guess flying ain't so high

Beans for breakfast once again
Hard to eat 'em from the can
Blue tick mattress, cold and greasy
I'm a hungry, nasty, lonesome man

The house burned down from the fire
That I built in your closet by mistake
After I took all them pills
But I got out safe in my Duck Head overalls

Beans for breakfast once again
I'm a hungry, nasty, lonesome man

I'D RATHER HAVE YOU

1986

I'd rather go to a rodeo
Than shopping on Rodeo Drive
I'd rather lay on the grass with you
And watch the planes than to have to fly

I'd rather have you
Than Ringling and Barnum & Bailey circus
With all three rings
And the high trapeze

And the lady on the horse
And the train that carries them through
Stacked up against all the gold in Africa
I'd rather have you

I'd rather share a hot dog with you
Than dinner with the president
Offer me a castle on a mountaintop
I'll take you in a tent

I'd rather be alone with you than to have my
very own satellite
To talk and sing and say everything to
everybody
Do whatever I wanna do
And to be number one on who is who, I'd
rather have you

I don't crave applause and praise
Or holidays with my way paid
I don't want to incorporate
Nor to be top rate nor a head of state

I don't want to play the didgeridoo
Nor the sitar or the kazoo
Just the two of us alone will do
I'd rather have you

I'd rather have tickets to the movies with you
Than the one that wins the lottery
Rather walk on the beach with you
Than to own all the ships at sea

I'd rather have you than the QE2 and the
Eiffel Tower,
The royal jewels and the Brooklyn Bridge
And the toll pay to go through
And throw in a Texas well or two, I'd rather
have you

Goodbye Ugly

Goodbye Ugly
you've embarrassed me too many times
So long Homely
Get out of my sight like you are my mind
You hurt my eyes to see you
I dont ever want to look at you again
Goodbye ugly
Dont even dare tell anyone we're friends

Hide your face in some dark hollow
With the rats and bats
And you might feel at home
— And just remember all the world is better off
If you are gone,
And in the dark somewhere alone
Go on gruesome
I cant wait to count the days that you'll be gone

Get Gone Grungy
Never more will your face make me sick
Hop to it Homely
All you're good for now is feedin lice and ticks
It cost so much to feed you
That your name aint in my budget anymore
Goodbye Ugly
Crawl out the hole that you crawled in
before

GOODBYE, UGLY

1986

Goodbye, Ugly
You've embarrassed me too many times
So long, Homely
Get out of my sight, like you are my mind
You hurt my eyes to see you
I don't ever want to look at you again
Goodbye, Ugly
Don't even dare tell anyone we're friends

Hide your face in some dark hollow
With the rats and bats
And you might feel at home
And just remember — all the world is better off
If you are gone
And in the dark, somewhere alone
Go on, Gruesome
I can't wait to count the days that you'll be gone

Get goin', Grungy
Never more will your face
Make me sick
Hop to it, Homely
All you're good for now
Is feedin' lice and ticks
It cost so much to feed you
That your name ain't in my budget anymore
Goodbye, Ugly
Crawl out the hole that you crawled in before

THE LITTLE WHITE CHURCH

1986

It must have been a piece of very hallowed ground
For many years ago they put a firm foundation down
And every Sunday morning every seat was always filled
At the little white church, just up the road, there on the right, at the top of the hill

There must have been a thousand brides and grooms walk the aisle
And many a mother praying for many a wayward child
And there was often weeping for a loved one, cold and still
In the little white church, just up the road, there on the right, at the top of the hill

It was there I learned songs like "Power in the Blood"
And "Standing, Standing on the Promises of God"
And "Jesus Saves, Jesus Saves"
In the little white church, just up the road, there on the right, at the top of the hill

By the pulpit at the altar many a knee has humbled down
There were many tears of joy for the lost sheep that was found
Many words of comfort preached that are comforting me still
From the little white church, just up the road, there on the right, at the top of the hill

Like a beacon to my soul are the lessons that I learned
A solid rock to hold on no matter where I turn
Hope and consolation are my promises still
From the little white church, just up the road, there on the right, at the top of the hill

It was there I learned songs like "Power in the Blood"
And "Standing, Standing on the Promises of God"
And "Jesus Saves, Jesus Saves"
In the little white church, just up the road, there on the right, at the top of the hill

The Little White Church

J. Cash
March 21 1986

It must have been a little piece of very hallowed ground
For many years ago they put a firm foundation down
And every Sunday morning every seat was always filled
At the little White Church, just off the road, there on the right at the top of the hill

There must have been a thousand bides and grooms walk the aisle
And many a mother praying for a many a wayward child
And there was often weeping for a loved one cold and still
In the Little White Church just off the road, there on the right at the top of the hill

Chorus
It was there I learned songs like Power in the Blood
And Standing Standing Standing on the promises of God
And ~~[illegible]~~ Jesus Saves Jesus Saves
In the Little White Church just off the road There on the right At the top of the hill

By the pulpit at the altar many a knee has humbled down
There were many tears of joy for the lost sheep that was found
Many words of comfort preached are comforting me still
From the Little White Church just off the road There on the right At the top of the hill

Like a beacon to my soul are the lessons that I learned
A solid rock to hold on no matter where I turn
Hope and Consolation are my promises still
From the little white church just off the road There on the right At the top of the hill

Repeat chorus

Cinnamon Hill Music
ASCAP

MAN IN WHITE

1986

I studied at the feet of a master
Gamaliel, we called him, the beauty of the law
I was born of the tribe of Benjamin, I was a Pharisee
And I could quote from memory the holy Torah

That day that the Nazarene was brought to trial
It was on a Sabbath eve, there was an earthquake when He died
Just another peasant preacher who came up from Galilee
Blaspheming troublemaker, we let Him be crucified

Then I thought that I would hear no more about Him
But His friends found His tomb empty
Claimed that He rose from the dead
Then they said He walked among them
With the nail wounds in His hands
That king upon a donkey with a thorn crown on His head

His followers kept growing in great number
And the one that they call Cephas mocked us in the judgment hall
And with the Greek named Stephen, we knew the gentiles had come in
I cast my vote against him, he was stoned I saw him fall

Then the friends of the Nazarene became united
And I became enraged, then led a slaughter zealously
I found their secret places, they were beaten, they were chained
But some of them were scattered, justified in fearing me

Then the Man in White appeared to me
In such a blinding light it struck me down
With its brilliance, took away my sight, then the Man in White
In gentle loving tones spoke to me
And I was blinded so that I might see the Man in White

But like the wind that blows the scattered sea
From Alexandria to Antioch, their congregation grew
I went to the high priest for letters of permission
To go to other cities, to see my mission through

Six days on the hot Road to Damascus
And just outside the city, in the middle of the day
A great unearthly light struck and overpowered me
Prostrate on the hot road, I was blinded where I lay

Then I thought I heard the rushing of great water
And a multitude of angels, singing sweet and heavenly
And through the sound of wind came a voice so soft and kind
Meant for only me to hear: "Saul, why do you persecute me?"

As I lay there on the ground, in my blindness
He asked me once again, and suddenly the voice I knew
So finally, I managed a trembling response
"Who are you, Lord?" I asked Him, but I already knew

"I am Jesus of Nazareth," the voice answered
"Arise, go to Damascus, on the street called Straight, will be
A place where you will wait for my servant, Ananias.
He will open up your eyes, you'll be a witness unto me."

So now I live to serve my master
As zealous in His service as I once was as His foe
And keeping His commandments given on Damascus Road
I go to all the world, and I let the whole world know

Then the Man in White appeared to me
In such a blinding light it struck me down
With its brilliance, took away my sight, then the Man in White
In gentle loving tones spoke to me
And I was blinded so that I might see the Man in White
And I was blinded so that I might see the Man in White

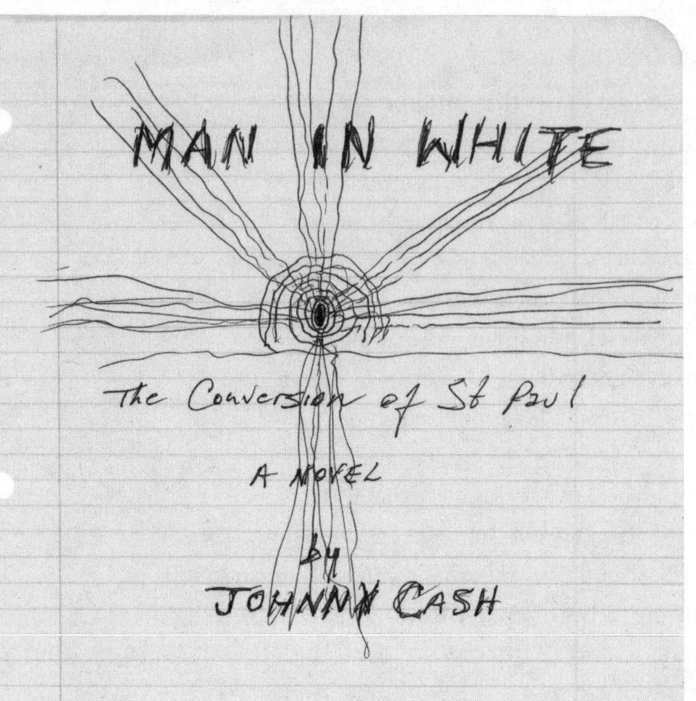
MAN IN WHITE

The Conversion of St Paul

A NOVEL

by

JOHNNY CASH

Chapter Heading

Peter and Saul

Saul learned a new word in Jerusalem: "Kristos" or Christ, the Greek word for Messiah.

He had heard the word, but long ago when as a child in Tarsus. The Greek speaking Jews called the Messiah "the Christ."

It had been a despicable word to him. The very idea that the Messiah of the Jews could even be mentioned in a Gentile tongue by another name was repulsive.

Though he read and spoke Greek fluently, to read the scriptures in anything but Hebrew, to debate the law, to quote from the torah, or to refer to God or Messiah in any tongue but hebrew would have been an abomination.

But now the word "Christ" took on new depth and new beauty, and a glory. Saul felt a new dimension in the word: The all-encompassing dimension of love. And the more Peter used the word when speaking to Barnabas or another Greek, or when addressing a Grecian Jewish assembly, the more comfortable Saul felt with it.

One day after nearly two weeks with Peter, Saul found himself saying, "Christ," and it was a joyous revelation when he realized the love he felt in just saying "Jesus Christ."

1981

The Re-Born Man

A Tale of the Apostle Paul

by

Johnny Cash

Describe Jesus!!!
Rev. 1.13–16
description of the
glorified Christ.

Also Jesus talks to Ananias –

Ac 9 !
Ac 22 !
Ac 26 !

Ph. 3.5
Paul of himself.
"of tribe of Benjamin etc.

Acts 26. 9–11
Acts 26. 12 Damascus Rd

Longest speech of Jesus!!

Sauls 1st sermon –

Paul goes to house of Judas, prays 3 days.

Ac 22.14 Ananias confirms Jesus earlier instruction.

Acts 8

to Cyprus Antioch etc.

1. Saul "consents" to Stephens death.
2. Great persecution, Church scattered.
3. Paul drags the christians out of their houses
4. Philip preaches and heals in Samaria
5. Peter and John go to Samaria
6. Simon the magician tries to buy Holy Spirit.
7. Simon repents, joins evangelists
8. Philip goes to Gaza, converts Eunuch. Baptizes.
9. Philip in Azotus & Caesarea.

AD 37 or 38

Acts 9.

Saul (Brought up in Jerusalem at feet of Gamaliel.) Ac 22.3

Ac 22.4

1. Wreaks havoc among Christs followers 1-2 – Ga 1-13
2. On Road to Damascus. 3. (Ac 22.5. Has letters) Ac 9.15
3. Struck down. Jesus appears, speaks 5-6. Ac. 22.6
4. Continues to Damascus. fasts & prays –
5. Jesus sends Ananias to Saul 10–15
6. Ananias lays hands on Saul, sees. 17-18
7. Saul preaches Christ in Synagogues 19–22

*8 Jews try to kill Saul 22–24

*9. Goes to Jerusalem – feared – befriended by Barnabas 26–28

10 Sauls life threatened. Sent by brethren to Tarsus. 29–30

11. Churches have rest – grow. 31

12 Peter goes to Lydda – raises Tabitha – (Dorcas) from dead. Stays with Simon Tanner heals Aeneas of palsy 32–43

*8A Escapes – Goes into Arabia, returns to Damascus stays 3 yrs.

*9A Stays with Peter 15 days Ga. 1.18

Ga 1,18

AD 40 or 41

Circumcision debated.

Paul in a trance in the Temple. Jesus speaks to him.

I'M ALWAYS MISSING YOU (TO JUNE)

1986

There's a spring at the back of the farm
Where I go walking alone
When I can speak to the birds that fly up from the field
Of clove and sagebroom

And then I cross the old fence
That goes down through the dogwoods
To where the big sycamore stands
I taste of the watercress ringing the spring
And I kneel down and drink from my hands

And I love the sound of the water
That comes from who could know where?
I sit on my rock as I survey my kingdom
But I'm always missing you there

The cry of the hawk and the sweet honeysuckle
And the breeze on the willows will do
At peace with the world — for only a moment
And then I'm always missing you

I wish we could share it without a word spoken
And worry about not a thing
You'd sit on my rock while I find arrowheads
And you'd sing along with the spring

That's how I picture it each time I go
So simple a thing we could do
Just walk through the fields
And share the sweet silence
Where I'm always missing you

ANGEL AND THE BADMAN

1987

There was a man whose deeds were dark as night
And quite by chance he rode into the light
A man, wild as a dust devil with no place to run
Livin' by his wits and by his gun

He met a girl like none he'd ever known
She cared not for the wild oats he had sown
And so he laid his gun down and set his spirit free
Began livin' in respectability

But his old ways of thinkin' wouldn't die
Could not forget the old creed he lived by
And the good and bad and the right and wrong kept fightin' for his soul
'Til his heart and mind both went out of control

But now the old saloon had lost its spell
What once was laughter now was livin' hell
And the hookers, guns, and drinkin' in his life were out of place
And in his mind he saw an angel's face

So he burned all his bridges in a day
And the devil deeds were done and laid away
And he rode out a better man than when he first rode in
And the angel got the badman in the end

AUTUMN

with Dave Daeger, Sara Watkins, and Sean Watkins

1987

Even now, the red and golden leaves
Are burnin' up the hills
And winter will come, the leaves will turn dark
As the snow begins to cover

But the earth will be one beneath
Holding the promised renewed spring
Then the green shoots of grass, flowers, weeds
Will burst through

Yeah, they'll burst through
The birdsong days of spring
As has been done
For eons past

The glory of growth, flowering in fruits
Will illuminate the land

When harvest falls, the red and golden leaves
Will burn up the hills
And I will walk in awe and wonder and
thankfulness
To once again witness this miracle

Autumn
Even now
The red and golden leaves
Are burning up the hills
And winter will come
The leaves will turn dark
As the snow begins to cover them
But the earth beneath
Will be warm
Holding the promised renewal
Of spring.
Then the green shoots
Of grass, flowers, weeds and herbs
Will burst thru the birdsong days
Of spring.
And as it has done for eons past
The glory of growth,
Flowering and fruits
Will illuminate the land
Then as harvest falls
The red and golden leaves
Will burn up the hills
And I would walk in awe
And wonder
And thankfulness
To again witness
This miracle

Oct. 87

TELECHRISTIANVISIONLESS

1987

I know there is a God. He makes His presence known in many ways. In the birth of a child, the eternally changing seasons, the gift of life, the exchange of love, the treasury of friendships. His sustaining grace during grief, and His countless, mysterious, unpredictable governing of events.

He is also a God of wrath, and to me this is one of His great mysteries.

Why does He not strike dead a TV preacher who blasphemes the Gospel by connecting its propagation to the amount of money sent in?

I know why He didn't strike me dead for the many times I turned from Him. He loved me and knew I'd repent. Yet He knows I'll fail Him again, so I guess I don't know.

Evil upon evil continues to be proven of certain ordained ministers, and rather than repent and humble themselves, they spend more millions of innocently donated money to fight back in the devil's own game.

They have allowed and promoted shame, which would supposedly fall upon the shameless shoulders of the carpenter from Nazareth.

The shame falls in the eyes of the world on the bride of Christ, his church. This is our ultimate injustice.

I, as a Christian, deeply resent this and accept no part in this ministerial televisionless, shameful conduct.

I only agreed to accept suffering for my own personal shameful acts and thoughts, which are known for the most part only by God.

He will and should punish me as surely as He will punish the others.

BON AQUA SPRING

1987

It's good water
The spring at the back of the farm
I walked across the new-cut hayfield
Over the barbed wire fence
Down the slope through the red October dogwoods

The sun had set when I reached the tree-lined slope
But I knew the trail down to the spring
In the deepening twilight I turned on my flashlight
Not to find my way
But to search the path for another arrowhead

I had found several here
Over the past fifteen years
But it hadn't rained lately
So there were none this time

I knelt at the spring flowing out of the rocks
I cupped my hands seven times
And drank (seven times)
(Just a little personal ritual of mine)
Walking back up the slope
I met a full moon rising
Such beauty

At the crest of the hill
Poplar and cedar trees
Seemed to mark the spot

I would build a house here
No one would see the house from any direction
If I ever do
Build that house, that is
I'll remember the spring daily
And drink from it
Seven times

At the crest of the hill
Poplar and cedar trees
Seemed to mark the spot.
I would build a house here
No one would see the house
From any direction.
If I ever do,
Build that house, that is,
I'll remember the spring daily
And drink from it.
Seven times.

Bon Agua Spring Oct. '87

It's good water
The spring at the back of the farm
I walked across the new cut hay field,
Over the barbed wire fence
Down the slope through the
Red October dogwoods.
The sun had set when I reached
The tree lined slope.
But I knew the trail down to the spring
In the deepening twilight
I turned on my flashlight,
Not to find my way,
But to search the path for
Another Arrowhead.
I had found several here
Over the past fifteen years.
But it hadn't rained lately
So there were none this time.
I knelt at the spring flowing out of the rocks
I cupped my hands seven times,
And drank seven times
(Just a little personal ritual of mine)
Walking back up the slope
I met a full moon rising
Such beauty

WATER FROM THE WELLS OF HOME

with John Carter Cash

1987

There's a stool along the road to freedom
Like a gypsy in a guilty cage
But rising has not always been bright
Destiny dreams are made

My days all run together
Like a timeless honeycomb
I find myself wishing I could drink again
Water from the wells of home
Water from the wells of home
Water from the wells of home

I've seen all your shining cities
Lean against the yellow sky
I've seen the down-and-out get better
I've seen many of strong men die

The troubled hearts in the worried men
Things that I've been shown
Keep me always returning to
Water from the wells of home
Water from the wells of home
Water from the wells of home

I want to come back some day
To the water from the wells of home
Lord, take me back someday
To the water from the wells of home

Water From the Wells of Home

As I stroll along the road to freedom
Like a gypsy in a gilded cage
My horizons have not always been bright
But that's the way that dreams are made
Days all seem to run together
Like a timeless honeycomb
I find myself wishing I could drink again
Water from the wells of home

Instrumental

I've seen all the shining cities
Lean against a yellow sky
I've seen the down and out get better
I've seen many a strong man die
Oh the troubled hearts and worried minds
And things that I've been shown
Keep me always returning to
To the Water from the wells of home

Instrumental

Always pray to go back someday
To the water from the wells of Home

John C
+ John R Cash

I DRAW THE LINE

with Rodney Crowell

1988

I have tasted honey from the heights of
paradise
I have eaten of the bread of ecstasy
I have often fallen to the lure of smoldering
eyes
And have given in to the wilder side of me

But I draw the line at going on
When I approach the danger zone
And I draw the line at going through
With anything that would lose me you

'Cause I won't give up the thing we've got
Nor give away my peace of mind
I'm often tempted, but for you I draw the line

I confess I'm human and I often fantasize
And I let my mind go loving 'round the town
But you should not forget, my heart is bigger
than my eyes
And I catch myself before it brings me down

And I draw the line at going on
When I approach the danger zone
And I draw the line at going through
With anything that would lose me you

'Cause I won't give up the thing we've got
Nor give away my peace of mind
I'm often tempted, but for you I draw the line

I sometimes take the low road when the hills
are hard to climb
And I know sometimes I play the fool
But I lock it in my heart that I am yours and
you are mine
And I straighten up before I break the rules

And I draw the line at going on
When I approach the danger zone
And I draw the line at going through
With anything that would lose me you

'Cause I won't give up the thing we've got
Nor give away my peace of mind
I'm often tempted, but for you I draw the line

I Draw the Line

I have tasted honey
From the hives of paradise
I have eaten of the bread of ecstacy
I have often fallen
To the lure of smouldering eyes
And I've given in to the wilderside of me

But I draw the line at going on
When I approach the danger zone
And I draw the line at going through
With anything that would lose me you
Cause I won't give up the thing we've got
Nor give away my peace of mind
I'm often tempted but for you I draw the line

I confess I'm human
And I often fantasize
And I let my mind go loving round the town
But you should not forget
My heart is bigger than my eyes
And I catch myself before it brings me down

I sometimes take the low road
When the hills are hard to climb
And I know sometimes I play the fool
But I lock it in my heart
That I am yours and you are mine
And I straighten up before I break the rules

JR Cash
Sept 1 88
[illegible]

A CROFT IN CLACHAN

1988

With the Campbells and MacDonalds, it was in their blood to fight
With each passing generation it became a man's birthright
But they always had one common enemy
Never would the English crown take Scottish independency

Oh, the battles raged in Glasgow and majestic Edinburgh
And they came with war machines and in the Highlands shots were heard
Then the people rose in union and the forces moved as one
And the clans all joined together to see English on the run

And in a tiny croft in Clachan sat a mother, Peg MacDunn
And she sewed a coat together for her sixteen-year-old son
And she cried as he was leaving, "Don't forget to keep you warm
And come you back to Clachan when the English are all done."

Now Rob MacDunn was ready as he left the croft behind
And he joined the Highland Pipe Brigade with one thing on his mind
That to keep his home and freedom he must face it like a man
So he marched in common cadence with his musket in his hand
And he met the hell of battle in the Highlands and the low
And the reason for the fighting long within his blood to know
In the middle of the rumble he was forward gaining ground
And the bagpipes still were piping as the dead lay all around

Then he moved with no direction 'til he faced the winds of north
And he boldly climbed the Highlands, further from the Firth of Forth
Then one freezing, blowing morning, came the cry of Peg MacDunn
"Back to my croft in Clachan, God has sent me home my son."

And in another croft in Clachan, 'cross the way from the MacDunns
With her face against the window sat a young girl, tired and worn
And she smiled a secret knowing as she breathed a prayer alone:
"I thank thee, Lord, for bringing Rob MacDunn back safely home."

Back to the croft in Clachan, he returned to peace again
He had gone a boy of sixteen, but he came back as a man

NEW MOON OVER JAMAICA

with Tom T. Hall and Paul McCartney

1988

There's a new moon over Jamaica
And the new year just got here, you see
There's a new moon over Jamaica
And I'm living with an old memory

So won't you come back to Jamaica?
You know, it isn't so far
Look up in the sky where you left me that night
I'll be standing right under that star

There's a new moon over Jamaica
And the new year just got here, you see
There's a new moon over Jamaica
And I'm living with an old memory

I said good evening to Venus
She said good evening, too
Out there somewhere, you know, I could swear
She sent a message of true love from you

There's a new moon over Jamaica
And the new year just got here, you see
There's a new moon over Jamaica
And I'm living with an old memory

A new moon makes someone feel happy
A new moon makes someone lovesick
I'm thinking of you, but what can I do?
New moons and new years and old loves don't mix

There's a new moon over Jamaica
And the new year just got here, you see
There's a new moon over Jamaica
And I'm living with an old memory
Just the new year, a new moon, and me

2nd

Baby is sweet to me
Doesn't mean to mistreat me
For I know she loves me
Like nobody else can do
I say I won't try again
That this time will be the end
~~But~~ But all I really want
is to be back in baby's arms

BACK in Babys Arms

Baby abuses me, mistreats ~~misuses~~ MISSUSES me
But loves me with a fire
That is beyond control
I dont know the reason why
I only know I almost die
Until ~~the~~ days alone go by
And I'm back in babys arms

Cho Back in babys arms
Where I know I belong
If only for a little while
I'll have the will to live
And carry on

Baby will do for me
The times baby's true to me
The days goes slow
Until I'm back in babys arms

BACK IN BABY'S ARMS

1989

Baby abuses me, mistreats
Misuses me
But loves me with a fire
That is beyond control

I don't know the reason why
I only know I almost die
Until the days go by
And I'm back in baby's arms

Back in baby's arms
Where I know I belong
If only for a little while
I'll have the will to live
And carry on

Baby will do for me
The times baby's true to me
The days go so slow
Until I'm back in baby's arms

Back in baby's arms
Where I know I belong
If only for a little while
I'll have the will to live
And carry on

Baby is sweet to me
Doesn't mean to mistreat me
For I know she loves me
Like nobody else can do

I say I won't try again
That this time will be the end
But all I really want
Is to be back in baby's arms

A BACKSTAGE PASS

1989

There were wackos and weirdos and
dingbats and dodoes
And athletes and movie stars and David
Allan Coe
There was leather and lace and every
minority race
With a backstage pass to the Willie Nelson
show

Kristofferson got an offer for a movie
Promoters closed another deal or two
Waylon got a call from his son Shooter
And he went home the minute he was
through

I moved with the mob at intermission
To the green room where you see who you
can see
There were has-beens and would-bes and
never-weres
Paupers, punks, and millionaires and me

And there were wackos and weirdos and
dingbats and dodoes
And athletes and movie stars and David
Allan Coe
There was leather and lace and every
minority race
With a backstage pass to the Willie Nelson
show

Hell's Angels blocked the traffic to the
building
In order for the beer truck to come through
And waitin' in the wings to sing with Willie
Were hopeful stars of flickering magnitude

There was a singer Willie knew back in the
fifties
Who once paid him fifty dollars for a song
There were women who once did and some
who still would
I heard one ask, "Did Connie come along?"

And there were wackos and weirdos and
dingbats and dodoes
And athletes and movie stars and David
Allan Coe
Leather and lace and every minority race
With a backstage pass to the Willie Nelson
show

I wish you could've been there
But maybe you were

FARMER'S ALMANAC

1989

Well, the farmer prayed for a better year
And the crops were good, like the Lord did
hear
But his barn burned down with winter near
The answer came in white and black
In the farmer's almanac, it says,
"If a man could have half his wishes
He could double his trouble."

A sweet old lady was eighty-four
When her kinfolks came for a month or more
Now from overwork she's on the other shore
Much too late was, y'all come back
And it says in the farmer's almanac, it says,
"Visitors and fish smell after three days."

Our leader was a silver-tongued man
He deceived the people of the land
And when he got caught he couldn't stand
It's a little offbeat and a little off-track
But it says in the farmer's almanac, it says,
"In rivers and bad government
The lightest things flow to the top."

Rod said, "I don't believe in God."
Rod died and lies beneath the sod
For God did not believe in Rod
Life is a troubled and a weary track
But it says in the farmer's almanac, it says,
"Feed your faith and your doubts will starve
to death."

The little boy followed the honeybee
And it flew straight to the honey tree
He got stung, but got the honey free
Consolation for the things you lack
Is in the farmer's almanac, it says,
"God gives us the darkness so we can see the
stars."

He came home three hours late from work
Said, "I had a flat and fell in the dirt."
She said, "You got lipstick on your shirt."
Well, it turned out like Jill and Jack
And it says in the farmer's almanac, it says,
"Lies have to be covered up, truth can run
around naked."

He said, "Honey, you know I'm true.
I just look at other women, that's all I do."
Then she caught him with her best friend,
Peggy Sue
Sometimes some women will look back
And it says in the farmer's almanac, it says,
"There's a lot of difference in window-
shoppin' and shopliftin'."

I sat down at a shoeshine stand
I had a real slow shoeshine man
I said, "You don't pop that rag like some of
'em can."
He looked at me and then he sat right back
It says in the farmer's almanac, it says,
"The trouble with the world today
Is there's too much poppin' and not enough
shinin'."

I SHALL BE FREE

1989

I don't wanna go to prison
I don't wanna be in jail
I don't want no badge and buckle
Bringin' me my meals and mail

I don't want to count the hours
When they ain't worth countin' for
I don't like to walk on a carpet
But I hate a concrete floor

So I'm trying to behave myself
I'm trying to act right
And I'm neighborly with my neighbor
And I say my prayers at night

But the thing that really matters
Is that you will care for me
And I just want you to know that if you do
I shall be free

I shall be free
I shall be free
I shall be free
I shall be free
If you ever do want me
I shall be free

I don't want to be a traveler
I don't want a suit and tie
I don't want to eat my supper
Seven miles up in the sky

I don't wanna be a chairman
I don't want a cellular phone
I don't want no gold in Switzerland
You are my precious stone

I'll be setting on dead ready
At the slightest nod from you
Want no kind of obligation
Not one thing I have to do

I will sleep out in your yard
So you will know where I will be
If you peek out your window and see me
I shall be free

I shall be free
I shall be free
I shall be free
I shall be free
If you ever do want me
I shall be free

I would give up my guitar
Give away my fancy clothes
I would cancel my engagements
I would cut out all the shows

I'd tear up my driver's license
I would burn up my road map
I would sit down by the phone
With your picture on my lap

I would sit out by the mailbox
Waiting for the morning mail
I'd be like an anxious puppy
Who just sits and wags his tail

You won't ever catch me sleeping, honey
That I guarantee
If you ever do want me
I shall be free

I shall be free
I shall be free
I shall be free
I shall be free
If you ever do want me
I shall be free

And just give me half a chance
And I will give the world to you
I would be and do most anything you
want me to

I will love you and protect you and
provide bountifully
I'll give you tomorrow if you give yourself
to me
And whenever that may be I shall be free

I LOVE YOU, LOVE YOU

1989

I love you, love you, I love you
Just in case you care, you know I do

I've done everything I know to do
To catch your eye and get a rise from you
I've said everything I know to say
Until I'm afraid that I'll scare you away

I've tried everything I know to try
And if you won't love me I'm going to die
I'll be anything I need to be
To make you want to bring your love to me

I love you, love you, I love you
Can't help it that I feel the way I do
I love you, love you, I love you
Just in case you care, you know I do

I'll quit anything I need to quit
Or I'll change anything to make it fit
I'll start anything I need to start
If that would mean you're giving me your heart

I love you, love you, I love you
Can't help it that I feel the way I do
I love you, love you, I love you
Just in case you care, you know I do

SONGS THAT MAKE A DIFFERENCE

1989

Hey, babe, do you remember, back in 1969
We gathered 'round the room, you sang yours and I sang mine
We took turns with the guitar, in the front and center seat
Shel and Kris and Dylan, and a couple off the street

Joni Mitchell cried on both sides now
We sang songs that made a difference
And we can again somehow

Everybody knew that this was quite a special night
Graham Nash was nervous in the hot seat, in the light
Joe South was total magic and we all walked in his shoes
Orbison and Rabbit cried and they rocked the country blues

Newbury, "San Francisco Mabel Joy"
We sang songs that made a difference
June was pregnant with my boy

Oh, I could make a living driving nails or driving trucks
Sleep beneath the bridge or in the streets, down on my luck
I'd stand the cold and hunger, if they'd let me hear the songs
Everybody write one that us bums can sing along

Keep it from the heart and down-to-earth
Sing the songs that make a difference
Give us all our money's worth

Keep it from the heart and down-to-earth
Sing the songs that make a difference
Give us all our money's worth

Kiss the Ladies Goodnite.

The party is ending
we sang and we laughed
The hours we planned on
Have sweetly slipped past
We talked and we danced
And we're feeling alright
So lets kiss the ladies goodnite

Its been twenty years
Since I heard these old songs
Wasn't it great
How the girls sang along
We all clapped our hands
And we did it up right
Now lets kiss the ladies goodnite

Me & you & Miss Dixie
And Linda & June
And Paul and John Carter
Surrounded the tunes
We've done it more
Than half way to daylite
Now Lets kiss the ladies goodnite

We sang and told stories
And Anna & Brack
Told a love story from 40 years back
A story so good that the whole place grew quiet
Now lets kiss the Ladies goodnite.
The kids are all sleepy
The dishes are done
We all agree that we've really had fun
We'll do it again
If the lord thinks its right
We'll kiss the ladies goodnite

KISS THE LADIES GOODNIGHT

1989

The party is ending
We sang and we laughed
The hours we planned on
Have sweetly slipped past
We talked and we danced
And we're feeling all right
So let's kiss the ladies goodnight

It's been twenty years
Since I heard those old songs
Wasn't it great
How the girls sang along
We all clapped our hands
And we did it up right
Now let's kiss the ladies goodnight

Me and you and Miss Dixie
And Linda and June
And Paul and John Carter
Surrounded them tunes
We've done it more
Than halfway to daylight
Now let's kiss the ladies goodnight

We sang and told stories
And Anna and Brack
Told a love story
From forty years back
A story so good
That the whole place grew quiet
And let's kiss the ladies goodnight

The kids are all sleepy
The dishes are done
We all agree
That we've really had fun
We'll do it again
If the Lord thinks it's right
Well, kiss the ladies goodnight

* REVIVAL *

1990–1999

THE EAGER NEWCOMER Cash had started in the narrow confines of a concrete box on the corner of Union and Marshall Avenues in Memphis, with the modest sign in the window reading SUN RECORDING COMPANY, a place known for pumping out rock and roll. From there, he conquered country music, spread the Gospel, spoke his conscience, climbed mountains, dwelled in the valley, and journeyed to the ends of the earth. The young Cash had simply dreamed for people to hear his songs. He managed to exceed that.

By 1990, a weary Cash was ready for his swan song, a closing of the circle. He continued to write — it was part of him; he could not stop — with his work, as always, reflecting, representing, and honoring the human condition in all its wonder and woe. "Drive On" told the story of an aging, disabled — and haunted — Vietnam vet. "She Sang 'Sweet Baby James'" harrowingly depicted the isolation and loss of hope of a struggling single mother. And in another of the countless examples of writing what he lived, "I Love You Tonight" spoke of a couple reaching the dusk of their day, but appreciating what was truly important all along. Written in the first person, it is easy to recognize the players in this valedictory. For a serene Cash, it was time to rest.

It turned out, though, that Johnny Cash had one more "return" in him. It seemed that his last chapter was forever being written. This time, like a thunderclap that had delayed its arrival until just the moment when the lightning had dimmed down to a flicker, there came a roar from the distant past. The noise was rock and roll.

Johnny Cash's election to the Rock & Roll Hall of Fame was a recognition of his presence back in the early days of the genre and the crossover popularity and influence that so profoundly affected the music forms. But seeing him performing onstage with the likes of John Fogerty, Keith Richards, and Little Richard (singing his classic "Big River") was a revelation: The elder statesman was still a vital force. In short order, the band U2 (the most popular rock group in the world at the time) was showing up at Cash concerts and inviting him to record with them. "The Wanderer," written by Bono "with Johnny's voice in my head," not only put Cash's voice in many, many other heads; it also deprived him of that retirement and changed his life and legacy forever.

The mythic collaboration between Johnny Cash and Rick Rubin upended previous notions of final acts. With a catalog extending back more than four decades, Cash had plenty of "oldies" to choose from if that was his wont, but producer and artist steadfastly refused to be part of the "nostalgia circuit." In a decade's time, Cash released four contemporary albums with Rubin, all earning acclaim and Grammy Awards. At the same time, the creative juices were flowing again. Although beset with health infirmities, especially failing eyesight and loss of mobility, Cash turned out brilliant pieces, including the introspective, autobiographical "Meet Me in Heaven," the achingly beautiful "Before My Time," and an elegy for his musical family, "Tears in the Holston River." Nearly blind, he memorized the words to each new masterwork as he formed it in his mind, then struggled to commit the lyrics to paper that he would never be able to read, leaving for posterity a treasure trove of material documenting this heartbreaking process and enormous achievement.

FRIENDSHIP

1990s

Awaking with scattered thoughts
And stumbling through the room
The birds announcing daybreak
A sweetness in the gloom

The morning functions, done by rote
Washed and finally dressed
A cup of coffee chasing now
My mental muddled mist

It was then I let myself
Recall a turmoil of yesterday
Last evening's trouble
Somatic demons slow to chase away

The sun comes up
So what is wrong?
My wristwatch doesn't care
And neither does the bird's song
Nor that flower growing there

Then it hits like muddy lava
Last night, born on evil wind
A hard word and a cold look
From he who was a friend

A close-kept friendship
That had been for twenty years or more
And now the years lie stinking
Like dead fish on the floor

Should I go see this friend today?
No, he won't take my call
All the chips have fallen
And the back's against the wall

Does he not feel the way I feel
And hurt the way I do?
We used to say we're both alike
You're me and I am you

Well, if I could hold heaven
If I could know its worth
I'd start a branch establishment
And run it here on earth

But not mine, that awesome power
Not mine, that holy strength
I barely can control
This old house's breadth and length

I gave it all to God
And I let Him have control
But God resounds, Rise up and heal
Thy friendship and thy soul

In sloth, I sit before the box
And let the hour pass
My mind a wandering raven
Newly flown and out of class

It isn't my place now, I say
I've done all that I can
It's time for him to come to me
And face me like a man

Face like what man, my canyon echoes
Come to you, facing what?
Perhaps he too is stricken
And his pride is all he's got

It isn't my fault, my anger screams
I did all I could do
It's up to him from this point on
It's he who has to do

I simply will not mention him
I'll go about my way
Minding my own business
Without a word to say

So there, that firmly is resolved
I stand just where I stand
And maybe someday he'll awake
And come out like a man

So now I've done it, that's the end
As far as I can see
But a still small voice says,
I thought you turned it over to Me?

My ego said, Go on and fix it
I've done my part
Not even you can warm
The chambers of his frozen heart

I'm just a man, I can do so much
And then I draw the line
And to that line I will retreat
With everything that's mine

I'll cast my nets and gather in
Ones who agree with me
A power vortex comfort zone
Where nothing disagrees

To bring rebuke upon my soul
To never make me doubt
I was the wise one and the true
And if you don't believe me, stay out

I'll go afar and pick and choose
Be cool and hold my peace
I'll have an army on my side
A regiment, at least

Who will say, "Did you hear about John
Getting stabbed in the back?"
And I'll humbly say, "Just forget it."
And I'll keep on wearing black

And to what end, I finally ask
Will I continue so?
How long can I make the world think
That I just let it go?

So far, God hasn't done a thing
Doesn't that prove that I'm right?
I dare not ask these questions
When I'm alone at night

For the stirrings of the conscience
And the trembling of the truth
Break loose on me like hormones
Break loose on the youth

The voice finally says, Well, finally
You're back to Me in the end
Go and see or write or call and say,
"Good morning, friend."

I AM READY FOR YOUR LOVE

1990s

Give up every notion
That my steam is running out
I've been up and I've been down
But I have not run out

The fire that burns within me
Often can't be seen at all
But do not be deluded
I'm still over six feet tall

I often am distracted
By demands imposed on me
Some personal attention now
Would set this tiger free

You ought to know
I'm ready for your love
What's that old and wearin' down
I hear so much about?

My get-up-and-go
Is gettin' up and goin' out
Don't expect complacency
I know what love's about

I won't brag but I still need
Your body in my arms
I have no intention to bring you
To any harm

I'm a-way past holding hands
And cooing like a dove
But right now
I'm ready for your love

I Am Ready for Your Love

Give up every notion
That my steam is running out
I've been up and I've been down
But I have not run out
The fire that burns within me
Often can't be seen at all
But do not be deluded
I'm still over 6 feet tall
I often am distracted
By demands imposed on me
Some special attention now
Would set this tiger free
You ought to know
I'm ~~[illegible]~~ ready for your love
What's ~~this ole~~ not old and wearin' down
~~[illegible]~~ I hear so much about
My get up and go
Is gettin' up and goin' out
Don't expect complacency
I know what love's about
I wont brag but I still need
Your body in my arms
I have no intention to bring you
To any harm
I'm away past holdin hands
And cooing like a dove
But right now I am ready for your love

I WOKE UP THIS MORNING

1990s

I woke up this morning
And I looked into the mirror
And I saw lines
I hadn't seen before
But I smiled back at the image
Of a walking, talking miracle
Who's lived two dozen lifetimes
Maybe more

So I found my book of numbers
And I called my inner circle
Of ones who have so long been tried and true
I said, "Let's get together now
'Cause I have really missed you.
It's been way too long since I saw you."

Just a few good friends

memo

I woke up this morning
And I looked into the mirror
And I saw lines I hadn't seen before
But I smiled back at the image
Of a walking talking miracle
Who's lived a dozen lifetimes, Maybe More
So I found my book of numbers
And I called my inner circle
Of ones who have so long been tried and true
I said lets get together now
Cause I have really missed you
It's been way too long since I saw you,

Just a few good friends

OLD FAMILIAR FEELINGS

1990s

I like my honey from the hives of home
And the berries from my own vine
I like to feel you beside me at night
And to hear you say you're still mine

I like the water from my own well
And peaches from my own tree
It all makes me feel that the Lord hung the moon
To watch over you and me

Old familiar feelings
Bringin' old love back around
Bundle me down in belongin'
Keepin' my feet on the ground

Old familiar feelings
Of fragrance and feelings and sound

Old Familiar Feelings

I like my honey from the hives of home
And the berries from my own vine
I like to feel you beside me at nite
And to hear you say you're still mine
I like the water from my own well
And peaches from my own tree
It all makes me feel that the Lord hung the moon
To watch over you and me

Old familiar feelings
Bringin old love back around
Bundle me down in belongin
Keepin my feet on the ground
Old familiar feelings
Of ~~And~~ fragrance and feelings and sound

SAILIN' HOME

1990s

We traveled across the highways in the sky
We smiled down on you when we sailed by
Autumn leaves have fallen and winter's comin' on
We're gonna spend it 'round the fires of home

We've been up and down the gray highway
Wakin' in a new world every day
I barely turn around and another year is gone
We've been around, but now we're sailin' home

Sailin' home, home, home, sailin' home
To family and friends, and you're invited to come along
Sailin' home, home, home, sailin' home
This mile is the sweet one, sailin' home
Get on board and bring along a song
Join in on my chorus, good and strong

Singin's free, and rich or poor, it doesn't mean a thing
I believe God loves you when you sing
Happy in this old familiar place
Happy just to see your pretty face
Wouldn't take a million for this feelin' comin' on
Returnin' once again now, sailin' home

Sailin' home, home, home, sailin' home
To family and friends, and you're invited to come along
Sailin' home, home, home, sailin' home
This mile is the sweet one, sailin' home
Get on board and bring along a song
Join in on my chorus, good and strong

Sailin' Home

We traveled 'cross the highways in the sky
We smiled down on you when we sailed by
Autumn leaves have fallen and winter's comin' on
We're gonna spend it 'round the fires of home
We've been up and down the grey highway
Wakin in a new world every day
I barely turn around and another year is gone
We've been around but now we're sailin home

Sailin' home, home, home, sailin home
To family and friends and you're invited come along
Sailin home, home, home, sailin home
This mile is the sweet one, sailin home

Get on board and bring along a song
Join in on any chorus good and strong
Singin's free and rich or poor it doesn't mean a thing
I believe God loves you when you sing
Happy in this old familiar place
Happy just to see your pretty face
Wouldn't take a million for this feelin' comin on
Returnin once again now, sailin home

Repeat Chorus

Well howdy-do, aloha - how you been
[illegible]
It's so good to see you once again
[illegible]
I would bet my boots you won't feel like a stranger
When we're all gathered round the fires of home
It's a very special time tonite
Your being here just makes it all right
[illegible]
[illegible]
I'll be content to be a rambler and a rolling stone
~~[illegible]~~ you are here when we come sailin home

SILK AND DENIM

1990s

She wore silk and denim
She wore silk and denim
From the top of her red head
To her red painted toes

The way she turned when I called her name
Her skirt whirled in circles
There were lacy little roses
On her red pantyhose

She looked like a fire coming
All except her eyes
They were bluer than lazuli
And deeper than the skies

They were full of love and welcome
They were kind and they were smiling
And I knew in a heartbeat
I would love her 'til I die

She wore lace and denim
She wore lace and denim
Lacy decorated bosom
Soft blue denim on her hips

I tried not to undress her
But my mind could not be passive
I fantasized my loving her
I kissed her on the lips

And the denim buttons opened
And the blue cloth fell away
She turned her back and held her hair up
Smiled a sweet okay

I fumbled with the lace buttons
And not one word did we say

Silk and Denim

She wore Silk and denim
" " " " "
From the top of her red head
To her red painted toes
The way she turned when I called her name
Her skirt whirled in circles
There were lacy little roses
On her red pantyhose

She looked like a fire coming,
All except her eyes
They were bluer than Lazuli,
And deeper than the skies
They were full of love and welcome
They were kind and they were smiling
And I knew in a heartbeat
I would love her till I die

She wore lace and denim
" " " " "
Lacey decorated bosom
Soft blue denim on her hips-
I tried not to undress her
But my mind could not be passive
I fantasized my loving her
I kissed her on the lips.

And the denim buttons opened
And the blue cloth fell away
She turned her back and held her hair up.
Smiled a sweet ok
I fumbled with the laces buttons
And not one word did we say

SITTIN' ON TOP OF THE WORLD

1990s

I'm never lonely, I'm never blue
I broke the shackles
Binding me to you
So now you're gone
And I don't worry
I'm sittin' on top of the world

Don't come around me
With that long face
I've got more women
Than I can chase

Woke up this evening
Put my blue jeans on
Don't tug my heartstrings
It's turned to stone

I loved the women
One or two at a time
You've gone and left me
It's eight or nine
You are gone
And I don't worry
I'm sittin' on top of the world

Sittin' on top of the World

I'm never lonely I'm never blue
I broke the shackles
Binding me to you
So now you're gone and I don't worry
~~I'm sittin~~ on top of the world

Don't come around me
With that long face
I've got more women
Than I can chase

Woke up this evening
Put my blue jeans on
Don't tug my heart ~~strings~~
It's [illegible]

~~Oh hear~~ I loved the women
~~At one~~ one or two at a time
~~So now~~ you've gone and left me
It's ~~always~~ eight or nine
You are gone and I don't worry
I'm sittin on top of the world

~~If you don't like my peaches~~
~~Don't shake my tree~~
~~Stay out of my henhouse~~
~~Let my chickens be~~
~~Now you're gone and I don't worry~~
~~I'm sittin on top of the world~~

WHAT WOULD I DREAMER DO?

with Gary Louris

1990s

What would I dreamer do?
Rainbow, it has its hue
See, it's long been hunted down
There are far too many clowns
Far too many carnivals

Some tell me, "Be like me."
No one's like you, you see
Hiding your secret side
All the hungry fools have died
And lock in the mysteries

Seems to be to fix up things
I should fly on brazen wings
Passing by all that conforms
Wearing no raincoat in the storm
And to hell with umbrellas

Put on a brand-new suit
I'd buy straw hat and boots
Live the accepted, normal life
Answer to "How's your wife and your
children?"

Should I wait in my seat
Watch as the blood heats?
I may know no other task
I won't wait, so please don't ask
Gotta go do something

I don't recall anyone
Task or duty, fail my line
Songs are nothing but the same
Say they're never listening
I'm hearing the music he's playing

Have it all figured out, I guess
I'm confused, all the rest
But I won't live 8 to 5
I'll be 8 to 5 alive
Even on the weekends

I've walked down a lot of streets
Get up and go when I eat
Throw away that business suit
Track mud on another man's carpet

WHAT WOULD I DREAMER DO
JOHN R. CASH

WHAT WOULD I DREAMER DO
THE RAINBOW ALREADY HAS ITS HUE
THE SEA HAS LONG BEEN SALTED DOWN
AND THERE ARE FAR TOO MANY CLOWNS
FOR TOO MANY CARNIVALS

SOME TELL ME, BE LIKE ME
NO ONE SHOULD BE LIKE YOU, YOU SEE
HIDE YOUR MYSTERIOUS SECRET SIDE
WHILE HUNGRY FOOLS HAVE DIED
UNLOCKING MYSTERIES

I PUT ON A NICE NEAT SUIT
HIDE MY STRAW HAT & BOOTS
LIVE THE ACCEPTED NORMAL LIFE
ANSWER TO MR. HOW'S YOUR WIFE
& YOUR CHILDREN

SEEMS TO ME TO FIX UP THINGS
I SHOULD FLY ON BRAZEN WINGS
PASSING BY ALL THAT CONFORMS
WEAR NO RAINCOAT IN STORMS
AND TO HELL WITH UMBRELLAS

WHY SHOULD I WAIT IN MY SEAT
PASSING TIME FOR A GLUTTON TO EAT
I MAY KNOW NO OTHER TASK
BUT I WON'T WAIT, SO DON'T ASK
I'LL GO DO SOMETHING

I DON'T RECALL, IF ANY OR WHAT
TASK OR DUTY FELL MY LOT
THEY SAY SONGS ARE FOR NOTHING BUT TO SI
SAY THE NEVER LISTENING - UNHEARING
WHILE THE MUSIC PLAYS

I DON'T HAVE IT ALL FIGURED I GUESS
MAYBE I'M CONFUSED AS THE REST
BUT I WON'T LIVE 8 TO 5
ARE THE 8 TO 5 ALIVE
EVEN ON WEEKENDS

SO, I'LL WALK A LOT OF STREETS
GET UP & GO, WHENEVER I EAT
THROW AWAY THAT BUSINESS SUIT
PUT NEETS FOOT OIL, ON MY BOOTS
AND TRACK MUD ON SOMEBODY'S
CARPET

WHO'S GONNA GREASE MY SKILLET

with John Popper

1990s

Who's gonna grease my skillet, when you're gone?
Who's gonna grease my skillet, when you're gone?
Who's gonna fire up my grill, when the heat needs turning on?
Who's gonna grease my skillet, when you're gone?

Who's gonna squeeze my juice, if you should go?
Who's gonna squeeze my juice, if you should go?
What you gonna do about it, when the pitcher's getting low?
Who's gonna squeeze my oranges, when you go?

Who are you gonna let squeeze your tangerines?
Who gonna put the hot to your collard greens?
My mouth is watering, thinking 'bout your butter beans
You're about the tastiest dish I've ever seen

Who's gonna feed you grapes by the bunch
And yummy little snacks, upon which to munch?
The breakfast pan is put away, but I've got me a hunch
You won't walk out on me without your lunch

Who's gonna grease my skillet, when you're gone?
Who's gonna grease my skillet, when you're gone?
Who's gonna fire up my grill, when the heat needs turning on?
Who's gonna grease my skillet, when you're gone?

Who's gonna grease my
skillett when youre gone

Who's gonna turn the heater on
When I'm cold to the bone
Who's gonna grease my skillet
when you're gone
Whos gonna squeeze my
juice if you should go.

What you gonna do about
it
If it drops down to
Who os gonna squeeze
my oranges when you go.
Who you gonna let
squeeze your tangerine

How about your grapefruits
Who's gonna help you wa

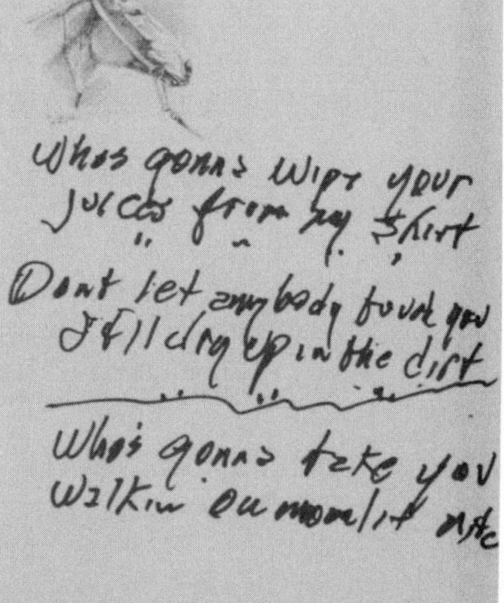
Whos gonna wipe your
juices from my shirt
Dont let anybody find you
Still drying up in the dirt

Who's gonna take you
walkin on moonlit nite

GOING, GOING, GONE

with Michael Forch, Robert Glasper, Ronnie James Tucker, and Anu Sun

1990

Liquid, tablet, capsule, powder, pill, smoke, vapor
Payoff's all the same in the end, payoff's all the same in the end
Liquid, tablet, capsule, powder, pill, smoke, vapor
Payoff's all the same in the end, payoff's all the same in the end

Going, going, going, now you're gone
Going, going, going, now you're gone
Going, going, going, now you're gone
Going, going, going, now you're gone

Pop the pill, medallion blinds
Spending time alone to ease my mind
It isn't fair that I have to suffer
How many jammers do I have to take?
It doesn't matter

Twenty thousand cells dead and blind
Down these likely valleys of my mind
Why can't the highs get higher?
Maybe you should go and get yourself a gun

Liquid, tablet, capsule, powder, pill, smoke, vapor
Payoff's all the same in the end, payoff's all the same in the end
Liquid, tablet, capsule, powder, pill, smoke, vapor
Payoff's all the same in the end, payoff's all the same in the end

Going, going, going, now you're gone
Going, going, going, now you're gone
Going, going, going, now you're gone
Going, going, going, now you're gone

You're my inventory, I'm just really
Trying to chase a high beyond the ceiling
Told me not to sleep a while, I don't like to feel it
Maybe I should go and get myself a gun

It isn't fair I have to suffer
For a little pleasure that doesn't matter
Why can't the highs get higher?
Maybe I should go and get myself a gun

Going, going, going, now you're gone
Going, going, going, now you're gone
Going, going, going, now you're gone
Going, going, going, now you're gone

Liquid, tablet, capsule, powder, pill, smoke, vapor
Payoff's all the same in the end, payoff's all the same in the end
Liquid, tablet, capsule, powder, pill, smoke, vapor
Payoff's all the same in the end, payoff's all the same in the end

GOING, GOING, GONE

(alternate version)

with Michael Forch, Robert Glasper,
Ronnie James Tucker, and Anu Sun

1990

Liquid, tablet, capsule, powder
Fumes and smoke and vapor
The payoff is the same in the end
Liquid, tablet, capsule, powder
Fumes and smoke and vapor
Convenient ways to get the poison in

Pop the pill and you don't hear
But there's a great explosion
Twenty thousand cells are dead and blind
Keep it up and very soon
A cold, dry wind is blowing
Down through the lifeless valleys of your
mind

Take the tiny crystals now
'Cause you don't need the stomach
Snort it, shoot it, ain't you having fun
Why can't the highs get higher
And why do the lows get lower?
Hey, maybe you should get yourself a gun

It isn't fair you have to suffer
For a little pleasure
You must relax, the red capsule will do
So nice to sleep a little while
But you don't like this feeling
So you lay a line of powder, maybe two
You do your inventory
And some of your drugs are missing
You know you didn't do near half that much
Turn on the ones who love you
Why are they afraid and crying
And why do they recoil to your touch?

Lock your door, tie down the blinds
And bring the lights down lower
You're only happy now when you're alone
How many downers will it take?
Oh well, it doesn't matter
You've long been going, going; now you're
gone

Going, Going, Gone

John R Cash

Liquid, tablet capsule powder
Smoke and fumes and vapor
The end is the end in the end
Liquid tablet capsule powder
Smoke and fumes and vapor
Convenient ways to get the poison in

up the nose
mainline the veins
Time release or ~~capsule~~ liquid

Pop the pill and you dont hear but there's a great explosion
Twenty thousand cells are dead and blind
Keep it up and very soon a dry cold wind is crying
Down through the lifeless valleys of your mind.
Take the tiny chrystals now dont worry about the stomach
Snort it, shoot it. Ain't you having fun.
Why cant the highs get higher and why do the lows get lower
And, oh yes, you were going to buy a gun.
It isnt fair that you should suffer for a little pleasure
You must relax a double shot will do
A moment of oblivion then you wake up pale and trembling
And you lay a line of powder, maybe two
You do your enventory and some of your drugs are missing
You know you didnt do nearly half that much
You turn on those who love you. They are pleading and they are crying
And why do they recoil to your touch
You lock your door. You close the blinds
And bring the light down lower
You're only happy now when you're alone
How many downers will it take? Oh well, it doesnt matter
You've been going going; now you're gone -

John R Cash
Loma Linda
Christmas 1990.

Going, Going, Gone

Liquid, tablet capsule, powder -
Fumes & smoke and vapor
~~If you've got the money~~
The payoff is the same in the end.
Liquid tablet capsule powder
fumes and smoke and vapor
Convenient ways to get the poison in.

Pop that pill and you dont ~~see~~ hear
But theres a ~~small~~ great explosion
Twenty thousand cells are ~~[illegible]~~ dead & blind
Keep it up and very soon
A ~~[illegible]~~ Dry Cold wind is blowing
Down through the lifeless valleys of your mind

Take the tiny crystals now
'Cause you dont need the stomach
Snort it, shoot it aint you havin' fun
Why cant the highs get higher
And why do ~~[illegible]~~ the lows get lower
Hey maybe you should ~~[illegible]~~ yourself a gun

It isnt fair you have to suffer
For a little pleasure
You must relax, the red capsule will do
So nice to sleep a little while
But you dont like this feeling
So you lay a line of powder. maybe two

Going Going Gone, Contd.

You do your enventory
And some of your drugs are missing
You know you didnt do near half that much
Turn on the ones who love you
Why are they afraid and crying
And why do they recoil to your touch?

Lock your door tie down the blinds
And bring the lights down lower
You're only happy now when you're alone
How many downers does it take?
Oh well, what does it matter
You've long been going going, now youre gone

John R Cash

I'M AN EASY RIDER

1990

I'm an easy rider
The wind is at my back
I'm an easy rider
The white line is my track

Every lane is a passing lane
And the right-of-way is mine
Let me on that straightaway
And I'll be fairly flying

I'm an easy rider
My wheels love to roll

I'm an easy rider
I ride a new road every day
I'm an easy rider
I will see you on my way

I got a number down in every town
In my little black book
And they understand that I'm a traveling man
So they don't think they got hooked

I'm an easy rider
I love that gray highway

I'm an easy rider
Oh Lord, I love to roll
I'm an easy rider
Moving's in my soul

I know a lady down in Little Rock
And I stopped for a little while
But I had to go because another I know
Is waiting for my smile

I'm an easy rider
I can't be in one place

REDEMPTION

1990

From the hands, it came down
From the side, it came down
From the feet, it came down
And ran to the ground

Between heaven and hell
A teardrop fell
In the deep crimson dew
The tree of life grew

And the blood gave life
To the branches of the tree
And the blood was the price
That set the captives free

And the numbers that came
Through the fire and the flood
Clung to the tree
And were redeemed by the blood

From the tree streamed a light
That started the fight
'Round the tree grew a vine
On whose fruit I could dine

My old friend Lucifer came
Fought to keep me in chains
But I saw through the tricks
Of six-sixty-six

And the blood gave life
To the branches of the tree
And the blood was the price
That set the captives free

And the numbers that came
Through the fire and the flood
Clung to the tree
And were redeemed by the blood

From His hands, it came down
From His side, it came down
From the feet, it came down
And ran to the ground

And a small inner voice
Said, "You do have a choice."
The vine engrafted me
And I clung to the tree

And the blood gave life
To the branches of the tree
And the blood was the price
That set the captives free

And with the numbers that came
Through the fire and the flood
I clung to the tree
And was redeemed by the blood

From His hands, it came down
From His side, it came down
From the feet, it came down
And ran to the ground

DEAR YOU

1991

I shall not mourn for my lost youth
For I was born to know the truth
And to be realistic, face the facts
And not look down, and not look back

So let it be and let it roll
I try to keep me in control
To say and do as I am called
And trust there's life to do it all

Discernment to do all things well
And give right good and give wrong hell
I would be sure, I'd be discreet
To choose the path that takes my feet

Upon the paths that they should go
And know the signposts I should know
To gain each goal and do each task
As well as God or man could ask

And all I ask is, at the end
You could say to women or men
Just one thing I'd have you tell
"He knew his duty. He did it well."

HAVE YOU EVER BEEN TO LITTLE ROCK

1992

Have you ever been to Little Rock?
Have you ever been to Little Rock?
Those Arkansas women
Born with beauty and grace
Up in the Ozark Mountains
The one they call Petit Jean
You can see God's country
Put a smile on your face

It's the land of my family
Down in Cleveland County
It's where my mama and daddy were born
Where the singing pines grow
They got some hot spring water
Down in the Ouachita country
Wash away your misery
You feel like Henry Ford

Right off the scenic highway
Shake the hand of a farmer
Have a cool watermelon
That weighs a hundred pounds
And in the Mississippi Delta land
They're growing rice and cotton
In the fields all week long
Saturday night in town

Yes, I love my people
And I'm proud of my raising
Sweet Arkansas memories
Until they leave me down
Have you ever been to Little Rock?
Have you ever been to Little Rock?
Those Arkansas women
Born with beauty and grace

Drive On, Dont Mean Nothin'

J.R.Cash

I got a friend named Whiskey Sam
Twenty five years ago was in Viet Nam
He said is my country a little off track?
It took em 25 years to welcome me back

But its better than not coming back at all
Many a good man I saw fall
And even now everytime I dream
I hear the men and the monkeys in the jungle scream

Drive on, Dont mean nothin' — my children love me and they understand
Cho And I got a woman that loves her man
So Drive on, Dont mean nothin

I was a grunt and I was wild
And I have seen the tiger smile
I spit in a bamboo vipers face
And I came out of that horrible place

I remember one night Tex and me
Sat in elephant grass and ate our C's

Cho But we chilled out and
A mortar fell ten feet away
And I carry schrapnel to this day
I came home but Tex did not
And I cant talk about the hit he got
I got a little limp when I walk
Got a little tremolo when I talk
But I finally found out who I am
I'm a grunt that survived Viet Nam
Cho

But I ha...
my rifle

SONG OF CASH

POST OFFICE BOX 508 • 700 JOHNNY CASH PARKWAY • HENDERSONVILLE, TENNESSEE 37077
PHONE (615) 824-5110 • FAX (615) 822-7332

DRIVE ON

John R. Cash

I GOT A FRIEND NAMED WHISKEY SAM
HE WAS MY BOONIERAT BUDDY FOR A YEAR IN NAM
HE SAID IS MY COUNTRY JUST A LITTLE OFF TRACK
TOOK 'EM TWENTY-FIVE YEARS TO WELCOME ME BACK
BUT, IT'S BETTER THAN NOT COMING BACK AT ALL
MANY A GOOD MAN I SAW FALL
AND EVEN NOW, EVERY TIME I DREAM
I HEAR THE MEN AND MONKEYS IN THE JUNGLE SCREAM

DRIVE ON, DON'T MEAN NOTHIN'
MY CHILDREN LOVE ME AND THEY UNDERSTAND
AND I GOT A WOMAN THAT LOVES HER MAN
DRIVE ON, DON'T MEAN NOTHIN', DRIVE ON

I REMEMBER ONE NIGHT, TEX AND ME
~~WALKED RIGHT UP ON TWO V.C.~~ Rappeled in on a hot L.Z.
~~BUT, WE HAD OUR 16'S ON ROCK AND ROLL~~
~~AND WE SEPARATED THEM FROM THEIR SOULS~~ But with all that fire
I was scared & cold
WE WERE CRAZY, WE WERE WILD
AND I HAVE SEEN THE TIGER SMILE
I SPIT IN A BAMBOO VIPER'S FACE
AND I'D BE DEAD, BUT BY GOD'S GRACE

DRIVE ON, DON'T MEAN NOTHIN'
MY CHILDREN LOVE ME ~~AND THEY~~ But they dont UNDERSTAND
AND I GOT A WOMAN ~~THAT LOVES~~ — Who knows — HER MAN
DRIVE ON, DON'T MEAN NOTHIN', DRIVE ON

~~A MORTAR FELL TWENTY FEET AWAY~~ It was a real slow walk
~~AND I CARRY SHRAPNEL TO THIS DAY~~ In a real sad rain
And nobody tried to be John Wayne
I CAME HOME, BUT TEX DID NOT
AND I CAN'T TALK ABOUT THE HIT HE GOT
I GOT A LITTLE LIMP NOW WHEN I WALK
GOT A LITTLE TREMOLO WHEN I TALK
BUT I FINALLY FOUND OUT WHO I AM
I'M A WALKIN'-TALKIN' MIRACLE FROM VIET NAM

DRIVE ON

1992

Well, I got a buddy named Whiskey Sam
He was my boonie rat buddy for a year in 'Nam
He said, "I think my country got a little off track.
It took 'em twenty-five years to welcome me back."

But it's better than not coming back at all
Many a good man I saw fall
And even now, every time I dream
I hear the men and the monkeys in the jungle scream

Drive on, it don't mean nothin'
My children love me, but they don't understand
And I got a woman who knows her man
Drive on, it don't mean nothin', it don't mean nothin'
Drive on

I remember one night, Tex and me
Rappelled in on a hot LZ
We had our 16s on rock and roll
And with all that fire I was scared and cold

I was crazy and I was wild
And I have seen the tiger smile
I spit in a bamboo viper's face
And I'd be dead but by God's grace

Drive on, it don't mean nothin'
My children love me, but they don't understand
And I got a woman who knows her man
Drive on, it don't mean nothin', it don't mean nothin'
Drive on

It was a slow walk in a sad rain
And nobody wanted to be John Wayne
I came home but Tex did not
And I can't talk about the hit he got

But I got a little limp now when I walk
And I got a little tremolo when I talk
But my letter read, from Whiskey Sam,
"You're a walkin', talkin' miracle from Vietnam."

Drive on, it don't mean nothin'
My children love me, but they don't understand
And I got a woman who knows her man
Drive on, it don't mean nothin', it don't mean nothin'
Drive on

I LOVE YOU TONIGHT

1992

It sure has been a party, hasn't it, baby?
We've really been down that road a time or two
We checked into the best hotels from San Francisco to Paris
And lived like royalty, me and you

But remember years ago in that church in Ottawa
We told God of our love and asked for His care
And so He made us happen and He blessed us
So if we were in the fold or out, He was always there

And I love you tonight
Even more than I loved you in the '60s
And I know that we are right
Even more than I knew it in the '70s

Oh, baby, ain't we a sight?
Can you believe we made it through the '80s?
And will we make the millennium?
Well, we might
I love you tonight

It's funny how we never settle down
Though we love our home and sitting by the fire
But we can't be at home for three days 'til we get itchy feet
And people always ask, "When are you gonna retire?"

But your people have always been my people
And you have always gone wherever I go
And when it's all over, I hope we will go together
I don't want you to be alone, you know

I love you tonight

It sure has been a party hasn't it baby
We've really been down that road a time or two
~~So we were often surrounded by thousands~~
~~But mostly it was just me and you~~
We checked into the best hotels
From San Francisco to Paris
And lived like royalty, me and you
But Remember ~~years ago in that church in~~ in Ottowa
We told God of our love and asked for his care
And so He made us happen and He blessed us
So if we were in the fold or out He was always there

Chorus
And I love you tonight
Even more than I loved you in the sixties
And I know that we're right.
Even more than I knew it in the seventies.
Oh baby aren't we a sight
Can you believe we made it through the 80s
And will we make the Millenium? Well we might
I love you tonight.

[signature]

HELLO OUT THERE

1992

Hello out there
This is planet Earth
Calling, calling, calling, calling, calling

Hello out there
Our net worth
is falling, falling, falling, falling, falling

We're the third from the sun
We are blue and white
Spinning, spinning, spinning, spinning,
spinning

If you wish upon a star
Wish upon us tonight
We're dimming, dimming, dimming,
dimming, dimming

Hello out there
We're in the Milky Way
Sailing, sailing, sailing, sailing, sailing

In this final fight
For life and peace
We're failing, failing, failing, failing, failing

Hello out there
You'll see a morning star
Gaining, gaining, gaining, gaining, gaining

And the alpha and
Omega will be
Reigning, reigning, reigning, reigning,
reigning

And the die is cast
And the lines are drawn
And the time is soon to be
When the angels sound their seven trumpets
Across the land and the sea

And the King will come and reign a thousand
years
And restore His earthly realm
And there will be no night
For He will be our light
Throughout eternity with Him

Hello out there
Hello out there
Hello, hello, hello, hello, hello

RETURN TO THE PROMISED LAND

with David Ray Skinner and Hugh Waddell

1992

There is harmony we've yet to see
There's love we get to share
Come, go with me to the Promised Land
So much is waiting there

Across the Sea of Galilee
In Canaan, we shall stand
Return with me to a brighter day
We must love and understand
And the sunset on the Jordan will paint us gold
As we return to the Promised Land

A place I know you will love to go
Come on, and let's depart
We go in search of perfect peace
And joy will fill your heart

Across the Sea of Galilee
In Canaan, we shall stand
Return with me to a brighter day
We must love and understand
And the sunset on the Jordan will paint us gold
As we return to the Promised Land

Like a Soldier Getting Over the War.

Last night I had a dream
That I was Driving Unfamiliar streets
Trying to find a spot that I remembered
An Old familiar nightmare
I've been having all these years
And now my years are well beyond September.

But the time that I was dreaming
Was when I was in my twenties
I was wild and my body in the fires of spring
Now each time ~~I~~ awake
My memory carries out the dream
You're there and I remember everything

Like a Soldier Getting Over the War
I'm a man getting over my wilder ~~[illegible]~~ Ways
Like a Bandit getting over his lawless days.
It's so much more like living than before
I'm like a Soldier Gettin' over the war.

At night when shades are falling
And the evening casts its shadows.
And the sounds are magnified within my mind
As I hear my own heart beating
And the life that's precious to me
I just wonder why I ever was that kind.

But the wild road that I rambled
Always seemed ~~there~~ to be, calling ~~to me~~
Everybody said a hundred times I should have died
Maybe that's why I'm so thankful
That you're lying here beside
So I have to believe that it's a road I had to ride.

HOUSE OF CASH

POST OFFICE BOX 508 • 700 JOHNNY CASH PARKWAY • HENDERSONVILLE, TENNESSEE 37077
PHONE (615) 824-5110 • FAX (615) 822-7332

A

<u>LIKE A SOLDIER</u>

John R. Cash

WITH THE TWILIGHT COLORS FALLING
AND THE EVENING LAYING SHADOWS
HIDDEN MEMORIES COME STEALING FROM MY MIND
AS I FEEL MY OWN HEAR BEATING OUT
THE SIMPLE JOY OF LIVING
I WONDER HOW I EVER WAS THAT KIND

BUT THE WILD ROAD I WAS RAMBLING
WAS ALWAYS OUT THERE CALLING
You ~~AND THEY~~ SAID A HUNDRED TIMES I SHOULD HAVE DIED
~~BUT NOW MY PRESENT MIRACLE But~~ you came down and touched me
~~IS THAT YOU'RE HERE BESIDE ME~~ And lifted me up with you
So ~~[illegible]~~, I BELIEVE ~~THEY WERE~~ it was a ROAD ~~THEY~~ I WAS MEANT TO RIDE

LIKE A SOLDIER GETTING OVER THE WAR
LIKE A YOUNG MAN GETTING OVER HIS CRAZY DAYS
LIKE A BANDIT GETTING OVER HIS LAWLESS WAYS
~~EVERY DAY IS BETTER THAN BEFORE~~ I don't have to do that anymore
I'M LIKE A SOLDIER GETTING OVER THE WAR

~~THERE WERE NIGHTS I DON'T REMEMBER~~ Nights and days that ain't rem.
~~AND THERE'S PAIN THAT I'VE FORGOTTEN~~ PAIN that's been forgotten
OTHER THINGS I CHOOSE NOT TO RECALL
THERE ARE FACES THAT COME TO ME
~~IN MY DARKEST SECRET MEMORY~~ That I thought were long forgotten
Faces ~~[illegible]~~ THAT I WISH WOULD NOT COME BACK AT ALL

IN MY DREAMS PARADE OF LOVERS
FROM THE OTHER TIMES AND PLACES
THERE'S NOT ONE THAT MATTERS NOW, NO MATTER WHO
I'M JUST THANKFUL FOR THE JOURNEY
AND THAT I SURVIVED THE BATTLES
~~AND THAT MY SPOILS OF VICTORY ARE YOU~~
And that my reward for victory is you.

LIKE A SOLDIER

1992

With the twilight colors falling
And the evening laying shadows
Hidden memories come stealing from my
mind
As I feel my own heart beating out
The simple joy of living
I wonder how I ever was that kind

But the wild road I was rambling
Was always out there calling
And you said a hundred times I should have
died
Then you reached down and touched me
And lifted me up with you
So I believe it was the road I was meant to ride

I'm like a soldier getting over the war
I'm like a young man getting over his crazy
days
Like a bandit getting over his lawless ways
I don't have to do that anymore
I'm like a soldier getting over the war

There are nights I don't remember
And pain that's been forgotten
And a lot of things I choose not to recall
There are faces that come to me
In my darkest, secret memories
Faces that I wish would not come back at all

But in my dreams' parade of lovers
From the other times and places
There's not one that matters now, no matter
who
I'm just thankful for the journey
And that I've survived the battles
And that my spoils of victory is you

I'm like a soldier getting over the war
I'm like a young man getting over his crazy
days
Like a bandit getting over his lawless ways
Every day gets better than a day before
I'm like a soldier getting over the war

POOR VALLEY GIRL

1992

She could never give up the homestead on the farm
Where they handed off tobacco in the big tobacco barn
And the long, straight rows that ran
From the house down to the road
That went to AP Carter's store, on the logging truck, she rode

She would sit and would gaze at the foggy mountaintop
As the swift hawk circled 'round the Clinch Mountain rocks
At the school down in Hiltons, she would read about the world
Created to be conquered by this Poor Valley Girl

Her mother was an Addington, from over Copper Creek
Her father was of sturdy stock; she was royal, but meek
Her laughter was infectious, her music was pure joy
She'd win the hearts of many men, as she did, many a boy

Her mother became famous, Maybelle and her guitar
With sisters, Helen and Anita, the family was four-star
June gave the world two daughters
And a son with auburn curls
And I thank God that He gave me
This sweet Poor Valley Girl

She would sit and she would gaze at the foggy mountaintop
Where the swift hawk circled 'round the Clinch Mountain rocks
At the school down in Hiltons, she would read about the world
Created to be conquered by this Poor Valley Girl

Poor Valley Girl

J. R. Cash

She could never give up the homestead on the farm
Where they handed off tobacco in the big tobacco barn
And the long straight rows that ran
From the house down to the road
That runs to AP Carters store on the logging truck she rode

She would sit and gaze at the foggy mountain top
As the swift hawk circled round the Clinch Mountain rocks
At the school down in Hiltons she would read about the world
Created to be conquered by this poor valley girl

Her mother was an Addington from over copper creek
Her father was of sturdy stock — she was royal but meek
Her laughter was infectous, her music was pure joy
She'd win the hearts of many men as she did many a boy
~~Her friends were [illegible] and Joyce, out from the [illegible] with her~~
~~Through pain and separation, they are always together [illegible]~~

Her mother became famous, Maybelle and her guitar
With sisters Helen and Anita, the family was 4 star
June gave the world two daughters
And a son with Auburn curls
And I thank God that He gave me
This sweet poor valley girl

She Sang Sweet Baby James

She had a heart full of love
~~Though her room was empty and cold~~
For her baby, for God, and James Taylor.
As she closed her eyes and she nursed it
She was a cowgirl, Truck driver and sailor

And she sang sweet baby James
And flew o're the mountains
The Turnpike and the sea.
And she longed for ~~her~~ a home in heaven.
~~And how long can eternity be~~
Or anywhere that heaven ~~could~~ could be
By the man she had long been abandoned
And the baby was all that she had
She was lonely but she was at peace.
But when singing it wasn't so bad.

SHE SANG "SWEET BABY JAMES"

1992

She had a heart full of love
For her baby, for life, and James Taylor
She nursed her baby, and she closed her eyes
She was a cowgirl, truck driver, and sailor

In her mind, she wasn't abandoned
Though the baby was all that she had
She was lonely at night when the babe was asleep
But when singing, it wasn't so bad

And she sang "Sweet Baby James"
And she flew o'er the turnpikes, the mountains, and sea
And she looked to the skies, where heaven should be
Said, "Could it be, there's no heaven for me?
The only difference in my life and hell are the flames."
So she sang "Sweet Baby James"

She had to work for a living
And her mom kept the babe every day
The driving paid minimum wages to all
And with so little carry-home pay...

But she'd take her own flights of fancy
Each time she found herself alone
She'd get on her dream song, and she'd sail away
With her baby, to find that new home

And she sang "Sweet Baby James"
And she flew o'er the turnpikes, the mountains, and sea
And she looked to the skies, where heaven should be
Said, "Could it be, there's no heaven for me?
The only difference in my life and hell are the flames."
So she sang "Sweet Baby James"

WELL ALRIGHT

1992

I met her at the laundromat
She was washing extra hot
I said, "Don't you need a little help
With that big load you got?"

She said, "No," but did a double take
And then she smiled and said, "I might."
As I rolled up my sleeves
I said to myself, Well alright

Well alright

I put it on automatic
And she sat down on the floor
She said, "Just keep it on medium hot."
I said, "I've done this before."

Then I opened up the dryer
And I set it on soft and light
She said, "Be gentle with my silk and lace."
And I said, "Well alright."

Well alright

Her clothes were in the basket
Folded down, so nice and warm
She headed for the door
And I said, "I will take you home."

She said, "I just live up the street."
I said, "It's a dangerous night.
Take my arm and I'll carry the basket."
And she said, "Well alright."

Well alright

The world's half full of women
And the world's half full of men
And sometimes one or the other
Opens up to let one in

But the one I met at the laundromat
That dangerous, beautiful night
Said, "Yes, I do, and yes, I will."
And I said, "Well alright."

Well alright

Well Alright

I met her at the Laundromat
She was washing extra hot
I said dont you need a little help
With that big load you got
She said no but did a double-take
Then smiled and said alright
As I rolled up my sleeves
I said to myself, Well alright!

Chorus M--- M--- M--- M--- M-- M--- M--- Well alright

I put it on automatic
And said I've done this before
With her back against the wall
She sat cross-legged on the floor
As I opened up the dryer
I put it on soft and light
She said put it on medium hot
And I said, well Alright.
I put it on Automatic
~~With her back against the wall~~
She sat ~~cross-legged~~ Down on the floor
~~Her cheeks were rosy when she asked~~
~~Have you done this before~~
I put the dryer on medium hot
And I put it on soft and light
She said be gentle with my satin Lace
And I said, "Well Alright"

> (She said keep it on medium hot
> I said I've done this before

Chorus Hm - Hmm - Hmm - Hmm - Hm Hm Hm Well Aright.

~~I could take you home~~
~~I could walk~~

~~come on I'll~~

…thes were in the basket
Folded down and clean and warm
She headed for the door
And I said I will take you home
She said I just live up the street
I said its a dangerous night.
Take my arm I'll carry the basket
She said "Well Alright"

Chorus Hm - Hmm - Hmm - Hmm - Hm - Hm - Hm Well Alright

~~After we put her clothes away~~

~~lovers meet at dancing~~

Well the world is full of women
And the world is full of men
And sometimes one or the other
Opens up to let one in.
But the one I met at the laundromat
That beautiful dangerous night
Said yes I do and yes I will
And I said, Well Alright

Chorus -

SOLDIER BOY

1992

Here comes the boy with the backpack on
He's going anywhere but home
Be some changes while he's gone
He's got a job to carry on

Here comes the boy in a dark green suit
Size 11 combat boots
He can run and he can shoot
He's got a gun that goes a-root, toot, toot

Here comes the jet with a tail of white
He'll be there before daylight
Got some wrongs to be made right
May not return, but I think he might

Here comes a ship sailing out to sea
Boys on deck for all to see
Waving bye to you and me
Keep the land and the water free

Soldier boy, walking boy, sailor boy, and flying boy
You won't be no boy no more after what you're going for
And all you women, thanks to you, doing what you have to do
Praying for you 'til you're through
Doodle, doodle, doo, doodle, doo, doo, doo

Here comes the boy with the backpack on
He's going anywhere but home
Be some changes while he's gone
He's got a job to carry on

Soldier boy, walking boy, sailor boy, and flying boy
You won't be no boy no more after what you're going for
And all you women, here's to you, doing what you have to do
Peace, because of all of you
Doodle, doodle, doo, doodle, doo, doo, doo

I STOP AND LOOK UP

1993

I stop and look up
And your hair's turning gray
I turn around twice
And our life's flown away

I just turned a page
And the end is in sight
And now's all we have
So love me tonight

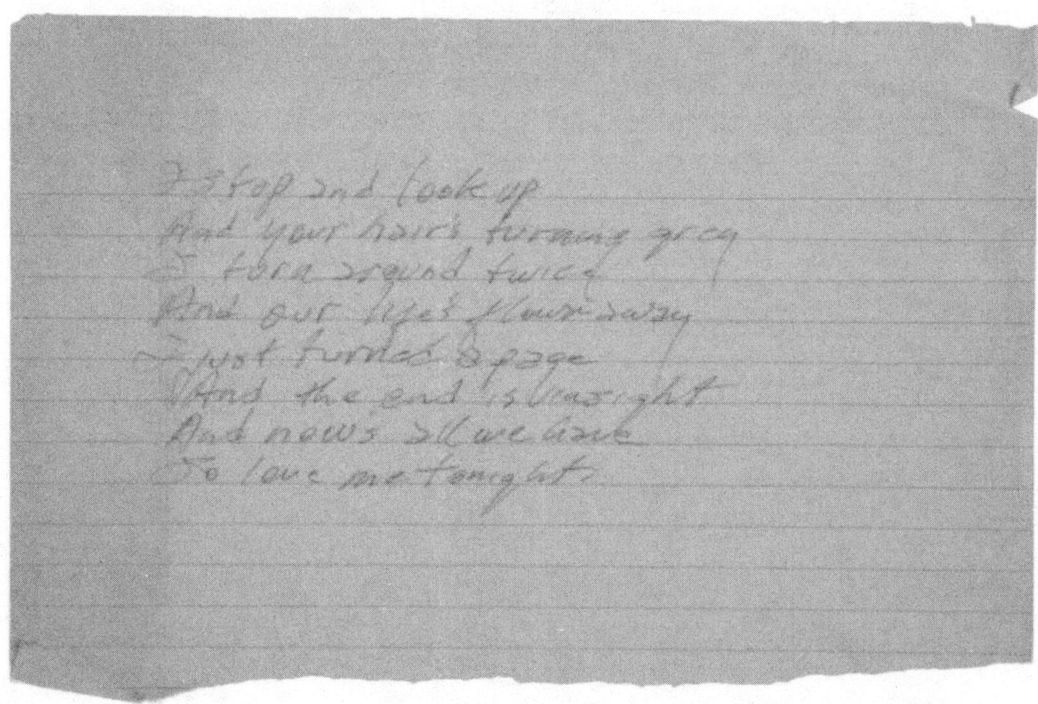

I stop and look up
And your hair's turning gray
I turn around twice
And our life's flown away
I just turned a page
And the end is in sight
And now's all we have
So love me tonight.

A

Delias Gone

I went up to Memphis. I met Delia there
Found her in her parlor, and tied her to her chair
Delias Gone – One more round – Delias Gone

She was lowdown and trifling and she was cold and mean
Kind of evil make me want to grab a sub-machine
Delias gone – One More – Round – Delias gone

First time I shot her – shot her in the side
Hard to watch her suffer – but with the 2nd shot she died
Delias gone – One more round – Delias gone

But jailer o – Jailer – Jailer I cant sleep
Cause All around my bedside I hear the patter – – –
Delias gone – One More round – Delias gone

So if your womans devilish ~~[illegible]~~ you can let her run
Or ~~But~~ you can bring her down and do her like Delia got Done
Delias gone – One more round – Delias gone –

DELIA'S GONE

originally by Blake Alphonso Higgs

adapted in 1993

Delia, oh, Delia
Delia, all my life
If I hadn't shot poor Delia
I'd have had her for my wife
Delia's gone, one more round
Delia's gone

I went up to Memphis
And I met Delia there
Found her in her parlor
And I tied her to her chair
Delia's gone, one more round
Delia's gone

She was low-down and trifling
And she was cold and mean
Kind of evil make me want to
Grab my submachine
Delia's gone, one more round
Delia's gone

First time I shot her
I shot her in the side
Hard to watch her suffer
But with the second shot she died
Delia's gone, one more round
Delia's gone

But jailer, oh, jailer
Jailer, I can't sleep
'Cause all around my bedside
I hear the patter of Delia's feet
Delia's gone, one more round
Delia's gone

So if your woman's devilish
You can let her run
Or you can bring her down and do her
Like Delia got done
Delia's gone, one more round
Delia's gone

Delia's gone, one more round
Delia's gone

LET THE TRAIN BLOW THE WHISTLE

1993

I don't want no aggravation
When my train has left the station
If you're there or not, I may not even know
Have a round and remember
Things we did that weren't so tender
Let the train blow the whistle when I go

On my old guitar, sell tickets
So someone can finally pick it
And tell the girls down at the Ritz I said hello
Tell the gossipers and liars
I will see them in the fire
Let the train blow the whistle when I go

Let her blow, let her blow
Long and loud and hard and happy
Let her blow
No regrets, all my debts
Will be paid when I get laid
Let her blow, let her blow, let her blow

You'll be left without excuses
For the evils and abuses
Down to the day from years and years ago
And have yourself another toke
From my basket full of smoke
And let the train blow the whistle when I go

Let her blow, let her blow
Long and loud and hard and happy
Let her blow
No regrets, all my debts
Will be paid when I get laid
Let her blow, let her blow, let her blow
Let her blow, let her blow, let her blow

Let Her Blow

I dont want no aggravation
When my train has left the station
~~[illegible]~~
~~[illegible]~~
If you're there or not I may not even know
Have a round boys and remember
Things we did that weren't so tender
Let the train blow the whistle when I go

On my old Guitar sell tickets
So someone can finally pick it
Tell the girls at the ~~[illegible]~~ Ritz I said hello
Tell the gossipers and liars
I will see them in the fire
Let the train blow the whistle when I Go

Let her blow, Let her blow
cho Long and loud and hard and happy, let her blow
No regrets, all my debts
Will be paid when I get laid
Let her blow, Let her blow

~~You'll be left~~ without excuses
For the evils and abuses
Down to today from years and years ago
Have yourself ~~[illegible]~~ another toke
From my basketful of smoke
Let the train blow its whistle when I blow.

TALK TO ME

with Marty Stuart

1993

If you wake up in the morning
Feeling all alone
When the neon lights from late last night
Have vanished in the dawn
If you need someone to lean on
If you need someone to care
Then you just call my name
And I'll be there

Talk to me, talk to me
I've got more love for you
Than you could ever need
Talk to me, talk to me
If it takes all night and it just might
It'll be all right with me

It's the same old story
When the sun goes down
You've told everyone to say,
"I ain't seen her 'round."
But somewhere in a corner
There's a shadow on the wall
If you keep running from me
You may catch me after all

Talk to me, talk to me
I've got more love for you
Than you could ever need
Talk to me, talk to me
If it takes all night and it just might
It'll be all right with me

HAPPY BIRTHDAY, PRINCESS

1994

We get old and get used to each other
We think alike
We read each other's minds
We know what the other wants without asking
Sometimes we irritate each other a little bit
Maybe sometimes take each other for granted

But once in a while, like today, I meditate on it
And realize how lucky I am to share my life
With the greatest woman I ever met
You still fascinate and inspire me
You influence me for the better
You're the object of my desire
The number one earthly reason for my existence

I love you very much
Happy birthday, princess

DEATH AND HELL

with John Carter Cash

1994

She stepped down from her carriage
At 10 Vermillion Street
I took off my roustabout
And slung it at her feet

We went into her parlor
And she cooled me with her fan
But said, "I'll go no further
With a fantasy-making man."

I said, "I'd walk on the Ponchartrain
For what you have today.
Just a drink from your deep well
And I'll be on my way."

She laughed and heaven filled the room
Said, "This I give to you
This body's wisdom is the flesh
But here's a thing or two."

Death and hell are never full
And neither are the eyes of men
Cats can fly from nine stories high
And pigs can see the wind

She let me make my pallet
In the moonlight on the floor
Just outside of paradise
But right in hell's back door

The image of her nibbled
At the eye of my soul
My dreams were a hurricane
And quite out of control

Then her voice came through the storm
"It's more than flesh I deal
And you will have to pay
For any wisdom that you steal."

I woke to tinted windows
In lavender and red
The first station of the cross
Was just above my head

I awoke to gargoyles
And a hard bench for my bed
Jesus Christ and Pontius Pilate
Were just above my head

Death and hell are never full
And neither are the eyes of men
Cats can fly from nine stories high
And pigs can see the wind

Death & Hell

Death and hell are never full
And neither are the eyes of men
Cats can fly from nine stories high
And pigs can see the wind.

She stepped down from her carriage at 10 Vermillion St
I took off my roustabout and laid it at her feet
We went into her parlor and she cooled me with her fan
But said I'll go no further with a fantasy makin man
I said I'll walk on Pontchartrain for a little time today
Just a drink from your deep well and I'll be on my way
She laughed and heaven filled the room said this I give to you
This bodys wisdom is the flesh but heres a thing or two

She let me make my pallet in the moonlight on the floor
Just outside of paradise but right in Hells back door
~~She took me in her parlor and she cooled me with her fan~~
The image of her nibbled at the edges of my soul
~~But said I'll go no further with a fantasy making man~~
My dreams were a hurricane and quite out of control
Then her voice came thru the storm its more than flesh a deal
And you will have to pay for any wisdom that you steal
I awoke to tinted windows and lavender and red
The first station of the Cross was just above my head.
I awoke to gargoyles and a hard bench for my bed
The first station of the cross was just above my head

Death and Hell

Death and hell are never full
And neither are the eyes of men
Cats can fly
From nine stories high
And pigs can see the wind

She stepped down from her carriage at 10 Vermillion St
I took off my roustabout and laid it at her feet
She took me in her parlour and she cooled me with her fan
But said I'll go no further with a music making man
I said lady I'll be good if you will let me stay
Just a drink from wisdoms well and I'll be on my way
She laughed and heaven filled the room, said this I give to you
~~The body knows no wisdom~~, but ~~[illegible]~~
This bodys wisdom is the flesh heres a thing or two
She let me make my pallet ~~on~~ the moonlight on the floor
Just outside of ~~[illegible]~~ but in hells back door
The image of her nibbled at the edges of my soul
My ~~dreams were~~ a hurricane and quite out of control
But I awoke to ~~[illegible]~~ gargoyles and lavender and ~~Red~~
The ~~second~~ station of the Cross was just above my head
I awoke to gargoyles and a hard bench for my bed
The second station of the Cross was just above my head
~~Her sweet voice came in the dream and she said [illegible]~~
Then came her voice thru the storm, its in the flesh I deal
~~you should know you'd have to pay for wisdom that you~~
You know you'll have to pay for wisdom that you try to steal

MEET ME IN HEAVEN

1996

We saw houses falling from the sky
Where the mountains lean down to the sand
We saw blackbirds circling 'round an old castle keep
And I stood on the cliff and held your hand

We walked trouble's brooding, windswept hills
And we loved and we laughed the pain away
At the end of the journey, when our last song is sung
Will you meet me in heaven someday?

Can't be sure of how it's going to be
When we walk into the light across the bar
But I'll know you and you'll know me
Out there beyond the stars

We've seen the secret things revealed by God
And we heard what the angels had to say
Should you go first, or if you follow me
Will you meet me in heaven someday?

Living in a mansion on the streets of gold
At the corner of Grace and Rapture Way
In sweet ecstasy, while the ages roll
Will you meet me in heaven someday?

In sweet ecstasy, while the ages roll
Will you meet me in heaven someday?

Meet Me in Heaven

E 1st fret

We saw houses falling from the sky
Where the mountains lean down to the sand
We saw blackbirds circling round an old castle keep
And I stood on the cliff and held your hand

We walked troubles brooding wind-swept hills
And we loved and we laughed the pain away
At the end of the journey when our last song is sung
Will you meet me in heaven someday

Cant be sure of how its going to be
When we walk into the light across the bar
~~But surely our spirits will be intertwined~~
Out there beyond the stars
But I'll know you and you'll know me
Weve seen secret things revealed by God
~~And weve been like children at their play~~
Should you go first or if you follow me
Will you meet me in heaven someday
And we ~~know~~ heard what the angels had to say

~~The [illegible] we made [illegible] eternity~~

~~Sitting by the river neath the tree of life.~~

Livin in a Mansion on the streets of gold
At the corner of grace and rapture way
In sweet ecstacy while the ages roll
Will you meet me in heaven someday

AS LONG AS THE GRASS SHALL GROW

with Peter La Farge

1996

I met you in the shadows and your face was all aglow
I remember it so well, though it was many years ago
We both knew something happened without a lot to say
But we had other lives and so we went our separate ways
But our hearts communicated and every time we passed
We were gradually building something that would forever last

As long as the moon shall rise
As long as the rivers flow
As long as the sun will shine
As long as the grass shall grow

My heart was calling for you when one night you came along
We danced around each other but then we sang our song
Our harmony was shaky, and the pitch not very true
But then you gave in to me and I gave in to you
We had to fight the world and we fought with all we had
We vowed to be together through the sweet times and the bad

As long as the moon shall rise
As long as the rivers flow
As long as the sun will shine
As long as the grass shall grow

I hear you whisper every night: "May I have this dance?"
And though I'm not light on my feet I always take the chance
We've gone through many storms and often walked through fire
But always our loving faith took us higher and higher
We know the mystery of life, it's love hard and long
I love you and I always will

As long as the moon shall rise
As long as the rivers flow
As long as the sun will shine
As long as the grass shall grow

COME ON DOWN

1996

Lord, I suppose
It's been a long, long time
Since Your beautiful feet
Have touched the ground

But if You're there
And hear my cry
Have mercy on me
And come on down

Show me a way
That's better lit
And hold my hand
As I walk in it

Give me mountains
I can climb
And take me up
One at a time

Speak for me
If my tongue gets loose
Help me not to cry
With any excuse

Please be my courage
When I'm weak and afraid
Be my judge and jury
When my debts are paid

Tell me You love me
Tell me You care
Please step down
The Golden Stairs

Take my hand
Lead me along
Try not to see
Everything I did wrong

Search me and try me
After Your will
Then reassure me
That You love me still

Lead me up the stairs
That the saints have trod
To Your father's house
The Kingdom of God

Come on down

If in Your love
I can be found
Have mercy on me
And come on down

NOW YOU'RE GONE

1996

Go from my window
Go from my door
I don't need you
Or want you no more
Now you're gone

I'll drink my coffee
I'll sip my tea
Stay away from my doorstep
Let my doorbell be
Now you're gone

Mississippi River is muddy and wide
I'll take this
You take the other side
Now you're gone

Ain't got nobody
To answer to
Ain't obligated
To especially you

Cold drink of water
And a shot or two
Ain't got nobody
To answer to

PASSIN' THROUGH

with Randy Scruggs

1998

Well, I have stood upon the mountain
I have seen the other side
I have wrestled with the devil
I have wrestled with my pride

I have been down in the valley
I have stood out in the rain
I have seen my love forsaken
Felt the pleasure and the pain

There's one thing that's for certain
One chord that rings true
It's a mighty world we live in
But the truth is, we're only passin' through

I have cried in tears of sadness
I have cried in tears of joy
I have found a life worth livin'
From the peace within the noise

I have turned my back on hatred
Lyin', prejudice, and greed
Found the future in the present
Found hope within a seed

If there's one thing that's for certain
Just one chord that rings true
It's a mighty world we live in
But the truth is, we're only passin' through

Passin' through, passin' through
It's a mighty world we live in
But the truth is, we're only passin' through

I have seen my bucket empty
Seen my well run dry
But there's water down the road
And I'm only goin' by

If I'm settin' on dead-ready
When my chances come to knock
I'll make it where I'm goin'
I'll be tall just like a rock

But there's one thing that's for certain
One chord that rings true
It's a wicked world we live in
But the truth is, we're only passin' through

Passin' through, passin' through
It's a mighty world we live in
But the truth is, we're only passin' through

BEFORE MY TIME

1999

I know that hearts were loving
Long before I was here
And I'm not the first to ever cry
In my bed or in my beer

There were songs before there was radio
Of love that stays and love that goes
They were writing melancholy tunes
And tearful words that rhyme

Before my time
Before my time

There were songs in old dusty books
Of love that's always been
Sweet lovers in their glory
Who are now gone with the wind

Old-fashioned love words spoken then
Keep coming back around again
Nothing's changed except the names
Their love burned just like mine

Before my time
Before my time

And in the dim of yesterday
I can clearly see
That flesh and blood cried out to someone
As it does in me

And there was some old song that said,
"I'll love you 'til I die."

Before my time
Before my time

But what the old-time masters had
Is what I feel for you
Love is love and doesn't change
In a century or two

If some way they had seen and knew
How it would be for me and you
They'd wish for love like yours
And they would wish for love like mine

Before my time
Before my time

TEARS IN THE HOLSTON RIVER

1999

On October 23rd, 1978
I lost a loved one and I confess I cried
In the joyous celebration of the lady and her music
There were tears in the Holston River
When Maybelle Carter died

Then walking down that river road
I saw crystal tear-shaped droplets
Silver beads of love sparkling on the riverside
And I'll just bet they turn to diamonds
For the love that was behind them
There were tears in the Holston River
When Mother Maybelle died

Then on January 8, 1979
We lost Sara Carter
And the pain was multiplied
Down below that old Clinch Mountain
We laid her at Mount Vernon
There were tears in the Holston River
When Sara Carter died

Then walking down that river road
I saw crystal tear-shaped droplets
Silver beads of love sparkling in the riverside
And I'll just bet they turn to diamonds
For the love that was behind them
There were tears in the Holston River
When Maybelle and Sara died

There were tears in the Holston River
When Mother Maybelle and Sara Carter died

EIGHT

✷ TWILIGHT ✷

2000–2003

JOHNNY AND JUNE did, indeed, make it to see the millennium turn. But no one has ever outrun time, and the finish line was approaching. It is not surprising that, as evening's shadows beckoned, his music's enduring constants remained, as if to both buffer him and provide the soundtrack to his passage home. These final years contained more of his signature interpretations — the consequence of needing to have old chestnuts and cherished favorites committed to memory rather than paper — but also some of his most arresting, significant, and intensely personal compositions. The depiction of the huffing and puffing of the train coming down the line in "Like the 309" as a metaphor for his own dire respiratory infirmities was at once wry and defiant. The ominous warnings contained in his adaptation of "Run On" ("God's Gonna Cut You Down") were the same admonitions given years before to the young cowboy named Billy Joe raised to an otherworldly plane. And "I Turn Around Twice" — a piece he could never commit to a recording, such was its stultifying pathos — is as heartrending as anything in his canon, made even more so by the knowledge that this would be the concluding story of his life when June died suddenly in May 2003.

In the middle of this frenzy, Cash produced his tour de force "The Man Comes Around," an utterly astounding account of the end-times, and the culmination of a journey that had begun in the dirt of the Depression even before he was born. No doubt echoing the Old Testament fever of his preacher forebears, he channeled his Creator and the Book of Revelation with such a mystical, awe-inspiring vision that even nonbelievers were surely reevaluating their position. Bono, of U2, who had been inspired by Cash to write his own chronicle of the apocalypse, would be so mesmerized that he took to calling him "Saint John." Johnny Cash would have vehemently rejected such a reference, but Saint John of the first century never had a better advocate. "The Man Comes Around" trumped all other testaments.

As eternity neared, the certitude never wavered. He had one final declaration in him, and that produced "My Lord Has Gone," a fitting conclusion to an epic quest to live and tell the fundamental truths of being a human in God's province. The body was weary and worn, but the spirit triumphed. With that, John R. Cash laid down his pen and turned the page.

MUSCADINE WINE

2000s

Right by the porch
In the honeysuckle vines
I found a jug
Of Muscadine wine

So I pulled the plug
And I took a little whiff
And said, "I can't handle
This by myself."

Before you could say
Zippety-doo
All my neighbors
Smelled it, too

In comes Casey
And Carey and Joe
With a how-de-do
And a hi-de-ho

Ain't you heard
Long as you live
It's a whole lot more
Blessed to give

And we all feel blessed
And mighty fine
Passing around
Muscadine wine

Right by the porch
In the honeysuckle vines
I found a jug
Of Muscadine wine.
So I pulled the plug
And I took a little whiff
And said I cant handle
This by my self.
Before you could say
Zippety-doo
All my neighbors smelled it too
In comes Casey & Carey
and Joe
With a how-de-do.
And a high-de-ho

Aint you heard
Long as you live
Its a whole lot more
blessed to give.
And we all feel blessed
And mighty fine
Passing Around
Muscadine Wine

FOREVER

2000

You tell me I must perish
Like the flowers that I cherish
Nothing remaining of my name
Nothing remembered of my fame
But the trees that I planted are still young
The songs that I sang will still be sung

you tell me that I must Perish
Like the flowers that I cherish
Nothing remaining of my name
Nothing remembered of my fame
But the trees that I planted
~~St~~ still are young
The songs I sang
Will still be sung

I TURN AROUND TWICE

2000

I thought you were the greatest thing
That I had ever seen in my life
And who'd have thought we'd make it
Like we made it, and I made you my wife

But it happened, as sometimes happens
We raised up a family and home
But I barely look up and there's snow in my hair
And I turn around twice and it's gone

The years and the good times
And our life together
I turn around twice and it's gone

I have seen your smiling eyes
Sparkling like a star in the sky
And I have seen your pretty face
Twisted down in pain when you'd cry

And the mountains . . . we climbed many a mountain
And fought and won, just you and I alone
But I barely look up and the sun's going down
I turn around twice and it's gone

The good days and sweet nights
And our life together
I turn around twice and it's gone

I never did believe it
When you told me you'd grow old gracefully
And I thought with time we both would change
And you'd no longer mean the world to me

But what happened was, you became my world
And everything would end if you were gone
But I barely look up and the world's at an end
I turn around twice and it's gone

The fire and the youth
And two lives locked together
I turn around twice and it's gone

I turn around Twice

I thought you were the Greatest thing
That I had ever seen in my life
And who'd have thought we'd make it
Like we made it and I made you my wife
But it happened, as sometimes happened
We raised up a family and home
But I barely look up and there's snow in my hair
And I turn around twice and its gone
The years and the good times
And our life together
I turn around twice and its gone

I have seen your smiling eyes
Sparkling like a star in the sky
And I have seen your pretty face
Twisted down in pain when you'd cry
And the mountains we climbed many a mountain
And fought and won just you and I alone
But I barely look up and the sun's goin' down
I turn around twice and its gone
The good days and sweet nights
And our life together
I turn around twice and its gone

I never did believe it
When you told me you would grow old gracefully
I thought with time we folks would change
And you'd no longer mean the world to me
But what happened was, you became my world
And every thing would end if you were gone
But I barely look up and the world's at an end
I turn around twice and it gone
The fire and the youth
And two lives locked together
I turn around twice and its gone

THE MAN COMES AROUND

2000

There's a man going 'round, takin' names
And he decides who to free and who to blame
Everybody won't be treated all the same
There'll be a golden ladder reaching down
When the man comes around

The hairs on your arm will stand up
At the terror in each sip and in each sup
Will you partake of that last offered cup
Or disappear into the potter's ground
When the man comes around

Hear the trumpets, hear the pipers
One hundred million angels singing
Multitudes are marching to the big
  kettledrum
Voices calling, voices crying
Some are born and some are dying
It's alpha and omega's kingdom come

And the whirlwind is in the thorn tree
The virgins are all trimming their wicks
The whirlwind is in the thorn tree
It's hard for thee to kick against the pricks

'Til Armageddon, no shalam, no shalom
Then the father hen will call his chickens
  home
The wise men will bow down before the
  throne
And at his feet they'll cast their golden
  crowns
When the man comes around

Whoever is unjust, let him be unjust still
Whoever is righteous, let him be righteous
  still
Whoever is filthy, let him be filthy still
Listen to the words long written down
When the man comes around

Hear the trumpets, hear the pipers
One hundred million angels singing
Multitudes are marching to the big
  kettledrum
Voices calling, voices crying
Some are born and some are dying
It's alpha and omega's kingdom come

And the whirlwind is in the thorn tree
The virgins are all trimming their wicks
The whirlwind is in the thorn tree
It's hard for thee to kick against the pricks
In measured hundredweight and penny
  pound
When the man comes around

The Man Comes Around

Spoken
You can be—first on the draw
You can kill—your mother in law
You can steal some pilgrims [illegible]
But you gotta know it'll be written down
When the man comes around—

V. 1.
Theres a man going 'round taking names
And decides who to free and who to blame
Everybody won't be treated all the same
There'll be a golden ~~ladder~~ stair coming down
When the man comes around

V. 2
The hairs on your head will stand up
When all you're trying to do is ~~sip~~ sip and sup
Will you partake of that last offered cup
Or disappear into the potters ground
When the man comes around.

1st Chorus
~~You will~~ hear ten million trumpets
Ten million angels will be singing
Multitudes are marching
To the big kettle Drum
Somewhere there are voices crying
Some are borning—Some are dying
Alpha and Omega
On the day of Kingdom Come

The Man Comes Around

2nd Chorus
The whirlwind is in the thorn tree
Ten virgins trimming their ~~lamps~~ wicks
The whirlwind's in the thorn tree
Its hard to kick against the pricks
Its that great gettin up morning
Coming down (slow)
When the Man Comes Around

Verse 3
Till Armageddon no shalam no Shalom
The father hen will call his chickens home
The wise will bow down before the throne
At his feet they will lay their golden crowns
When the Man comes around

Verse 4 spoken
Whoever is unjust let him be unjust still
Whoever is righteous let them be righteous still
Whoever is filthy let them be filthy still
Listen to the words that are written down
When the man comes around

~~Repeat 1st Verse Repeat 2nd Verse~~ (Type out) Repeat 1st Chorus
(Type out) Repeat 2nd Chorus
Repeat 1st Spoken

He is alpha and omega the beginning
And the end.

Theres a city lies foursquare
And ~~it~~ in its books the names
are written there

Sapphires and jasper and emeralds and
beryl and amethyst and topaz and
pure gold and pearls
! The bright and morning star

FIRST CORINTHIANS 15:55

2002

O Death, where is thy sting?
O Grave, where is thy victory?
O Life, you are a shining path
And hope springs eternal, just over the rise
When I see my redeemer beckoning me

Oh, row my ship over the waves of your sea
Let me find a safe port now and then
Don't let the dark one in your sanctuary
Until it's time to pack it in

Oh, row, row my ship
With the fire of your breath
And don't lay a broadside on your ship as yet
Blow ye warm winds
When it's chilly and wet
And don't come too soon yet
For collecting my debt

O Death, where is thy sting?
O Grave, where is thy victory?
O Life, you are a shining path
And hope springs eternal, just over the rise
When I see my redeemer beckoning me

Oh, let me sail on
With my ship to the East
And keep my eye on the North Star
When the journey is no good for man or for beast
I'll be safe wherever you are

Just let me sail into your harbor of lights
And there and forever to cast out my line
Give me my task
And let me do it right
And do it with all of my might

O Death, where is thy sting?
O Grave, where is thy victory?
O Life, you are a shining path
And hope springs eternal, just over the rise
When I see my redeemer beckoning me

(1)

~~O' Death where is thy sting~~
~~O' Grave where is thy victory~~
~~O' [illegible] I see a shining sea~~
~~[illegible] the same~~ your victory
Sail my ship over the waves
of your sea
let me find a safe port
now and then
Dont let the dark one in your sanctuary
Until its time to pack it in
Blow Blow with the power of your breath
And dont lay a broadside
On your ship as yet
Blow ye warm winds when it's
Chilly and wet
And dont come too soon
for collecting your debt

2.

Sail me on into that sweet rivers mouth
That flows from the golden throne
Put me to berth in some slip
To the South
Where all of my loved ones have gone
Light house with unearthly ligh
Cast out all traces of night
Show me my mansion & long for the sight
Where I'll never be alone
Sweet sweet that sweet voice of peace
Heave to
That voice calling me
And hope springs eternal
Just over the rise
And there stands my victory

O Death—etc.
~~O Grave [illegible] victory~~
~~Joy in the [illegible]~~

1st Chorus

Oh Death where is thy sting
O Grave where is thy victory
O'Life there is a shining path
O'joy in the morning
When you call me in
From off of your shining sea.

2nd Chorus

~~O Death where is thy sting~~
~~O Grave where is thy victory~~
~~O Joy in the morning~~
~~When He calls me in~~
~~From off of the shining~~

2nd Corinthians 5:55
Oh Death where is thy sting
O Grave where is thy victory
end of 2nd verse

Sweet sweet
Sweet ~~peace~~ voice of peace
Heave to
That voice calling me
Hope springs eternal
Just up on the rise
And there stands my victory

~~3rd~~ Chorus Cont. 2nd Verse
~~Oh Death where is thy sting~~
O' ~~Grave where is thy victory~~

Sweet, Sweet 2nd Chorus
The sweet voice of peace
Heave to
That voice calling me
Hope springs eternal
Just over the rise
And there stands my victory

Last

O Death where is thy sting
O Grave where is thy victory
Hope springs eternal
Just over the rise
And there stands my victory

I CAN SEE

2002

Have you heard the news?
There's a young Jew
Who claims to be the son of God
He's been walking in Jerusalem
On the streets that the prophets trod
I followed Him from Galilee
And the things upon my way
If I hadn't seen with my own eyes
I wouldn't believe a word you say

He touched a blind man with mud in His
hand
And He spit upon the mud
People were laughing at Him now
But He was doing good
He put the mud on the blind man's eyes
And then took it away
Then the man opened his eyes
And this is what he had to say

"I can see — I can see — I can see.
I've been healed by the man from Galilee.
My world was dark as night
But the man gave me my sight.
I can see — I can see — I can see."

You might have heard about the word
He spoke over fish and bread
Just five loaves and two little fish
He said a prayer and thousands were fed
He gave God the credit
And then said, "Follow me.
I've come to break your bondage
And set your captors free."

I followed Him 'til the trail grew dim
And now He's sentenced to die
I think of all the good He's done
And see no reason why

But then I realize His sacrifices
Are personally for me
To give me sight and life to my soul
Now, praise God, I can see

I can see — I can see — I can see
I've been healed by the man from Galilee
I've been set free from the chains
Of sin and all its pain
And I can see — I can see — I can see

Have you heard the news?
There's a young Jew
Who claims to be the son of God
He's carrying His cross in Jerusalem
On the streets that the prophets trod
I followed Him from Galilee
And the things upon my way
If I hadn't seen with my own eyes
I wouldn't believe a word you say
I can see — I can see — I can see

I CAN SEE

John R. Cash

Have you heard the news
There's a young Jew
Who claims to be the Son of God
He's been walking in Jerusalem
On the streets that the prophets trod
I followed Him from Galilee
And the things upon my way
If I hadn't seem with my own eyes
I wouldn't believe a word you say

He touched a blind man
With mud in His hand
And He spit upon the mud
People were laughing at him now
But He was doing good
He put the mud on the blind man's eyes
And then took it away
Then the man opened his eyes
And this is what he had to say

I can see - I can see - I can see
I've been healed by the man from Galilee
My world was dark as night
But the man gave me my sight
I can see - I can see - I can see

Have you heard the news
There's a young Jew
Who claims to be the Son of God
~~He's walking in Jerusalem~~ He's carrying his cross in Jerusalem
On the streets that the prophets trod
I followed Him from Galilee
And the things upon my way
If I hadn't seen with my own eyes
I wouldn't believe a word you say
I can see - I can see - I can see

I Can See

1st
Have you heard the news
There's a young Jew
Who claims to be the Son of God
He's walking in Jerusalem
On the streets that the prophets trod
I followed him from Galilee
And the things upon my way
If I hadn't seen with my own eyes
I wouldn't believe a word you say
He touched a blind man
With mud in His hand
And He spit upon the mud
People were laughing at him now
But He was doing good
He put the mud on the blind mans eyes
And then took it away
~~The blind man opened his eyes~~

Then the man opened up his eyes
And this is what he had to say
Cho I can see - I can see - I can see
I've been healed by the man from Galilee
My world was dark as night
But the man gave me my sight
I can see - I can see - I can see

2. You might have heard
About the word
He spoke over fish and bread
Just five loaves
And two little fish
He said a prayer
And thousands were fed
~~[illegible]~~ [illegible]
~~[illegible]~~

He gave God the credit
And then said follow me
I've come to break your bondage
And set your captives free

I followed him till the trail grew dim
And now he's sentenced to die
I think of all the good he's done
And see no reason why
But Then I realize his sacrifices
Are personally for me
To give me sight
And life to my soul
Now praise God I can see
Cho I can see - I can see - I can see
I've been healed by the man from Galilee

I've been set free from the chains
Of sin and all its pain
And I can see - I can see - I can see

Have you heard the news
There's a young Jew
Who claims to be the Son of God
He's walking in Jerusalem
On the streets that the prophets trod
I followed him from Galilee
And the things upon my way
If I hadn't seen with my own eyes
I wouldn't believe a word you say
I can see... etc repeat cho

GOD'S GONNA CUT YOU DOWN

traditional

adapted in 2003

You can run on for a long time
Run on for a long time
Run on for a long time
Sooner or later, God'll cut you down
Sooner or later, God'll cut you down

Go tell that long-tongue liar
Go and tell that midnight rider
Tell the rambler, the gambler, the backbiter
Tell 'em that God's gonna cut 'em down
Tell 'em that God's gonna cut 'em down

Well my goodness gracious, let me tell you the news
My head's been wet with the midnight dew
I've been down on bended knee
Talking to the man from Galilee

He spoke to me in the voice so sweet
I thought I heard the shuffle of angels' feet
He called my name and my heart stood still
When He said, "John, go do my will!"

Go tell that long-tongue liar
Go and tell that midnight rider
Tell the rambler, the gambler, the backbiter
Tell 'em that God's gonna cut 'em down
Tell 'em that God's gonna cut 'em down

You can run on for a long time
Run on for a long time
Run on for a long time
Sooner or later, God'll cut you down
Sooner or later, God'll cut you down

Well, you may throw your rock and hide your hand
Working in the dark against your fellow man
But as sure as God made black and white
What's done in the dark will be brought to the light

You can run on for a long time
Run on for a long time
Run on for a long time
Sooner or later, God'll cut you down
Sooner or later, God'll cut you down

HANGMAN

with Marty Stuart

2003

I killed another man today
It's hard to believe
I lost count at thirty
And I've grown too numb to grieve

The bottle helps me cope
When I lay down at night
And when the dope rolls through my veins
It all fades out of sight

Hangman, hangman
That's my stock and trade
Hangman, hangman
Sending bad men to their graves

Who killed who, I ask myself
Time and time again
God have mercy on the soul
Of this hangman

There's a woman down the street
Named Rosalie MacFall
She don't ask me any questions
When I come to call

Her body keeps me warm
Her words are soft and kind
She holds me in her arms
'Til the bad dreams leave my mind

Hangman, hangman
That's my stock and trade
Hangman, hangman
Sending bad men to their graves

Well, who killed who
I ask myself, time and time again
God have mercy on the soul
Of this hangman
God have mercy on the soul
Of this hangman

LIKE THE 309

2003

It should be a while before I see Doctor Death
So, it would sure be nice if I could get my
breath
Well, I'm not the crying, nor the whining kind
'Til I hear the whistle of the 309
Of the 309, of the 309
Put me in my box on the 309

Take me to the depot, put me to bed
Blow an electric fan on my gnarly ol' head
Everybody take a look, see I'm doing fine
Then load my box on the 309
On the 309, on the 309
Put me in my box on the 309

Hey, sweet baby, kiss me hard
Draw my bathwater, sweep my yard
Give a drink of my wine to my Jersey cow
I wouldn't give a hoot-and-nail for my journey
now
On the 309, on the 309

I hear the sound of a railroad train
The whistle blows and I'm gone again
Hit man, take me higher than a Georgia pine
Stand back, children, it's the 309
It's the 309, it's the 309
Put me in my box on the 309

A chicken in the pot and turkey in the corn
Ain't felt this good since Jubilee morn
Talk about luck, well, I got mine
Asthma comin' down, like the 309

Write me a letter, sing me a song
Tell me all about it, what I did wrong
Meanwhile, I will be doin' fine
Then load my box on the 309
On the 309, on the 309
Gonna get outta here on the 309

Like the 309

It should be awhile
Before I see Dr. Death
So, it would be nice
If I could get my breath
I'm not the crying
nor the whining kind
Till I hear the rattle
Of the 309

...ar the rattle of a RR train
...whistle blows and I'm gone again
...would make me higher
...n a Georgia pine
...d Bark children it's the
309
...the 309
...the 309
...thma coming down

309
...n the pot
...key in the corn
...this good
...'lee shone
...t luck
...t smile
...ma coming down like the 309
...309

...ming down
...own the track
...ing a song
...be awhile
...train comes along
...ga to smile
...y mine
...re over
...309

309
...to the Depot
...to bed
...electric to a
...gnarly old head
...body take a look
...I'm doing fine
...d my box on the 309
...309
...s' Comin down like the 309
...me I heard that whistle blow
...der can you hear it 6' below
...wonder if you hear
...ing of mine
...comin' down
...the 309
Asthma comin' down
Put it Here

309
I had a woman
Awhile back
Down a long mainline
Down a short side track
Nothing could replace
This love of my mine
But Asthma coming down like the 309
Like the 309
Asthma coming down like the 309
309
I like you
And you like me
And we're both alright
At MDC
Come September
We will meet some time
But Asthma coming down
Like the 309
Asthma

309
...letter
...a song
...about it
...d wrong
...fine
...t coming down 309
...zid
...chicken
In the yard
Give my grazy cow
A drink of wine
Asthma coming down Like 309

309
I know a woman
...eyes so deep
...keep me
...asleep
...no direction
...and no sign
...Asthma coming down like the 309
...309
...ma coming down
...tell me that I don't
...well
...I don't give
...in hell
...called
...fine
...Asthma coming down
Like the 309
Asthma

...at this country
...the wealth they got
...is a chicken in every pot
...with water so sweet
...the air so fine
...Asthma coming down Like the 309
...Like the 309
...Bertha coming down like the 309
Hey 309

MY LORD HAS GONE

2003

My Lord has gone to make a place for me
My Lord has gone to make a place for me
He's gone to build a mansion just for me
A mansion that will stand eternally

I dreamed that I was walking by the sea
By the sea, the Sea of Galilee
Through tear-filled eyes, He said, "Follow me."
Walking by the Sea of Galilee

Then I saw Him on the road to Jericho
On the road to Jericho
He picked a broken man up from the road
Then He said, "I've healed you, go
Down the road to Jericho."

They laid palms before Him on the way
They laid palms before Him on the way
There they crucified Him on that day
And He had not one single word to say

My Lord has gone to make a place for me
Gone to make a place for me
I've read about how great it's going to be
It will stand eternally
It will stand eternally

One day He'll come down from heaven just
for me
He'll come down from heaven just for me
Then I'll finally see Him face-to-face
When I rest in His amazing grace

My Lord has gone to make a place for me
My Lord has gone to make a place for me

INDEX OF SONGS

ACKNOWLEDGMENTS

Thank you to Trey Call, Jason Preston, Darren Julien, Skye Ridge, Julien's Auctions, Cathy Sullivan, Tiffany Dunn, Michael Szczerban and the entire team at Voracious, Steve Troha, Jeff Kleinman, Sophie Brett-Chin, and all who contributed to bring this book to life.

ABOUT THE AUTHORS

JOHNNY CASH (1932–2003) was an American singer and songwriter who became one of the most important, influential, and respected artists in the history of music. From his monumental live prison albums to his commentaries on the American spirit to his mesmerizing canon of gospel recordings and his late-life artistic triumphs of will and wisdom, Cash's impact on our culture is profound and continuing. He blended country, rock, blues, and gospel in his music, ushering in the Countrypolitan and Outlaw country movements. He was also a successful actor, writer, and activist. A statue of Cash was unveiled in the U.S. Capitol in 2024, gifted by the state of Arkansas. He is the first musician to be represented in the National Statuary Hall.

JOHN CARTER CASH is the only son of Johnny Cash and June Carter Cash. He is a singer and a songwriter and has produced five Grammy Award–winning albums. He owns and operates the Cash Cabin Studio in Tennessee and is the author of *House of Cash: The Legacies of My Father, Johnny Cash*.

MARK STIELPER has chronicled the life of the Man in Black for nearly forty years. Cash called him "my vault" and said, "He knows more about me than me." Stielper has collaborated on more than two dozen Cash biographies and documentary films and given lectures across the United States, including at the Rock & Roll Hall of Fame, the Country Music Hall of Fame, and the Johnny Cash Museum. His most recent work was the companion to this book, *Johnny Cash: The Life in Lyrics*.